SELF-DIRECTED BEHAVIOR

Self-Modification for Personal Adjustment

THIRD EDITION

SELF-DIRECTED BEHAVIOR

Self-Modification for Personal Adjustment

THIRD EDITION

David L. Watson
Roland G. Tharp
UNIVERSITY OF HAWAII

Brooks/Cole Publishing Company

Monterey, California

Brooks/Cole Publishing Company
A Division of Wadsworth, Inc.

Printed in the United States of America

10   9   8   7   6   5   4   3   2   1

Library of Congress Cataloging in Publication Data

Watson, David L   1934–
    Self-directed behavior.

    Bibliography: p.
    Includes index.
    1. Behavior modification.   2. Success.   I. Tharp,
Roland G., 1930–   joint author.   II. Title.
BF637.B4W38   1981   158'.1   880-24411
ISBN 0-8185-0443-9

Subject Editor: *Claire Verduin*
Production Editor: *Fiorella Ljunggren*
Designer: *Jamie Sue Brooks*
Illustrations: *Ron Grauer*
Technical Illustrations: *Lori Heckelman*
Typesetting: *Graphic Typesetting Service, Los Angeles, California*

For our parents,
Faye and Manly Watson
Berma and Oswald Tharp

Preface

This book is designed to acquaint you with a general theory of behavior, to guide you through exercises for developing skills in self-analysis, and to provide you with concrete information on how to achieve the goals you hold for yourself. The most important goal of this volume is to help you, the reader, achieve more self-determination, more "willpower," more control over your own life.

The book can serve as a textbook in psychology courses but does not depend on a formal course structure. Any reader can use it for self-instruction; no "prerequisites" are necessary. Clients of therapists or counselors can use it as an adjunct in planning their own self-change.

You should be warned about one possible side effect: you may become interested in the science of behavior. A number of people do find themselves delving deeper into the subject as a result of studying this material and in response to the experiential learning that can result from the self-change process.

The vehicle for learning will be your own self-analysis, your own program for implementing your values. Throughout, you are urged to accompany your reading with your own self-improvement project. In a sense, your daily life will become the laboratory in which you will study and develop your own behavior.

Foreword to the Professional

It is now several years since this book's first edition was published. Self-directed behavior change was originally the offspring of behavior theory, behavior therapy, and behavior modification. Accordingly, the first edition heavily emphasized issues of reinforcement and conditioning. In the early 1970s vicarious- and observational-learning issues received much attention, and the second edition reflected that concern. Those years also saw considerable advances in the field of cognitive behaviorism. Those developments, too, were incorporated into the second edition of our book.

In the last four years self-directed behavior has retained its full vitality as a research field in psychology. Theoretical and research treatments of various areas of the field continue to multiply, although case studies are less in evidence—no doubt a sign of the field's maturity. This continuing vitality, movement, and change are the rationale for this third edition.

There is one development, among all those that have occurred in these last few years, that we consider exceptionally interesting: cognitive behavior therapy has turned increasing control of change techniques over to clients. Self-instructions, self-observations, and self-goal setting have become vital to the practice of the parent disciplines of behavior therapy and behavior modification. In a sense, then, the child has become the parent, and, generally, the major movements in behaviorism are now coming about through the study of self-change processes.

A prime example of this extraordinary development is the incorporation into behaviorism of the theory and research of the role of language in behavior, particularly in the area of verbal self-control. The inclusion of this domain into the literature on self-directed change has brought about a more comprehensive understanding of self-directed behavior and has led us to a major reorganization of the text, which reflects these recent developments. Theory and research in verbal self-control are now presented as one major construct for understanding the *antecedents* of behavior. In the previous editions we had to present a discussion of behavioral consequences first, because an understanding of contingent consequences was necessary in order to grasp the concept of antecedent discriminative stimuli. This distortion of logical order, which has been distressing to us as well as our readers, is no longer necessary, since a coherent theory of behavior change that can be discussed in A-B-C (antecedents-behaviors-consequences) sequence is now available. Old friends of *Self-Directed Behavior* will welcome the resulting reorganization of the book.

As part of the same issue, cognitive strategies for self-change occupy even more space than in the previous editions. These cognitive strategies are tactics of verbal self-control and are so discussed and justified.

Behavioral consequences—self-reward and self-punishment—have not been supplanted by these new developments but have been enriched in their applications and understanding. Many students have learned their basic behavior theory from the previous editions of this text. In this latest revision we have retained the treatment of classical and instrumental conditioning intact as part of our continued attempt to reflect the state of the art.

In sum, "behaviorism," which is becoming increasingly indistinguishable from "empirical psychology," is not a static body of knowledge. Rather, it is a series of progressively broader inquiries spiraling further and further away from the narrow confines of conditioning. This and the previous revision have been necessitated by the expansion of the field. We have no doubt that the future will see yet another edition with further reorganization, extension, and update.

From a practical point of view, we have retained the basic intention of the book: to teach the principles of self-directed behavior, so that they may become coping mechanisms for life. The specific goal selected by a student for the study project is therefore treated as a vehicle for learning a general skill. But students do choose goals that are valuable to themselves and often ask for specifics about weight loss, assertiveness, the control of fears, and the like. There is a proliferation of specific how-to books for all sorts of problems; interested students will find a list of them in Chapter 2. But to help students apply the general to the specific, we have added a new feature to the book— "Tips for Typical Topics." These tips, which can be found at the end of most chapters, suggest specific applications of the general principles and procedures treated in the chapter. The topics covered are the same throughout the various chapters, allowing the student to follow the practical applications to problem behaviors from beginning to end. These topics are also listed in a special index at the end of the book.

Acknowledgments

For this edition we are particularly indebted for the excellent critical analyses provided by Donna M. Gelfand of the University of Utah, Yaakov M. Getz of Indiana University Northwest, Melvin M. Hoffman of California State University at Northridge, John R. Lutzker of Southern Illinois University, Steve Mozara, Jr., of Galveston College, Dan Perkins of Richland College, Lynn P. Rehm of the University of Houston, and Richard D. Tucker of the University of Central Florida.

Our greatest debt of gratitude is to all our students at the University of Hawaii. Their self-change projects have taught us much and made this edition, like the previous ones, possible. The list of their names has grown too long to cite. We have always disguised the identities of their case studies appearing in the book; we hope that in this anonymity each will accept our symbolic tribute to the Unknown Student.

David L. Watson
Roland G. Tharp

Contents

Chapter 1 Adjustment, Personal Goals, and Self-Management 2

Self-Direction and Willpower   5
Personality, Behavior, and Situations   6
The Process of Self-Management   11
Research in Self-Management: Does It Really Work?   16
Chapter Summary   19
Your Own Self-Direction Project: Step One   20
Tips for Typical Topics   20

Chapter 2 Specifying the Goal and Building Commitment   22

The Goal as Behaviors-in-Situations   23
Tactics for Specifying Behaviors-in-Situations   24
Building Commitment   35
Your Own Self-Direction Project: Step Two   42
Tips for Typical Topics   43

Chapter 3 Self-Knowledge: Observation and Recording   46

Structured Diaries   47
Frequency Recording   54
Rating Scales   62
The Reactive Effects of Self-Observation   67
Dealing with Problems in Getting Records   70
Self-Recorded Data and Planning for Change   74
Your Own Self-Direction Project: Step Three   79
Tips for Typical Topics   80

Chapter 4 Behavior/Environment Relationships   82

Language, Thinking, and Behavior   83
Consequences   86
Antecedents   93
Respondent Behavior   97
Modeling   101
Your Own Self-Direction Project: Step Four   102

Chapter 5 Antecedents   104

An Introduction to Chapters 5, 6, 7, and 8   105
Antecedent Control   106
Identifying Antecedents   106
Avoiding Antecedents   110
Changing Chains   113
Arranging New Antecedents   118
Building New Stimulus Control: The Physical and Social Environments   125
Your Own Self-Direction Project: Step Five   128
Tips for Typical Topics   128

Chapter 6 Developing New Behaviors   132

Shaping: The Method of Successive Approximations   133
Incompatible Behaviors   138
Coping with Anxiety and Tension   143
Relaxation   146
Developing New Behaviors through Practice   156
Developing New Behaviors through Modeling   160
Mastery in the Real World   161
Your Own Self-Direction Project: Step Six   161
Tips for Typical Topics   162

Chapter 7 Consequences   164

Discovering and Selecting Reinforcers   166
How to Use Reinforcement   178
Extinction   191
Self-Punishment   193
Reinforcement in Plans for Self-Direction   198
Theory and Research in Self-Directed Consequences   203
Your Own Self-Direction Project: Step Seven   205
Tips for Typical Topics   205

Chapter 8 Planning for Change   208

Combining A, B, and C Elements   209
The Features of a Good Plan   213
Formulating the Plan   217
Your Own Self-Direction Project: Step Eight   223
Tips for Typical Topics   223

Chapter 9 Is It Working? Analyzing the Data   224

Making a Graph   226
Analyzing the Data   231
Tinkering and Troubleshooting   237
Your Own Self-Direction Project: Step Nine   242

Chapter 10 Termination   244

Evolving Goals   245
Formal Termination: Planning to Maintain Gains   248

Dealing with Problems   252
Long-Term Projects   256
Your Own Self-Direction Project: Step Ten   257

Chapter 11 Uses and Limits of Self-Directed Change   258

The Limits of Self-Directed Change   259
Seeking Professional Help   262
Helping Others   265
Self-Management as a Lifelong Practice   267

References   269
Name Index   283
Subject Index   288
Topic Index   293

SELF-DIRECTED BEHAVIOR

Self-Modification for Personal Adjustment

THIRD EDITION

CHAPTER 1

Adjustment, Personal Goals, and Self-Management

GOAL:
To introduce the basic ideas and assumptions of self-directed change.

OUTLINE:
Self-direction and willpower
Personality, behavior, and situations
The process of self-management
Research in self-management: Does it really work?
Chapter summary
Your own self-direction project: Step one
Tips for typical topics

To arrange, to harmonize, to come to terms; to arrange the parts suitably among themselves and in relationship to something else—that is the definition of adjustment. Adjustment can mean harmony among the parts of the self—harmony of thoughts, feelings, and actions. The person who is torn by internal contradictions, the person who wants love but hates people, is not balanced or happy. In common language, such a person might be called badly adjusted or disturbed. Significantly, a synonym for mentally ill is unbalanced.

Adjustment can also mean harmony between the self and the environment. If someone is out of phase with the world around, we may speak of him or her as out of touch, gone, way out—terms that show our understanding that the maladjusted person is not in harmony with the environment. Of course, there are times when one doesn't want to be in tune, when it is best to be a rebel, a protester, a hermit, an individualist.

But when should we rebel, and when should we conform? When should we insist on our personal values, and when should we change our values because they are unproductive? Consider the issue of *shyness*. Is shyness good or bad? If you are shy, should you try to change? Shyness can be described as a problem—"I'd like to make new friends, but I am afraid to try"—or as an advantage—"Being shy gives me a chance to stand back and get to know others before I get too involved. Besides, no one ever thinks I'm obnoxious" (Zimbardo, 1977). Shyness itself is neither good nor bad. Whether it is good or bad *for you* can be determined only through a personal value judgment.

When we say that someone is "badly adjusted," we are also making a value judgment; in fact, we are saying that the person should not be doing something or should be doing something else. We make value judgments about our own behavior, too. You may conclude that you are too shy in

3

certain situations and that you would like to be more outgoing. You may feel, for example, that the quality of your life would be improved if you were less shy when meeting new people. If you talked to them a bit more and smiled a bit more, you might make new friends, which you would like. If that is your own value judgment about your shyness, you would probably want to develop more social confidence.

But can you? Do you have the skills to change? If you don't, people who can make a decision to change themselves and then do so probably seem a marvel to you. For example, if you are overweight and a slim friend says "Yes, I decided I was about five pounds overweight, so I just took them off," you listen with mouth agape—you who have been trying unsuccessfully for years to do the same thing!

All of us have some goals we cannot reach "just like that." Most of us have skills for certain situations but not for others. The person who easily sheds weight might have great difficulty shedding shyness. In a sense these abilities, or skills, to change ourselves in the direction of our values are the same skills that make up good adjustment.

Your pattern of good adjustment must be responsive and changing if you are to hold your chosen course. Like the rudder of a ship, your behavior must adjust to the currents and tides of the environment and to your own maturing values and goals. You, the pilot, must be in a constant and dynamic interplay with the environment.

Steering any course takes skill; adjustment itself is better seen as a skill than as a condition. Self-direction is the skill of actualizing one's values. Self-direction includes choosing goals and designing strategies to meet them, evaluating outcomes, changing tactics when needed, and solidifying new gains. Self-direction is the combination of the skills by which goals are achieved.

The purpose of this book is to present these skills of personal adjustment. As you will see, there is a strategy for achieving change itself. The same principles can be employed for losing weight, for becoming less shy, or for giving up smoking. The same principles are involved in gaining skills at tennis, in taking examinations, or in reducing anxiety. Although we'll deal with specific

---

BOX 1-1
How to Study This Book

Begin each chapter by reading the outline, printed on the opening page of the chapter. Even though one or two terms may not be completely clear to you until you have read the text, the outline will help you see the relationships among ideas, and that will make learning easier. There is a summary at the end of each large section of each chapter; read the summary first, then read it again after you have finished that section. Then close the book, and say out loud the major points discussed in the section you have just read. If you can't remember them all, go back and check them. These steps will help you learn.

problem areas, our essential goal is to teach you the basic skills for maintaining good adjustment. As in all teaching, our success will also depend on you, the learner. All skills begin at simple levels and rise to higher ones. Understanding requires effort and study; perfection requires practice. Specific exercises are suggested at the end of each chapter, and it is very important that you carry out these practice assignments. Like someone who is learning to ride a bicycle, you must actually ride, be willing to wobble a bit, and even take a fall. That's the only way you can learn to ride "just like that."

SELF-DIRECTION AND WILLPOWER

Is it really possible to learn self-direction? The answer is *yes*. You can increase the control you exercise over your own behavior and your own life. Obviously you can't control all events in your life; we are all limited by lack of talent, energy, or plain good luck. But within broad limits you can direct yourself toward your chosen goals.

There are clearly people who are excellent managers of their lives. They aren't overweight, they aren't too shy, they are in charge. By analyzing the ways these good managers achieve their goals, we can establish principles and techniques we can all use. And there has been considerable research in the last few years on methods of teaching these techniques. The parent disciplines for these studies are called *behavior analysis* and *behavior therapy* or *behavior modification*. These disciplines study the relationships among human behavior, thoughts, and environment. Research has led to the discovery of principles that could be applied to self-direction, resulting in a body of knowledge that describes how self-direction occurs and how it can be increased.

Some people tell us "I can't learn this, I have no willpower." These folks speak as though "willpower" involved something like standing in the face of temptation, fists clenched, jaws tight, finally refusing to do what one shouldn't do, even though one wants to do it. But people with effective willpower don't get into that kind of situation in the first place. They use foresight, self-analysis, and planning to avoid having to face irresistible temptations. This point (certainly not a new one) can be found in many ethical and religious systems. St. Paul and St. Augustine and St. Thomas Aquinas, for example, taught that to avoid sin one should avoid the occasion for sin.

For each of us there are irresistible "temptations"; that is, there are situations in which we make choices for immediate pleasure that go against our long-range goals. Laboratory research has shown that this is true even for mice (Ainslee, 1975). And it has been a topic of concern from time immemorial. Our own mythology shows, for example, how one wily man scored a victory over temptation. In Homer's *Odyssey*, written around 800 B.C., Odysseus and his crew had to sail through the straits where the Sirens sang. Their song, so alluring that it was irresistible, drew sailors to their deaths on the rocks. Odysseus didn't want to miss hearing their wonderful music, and yet he didn't want to be confronted with the irresistible temptation to sail too close. A shrewd man, he used a clever strategy to achieve both goals. First, he had his men lash him to the mast and ordered them to keep him there until they had sailed through the straits, no matter how much he might beg to be set free. Then he stopped the ears of his sailors with wax, so they couldn't hear the music and would row on (Ainslee, 1975).

This same strategy—preventing a behavior we do not want—is used, for example, by many of us every night that we set our alarm clock. The crucial element is to make the desired choice when we have the opportunity to choose correctly—before the Sirens sing, not while they sing; before we are sleepy, not in the drowsy morning hours (Rachlin, 1974).

PERSONALITY, BEHAVIOR, AND SITUATIONS

We all tend to see ourselves as consistent beings. Although we realize that in different situations we may act somewhat differently, we feel that our personality doesn't change, no matter what the situation. You might say, for example, "I tend to be a tense person. I get tense particularly when I'm taking an important test or going for a job interview." This type of self-description involves two elements: the kind of personality you have (tense) and the kind of situations you encounter (tests or interviews). But current research shows that, when thinking about their actions, most people *over*emphasize consistency and *under*emphasize the effects of different situations.

Trait Theory

Scientific psychology, too, overemphasized consistency in the first decades of theory and research in human personality. *Trait theory* is the name given to this original position. The basic assumption was that people possess underlying personality structures, or *traits* (distinctive characteristics thought to be long lasting and consistent in most situations), that account for their behavior (Mischel, 1968). If you were a trait theorist, you would describe someone's personality by listing his or her traits—for example, "My friend June is intelligent, achievement oriented, aggressive, sensitive, sensual, and emotionally cool." Each item describes one of June's traits, and, if you could list all of them, you would describe her total personality.

Often trait theorists have assumed that human actions stem only from inner conditions of the person's mind (Kazdin, 1975a) and that the situation has little influence. Consequently, if you want to achieve personal adjustment and other goals, you need to change your inner traits. But this approach results in a serious problem: we often don't know how to make these changes. Suppose you had the "nervous habit" of pulling your hair. Trait theory might advise you, first, to discover the inner trait that leads to hair pulling and then change that trait. This makes your task of changing much more complex than if your goal were expressed simply as "Change the act of hair pulling."

You, as a follower of trait theory, might say "But I really am a nervous person, and that's probably why I pull my hair. Shouldn't I try to get rid of the nervousness as a trait, instead of focusing on the one act of hair pulling?" You could describe other situations in which tension occurs—for example, "I'm nervous about meeting new people. And when I speak in front of a group. And in exams. And I pull my hair. I know I'm a nervous person because it shows up in various situations."

We would then say that you have put a *label* on your actions in these different situations. Do you think that you have explained your actions better by using this label, *nervousness?* Suppose you said simply "Here is a list of situations in which I am sometimes nervous." What would be lost?

As a matter of fact, if your goal is to be less tense, something would be gained. Inventing a label and applying it to yourself brings no benefit, but changing your reactions to the particular situations does. You cannot change a trait like "nervousness," because it is nothing more than an abstraction, a label you apply to yourself. Changing yourself always means changing behaviors in specific situations.

The same idea applies to willpower. If you observe yourself, you may find that there are certain things you can do—for example, resist smoking although you used to smoke or get your assignments done on time—and certain things you don't seem to be able to do—for example, follow a diet or exercise. You could say "Well, I have a bit of willpower, but I could use more." But what would be gained? This line of thinking puts all the emphasis on your inner personality and ignores the situation. Yet, often the best way to gain control over yourself is to control the situation, as Odysseus did.

The Medical Model

Trait theory has often been used to deal with questions of human adjustment. Questions such as "Where does badly adjusted behavior come from?" and "Why are some people badly adjusted?" have been answered in terms of inner personality. Physicians, too, have looked at problems of adjustment from this general perspective and have considered these problems analogous to those in physical health—that is, as similar to diseases. This has been called the *medical model* of adjustment (an interesting history of the medical model can be found in Ullman & Krasner, 1975). This model has become so entrenched that you may use this way of thinking without realizing that there are better alternatives.

The basic characteristics of this model are the concepts of inner cause and outer symptom. Suppose, for example, that you have a fever of 102 degrees and go to a physician for help. The way the doctor looks at your fever is to see it as a symptom, or signal, that there is something wrong inside you. Therefore, the doctor will not try just to eliminate the fever, for that would be taking care of the symptom and leaving the inner illness untreated, but will try to discover and eliminate the inner problem. If the inner problem can be eliminated, the outer symptom—the fever—will also disappear. For the medical model, inner problems cause outer symptoms and the proper course of treatment is to eliminate the inner problem. Of course, physicians do sometimes give treatment that provides symptomatic relief, but whenever possible they seek to eliminate the basic problem.

How does this model shape the thought of people who deal with issues of adjustment? First, what is the analog of the fever (the symptom)? Since "adjustment" deals with issues of behavior, some problem in behavior will take the form of the "symptom"—that is, the fever. For example, you might be unable to concentrate while studying, and this could be serious enough to interfere with your work in school. If you talked with someone—a friend or a counselor—about your problem and this person looked at it from the viewpoint of the medical model, he or she might view your lack of concentration as a symptom of some inner problem. The person would attempt to discover this "inner problem" and then "treat" it.

The nature of this supposed inner problem has been seen differently by different theorists. Sigmund Freud, the father of psychoanalysis, viewed behavior problems as symptoms of inner sexual conflicts or frustrations. Later theorists agreed that the inner problem was conflict but denied that it was necessarily sexual. They argued that any unresolved inner problem can lead to outer problems in behavior.

Perhaps the major advantage of the medical model is that physicians have searched for the medical reasons for some behavioral problems— for example, in some forms of mental retardation or diseases of the nervous system. Further, physicians have discovered symptomatic treatments, such as drugs to reduce anxiety or depression, that are effective in alleviating the suffering that so often accompanies major psychological disturbance.

But the medical model has limitations, similar to those of trait theory. The person's inner characteristics—the "inner cause"—are emphasized at the expense of external situations. For example, should the fact that a kid from a slum becomes a juvenile delinquent be interpreted as a sign of some inner malfunctioning or as the result of living in that neighborhood? (Probably both.)

Second, the medical model doesn't help you understand your own striving toward goals. For example, if you are making no progress toward some major goal, such as selecting a career, does that mean that you have some psychological disease? There is no research evidence that supports this explanation. Was Odysseus psychologically "healthier" than average, or was he perhaps simply more skilled at self-control?

Last, the research on psychological treatments based on the medical model is not encouraging. There is scant evidence that such treatments are actually helpful (Levitt, 1971; Rachman, 1971). Physical treatments such as drugs often do have an effect, but psychological treatments based on the medical model are at best very weak. The proof of the pudding is in the eating.

The Behavioral-Skill Model

In view of the serious problems inherent in both the trait theory and the medical model, we prefer to use a behavioral-skill model in thinking about personal adjustment and self-management. This means thinking about both inner characteristics and the situations in which actions occur. Goals are defined in terms of particular behaviors in particular situations.

Sometimes your goal is to stop behaving in a certain way. For example, you may become nervous every time you take a test, and this anxiety may interfere with how well you perform. If you were calm, you could remember more, think more clearly, and, more generally, perform at a higher level. Your goal, then, is to eliminate the behavior of nervousness in the situation of taking tests.

Sometimes your goal is to start behaving in a certain way. You may not be studying enough, and, as a result, you may not be doing well in school. Your goal is to increase the behavior of studying in the situation of the library or in the situation of your own room.

In either case—increasing or decreasing a behavior—it is the relationship of the behavior to its situation that you must analyze and control.

Behavior and the Environment

If you are very shy, just seeing a roomful of strangers at a party is enough to make you feel uncomfortable. Nothing bad has actually happened, but you feel nervous. You think "I don't know anybody here!" Feelings and thoughts of discomfort have been cued by the sight of a roomful of strangers. This party isn't for you, you think. Suppose you flee. Immediately your nervousness begins to dwindle. You feel relaxed, and your thoughts turn to where you'll go next. Fleeing had consequences: you feel better. This means that you are more likely to do something similar the next time you're in that kind of situation, because you've learned the benefits of flight.

Your behavior and thoughts are always imbedded in a context—the situation. Situations can arbitrarily be divided into two elements: the events that come before a behavior and those that come after it. In psychology these are called *antecedents* and *consequences*. They have been extensively studied by psychologists, and we know that both affect behavior. Antecedents are the setting events for your behavior. They cue you or stimulate you to act and feel in certain ways. They can be physical events, thoughts, emotions, or inner speech. Consequences affect whether you repeat certain actions or not. In B. F. Skinner's language, they reinforce behavior or fail to do so. And they affect how you feel. Consequences, too, can be physical events, thoughts, emotions, or inner speech. The antecedent for the behavior of the shy person is seeing the roomful of strangers and thinking "Panic!" The consequence is fleeing, which makes the person feel better and is therefore reinforcing. A simple way to remember this idea is to remember A-B-C: Antecedents-Behavior-Consequences.

What we do in a particular situation—how we behave—is determined by the nature of the situation. Changes in our environment produce changes in our behavior. Suppose, for example, that you are at home. There are certain things you will do there that you wouldn't do in other physical surroundings, such as school. You might take a nap at home, but you wouldn't do so in a classroom. Or suppose you are on a picnic; you would do things there that you wouldn't do at a formal dinner. Or suppose your girlfriend or boyfriend has just kissed you; that behavior will affect what you do next.

Because behavior is a function of the environment, changes in your physical surroundings or in your social circumstances or in the behavior of others will produce changes in your behavior. Of course, this is not a simple one-way relationship. Our behavior can affect our environment as well as be affected by it. The changes that result in the environment in turn affect our later behavior.

One of our undergraduate students, John, was an effective student and already the night manager of a grocery store. He had many male friends, found time for some weekend basketball, and played the piano. But he had one goal that remained unachieved; he was lonely for female friendship and felt pessimistic about his future love life. John analyzed his behavior in terms of situations. When he met a woman for the first time, he was able to talk comfortably and easily until or unless he felt the woman was attractive to him. When the situation was talking-to-an-attractive-woman, John behaved quite differently—stiffly and with reserve, so that others saw him as being aloof and as feeling superior. The sequence of events was generally the following. At the beginning, John would talk, comfortably and easily, to an interested new acquaintance; very quickly he would be talking, uncomfortably and stiffly, to an attractive, irritated woman—a woman made irritated by his own unfortunate embarrassment. In this changed environment resulting from his earlier actions, John's subsequent behavior also changed. When the woman was interested, John talked—easily at first and then increasingly stiffly; but, as she grew angrier and angrier, he became hurt, puzzled, and quieter. His behavior changed his situation, which in turn produced his new behavior.

All of us are constantly involved in interactions like this, interactions in which an environmental situation evokes behavior from us that in turn affects our situation. This kind of process is continuous in our lives and is determined not only by the reactions of specific others but by any kind of social or physical environment. Therefore, adjusting always involves changing the way our environment and our behavior in that environment relate to each other. The changes may come quickly, minute to minute, or extend over very lengthy periods.

Behavior and Learning Experiences

The effects of situations—antecedents, behavior, and consequences—are influenced by the learning experiences the person has had in similar situations. Standing on the top of a cliff, one person—who has learned to be nervous of heights—will feel fear and back away; another person—who has had no experience of fear of heights—will exclaim "What a view!" Different learning experiences produce different behaviors even when we are dealing with the same antecedent or consequence.

Our student John (who later undertook his own self-modification program) told us that he had profited from observing the behavior of a friend who was not at all nervous or backward when dealing with an attractive woman. John was struck by the great difference between his own behavior and that of his friend in the same situation. The point was that John's learning history had been very different from that of his friend; consequently, each young man behaved and felt in his own learned way in a specific environment.

The fact that behavior has to be learned does not imply that, once you are an adult, all you do is produce behaviors that you learned as you were growing up. New or changed situations may produce new behavior. For example, a young woman who has just become a mother finds herself in a relatively novel situation. She has a real, breathing baby to cope with, and she will learn new ways of behaving as she deals with the novel situation. Some of her behavior, however, will have been learned in the past. She didn't come to motherhood completely naive. Probably she had already developed certain ideas, attitudes, and specific ways for dealing with babies. For example, she may have had practice in caring for someone else's baby, she may have observed others caring for theirs, or she may have read books about child care.

The effect of the environment, then, is to evoke behaviors already learned and to teach new behaviors. The implication is clear. Adjustment reflects learned behaviors in specific situations, and you deal with your problems in adjustment by dealing with what you have learned (or not learned) to do in a particular situation. Therefore, in the process of self-modification, you set out to produce new learning for yourself in specific situations. To modify your own behavior—to bring it under control or determine its course—you'll have to seek to learn new behaviors for particular situations.

To change yourself, you need to develop the ability to change the antecedents and consequences that affect your behavior. This means that you must first notice them and then devise a way to change them.

THE PROCESS OF SELF-MANAGEMENT

Successful self-management always contains certain crucial elements: self-knowledge, planning, information gathering, and modification of plans in the light of the information available. There is a definite sequence in deliberate self-direction. Most self-change programs involve these steps:

1. Selecting a goal and specifying the behaviors you need to change in order to reach the goal. These are often called the *target behaviors.*
2. Making observations about the target behaviors. You may keep a kind of diary describing those behaviors or count how often you engage in them.

You discover the events that stimulate your acts and the things that reward them.

3. Working out a plan for change, which applies basic psychological knowledge. Your plan might call for gradually replacing an unwanted action with a desirable one. You might change the way you react to certain events. You might arrange to be rewarded for certain behaviors.

4. Readjusting your plans as you learn more about yourself. As you practice analyzing your behavior, you can make more and more sophisticated and effective plans for change.

Antecedents (A)	Behavior (B)	Consequences (C)
You can change the setting events for a behavior by building in antecedents that lead to wanted behavior and by removing antecedents that lead to unwanted behavior.	You can change actions, thoughts, feelings, or behaviors directly, by practicing desirable ones or by substituting desirable alternatives for unwanted acts.	You can change the events that follow behavior by reinforcing desired actions and not reinforcing unwanted behavior.

Figure 1-1.   Analysis of self-management: The A-B-Cs of change.

Carrying Out a Self-Change Project

So that you can better understand the processes involved, here is the report of one of our students who carried out a self-change project in our class. His name is Dean and he is a 20-year-old college student. Dean's experience with his plan for self-directed change is presented largely in his own words, along with our comments.

"I started off with this feeling that I don't make the right impression on people. I got that feeling a lot. I tried to notice when it was happening and made notes in my diary. It usually happens when I don't express myself very well. When I can't think of the right words, what do I do? I swear. I swear a lot. My foul language has gotten to be a habit. It turns people off and makes me feel stupid. I think that if I could stop swearing I'd become more articulate. So that's my goal."

Dean has taken the first step in self-direction; he has translated a vague sense of dissatisfaction into a concrete goal. He has expressed his personal values in terms of a specific behavior.

Dean writes: "I used a 3 × 5 card to count how often I swore. I found that I swore approximately 135 times in one week. I'm sure I missed some, but I don't think I missed very many. The card was in my wallet, which I take everywhere with me.

"I noticed that just making the count cut down how much I swore. Every time I had to make a mark on that card I felt guilty. So I was more careful in trying not to swear. 135 per week is just an approximate figure. But it would be higher if I hadn't counted it."

Dean has taken the second step in self-direction: making a specific count of his problem behavior. He was wise to get this record before attempting a change. To begin an improvement program before getting careful information usually results in failure. Dean wouldn't have known enough to successfully improve unless he had carefully observed himself. Also, his counting record made it possible for him to measure the success or failure of his eventual program.

"After counting my swearing for a week," Dean continues, "I narrowed my behavior down to a specific situation. The situation in which my swearing occurred the most was when I was with the guys at work. I am a food runner at a restaurant; I replenish the food on the buffet line. All of us in the kitchen swear all the time; there, swearing is like another language."

Often self-observation results in the realization that the target behavior occurs, or fails to occur, because of specific circumstances. This makes change easier because you can change the circumstances. And that is what Dean did, as we will see in a moment. Notice that you have to make the self-observations in order to discover the circumstances.

Dean goes on: "I really enjoy using my car radio when I'm driving. You don't know how difficult it is for me to drive without music! I fixed a plan so that I had to earn the right to listen to the car radio by cutting down on my swearing."

This is a kind of self-punishment. If he swears too much, Dean will take away one of his favorite activities—listening to the radio. We usually recommend against self-punishment, because, as you will see, it often doesn't work. We will also see that self-direction skills can identify and overcome some inevitable errors, like Dean's self-punishment.

Then Dean says: "I needed something to bridge the time between my performing the desired act and my getting to listen to the car radio. So I worked out a 'point system.' For every hour that I didn't swear, I would get one point. I work six hours per night. I decided that I had to get all six points if I wanted to listen to the car radio while I was driving home from school or work. If I got only four points, then I couldn't use the radio until next morning on the way to school. Less than four points, no car radio till the next afternoon.

"But I wasn't making the points. Too much swearing still. So I decided to avoid going into the restaurant kitchen while I was working on this plan. We can't swear when we're out on the dining-room floor, so this way I would avoid the situation that led to a lot of swearing. When I had to go back to the kitchen to get more food, I'd tell myself 'Remember, don't swear.'"

Dean's idea to use points is a good one, as the point system helps him bridge the gap until the time for listening to the radio comes. He found that self-punishment didn't work, however; he still swore. He might have quit at this point, but he thought again and decided to avoid the situation in which he was tempted to swear—an excellent idea. Later, he will have to deal with that temptation directly; but in the early stages of his plan it is a wise technique. His verbal reminder to himself is another effective device.

Dean's project was a success. Two months later, his swearing was near zero, and he had learned to cope with the "tempting" situation of the kitchen. At the semester's end, he intended to begin a new plan, this time to increase accurate self-expressions of opinion and feelings. He did, and now he continues to work toward his long-range goal of becoming more articulate.

Applying Principles

What makes a plan to change, like Dean's, different from any New Year's resolution? Is a self-direction plan only a resolution to do better? Sometimes we can just make up our minds to change and do it: "I turned over a new leaf!" or "I made a New Year's resolution." But of course it is not always so easy. If it were, there would be only self-satisfied people in the world. Most people, however, are not completely pleased with themselves. Something more than good intentions is needed. That something more is a correct, self-conscious application of the principles of human-behavior change.

Self-direction is, itself, a set of techniques that must be learned. To see if you are beginning to learn, evaluate the following report, which is a first effort at self-modification by another of our students. Is it a good plan? Does it make sense to you?

Bryan, a 20-year-old college junior, writes: "I'm a nail biter, but I wish I weren't. It's embarrassing, sometimes it's painful, and it seems childish to me—something that is OK when you're a kid, but not now.

"*Target behavior:* reduce nail biting to zero.

"*Count:* I counted for three weeks. The frequency of nail biting ranged from one to eight times a day, with the average about four or five at first, but during this last week it's down to two times a day. I think counting the biting makes me more aware of it, and sometimes I stop where I would have gone ahead and bitten them before.

"The situations that seem to produce more biting are (1) watching TV, (2) being bored, almost anywhere, and (3) listening to lectures. I don't see any way I can change these situations, since I don't want to give up TV, I have to go to lectures, and how can anybody completely avoid being bored?

"*Plan for changing:* I have signed the following contract and put it up on the mirror where I see it every morning. 'I promise not to bite my nails at all each day. If I don't bite my nails all day, then (1) I get to eat dinner and (2) I get to see my girlfriend that night. If I refrain from biting my nails all week, I get to go out Saturday night, which I usually do. Otherwise, I must stay home. Signed, Bryan W.'"

In our opinion, this case has some good points and several bad ones. The good points are that Bryan has an accurate count of how often he bites his nails and that he knows the situations in which he is likely to bite them. One of the bad points—bad because it decreases Bryan's chances of success— is that he intends to take away one of his major joys (being with his girlfriend) if he bites his nails, and we suspect that he won't stick to this intention. A second bad point is that he has no plan for developing any behavior that will replace nail biting, which would make quitting much easier. By the end of the book, you'll be better able to judge the quality of possible plans. Even now, it is a good learning technique to begin thinking critically about the many cases that are included in this book as examples.

Adjusting and Changing Plans

If Bryan is going to successfully change his nail-biting habit, he will have to change his plan as he learns more about the art of self-management. Very often people start with an apparently sound plan, but, as they actually try it, they find that it needs adjusting. Plans must be adjusted as one finds parts that are not working. Sometimes an entire plan must be redesigned, as our third case illustrates.

Claudia felt she wasn't studying enough. "I knew my study habits were dreadful; I study hard only when some deadline is about 12 hours away. I decided to reward myself each time I completed an assignment early by allowing myself to perform one of my favorite activities—playing the guitar, reading the newspaper, memorizing a limerick, doing a crossword puzzle, or resting. Six completed assignments would allow me to watch my favorite TV program.

"This plan worked fabulously for one day and fairly well for three more. After that it fell apart completely. I began indulging in my rewarding activities whether I had studied or not and quit keeping records of my studying. I was just too busy with my job and hobbies to study more. I began to wander through my studies, falling farther and farther behind. But I knew I'd never get into veterinary school unless I studied more.

"I thought about it a great deal, and I realized that I hate studying because it cuts into my free time so much. The basic problem is that I don't have enough free time. I feel trapped in duties. So I have decided to change my plan. My goal right now is to schedule my daily activities efficiently, so that I will manufacture more free time."

Claudia's new plan called for specific, regular study times, work times, and play times. At the end of the day, she scheduled a late TV show, which she allowed herself to watch only if she had kept her daily schedule.

It often happens that once you begin a plan you realize that you need to change some of the details (like Bryan) or even that you have to reorient the goal of your plan entirely (like Claudia). Start with a simple plan that seems to meet your needs. Then find out what interferes with success. That will tell you what the new, changed plan should be.

But will any plan work? Can you change yourself?

RESEARCH IN SELF-MANAGEMENT: DOES IT REALLY WORK?

A number of successful cases of self-management have been reported in the professional literature. People have been successful at:

studying better (Richards, 1976);
controlling weight (Mahoney, Moura, & Wade, 1973);
handling anxiety in social situations (Rehm & Marston, 1968);
controlling "nervous habits" like scratching, nail biting, and hair pulling (Watson, Tharp, & Krisberg, 1972; Perkins & Perkins, 1976);
overcoming mild depression (Tharp, Watson, & Kaya, 1974);
speaking up in class (Barrera & Glasgow, 1976);
relaxing (Rosen, 1977);
enhancing creativity (Meichenbaum, 1975);
reducing aggressiveness (Novaco, 1976);
exercising (Sherman, Turner, Levine, & Walk, 1975; Kau & Fischer, 1974).

We should be cautious, however, in assessing these favorable reports (Glasgow & Rosen, 1978). By their very nature, clinical work and most research projects imply the presence of an adviser, a counselor, or at least an experimenter, who has, of course, some influence on the self-help program. Furthermore, clinical cases don't prove conclusively that you can succeed at increasing your self-direction, since not all alternative explanations for these successful cases have been ruled out by careful experimentation. But note that it is not the validity of the principles that is in doubt. In fact, there is a very large amount of experimental evidence supporting the principles that underlie self-direction and a modest but growing literature detailing the elements that increase success in self-direction.

Certainly not every problem will yield to self-management; not every reader will master self-control. But it is the purpose of this book to detail those procedures that will make that mastery more likely. Let's ask again, in the light of these comments, the question we posed a little earlier. What is the likelihood of *your* success? Or, to put it in a different way, can you learn self-change techniques in a course like the one you are attending now?

In a class designed by Manuel Barrera and Russell Glasgow (1976) at the University of Oregon, 20 students carried out self-change projects using this text. At the end of the semester 70% rated their project as "extremely valuable" and another 25% rated it as "of some value." Three months later 83% said either that they were still improving or that they had not lost ground since the end of the course.

In another study carried out by Paul Payne and Roger Woudenberg (1978) at the University of Cincinnati, 63 students attending a similar course and using this text attempted self-change projects on problems like weight control, smoking reduction, nervous habits, bad studying habits, and social problems. The researchers measured changes from the onset of the project to its completion at the end of the semester. For each type of project they compared the students' success rate with success in the same types of projects when supervised by professional helpers, as reported in the research literature. They concluded that overall the self-change projects were as effective as individual or group-treatment procedures administered by a professional.

Everett Worthington (1979) of the University of Missouri taught self-modification to 40 students in his psychology-of-adjustment class and measured its effect. He found that "classroom-based self-modification projects apparently produced and maintained changed target behaviors and changed emotional reactions to the target behaviors" (p. 93).

Scott Hamilton (in press) at Colorado State University taught self-change techniques to 72 students, using this text. He reported that 83% of the students met their preestablished goals for behavior change. He also found that having a successful experience with self-modification increased students' expectancies of success in future projects.

There have been other systematic reports on whole classes who learned self-management; these reports have been summarized in detail by Robert Menges and Bernard Dobroski (1977), who conclude "The studies . . . provide some evidence that the subject matter of behavioral psychology can be taught at a level which facilitates successful self-modification projects" (p. 172). Michael Perri and Steve Richards (1977) studied the difference between people who succeeded at self-management and those who did not. They found that successful people used *more* techniques and for a longer period of time. The particular techniques you use will depend on the things you want to change, but the message is clear—to increase your chances of success, use as many different techniques as you can, and be ready to use them long enough to have an effect.

BOX 1-2
A Tic-Like Behavior Case Study Emanating from a Self-Directed Behavior Modification Course

In the journal *Behavior Therapy,* Pawlicki and Galotti (1978) report the case of a student who, as a project in a course such as the one you are taking and using this text, successfully changed a serious tic. This case is a nice illustration of the process of self-modification. Here is the original research report:

> The subject was a 23-year-old male undergraduate student with a problem behavior of teeth grinding, observed most often during periods of concentration such as reading, note taking, and letter writing.
> Baseline . . . [the period in which a behavior is observed but not deliberately changed] . . . was easily accomplished by carrying around an index card and making a mark every time the teeth-grinding behavior was noticed. Sometimes teeth grinding would happen unconsciously and, to combat this, the subject asked his girl friend for assistance in keeping an accurate baseline.

(Box 1-2 continues)

BOX 1-2 *(continued)*

The initial baseline period lasted 10 days with a mean of 42 occurrences per day. A written contract was designed by the subject, stating his goal to maintain the target behavior at a level of zero. The contract utilized the techniques of coveranting [changing thoughts], reinforcement, mild punishment, and alternative response training.

In addition to the instructions written in the contract on how and when to coverant, there was a list of five negative [thoughts] followed by a list of five positive [thoughts] which was memorized by the subject. Also included in the formal contract was an agreement whereby the subject would receive a positive reinforcement each evening if a reduction of 10 or more teeth-grinding behaviors had occurred since the previous evening. However, after the first three days of program implementation, a decrease of 10 occurrences of teeth grinding in one day seemed a somewhat unreasonable demand to be met. The contract was therefore changed to five occurrences. Another step included in the program was the use of mild punishment. . . . In addition, an attempt was made at alternative response training. Whenever the subject noticed teeth-grinding behavior, he would stop and consciously practice relaxing his jaw muscles and concentrate on how much better they felt.

The number of occurrences of teeth grinding decreased from 32 times to three times in only 10 days with a mean of 15 occurrences per day. These results were in themselves very gratifying to the subject who "no longer felt the need to grind my teeth." At Day 20, the contract needed to be altered slightly since the number of occurrences was below the five that were needed for reinforcement that evening. The reduction needed to gain reinforcement was changed to three occurrences. . . .

After a slight increase in teeth grinding at Day 21, the behavior steadily decreased until the goal of zero occurrences was maintained consecutively from Day 24 on, with the exception of one occurrence on Day 26. Beyond Day 30 of the program, the subject discontinued the program contingencies and continued with a less formal observation of his target behavior. A 6-week follow-up indicated that the teeth-grinding behavior was occurring at a rate of less than three times per week.

The importance of the above findings appears to be twofold. First, the subject did not face the difficult task of generalization from "therapeutic sessions." Second, through the process of self-administration, the subject was able to record a behavior that may have been difficult to otherwise accurately record. A still more sensitive observation was gained through his girl friend's assistance. The sensitivity of the program is also illustrated in the subject's responsiveness to variations in the occurrence of the target behavior. Through the subject's intimate involvement in the construction of the program, he was able to modify the plan without outside consultation.

From "A Tic-Like Behavior Case Study Emanating from a Self-Directed Behavior Modification Course," by R. Pawlicki and N. Galotti, *Behavior Therapy*, 1978, *9*, 671–672. Reprinted by permission.

BOX 1-3

Unsuccessful Self-Treatment of a Case of "Writer's Block"[1]

It would be misleading to suggest that everyone who tries self-modification is successful. There are, however, very few published examples of unsuccessful cases, as journals are not much interested in publishing them. Here is one, in its entirety:

THE UNSUCCESSFUL SELF-TREATMENT OF A CASE OF "WRITER'S BLOCK"

DENNIS UPPER

Veterans' Administration Hospital, Brockton, Massachusetts

REFERENCES

---

[1]Portions of this paper were not presented at the 81st Annual American Psychological Association Convention, Montreal, Canada, August 30, 1973.

Reprinted with permission from *Journal of Applied Behavior Analysis, 7,* Dennis Upper, "Unsuccessful Self-Treatment of a Case of 'Writer's Block,'" Copyright 1974, Pergamon Press, Ltd.

CHAPTER SUMMARY

Psychological adjustment is determined through a value judgment one makes about the relationship between a person and the environment. The skills necessary to change oneself in the direction of one's values are the same skills that make up adjustment. The purpose of this book is to present such skills. One can think of these skills as personal characteristics—willpower for example—but it is more helpful to think of them as both the characteristics of the person and the situation in which action occurs.

As you strive toward self-change, you need to change your actions in the context of particular situations. Your behavior, thoughts, and feelings are embedded in contexts—the things that go before them (the antecedents) and the things that come after them (the consequences). A-B-C relationships are established through learning. The environment evokes behaviors already learned and teaches new behaviors. In the process of self-change you produce new learning for yourself in specific situations.

You are more likely to be successful if you use a variety of techniques for a certain period of time and if you follow the exercises at the end of each chapter in this book. Research in self-modification has shown that students can learn the principles of self-change and carry out successful projects.

YOUR OWN SELF-DIRECTION PROJECT: STEP ONE

There's a big difference between knowing ideas well enough to pass a test on them and knowing them well enough to use them in your daily life. To reach this more advanced stage, you must practice self-change.

Make a list of several personal goals. These can be major, long-term goals or minor, shorter ones. They should, however, be important to you. You won't learn much by trying to change something trivial about yourself. Think over your list for a day or two, perhaps adding some goals to it or changing some. Then select one goal for a learning project. Our advice as you take this step is that you remain flexible in your choice. Some projects that seem simple turn out in practice to be quite complicated, and apparently complicated projects sometimes turn out to be simple. The main purpose is to learn the steps and techniques of self-management by practicing them. The best project for learning is one that is important enough to you to make it worth going through most of the steps in the book.

For your project, should you select one of the really difficult tasks in your life, or should you choose something you feel will be easy to bring under control? There is no clear answer, but here are some considerations. If you are involved in a difficult problem—for example, a weight problem or smoking or drug abuse—you should know that, although here you may be able to learn self-control, reaching your goal and maintaining it are likely to take longer than one semester. If you are overweight, for example, you will have to change several different things about your pattern of overeating and un-derexercising. A "major project" may mean selecting only some aspects of the problem to work on, and it may not be possible to reach the entire goal in one semester. Will that discourage you? Will you quit just when you should keep going? If you try for a less ambitious project, you may achieve complete success; but, if success comes too quickly, will you learn enough about the process? So there is an argument for and an argument against the very chal-lenging and the very easy; both have advantages. You alone can decide.

TIPS FOR TYPICAL TOPICS

Most chapters end with a section called "Tips for Typical Topics," in which we point out how you can apply the ideas discussed in the chapter to the more common kinds of self-management projects. Here's a list of common topics in our classes in self-management:

overeating, smoking, drinking, and drug use
studying and time management
family, friends, lovers, and coworkers
assertion
the other sex
specific fears
depression

These end-of-chapter suggestions are not intended as substitutes for reading and thinking about the ideas offered in the chapter. For each topic, the "Tips" section will call only specific things to your attention. These specific tips should be integrated into your overall emerging plan.

BOX 1-4
Criteria for a Good Project

Your instructor will probably tell you that success or failure in your self-change project is less important—even to your course grade—than your sophistication in carrying out the project. Sophistication (or complexity) refers to the number of different techniques you try and to the relationship between the techniques and your self-observations. If you observe yourself carefully, you will be able to use more techniques. Sheer effort also makes a difference. If you want to take on a difficult project, check with your instructor to be sure that she or he realizes that the project is a difficult one and will grade you on sophistication and effort, not just on success.

Here are some tips for getting a better grade:

Make careful observations. Try to learn about the actual A-B-C relationships in your behavior.

Use a variety of techniques. These techniques for change are grouped under the A-B-C headings. Try to use some techniques from each category.

Change your plans as you find out what works and what doesn't work. You will want to tinker with your system. This is discussed throughout the book and summarized in Chapter 9.

Be persistent. Keep trying to effect a change, and change your plans as you learn more about yourself and your A-B-C relationships.

Be well organized in your final report. Here is a possible outline for the report:

The goal you selected (from this and the next chapter).
Your observations about your behavior (from Chapter 3).
Your first plan to change. Draw on ideas from Chapter 5, 6, and 7. Try to use several kinds of techniques. Show your results (see "How to Make a Graph" in Chapter 9).
Your second plan for change. If the first plan is not completely successful, readjust, tinker with the system, or draw up a new system altogether. Show your results.
Your plans for the future—what you will do to maintain your gains.
Final conclusions.

CHAPTER 2

Specifying the Goal and Building Commitment

OUTLINE:

The goal as behaviors-in-situations
Tactics for specifying behaviors-in-situations
Building commitment
Your own self-direction project: Step two
Tips for typical topics

Any good beginning in self-direction projects requires two things: a clear
specification of the goal and a strong commitment to the act of self-change.

THE GOAL AS BEHAVIORS-IN-SITUATIONS

All of us use abstract words like *aggressive, dependent, strong,* or *ambitious*
to describe personality traits or motives. Words of this kind pose two problems: they don't specify the situations in which behaviors may occur, and they
don't specify particular behaviors. Also, these words seem to imply that behaviors exist independently of their environmental setting. The use of such
abstract words comes from the belief, which we discussed earlier, that people
possess traits that are the same in every environment. Thus you might say
"I'm an independent person" or "I'm not very sociable." But this kind of
language is misleading, because you may act independently in one situation
and dependently in another. A student, for example, might be quite emotionally dependent on his girlfriend but rather independent in his schoolwork
and relationships with his professors.

Even if your problem relates to pervasive inner feelings—a sense that
"something is wrong inside"—you should still think of it as emotional-reac-
tions-in-particular-situations. You might think "I'm nervous and depressed.
I'm getting neurotic." But a better formulation—one that can help you
change—would be "At work, after I finish a big task, I get depressed" or "At
night in the dorm I seem to feel nervous."

In other words, *it is necessary that you think of your behavior in combination with the situation in which the behavior occurs.* You have to be very
specific, because you can change only specific things in specific situations.
Regardless of the type of problem or goal you are dealing with, you must
have well-defined objectives that are specified in terms of particular behaviors

23

in particular situations. That should be your goal for this chapter. Here are several tactics that will help you specify your goals along the lines just described.

TACTICS FOR SPECIFYING BEHAVIORS-IN-SITUATIONS

Tactic One: Make a List of Concrete Examples. Suppose you're dissatisfied with yourself. "I'm too self-centered" you think. This self-statement doesn't tell you what to change, though, because it is too vague. Try giving yourself a concrete example of the problem such as "I talk about myself too much when I'm with my friends." As you can see, this is much more concrete than "I'm too self-centered," since it specifies both the behavior and the situation in which the behavior occurs.

"I'm insecure" is another example of a vague statement. Peter, a divorced transfer student, said that he was "insecure" and wanted to change that. Two examples that came to his mind were: (1) a time when he had left a party early because he didn't know anyone there and felt too shy to introduce himself and (2) a time when he had not asked out a new acquaintance he wanted to date for fear she would say no. These examples were specific; they allowed Peter to focus his attention on the concrete problem behaviors and on the situations in which they occurred.

Tactic Two: Look for Examples in Your Daily Life. Sometimes providing yourself with two or more examples of the behavior in question will make you more aware of the kinds of situations in which the behavior occurs. A young woman reported "I'm too rude." We pointed out that, with that statement, she was telling us nothing about the circumstances of her rudeness; in fact, she wasn't even saying what she meant by "rude." Then we asked her "Can you give an example of your rude behavior?"

"Sure," she answered promptly. "Yesterday my friend asked to borrow my pen. It was my best pen, and I was afraid I wouldn't get it back. I think I said no rather abruptly."

"Okay. Can you give us another example?" we said.

She paused. "A guy who lives down the street also goes to the university. Two days ago he called and asked if he could have a ride to school. But I didn't want to go so early. So I just turned him down with no explanation."

This dialog illustrates a process. The woman began with a vague, abstract statement—"I'm too rude." Yet, when she was asked to give examples, she gave examples that were quite specific. In other words, she turned a vague and hardly useful observation into a clear and productive statement about her behavior and the specific situation in which the behavior occurred.

In thinking about the examples from your daily life, you can often extract the common elements that tie them together. For example, the "rude" woman thinks to herself "It's not that I am always rude. But when people seem like they're pushing me and I'm afraid they will take advantage of me, then I'm rude." Now that she has more clearly labeled the kind of situation in which her rudeness occurs, she can begin to change the way she reacts in that sort of situation.

Tactic Three: List the Details of Your Problem. The two tactics suggested above are based on the principle that to solve problems you must attend to the details of problems (D'Zurilla & Goldfried, 1971). What details are involved in your feelings of "insecurity"? Do you feel nervous? Do you fail to talk or to look people in the eye? Do you brag? State the problem, as well as your goal, in detailed terms that are objective, clear, and complete (Hawkins & Dobes, 1977). For example, if you feel depressed and helpless, list the details: moping, self-criticizing, inactive. Each detail specifies a goal for change.

Often our thinking about a problem is unfocused. Listing the details will help you see precisely what your target goal should be. For example, a man who was trying to give up smoking listed the details of each situation in which he had given in and taken another cigarette. His list looked like this: "I really was craving a cigarette. I told myself 'I can handle it, I'll smoke just one.' This happens only at parties or during the day if I feel that I've been working too hard and deserve a break." You can see from these details that he needn't worry every minute of his life about smoking. But there are specific situations that greatly increase the chances that he will go back to cigarettes, and it is those times that define his problem for him.

Research in problem solving suggests that people who list details improve their problem-solving ability, compared with those who do not (Presbrey, 1979). We suggest making a list of the details of your problem, then selecting those that seem critical to its solution. For example, a woman who was unsuccessfully trying to lose weight listed these details: "I can usually keep breakfast small. I can resist eating once I go to work. If I take my lunch, I can make it light. I don't mind being hungry at work, because I'm so busy I don't much notice it. Toward midafternoon I get very hungry. On the way home on the bus I often feel like I'm starving. When I get home I'm frantic. I go straight to the fridge and eat about three-quarters of a supper. Then I cook a meal and eat that. So I end up gorging in the evening. And on weekends I never stick to the diet. As soon as I get hungry, it's straight to the fridge." This list of details suggests a clearer definition of her problem than a simple "I can't stick to my diet." There were times when she could stick to it and times when she could not. She began her self-change project by attacking those times when she was not staying on the diet.

Tactic Four: Become an Observer of Yourself. It is true that, when you try to describe your behaviors, you often begin with a vague trait term. You somehow feel that you are "aggressive" or "dependent," without knowing exactly what behaviors you mean when you use these terms. When this happens, you need to become an observer of yourself.

A critical step in specifying the problem is to stop speculating about your behavior and start actually observing it. Your thoughts about your problem will probably remain overly vague until you begin to actually watch yourself behaving in various situations.

Not only should you actually observe your own behavior, but you should keep notes of your observations. You might keep a narrative account of your daily life or simply note instances of behavior that seem related to the problem. Your goal is to gather enough observations of your behavior in various situations to enable you, when you sit down to read over your notes, to see some pattern emerging.

The best way to make these observations is to write down your behaviors and the situations in which they occur as soon as you think you have an instance of the problem. Suppose that, in the example above, the woman hadn't been able to specify situations in which she was rude and decided to follow our advice and begin to actually observe her behavior. When the student who lived down the street called to ask for a ride to the university and she responded with her rude "No!" she would have asked herself "Was that an instance of being too rude or not?" If she had decided that it was, she would have observed that her rudeness occurred when someone asked for a ride to school. The next day, when her friend asked to borrow her pen and she responded ungraciously, she might have asked again "Was that another example of rudeness?" In other words, she would have set out to observe all instances of rudeness, but in time she would have come to realize that her problem was more specific.

Another of our students, Marie, began by stating that her problem was "overdependence" on men. She couldn't think of any examples, so she started off by making observations and writing down details of the problem. On a date a few days later, her friend asked her if she wanted to go to see a particular movie. Marie didn't want to go but went anyway. So she asked herself if that was an instance of being too dependent. A few days later another date took her bowling—something that, she confided to us, she hated. She counted that as another instance of overdependence. Soon afterward Marie reported that she could see now what her problem was: she tended to do whatever her companions wanted to do, for fear of contradicting their wishes, even though sometimes she didn't want to do it. From a vague statement of "overdependence," Marie had come to realize that her problem could be expressed as a specific behavior in a particular situation—going along too often with her dates' wishes even when she didn't want to.

When the Problem Is Nonperformance of Some Behavior

Sometimes your goal is to start doing something that at present you're not doing. For example, you may realize that you are failing in college because you're *not* studying. What can you do? The same general strategy of specifying the problem applies; you should specify the situation in which you *want* the behavior to occur: "My goal is _____ in _____ ."

(what you want to do)   (situation)

Paul, a student who had such a problem, kept a journal to record these situations. It had entries like this: *"Wednesday. Roommate went out. Room quiet. Got out the history text and turned to the assignment. Remembered baseball game was on TV and started watching it. Tried to study between innings but gave it up. Studied about five minutes the whole afternoon. Thursday. Went to the library to study. Saw Karen. Didn't study."*

These observations do specify two situations in which studying would have been desirable: "room quiet in the afternoon" and "went to the library." But the journal also contains other valuable information; it tells our student what he did instead of studying. Paul was not simply "not studying"; he was actively performing behaviors that made studying impossible. In other words, as far as studying was concerned, he was performing the "wrong" behaviors. So his task of problem specification was not really different from those we have discussed earlier—specifying the situation in question (for example, "room is quiet") and then specifying the behavior in question (for example, "watching TV instead of studying").

Remember that you should specify not only the situation and the fact that the desirable behavior is not occurring but also the behaviors that do occur instead of the ones you want. Thus, Paul should first specify the situation in which he wants the behavior to occur—when he is alone in his room or when he is in the library—and then observe what occurs *instead* of the desired behavior. He wants to increase studying, but to do so he has to see what he does that interferes with it.

When the Problem Is Getting Rid of Some Undesirable Behavior

Paul could express his goal in two different ways: (1) "I want to quit goofing off and study more" or (2) "I want to increase studying in those situations in which I should study." The second way is better, because it expresses the goal in terms of some behaviors that need to be increased. Trying simply to stop doing something is like trying to think of nothing. Your strategy should always be to *increase some desirable behavior.* Even if the problem is that you are doing something you want to stop, your strategy should be to specify a desirable alternative behavior.

For Paul, specifying a desirable alternative was easy. By making records of his behavior, he saw that when he was alone in his room he watched TV and that when he went to the library he talked with Karen. For each of those two situations, he could name the desirable alternative behavior—he should have studied. His intervention plan would *not* be to decrease directly the undesirable behaviors of watching-TV-when-alone-in-room or talking-with-Karen-in-library but, instead, to increase the desirable behaviors of studying-when-alone-in-room and studying-when-in-library. He therefore set up a plan to increase studying in these two situations.

It is always best to attempt to specify your problem in terms of some desirable behavior that you would like to increase.

Laura came to one of us complaining that she was bothered by frequent feelings of depression. She had begun searching for possible causes of these upsetting feelings and found that a great variety of things seemed to produce depression. A friend would mildly criticize her, her cat would briefly disappear, her new clothes would be slightly soiled—many relatively meaningless events seemed sufficient to set off hours of unpleasantness. Laura had the feeling that it would take her a lifetime just to specify all the situations leading to depression, much less to do anything about them. When asked to specify a desirable alternative, she replied that feeling good was an alternative. We suggested that she search for events that made her feel good and that she keep in mind the goal of attempting to increase them.

When You Aren't Sure What to Do

Suppose you're not reaching some goal but aren't sure what to do to reach it. A young woman with ambitions to be a poet complained to us that she never seemed to get around to writing poetry. "Do you have a schedule for writing?" we asked. We pointed out that all writers must discipline themselves to set aside some time in which they sit down at the typewriter, whether they feel "inspired" or not, and suggested that she choose a specific hour, every other day, to do nothing but write poetry. She seemed to agree, but, just as she was leaving, she turned back to say "Actually I tried something like that last week, but I couldn't keep the schedule." She went on to explain that she did understand what had happened. She had begun to worry about how her poem would sound to other people before she had even written the lines. This prevented her from writing and made trying to write very unpleasant.

"What is the full chain of actions that would produce your goal?" we asked. After a few moments she was able to state the chain precisely: keeping a firm schedule for writing, developing a feeling of confidence, and concentrating on the poem itself rather than on the readers' eventual reactions. She decided to choose the last link of the chain as her self-directing project, and in time she was able to develop good concentration. As a consequence, she became more productive.

If you aren't sure what to do to reach a goal, there are additional tactics available. You've just seen an illustration of the next one:

Tactic Five: Specify the Chain of Events That Will Produce Your Goal. The things that "happen" to you are the result of a series of causes—more specifically, of a chain of behaviors (behaviors of your own and of other people) that, once set in motion, seems to lead inexorably to its conclusion.

You are probably now involved in some such chain, which is leading to repeated frustration of your goal. The case of the young poet illustrates such a chain. But remember that even your new, adaptive behaviors will also occur in chains-of-events. Therefore, your task in designing a plan for self-direction will involve specifying not only the simple, targeted behavior, but the chain that would produce it.

A shy young man told us in conference, "I do want to date more, I really try in spite of disappointments. I set up situations where I can meet girls, but at the last minute I get anxious and tongue-tied, and I chicken out. What should I do?"

We gave him the assignment of producing two written chains-of-events: the current one and a hypothetical one that would produce his goals. He brought back an excellent analysis.

"Here's an example. I have spotted a girl in your class I'd like to know. I want to begin an acquaintance in a gradual way, by sitting next to her and having a brief conversation."

Now	Goal
1. I am scared [censored].	1. I tell myself "My boy, you're a wonder and potentially magnetic to women."
2. I sit down.	2. I sit down.
3. She looks at me.	3. She looks at me.
4. I say "Hi" and panic. I look away.	4. I say "Hi" and ask her what she thinks of the course.
5. That's the end. I feel stupid and worthless.	5. She answers.
	6. I reply calmly and hopefully with wit and charm.
	7. I walk out with her after class.
	8. I'm on the way!

As we will discuss in the chapter on antecedents, this student will probably want to change both ends of the chain (Frankel, 1975). For now, this sample illustrates the power of a careful chain-of-events analysis. The student can now work on those behaviors that will lead eventually to his goal.

Tactic Six: Get Advice. Chain-of-events reasoning depends on knowing the critical behaviors, and sometimes these important links won't occur to you. At other times you may really not know how to perform a needed behavior. In such cases, the advice of others may be helpful. Friends, family, or others you respect may sometimes help you over difficult moments in your self-analysis.

This is particularly true in the stage of problem definition. If you are unable to determine your own contribution to an unsatisfying chain of events, someone who you think handles these chains well may be able to offer advice. For example, a man who often felt ill at ease at social events noticed that his friend seemed perfectly comfortable at the same gatherings. So in private he spoke to her: "What do you do at these things? I always feel awkward. How do you deal with that?" His friend explained that everyone she met knew something interesting that she didn't know, so, instead of making "small talk" at parties, she tried to find out the areas of expertise of the people she talked to and drew them out on their own topics.

In seeking advice, you should remember that it is advice you want, not punishment. Suppose your adviser suggests that you are really behaving stupidly. A polite and very appropriate comment on your part would be "Don't tell me I'm a stupid jerk. Tell me what behavior I could change so I would *not* be a stupid jerk." On the other hand, it will be just as useless to have an adviser assure you that nothing is the matter with you and that you are really wonderful. If you turn to advisers, you may have to teach them the principles and language of self-directed behavior. You can't assume that everyone understands behavior/environment relationships or the necessity for precise specification of events.

When asking for advice, hear out the person without interrupting or expressing disagreement. If you disagree, hold your disagreement for the moment; you may change your mind later. Remember that it is very difficult to assimilate negative comments about yourself as soon as they are made, so don't punish the person whose advice you have requested (Williams & Long, 1975).

Be precise in your requests. Don't ask "Am I a social failure?" Ask instead "Can you give me some advice on how to feel comfortable with the other sex?" or something even more precise. If you know that negative comments and criticism are going to hurt you too much to be worth getting, then ask for positive criticism. Ask for comments on how you can improve rather than on what you do wrong (Williams & Long, 1975). Last, be sure to ask the advice of someone whose opinion you respect and who is likely to be sophisticated enough to give good, specific advice without punishing you.

Tactic Seven: Think of Alternative Solutions. D'Zurilla and Goldfried (1971) suggest that you think of several alternative solutions to the problem and then select one or more to implement. Our first thoughts are often not the most creative. If you think of several solutions, a better one will likely occur to you. It's helpful here to use a technique called *brainstorming*. The technique has four simple rules: (1) Try for quantity—quality will follow. (2) Try not to criticize. If you greet every idea with a "Yes, but . . . ," you will dry up your well. Criticism can come later; for now, blow it all out. (3) Try to be freewheeling. Some ideas will be unrealistic or even weird, but don't criticize now. (4) Try to improve ideas by combining them. The case described in Box 2-1 illustrates this approach.

BOX 2-1

The Case of the Worn-Out Student

Ruth is 26 years old, married, working, and going to college. She first majored in elementary education, then added a second major—general science—to increase her chances of getting a teaching job. Her first attempt to state the problem was vague: "I'm losing my motivation for school. I've become too emotional. I argue with my husband too much. I can't really get into my science projects, even though I love the field." We suggested to Ruth that she list all the details of her problem, searching for a specific goal. She wrote:

> I feel that the arguments with my husband are due to my being upset about school work.
> My generally bad moods are also reactions to school.
> I haven't been going to classes regularly.
> I feel under a lot of pressure from the buildup of assignments.
> My study habits are deteriorating.
> Classes just don't seem as important to me as they used to.
> I am spending more time playing tennis.
> The pressure is strongest in the two graduate courses in education. I am having trouble with these two courses. I'm actually getting frightened. The most difficult is History of Education.

Ruth then brainstormed several possible solutions to her problem:

> I could drop out of school.
> I could change my major, go back to elementary ed.
> I could drop the education courses and forget about graduate school.
> I could find someone to help me with my studies.
> I could sell my car, so I couldn't get to the tennis courts.
> I could go to a hypnotist.

After thinking about various solutions, Ruth decided to drop History of Education. This would take off the greatest pressure. She could then concentrate on catching up and doing well in her other courses. Note that at the beginning she had difficulty specifying her problem but that, by listing details and brainstorming several solutions, she improved her specification enough to formulate a reasonable plan. Ruth told us that, before going through this process, she would never have considered dropping that course.

When Your Goal Is Not a Behavioral One

There are times when your goal is not a particular behavior but some result you want to achieve—being up on your homework, having no extra pounds around your waist, or having a stack of your own completed poems. For some of these results, the behavior you have to change is obvious: for example, the stack of finished poems will grow if you increase the time you spend writing them. But for other results, what you need to change may not be so obvious. For example, if you want to lose weight, what behavior should you change? Of course, you have to go on a diet. But, unless you change some of the behaviors that led to your being overweight, you will regain whatever weight you lose on a diet.

Even if your goal is not a specific behavior, it is still true that reaching your goal will require changing certain behaviors. To lose weight, you will have to eliminate snacks, cut out high-calorie foods, push away from the table earlier, stay away from leftovers, eat smaller meals, and so on. To keep weight off, you have to change other behaviors. For example, you have to exercise regularly. Overweight people do many of the following things. They buy fattening foods and keep them around; they eat to avoid waste; they pile too much food on their plates; they eat very rapidly and while doing other things, such as reading or watching TV; they eat when they are emotionally upset (instead of making some other nonfattening response); and they eat just because of the time of day (Mahoney & Thoresen, 1974; Stuart & Davis, 1972). They rarely weigh themselves and don't exercise enough. Also, they often skip breakfast. They starve themselves and then gorge (Mayer, 1968). In the long run, all or most of these behaviors will have to be changed if the person is going to get permanent weight control.

Suppose an overweight person asks the question "What would I be doing if I were at my goal of being slim?" The answer is spelled out in the paragraph above: change all the behaviors that contribute to the problem, and don't fall back on them. Each of the things an overweight person does is a particular action. The goal of slimness is not a behavior, but, to reach it, each of the necessary behaviors has to be developed. You may have been surprised reading about some of these behaviors. Most overweight people don't realize that, in order to get permanent weight control, they have to change each and every one of certain kinds of behavior.

The most important part of a strategy for any "nonbehavioral" goal is to realize that, to reach the goal, you must change certain behaviors. You need to eliminate some old behaviors that contribute to the problem and to develop some new ones that help you reach the goal.

An important step is to start observing yourself; it is important, however, that you keep doing it over relatively long periods of time. If, for example, you begin to keep track of the food you eat, you'll notice patterns, and for the first time you'll see the relationship between something you do and the pounds you gain. For instance, you finally realize that, each time you get down in the dumps, you eat. If you keep records of your behavior in social situations, you'll start seeing things you do that put others off and discovering things you can do that will make you more attractive.

The point of long-term self-observation is that you begin to see relationships between what you do (or don't do) and the goal you want to reach. You become a "scientist of yourself," looking for aspects of your behavior that have been contributing to your not reaching the goal and searching for new behaviors you can develop that will help you reach your goal.

Self-analysis should be applied to any kind of complex goal, every time you aren't sure you know what to do. Suppose you feel you're concerned with the question "Who am I?" Ask yourself "If I knew, what would I be doing?" That tells you what your goal is. It is through self-analysis that you will be able to answer the essential questions "What acts do I perform, what thoughts do I have, that keep me from reaching that goal?" and "What behaviors do I need to develop in order to reach my goal?"

Successive Approximations to a Goal

As you learn more about how your own thoughts or actions interfere with the goal you want to reach, you generally go through a series of self-discoveries. One of our students, Michael, was often depressed. He began a self-change project with only a vague idea of how to go about reaching his goal of getting rid of his depressions. His first step was to keep a record of the situations that made him depressed. This record told him that all such situations seemed to stem from daily frustrations. Michael then began to study his reactions and discovered that, once frustrated, any additional disappointment would make him depressed. He continued to study himself, now asking "Why do frustrations make me feel so bad?" His answer was that he seemed to brood over his frustrations. For example, if his child misbehaved, he'd find himself thinking—often for hours at a time—that he was a terrible father and that he was responsible for raising a spoiled child. He decided that brooding was self-defeating and, what is more, unnecessary.

It took Michael about two months to get to this point. But then he made what he felt was a breakthrough. "All along I've suspected that not all frustrations have the same effect. My kid isn't really at the root of the problem. It's my own self-esteem; that's what the problem with me is. When I get frustrated in my self-esteem, all other frustrations seem to be magnified." We asked what "frustrated self-esteem" meant in terms of behavior. After more self-observation, Michael decided that he evaluated himself against people who were doing the very best. In his job as a salesman, he would notice that the top people were achieving certain sales levels, and then he would feel bad because he couldn't do the same. "My standards for myself are too high" he concluded. "Always comparing myself to the absolute best leads to unhappiness. I seem to think that, if I'm not the very best, I'm no good at all." So he set out to change the process of comparing himself to the best.

Before he embarked on a self-change project, all Michael knew was that he was unhappy and too easily upset by frustrations. Over a period of several months through self-observation and thinking, he learned much more about how his own actions and thoughts contributed to his problems. Like Michael, in order to learn what you do or don't do that interferes with your goal, you may have to go through a period of successive approximations. You do this through self-observation and thinking about the meaning of your observations.

People who are successful at self-change often change the target of their self-change efforts several times. For example, people seeking permanent weight control might start off with the goals of acquiring the habit of counting their calories, exercising a little more, and trying to lose some weight. As they learn more about their personal eating habits, these people set new targets for themselves—eating more slowly and only low-calorie foods. Later, after learning that they eat supper just because it's there, whether they're hungry or not, they develop another target—eating supper only when they are hungry. Still later, yet another target—not eating when depressed—is taken up. And so on. As you learn more about yourself and about the actions that support or hamper your progress, you add new target behaviors.

Living means adjusting; as we go through life, we take up new goals and discard old ones. This is a process that applies to conscious self-direction too. Michael's first target was to learn about his reactions to frustration. As he worked at this target, he discovered that his problem was frustrated self-esteem. This discovery led to other discoveries about himself—more specifically, that frustrated self-esteem was the result of his comparing himself to people who were the very best in their jobs and thus evaluating himself negatively. In turn, this new awareness led Michael to a new goal—avoiding comparisons that frustrated his self-esteem.

As your understanding of yourself deepens with self-observation, so will your understanding of the appropriate techniques for change. There are two questions you need to ask and reevaluate throughout the process of self-change. One is "What is the target I should be working on?" and the other is "What techniques should I use to get to that target?" Self-understanding and a knowledge of techniques will permit you to give more and more sophisticated answers to both questions.

For complex goals, where do you begin? How do you know where you should start—which of several possible behaviors should be your first target? The basic rule is: start by making self-observations, because the most important part of a self-change plan is getting data about yourself. If weight control is your goal, your first subgoals are to start counting calories and to observe your eating behaviors. If eliminating depression is your goal, your first subgoal is to study yourself to find out what sets off the depression.

Summary

You must have well-defined objectives that are specified in terms of particular behaviors in particular situations. To specify behaviors-in-situations, four tactics have been suggested: (1) make a list of concrete examples; (2) look for examples in your daily life; (3) list the details of your problem; (4) become an observer of yourself. The aim is to be able to fill out this sentence:

My goal is to change _____ in _____ .
                              (thought, action, feeling)   (situation)

When the problem is nonperformance of some behavior, specify the situations in which the desired behavior is to occur, and note the undesired behaviors you now perform. When the problem is eliminating an undesirable behavior, increase some desirable alternative act.

If you are uncertain about a behavior, a situation, or a goal, there are additional tactics you can use: specify the chain of events that will produce your goal, get advice, and brainstorm alternate solutions to the problem. If your goal is not behavioral, you can still reach it through changed behaviors. With complex problems, you are likely to move through a series of approximations to your goal as your self-understanding deepens.

BUILDING COMMITMENT

Even with the most detailed and specific plan, during the process of self-change two kinds of problems are bound to arise: you will sometimes be tempted to go astray, and you will sometimes grow weary of the work involved in changing. The effective self-director realizes that these two problems will occur and plans for them in advance. This section discusses how you can build commitment to change and how you can anticipate and neutralize inevitable temptations and boredom. Commitment to change is not something you have; it is something you *do* (Coates & Thoresen, 1977). Commitment itself is a behavior—or, rather, a complex set of behaviors—one of which is careful and honest self-examination.

The Advantages of Not Changing

Tim had a "terrible temper" and wanted to change it. As a first step, he kept records of his angry outbursts, noting what happened as a result of them. He had expected to find that people resented his outbursts and that he felt guilty after his blowups; what he didn't expect was to also discover that he often got his way and felt less tense after such blowups. Thus, Tim realized that, in the short run, he got something out of his "terrible temper" but that, in the long run, his outbursts were quite costly to him. Having assessed the pros and cons of the situation, Tim could rationally ask himself "Do I really want to change? Do I want to lose the occasional advantage of my terrible temper?"

When you cannot readily change some problem behavior or reach some desired goal, it may be because the immediate payoff of the "problem" behavior is greater than you suspected. People who bite their nails find comfort in their habit. People who overeat enjoy the feeling of a very full stomach. People who don't exercise enjoy the comfort of inactivity. Those people who don't get much work done enjoy the freedom of not working on a schedule. People who continue to withdraw don't have to face their anxieties about meeting other people. Any behavior that continues offers some advantages, no matter how slight and temporary. Therefore, *you must ask yourself "What will I lose by changing?"*

Here's what one student wrote about the payoffs of his habit of putting himself down: "Maybe I really believe the bad things I say about myself. Perhaps other people, too, believe them and will think I'm vain if I don't say them. Maybe my modesty is appealing. Maybe people pay attention to me because I make a lot of self-effacing statements. Maybe I do it to keep others from putting me down first. If I stopped, I would lose all these advantages."

Many times we are unaware of the reasons for problem behavior until we try to change it. It is when temptation knocks that we become particularly aware of the advantages of not changing. An overeater told us "It wasn't until I tried to stop snacking that I realized how I use between-meal snacks to cheer myself up. Then I saw that I really got a lift from food. There are advantages to overeating." When you embark on a program of self-change, all the negative consequences of changing may not occur to you, but they will appear later in the form of temptation. Again, ask yourself "What will I lose by changing?" (Coates & Thoresen, 1977; Janis & Mann, 1977). You can answer this question by making a list of all the negative consequences of changing. For example, increasing your study time is going to decrease your leisure time, and that may or may not be worth it to you. Many people fail to change themselves not because they lack willpower but because they haven't faced the cost of changing. When the time comes to give something up, they aren't ready, they haven't thought about it, so their "willpower" fails: "Wait a minute, I can't watch TV tonight because my plan calls for studying. This is a terrible plan."

Now let's look at the positive: *What will you gain from changing?* Write a list of all the positive consequences of changing. For example, "If I stopped putting myself down, I wouldn't feel depressed so easily. I think that some people would like me more. I would be able to see myself in a different light, perhaps more clearly. I would be happier." Or "If I stopped overeating, I would lose weight. I would look and feel better. My health would improve. I would be more attractive. I would like myself more. I would find other ways besides snacking to cheer myself up."

After making the two lists of the positive and negative consequences of changing, you are in a better position to make a rational decision about changing. Another reason for making your lists at this point is to solidify your commitment to try to change. It's best to think now of reasons for not changing than later, when you're surprised by temptation.

If, after having assessed the positive and negative consequences of your plan for change, you have come to the conclusion that you do want to change, there is still another important question you need to ask: can you do it?

Your Beliefs about Changing

Lou is asked to give a talk to the pledges of her sorority. "Oh, I couldn't do that. I'd get nervous. I'd be tongue-tied. I can't talk in front of groups." And, of course, she can't. John, who is on a diet, is invited to a friend's for dinner. Confronted with a tray of delicious, high-calorie food, he thinks "There goes my diet. I can't resist this." And, of course, he can't.

Our beliefs create our reality. Lou makes herself incapable of speaking before a group; John makes himself unable to resist fattening food. What you believe about your ability to change will affect how hard you try to change, and that, in turn, will affect your chances of success (Bandura, 1977). Perhaps Lou imagined herself talking before a group. Immediately she felt nervous and even noted certain physical changes indicating great tension. So she gave up. Her belief that she couldn't give the talk influenced—even determined— her decision to turn down the invitation. She could have braved it through, telling herself that the imagined threat was greater than the actual risk, and given the speech. But her belief in her inability led her to give up as soon as she encountered the first difficulty.

It's not that the belief that you can cope eliminates all difficulties; what it does do is to make you try harder when you attempt to cope with the diffi- culties. Research demonstrates. that people who are trying to stop smoking, as well as people who are trying to lose weight, persist longer and succeed more if they believe that their efforts can produce change (Chambliss & Murray, 1979a, 1979b).

What do you believe about your present goal for self-change? Do you think that you can reach it?

Yes _____   No _____   Uncertain _____

If you said yes too easily, it could be that your project is too easy. Being uncertain is reasonable, but being certain that you cannot change is self- defeating. As the philosopher Spinoza stated 300 years ago, "So long as a man imagines he cannot do something, so long as he is determined not to do it, then it is impossible for him to do it." How many smokers have you heard say "I can't quit" and seen them make no further effort? How comfortable! If you are sure you can't change, you are not obliged to try.

You can become aware of some specific beliefs that will affect your com- mitment by answering these questions:

1. Are you willing to read through carefully to the end of the book?
   Yes _____   No _____
2. Are you willing to try the ideas suggested in this book and then evaluate them?
   Yes _____   No _____
3. At the end of each chapter there is an exercise in which you apply the ideas discussed in that chapter to your own self-change project. Are you willing to do these exercises?
   Yes _____   No _____
4. Finally, are you willing to commit yourself to a self-change learning program that will take some effort and time?
   Yes _____   No _____

If you have carefully thought about the advantages versus the disadvan- tages of changing, you ought to be able to answer yes to the questions above. If you are not willing to say yes, then perhaps you should pick another project.

Thinking about the advantages of not changing and thinking about your beliefs about change are part of the behaviors of commitment. As you progress, you will meet temptation, and, like Odysseus, it is best if you are prepared. Two things you can do to be prepared are to give yourself reminders and to use others to remind you.

Giving Yourself Reminders

There will be some difficult times—times when you will too clearly hear the Sirens singing. It is at those times that you need to remind yourself of your goal (Lazarus, 1971; Graziano, 1975). For example, a woman who had taken up jogging to lose weight and be healthier found that, while jogging, she was thinking "This is stupid—and so boring. I'm going to quit." She realized that these thoughts were self-defeating, so she would remind herself "I really want to look better, and the best way is to jog. So it's worth it. I won't quit." A student wanted to get better grades so he could have a better chance of getting a good job after college. But at times the temptation to do something else instead of studying was great—for example, when his friends asked him to play basketball in the afternoon. When that happened, he reminded himself "No, I really do want to improve my grades, and that means I have to study now."

The trick is to remind yourself of your goal when you are tempted. Expect temptation; it will come. Be prepared for it by being prepared to remind yourself of the goal you want to reach: "As much as I would like to eat this chocolate cake, it will blow my diet for the whole day, and I really, really want to lose weight"; "It would be a relief to tell him to go to hell, but I really do want to learn to deal with people in a friendlier way"; "I'm thinking of giving in and watching TV. But I watch too much TV; I do want to cut down"; "I am tired, and it would be easy to say 'No, I don't want to make love tonight,' but I really do want to be more loving."

Your self-reminder can include all the advantages of reaching your goal: "I'll feel so great when I have caught up on my homework—free as a bird!" "I'm going to look terrific when I have lost ten pounds—slim and sexy!" "I'm going to enjoy having new friends. So that's worth overcoming my shyness and going to the party."

You can see that this kind of reminder will work only if you really do care about reaching your goal. You can also see that you will be tempted to think "Well, just this one time . . ." But life can become a string of just-this-one-times, and, before you know it, years have gone by without your being a step closer to your goal. Lots of smokers go to their (early) graves thinking "Some day I'm going to give up cigarettes." So, you need to have a reminder for the just-this-one-time situation: "I'm always telling myself 'Just this one time.' But I really do want to . . . (reach that goal). So this time I won't . . ."

Once you have begun to be successful in your self-change, you can remind yourself, when dealing with temptation, "I've put in a lot of work, and I don't want to blow it now. I really do want that goal." For example, the once-fat person sitting down to a Thanksgiving feast thinks "I could regain five pounds right here. But I've put a lot of effort into losing that weight, and that's worth more than masned potatoes." The Greek Stoic philosopher Epictetus gave much the same advice in 100 B.C.: "First say to yourself what you would be, and then do what you have to do."

Prepare a written list of self-reminders you can use when temptation strikes.

Using Others: Getting a Little Help from Your Friends

John has been trying very hard to cut down on his drinking. Tonight he and his wife are getting ready to go to a party. John says to his wife "Do me a favor. I'm going to be tempted to drink too much tonight, and you know I want to stop that. So, if you see me taking a second drink, would you remind me, please, that I really want to cut down?" Research by Richard Passman (1977) suggests that you can increase your chances of success if you prearrange with someone else to remind you when you are faced with temptation. Groups such as Weight Watchers and Alcoholics Anonymous sometimes work in this fashion (Stuart, 1977). The basic idea is to ask someone who will be present when you are tempted to remind you of your goal and of your self-change program.

Recall our earlier injunction that you should not ask for punishment. John doesn't want his wife to tell him he's a lush and a bum because he has taken a second drink. He wants her to remind him of his own resolve not to drink too much. If others misinterpret the task, thinking that it is punishment you need, remind them that's not so: you are asking for a reminder of your own goal, nothing more. Also beware of the tendency to punish the person who does the reminding: "I know it's my second drink! I'm not stupid!" Sometimes one feels like lashing out at the reminder, because it is frustrating and embarrassing. But, in John's case, for example, he should remind himself again "It's true, I really do want to cut down drinking" and thank his wife for being helpful.

In its most recent recommendations on how to stop smoking, the American Cancer Society suggests that you tell all those you come in contact with that on a certain date you are going to stop smoking and that you ask them to notice whether you do it or not. This is the same strategy we suggest. Realize that you will be tempted to break your resolve at some point in the future, and ask people who will be around when that happens to remind you of your goal.

Sometimes, when we present this idea to a class, some of the students are shocked: "You mean, I'm supposed to tell people to bug me?" "No," we reply, "to remind you of your goals."

Escape Clauses (Good and Bad)

At the beginning of self-change projects, people tend to be vague about their intentions. They may say "No more getting drunk (or stoned)!" Their real intentions, however, may include an unstated escape clause—for example, "except at parties, when I really feel like it." Many people are horrified at the thought of having others remind them of goals; this feeling probably indicates that an unstated escape clause is part of the actual intention.

Some goals allow more reasonable escape than others. For example, you can increase your studying and still allow plenty of time for leisure; you can plan your time carefully and also include free, unscheduled periods. You can lose weight and still enjoy nice food. Most people who are addicted to tobacco, alcohol, or other substances, however, cannot afford any escape clause, because just one slip may reactivate the craving to an irresistible level. The danger with all escape clauses is that they may be so generous as to destroy the effects of a plan—the classic example being the dieter who never sticks to the diet. On the other hand, the danger of not including *any* escape clause is that a plan may be so rigid as to become absurd and obnoxious, as the following example illustrates.

One of our students, during his first conference, reported that he had begun a time-management plan. He liked the sound of it—"time management"—because it made him think of efficiency and self-respect, as well as a change in his self-perception of laziness, drifting, and underachievement. He had always been more intelligent than his grades suggested; but during high school he hadn't needed to study and had never developed discipline in his daily routines. Time management! This offered him a vision of regular, efficient days, controlled energy, and a brighter future. The plan lasted eight days before he scrapped it, and he never wanted to hear the expression *time management* again. "I can't live like that" he said. "I don't even want to live like that. I'll do some other project, but that schedule stuff is crazy." We gradually reconstructed his "crazy" plan, and he was right: the schedule was awful. He had blocked out every waking moment, from brushing his teeth in the morning to waiting at the bus stop, 30 minutes for lunch, Monday-night football and the 6:00 P.M. news (only) on television. He had even restricted the times he spent talking with his girlfriend on the telephone. Every moment was rigidly dictated by his time-management schedule.

"The flaw in your plan is clear" we said. "You didn't include your favorite activity." "What's that?" he asked. "Being unscheduled. After some years of doing whatever comes up at the moment, it should be obvious that you really enjoy this relaxed, casual approach to your time. And who doesn't? Your plan's flaw is that you haven't scheduled some unscheduled time. That can be done too." We pointed out late-afternoon blocks that could have been labeled FREE on his schedule. In this instance, we urged him to include an "escape" section in his time-management plan. Without it, the personal cost for someone with a long history of casual days was too great.

The important point, however, was to make the escape clause explicit. Some plans should have no escape clauses; but any plan should clearly state all intended escapes, whether or not they are wise. If you really intend to overeat every Sunday when you are with your parents, say so. If this escape will cause havoc with your diet, you can then make an intelligent choice as to which is more important: mom's cake or faster weight loss. A concealed escape clause will ultimately destroy the plan altogether.

Here is an example of a good, clear statement with an intelligent escape clause built into it by a young woman who had a tendency toward frivolous, impulsive spending:

Goal: Sticking to the budget	
Included	*Not included*
1. Make a revised budget at least every other month (because of inflation). 2. Write down every expenditure in notebook; don't forget the drugstore. 3. Transfer expenditures from notebook to ledger, and add everything up. It's no good if I don't add them up. See how it matches the budget. *Every month!* on the 1st.	Don't have to write down what I spent out of the $20 a month that I put in my bag's zipper pocket. *Need some fun!*

Is there an escape clause in your actual intentions?

Yes _____   No _____

If you detect one, make it explicit.

The Self-Contract

As you build commitment to your goal for change, we have a final suggestion: write out each element of your plan as a *self-contract*. You are now ready to write out the first paragraph of the contract, which is the statement of your true intention. In Chapters 3 to 8 you will be able to add more details and elements to your self-contract at the end of each chapter. For now, write your goal and intentions as clearly as possible. Then add "I am willing to change my behaviors as necessary to reach the goal I have chosen and will carry out the steps suggested in the text. Specifically, I am willing to do the work suggested in this chapter and in Chapter 3." Then sign your name.

Does this help at all? Griffin and Watson (1978) carried out an experiment in self-contracts in a college course in which the students had to take a large number of tests. Experience had shown that, as the semester progressed, a larger and larger number of the students were not taking quizzes or were taking them unprepared. Griffin and Watson had half the students, randomly selected, write a self-contract in which they promised themselves that they would prepare for the tests and take them. The other half had no self-contract. The results showed that those students who had made the self-contract took a larger proportion of the tests and were better prepared. Similar results were obtained in an experiment on learning better study skills (Seidner, 1973, reported in Kanfer, 1977). By itself, a self-contract won't keep you from temptation, but it is one more effective way of building your commitment to do the work of self-change.

Summary

Commitment is not something you have, it is something you do.

First, ask yourself "What are the advantages of not changing?" and make a list of them. Then make a list of the advantages of changing. Ask yourself whether you are really willing to give up the things you will lose if you indeed change.

Second, remember that your beliefs about changing will influence your persistence in trying to change. If you believe that you don't have the ability to change, you will make little effort; failure will follow; and your belief will be confirmed. Be sure you can answer yes to the questions on page 37. Choose a goal and design a plan that you can believe in.

Third, prepare yourself to cope with temptation; it will surely arise. Remind yourself of your goal when you are tempted: "I really do want to . . . (whatever your goal is), so I won't give in to temptation this time." Remind yourself of the advantages of reaching your goal.

Ask others to remind you. Be sure that you get only a reminder, not punishment, and that you don't punish the person who does the reminding. Asking others to help you means that you have to face up to any escape clauses you have been building into your self-change plans. Acknowledge any escapes in your intentions, make them explicit, and decide whether these escapes should be included in your plans.

Now write yourself a self-contract detailing the work you are about to begin in order to achieve self-change.

YOUR OWN SELF-DIRECTION PROJECT: STEP TWO

Before going on to Chapter 3, you should do the exercises suggested here for specifying the problem and building commitment.

Part One—Specifying the Goal

You should now specify your goal as some behavior-in-a-situation that you wish to decrease or as some behavior-in-a-situation that you wish to increase. Ideally, even if you want to decrease some undesirable behavior, you should be able to state as your goal an *increase* of some other behavior that is incompatible with the undesired one. You should specify a category that includes all instances of the target behavior, so that you can identify an instance of the behavior when it occurs. If now you can't state your problem as behavior-in-a-situation, you should go through each of the procedures in this chapter, step by step, for your own chosen goal.

My goal is to increase _____ in _____.

(behavior)   (situation)

Part Two—Building Commitment

Make a list of the advantages of not reaching the goal you indicated above and a list of the advantages of reaching it. You should assess your own beliefs about the possibility of change by answering the questions posed in the preceding pages. State the self-reminders you will use when tempted to avoid working toward your goal. List the people you will ask to remind you of your goal when you are avoiding working toward it. Write the following: "I am willing to change my behaviors as necessary to reach the goal I have chosen and will carry out the steps suggested in the text." Then sign your name.

This series of acts doesn't mean that you are permanently committed to your first choice of a goal. You may decide to change as you progress. In fact, you should expect to change in some ways. The point of this promise is that you start with a goal that is important enough for you to actually perform the steps toward self-direction.

When you have completed both parts of step two, go on to the next chapter.

TIPS FOR TYPICAL TOPICS

This "Tips" section lists popular books devoted to one topic only. Consult the suggested books if you develop an interest in that specific topic. Be aware, however, that the best strategy is to learn the *general* principles of self-direction, so that you can develop solutions to whatever problems life presents.

Smoking, Drinking, and Drug Use.   There is considerable disagreement in the literature with regard to whether one should stop "cold turkey" or reduce consumption gradually. This issue will be discussed in Chapter 6 in the section entitled "Shaping: The Method of Successive Approximations." It is especially important that in self-contracts dealing with this issue any implicit "escape" intentions be made clear and explicit. Because substance abuse is highly situation-specific, you should anticipate instances of great temptation. Use others to remind you of your commitment during those more difficult times.

The following books contain useful ideas: *How to Control Your Drinking,* by William Miller and Ricardo Munoz (Englewood Cliffs, N.J.: Prentice-Hall, 1976); *Become an Ex-Smoker,* by Brian Danaher and Edward Lichtenstein (Englewood Cliffs, N.J.: Prentice-Hall, 1978); and *Break the Smoking Habit,* by Ovide Pomerleau and Cynthia Pomerleau (Champaign, Ill.: Research Press, 1977).

Weight Loss.   Weight loss is a complex goal, and it may be desirable to break it down into subgoals, such as weighing oneself once a week, counting calories accurately, instituting an exercise program, and so on. Begin by observing and recording every behavior-in-situation that pertains to your weight.

Many books on weight control are available. Among the better ones are: *Take It Off and Keep It Off: A Behavioral Program for Weight Loss and Healthy Living,* by D. Balfour Jeffrey and Roger Katz (Englewood Cliffs, N.J.: Prentice-Hall, 1977); *Permanent Weight Control: A Total Solution to a Dieter's Dilemma,* by Michael Mahoney and Karen Mahoney (New York: Norton, 1976); and *Slim Chance in a Fat World: Behavioral Control of Obesity,* by Richard Stuart and Barbara Davis (Champaign, Ill.: Research Press, 1972).

Time Management.   Careful scheduling of available time, according to one's priorities, is a goal of many busy students. It is almost certain that you will need to include some "free"—that is, unscheduled—time in your schedule. The philosopher Mortimer Adler, for example, affirms that the busier a person is, the more important it is that he or she schedule some amount of time—even if it is only 30 minutes a day—devoted to doing nothing. During these "nothing" times, the mind is free to drift, relax, and create. This is an example of the value of an "escape" element in a plan.

An excellent source book for time management is *How to Get Control of Your Time and Your Life,* by Alan Lakein (New York: New World Library, 1974).

Studying and Career Planning.   A wonderfully wise book for college students is *On Becoming an Educated Person,* by Virginia Voeks (Philadelphia: Saunders, 1979). The best book for improving study techniques is *Effective Study,* by Francis Robinson (New York: Harper & Row, 1970; 4th ed.).

Family and Lovers.   Probably the best books on being a parent are *Living with Children: New Methods for Parents and Teachers,* by Gerald Patterson and Elizabeth Gullion (Champaign, Ill.: Research Press, 1971), and *Effective Parents, Responsible Children,* by Robert E. Eimers and Robert Aitchison (New York: McGraw-Hill, 1970).

One of the best books on strained relationships with spouses is *A Couple's Guide to Communication,* by John Gottman, Cliff Notarius, Jonni Gonso, and Howard Markman (Champaign, Ill.: Research Press, 1976). *Treat Yourself to a Better Sex Life,* by Harvey Gochros and Joel Fischer (Englewood Cliffs, N.J.: Prentice-Hall, 1980), is an excellent book on how to improve sexual relationships.

Assertion.   A frequent goal is to become increasingly able to stand up for one's own rights and be less timid and helpless. Note that this ability, which is called *assertion* by psychologists, does not mean aggressiveness or hostility. There are several good sources on the topic of assertion, such as *Your Perfect Right: A Guide to Assertive Behavior,* by Robert Alberti and Michael Emmons (San Luis Obispo, Calif.: Impact, 1974); *Asserting Yourself: A Practical Guide for Positive Change,* by Gordon Bower and Sharon Bower (Reading, Mass.: Addison-Wesley, 1978); and *Don't Say Yes When You Want to Say No,* by Herbert Fensterheim and Jean Baer (New York: McKay, 1975).

The Other Sex.   Although there are numerous books on how to make a great impression on the other sex, they are mainly popular, common-sense books. There is no book on improving one's relationships with the other sex that covers all the areas involved in this endeavor. For example, you may have to learn to relax (see Chapter 6), to monitor your thoughts (see Chapters 3 and 5), and to develop new behaviors (see Chapter 6). One nice little book on a related topic is *Shy?* by Michael Girodo (New York: Pocket Books, 1978).

Depression.   You will need to pay particular attention to observing your own thoughts and automatic reactions to situations (Chapters 3 and 5) and to increasing the rewards in your life (see Chapter 7). The two books that treat these topics are *Coping with Depression,* by Aaron Beck and R. L. Greenberg (New York: Institute for Rational Living, 1974), and *How to Control Your Depression,* by P. Lewinsohn et al. (New York: Prentice-Hall, 1979).

CHAPTER 3

Self-Knowledge: Observation and Recording

GOAL:
To teach the basics of self-observation.

OUTLINE:
Structured diaries
Frequency recording
Rating scales
The reactive effects of self-observation
Dealing with problems in getting records
Self-recorded data and planning for change
Your own self-direction project: Step three
Tips for typical topics

Self-knowledge is the key to self-direction. Your behaviors—your actions, thoughts, and feelings—are embedded in situations, and each of these elements must be carefully observed. Self-observation is the first step on the road to self-directed behavior: we have said it several times, but it needs repeating, because it is the step most often omitted in our ordinary lives. Most of us assume that we understand ourselves, and we rarely feel that we need to employ any systematic self-observation techniques. For that reason, real surprises may be in store for the person who begins careful self-observation. Genuine discoveries can and will be made.

Self-observations are often quite inaccurate. A group of people who wanted to lose weight were asked by an experimenter to tell him how much they ate. Many assured themselves and the researcher that they "really didn't eat very much." Then each person was asked to remember and write down *everything* he or she had eaten in the preceding two days. They did, and it seemed indeed that they were not overeating. The researcher then put them all on a diet that consisted simply of eating what they had reported having eaten in the preceding two days. Every one of them began to lose weight (Stunkard, 1958)!

In order to change yourself, you have to know what you're doing. The purpose of this chapter is to present a set of techniques for gaining knowledge about your behaviors, thoughts, and feelings and about their relationships to specific situations.

STRUCTURED DIARIES

In Chapter 2 you began to formulate your goals and values in terms of specific acts performed in specific situations. Before you begin a plan for change, it is necessary that you understand your current performance and that you discover those situations that are now affecting your target behaviors. Then you can take steps to bring them under control. To achieve the first goal, better self-understanding, many people use a structured diary.

A *structured diary* is a record you keep that records not only your behaviors but their antecedents and consequences as well. Recall from Chapter 1 that you can think of your behavior as embedded in a situation. The antecedents come before your behavior, and the consequences come after it. A-B-C: Antecedents-Behavior-Consequences. This is not the kind of diary in which you write down random thoughts or musings about the day. The diary entries are made in connection with your goal for change. A very important point: you don't wait until the end of the day to write your entries. As soon as you realize that some relevant behavior has occurred, you note the behavior, as well as what happened before and after it.

This diagram gives you an idea of how you go about keeping your diary and of the kinds of questions you must answer to write your entries (Hay & Hay, 1975; Thoresen, 1975).

Antecedents (A)	Behaviors (B)	Consequences (C)
When did it happen? Whom were you with? What were you doing? Where were you? What were you saying to yourself?	Actions, thoughts, feelings	What happened as a result? pleasant or unpleasant?

The reason for keeping this kind of diary is that it will allow you to see what kinds of situations have an effect on your target behavior.

A man began to keep a record of what he called his "sulking." Here are two entries from his diary.

Antecedents (A)	Behaviors (B)	Consequences (C)
Sunday morning Was in a bad mood.	Sulking (not talking; feeling sorry for myself).	Judy [his wife] paid a lot of attention to me.
Tuesday afternoon Feeling frustrated about my work.	Sulking.	Judy held me close and we talked.

The diary for several other days showed the same kind of pattern. Chapter 4 describes in technical terms what is happening here, but even without knowing the technical terminology you can notice that the man's sulking seems to get him love and attention (pleasant experiences) from his wife. What effect might that have on the man's sulking?

Joan, a young office worker, was concerned with her feelings of inferiority and defensiveness, especially with a Ms. X. Her structured diary looked like this:

Antecedents (A)	Behaviors (B)	Consequences (C)
Monday afternoon X acted arrogant in the elevator.	I said some stupid sarcastic things.	Felt bad.
Wednesday morning X gave me a superior look from across the room.	Got unreasonably angry at her.	Had to leave the room.
Friday morning With X, doing paper work. What a know-it-all!	I was very careful; didn't look good in the exchange.	Hated myself for getting so upset.

When she analyzed her structured diary, Joan was able to see that, whenever Ms. X appeared to feel superior, she (Joan) became angry and her anger was self-defeating. Later, Joan was able to devise a plan for a more adaptive, less defensive response to Ms. X.

An older woman wanted to take up jogging but noticed that very often she didn't do the jogging she meant to do. She kept a structured diary on the A-B-Cs of not jogging:

Antecedents (A)	Behaviors (B)	Consequences (C)
Sunday morning It was drizzling.	Didn't jog.	Felt good at first but guilty later for not jogging.
Tuesday after work Had worked hard all day and felt tired.	Didn't jog.	What a relief! No running! Then felt guilty and lazy.
Saturday morning Thought I would rather work on my African violets.	Didn't jog.	Ditto. (Liked the way the violets looked after repotting them, though.)

The pattern was clear; each time she felt she should jog but didn't, first she felt relieved and then guilty. At this point she had to face her value conflict about jogging: did she really want to jog?

The Mechanics of Diary Making

As soon as you realize that you have performed some undesired target behavior or failed to perform some desired one, make an entry in your structured diary. Describe the physical setting, the social situation, your thoughts, and the behavior of other people. Journalism students learn that, to write a good story, they must answer five questions: Who? What? Where? When? Why? In order to keep a good structured diary, you must answer these same questions.

Be sure you make the diary entries as soon as the target behavior occurs or fails to occur as it should. Don't wait, because, if you do, you will surely overlook some important details. For example, if the sulking man had waited until the evening to write down what happened when he sulked, he might have realized that his wife was always present, but this thought would have only confused him, unless he had also remembered very specifically what his wife did right after he began sulking.

Here is a selection from the structured diary of a father whose goal was to stop spanking his children and start using nonphysical punishments. As soon as he had disciplined the children, he made an entry in his diary:

Antecedents (A)	Behaviors (B)	Consequences (C)
April 3 Saturday morning at breakfast table. Kids did a lot of bickering.	I spanked both of them.	Made them even more cross.
April 6 Came home from work feeling pretty tired. My boy talked back to me.	Started to spank him but stopped. Grounded him for an hour instead.	Felt pretty good about that. Was glad I didn't hit him. He calmed down while he was grounded.
April 10 Had an argument with my wife. Then in the car the kids started acting up and quarreling.	Spanked them— actually, slapped them.	It spoiled our whole outing. I felt guilty. They felt rotten.

You can see what conclusion this man may draw from his diary: he feels better when he doesn't spank. But also note that it's not simply the behavior of the children that determines whether he spanks them or not. An argument with his wife or a hard day at work has an influence on his behavior as well.

Recording Thoughts and Feelings

Thoughts and feelings can also represent your target for change. A young woman reported: "I often put myself down in my thoughts. I'll do something rather well, and then I hear myself saying in my mind 'Pretty good for a basically mediocre person.' This makes me feel bad and seems unnecessary." So she began to record these "self-putdowns," together with the situations that preceded and followed them. A clear pattern emerged: her negative thoughts followed small successes and were followed by a feeling of dissatisfaction.

Thoughts too can be the antecedent of some problem behavior. They precede it. For example, the shy person thinks "She's not going to like me" and makes a fumbling approach to a potential new friend. The softball player visualizes striking out and, as a result, clutches up. The student who wants to speak up fantasizes the whole class snickering at her question and so remains silent. The would-be friend imagines the other person saying no to a request for a date and doesn't ask.

When you keep a structured diary, the relationship between thoughts and problem behaviors will become clear. For example, you may record your thoughts in the B column, like this:

A	B	C
	Told myself I was really only average at best.	

and then look for the antecedents and consequences of this target behavior.

Or you may record your thoughts in the A column as antecedents, like this:

A	B	C
Saw this attractive woman and said to myself "Nobody that attractive is ever going to like me."	Didn't introduce myself.	

Thoughts can be visual as well as verbal. Many people have short, visual fantasies, like film clips projected in their imaginations. For example:

A	B	C
Saw this attractive woman, then had a fantasy that I smiled at her but she completely ignored me.	Didn't introduce myself.	

One of our colleagues, a history professor, had begun writing history books for children instead of research articles. He told us that a number of times, while writing, he had the following fantasy. A distinguished historian and senior professor in his own department would come into his office, look at his desk, read over his shoulder, and snidely remark "Children's stories? You're really out of your mind!" This fantasy, with many variations, was often played out in our friend's imagination. The antecedent was the fact that he was working on children's books. The consequence was that he became nervous, stopped writing, and went to check his mail. He noted that the fantasy was probably a reflection of his ambivalence about writing children's history books when he should have been doing the "more serious" work of scholarship. He also noted that he was glad he had kept a record of these fantasies, because it allowed him to face up to his ambivalence and ask himself if he really believed that a children's history book was any less valuable than more traditional research articles.

If you are going to record your thoughts or fantasies, it is particularly important that you record them as soon as they occur. Our students who have tried to wait to note them in the structured diary remark that it is quite difficult to remember enough important details to see what effect the thought has on one's actions or feelings.

Thoughts may or may not be an important feature of your target behavior or of the related situation. But even if they are not, a certain amount of this kind of self-observation is worth the effort, because, if your thoughts and self-statements are problematic, they too can yield to self-directed behavior change.

What the Diary Tells You

People working on consummatory behaviors—such as overeating, drinking, or smoking—will find that many situations that at first glance seem unrelated to the problem are in fact closely connected to it. For example, a smoker who kept a structured diary centered around the question "Why do I light a cigarette?" found that all of the following situations stimulated smoking: any social gathering; a cup of coffee; being bored, angry, depressed, or excited; certain times of day; and after every meal. Overeaters, too, will find that they eat in response to situations like these rather than in response to an internal feeling of hunger.

If you don't believe that a situation can control your behavior, watch people who are trying to stop smoking when they are in certain settings—for example, during a morning coffee break when others are smoking. You will then realize that situations like this one can have a very strong effect on people. The point of the structured diary is to find out which situations are affecting your behavior.

Often time and patience are required to discover the pattern of antecedents and consequences. A young man was concerned with his rudeness, or, as he put it, "telling other people what I think of them, which is often unflattering." On page 53 are some entries from his diary.

After making observations of this kind for two weeks, this young man was able to establish a category of the situations that seemed to produce his undesired behavior: "When people disagree with my personal philosophy, I tend to tell them off." This doesn't imply that his philosophy was either good or bad. It does imply that disagreement with it seemed to stimulate the response of "telling people what I think of them." He felt that his response was

A	B	C
Tues. morn. John said he was pretty happy about school election results.	Told John he was being dumb	Hurt his feelings
Wed. eve. Ellen said she thought the people who were making the most difference in the world were scientists.	Told her she was "full of bull."	She said I was too ignorant to argue intelligently.
Fri. morn. Prof. B told me I *should* do the assignments.	Told him he was an authoritarian old man.	I don't think it helped my grade.
Sat. nite My date said she was looking forward to marriage and having a family.	Told her she was hopelessly middle class, unliberated, and dumb.	She was very angry. Said she wouldn't go out with me again.
Sun. aft. Don't know what happened.	Told John he was dumb.	He left. I was disgusted.

undesirable because it often angered others, with the result that they stopped showing any interest in his personal philosophy (or, for that matter, in anything else he said). But it took him several days of keeping the structured diary to understand the category of situations that led to his unwanted target behavior.

Discovering the patterns in your own diary may take time and patience, because you may need to make many entries. This is not unusual, and the process can be most helpful in achieving eventual self-direction. Often this analysis will shift your focus of interest from the original behavior of concern to some feature that seems to influence it. Here is a good example of this process.

An elementary school teacher was observing her patterns of depressed feelings. She wrote: "I was in my yard gardening, which usually makes me feel very happy. But I began to feel uncomfortable and stopped to think why. It felt like depression, but there was nothing to be depressed about. So I wondered about what I had been thinking just before I felt depressed. And then I remembered that, a minute before, I had imagined this scene: I'm in my classroom, at the beginning of next year, and I'm teaching fifth grade (just as I will be) instead of my usual third. The class is a shambles. The kids aren't understanding anything, they are misbehaving, and I can hear the principal coming down the hallway. She comes in the door, stands, and glowers at me . . .

"I imagine things like this often. I even have a name for them—my incompetence fantasies. And I believe they do depress me. So I'm going to record instances of fantasies about incompetence, find out what sets them off, and try to get rid of them." She then moved "incompetence fantasies" to the center column of her diary and recorded antecedents and consequences of her fantasies.

The young woman who recorded "self-putdowns" reported that at first she didn't think of them as putdowns. "I just felt I was being properly modest or was being realistic in my self-evaluations. But after a while I saw that what I was really doing was putting myself down. It went beyond modesty or reality, and it was making me unhappy." You learn to make this kind of differentiation by keeping records and thinking about them.

When you search for antecedents and consequences, others may be helpful. Many couples use the following technique to iron out their difficulties. After a series of arguments, they will sit down and discuss "just what is wrong." The woman may offer suggestions about the man's behaviors that evoke her undesired reaction, and the man may counter with ideas about things the woman does that serve as antecedents of his undesired behavior. Even if your target problem is not an interpersonal problem, you may want to try seeking the advice of another who has the opportunity to observe your behavior and its possible situational determinants.

Summary

Situations can be divided into antecedents and consequences of behavior. To identify both, keep a structured diary, in which you record the behavior and its antecedents and consequences.

Antecedents (A)	Behaviors (B)	Consequences (C)
When did it happen? Whom were you with? What were you doing? Where were you? What were you saying to yourself?	Actions, thoughts, feelings	What happened as a result? pleasant or unpleasant?

Entries should be made as soon as possible after the event. The diary will tell you what situations affect your actions, thoughts, and feelings. These entries give you ideas for changing your behavior by changing the situations.

FREQUENCY RECORDING

Some psychologists have suggested that self-direction is a process of "personal science" (Mahoney, 1974). If you keep that definition in mind, you can see that the structured diary is a source of promising hypotheses about your behavior. Your next step in that process of personal science is to start collecting systematic observations in order to prove or disprove your hypotheses.

Simple Counting

The simplest kind of record keeping is a straightforward count of how often you do something. One of our students wanted to know how often he practiced his music. He kept a chart in the same drawer where he kept his recorder and music sheets. The sheet looked like this:

Recorder playing

	Week 1	Week 2	Week 3	Week 4
Mon	✓	✓	✓	
Tues				
Wed	✓		✓	
Thurs		✓	✓	
Fri	✓	✓	✓	
Sat				
Sun				

Whenever he took out his recorder to practice, he made a mark on the sheet. By looking at his sheet, he could see how many times per week he practiced and could ask himself whether it was enough. Also, if he later decided that he wanted to increase his practicing, he would know exactly the level he was starting from. But the chart yields even more pieces of information. Just by glancing at it, our musician would notice that he never seemed to practice on Tuesdays, Saturdays, or Sundays. This observation would lead him to ask the more sophisticated question "Why don't I practice on those three days?" This would be, of course, a step forward, because he could then determine what it was that interfered with his practicing on those days.

It is important that you be accurate in your counts. If your target behavior is to increase the amount of time you study, you begin by counting the number of minutes you spend each day *actually* studying. Suppose you sit down, open the book, and, instead of reading, daydream for five solid minutes. Since you count only the time spent doing the target behavior (studying), when you snap back to reality, you say to yourself "Well, I didn't really study for those five minutes, so I won't count them." And if you had written on your daily record "Began studying at 7:45 P.M.," you would change it to "7:50 P.M."

In this kind of situation, you're likely to think that you are studying a certain number of hours, when in fact you study much less. Keeping an accurate score of all the times your attention drifts away is not all that easy. One way to increase accuracy is to ask another person to record along with you. If you are clearly not studying for a ten-minute period and are so inattentive that you neglect to note it, your friend may.

Maureen, a sophomore, decided to record the number of minutes she actually spent studying *and* the number of minutes she was "ready to study." Her chart looked like this:

	Mon	Tues	Wed	Thurs	Fri
Ready to study	45	30	35	50	0
Actually studying	15	10	20	30	0

Maintaining a strict count like this helps you understand the difference between engaging in the actual target behavior and engaging in other, related behaviors. You might come to realize, as in this example, that you spend a large amount of time doing things that are not your target behavior. Getting "ready to study" is not studying. By keeping a strict count of the amount of time you actually engage in the target behavior, you can learn what it is that you are doing instead of the desired behavior and how that interferes with it.

Maureen recorded the *duration* of her behavior. This is desirable whenever the length of time of the behavior is an issue. The music student above might have recorded not only how many times a week and when he practiced but also how long he practiced each time. There are certain behaviors, of course, for which a simple count of the frequency is enough—number of cigarettes smoked, number of rude answers, or number of defeatist self-statements.

A student wanted to increase her vocabulary. When she encountered a word she didn't know, she wrote it down in her notebook. Later she looked up its meaning in the dictionary. Inside the dictionary she kept a chart like this:

Number of words looked up		
Mon ___✓___	Mon ___✓___	Mon ___✓✓___
Tues ___✓✓___	Tues _____	Tues ___✓___
Wed ___✓___	Wed _____	Wed _____
Thurs ___✓✓✓___	Thurs ___✓✓___	Thurs ___✓___
Fri ___✓___	Fri ___✓___	Fri ___✓✓✓___

You can combine counting with a record of the kind of situation in which the behavior occurs. By using a code mark for the situation, you keep a record of how much you do something in particular situations. For example, a woman who wanted to quit smoking counted the cigarettes she smoked each day. She also noted the situation in which her smoking occurred, using this code system:

E (for eating) after or during a meal
S when nervous in a social situation
D while driving her car
O other times

On the first day her 3 × 5 card looked like this:

Smoking record—Monday, December 7		
Morning	Afternoon	Evening
E E D O S S S E	O S S D S E E E	E O

Her records for several days were very consistent, and she was able to plan an intelligent antismoking program that concentrated on eating and social situations.

People doing self-change projects count a lot of different things about themselves. For example:

An office worker recorded the number of thoughts she had when dealing with rejection by others.

A woman counted the number of hours per day that she watched TV.

A father counted how much time he spent with his children.

A writer made a note of the exact time she began her daily writing, carefully noted each time she took a break, and, at the end of her scheduled writing period, marked down the total time spent writing.

A jogger kept track of how many miles he ran each week. Another jogger kept track of the number of hours she ran per week. A third recorded the number of times he ran each week.

A woman working on her budget kept track of all her daily purchases.

A man recorded all instances of impulse buying.

An overweight man counted daily instances of "eating errors," when he ate something he knew he shouldn't have eaten.

Many dieters have recorded total calories per day.

A knuckle cracker counted number of cracks per day.

A skin scratcher recorded the number of hours she could go without scratching.

A student kept track of the number of times per week that he said something nice to his parents.

Note that people don't record just instances of unwanted behavior. Whenever possible, they record positive things as well. For example, a dieter kept records of the times he avoided the temptation to eat too much, as well as the times he gave in to the temptation. A mother recorded the times she avoided spanking her kids and thought of some more positive response, as well as the times she hit them. This kind of recording allows you to see when you make progress and when you don't. For example, if, while on a diet, you stick to it for six days and then gorge, you should feel good about the six days even if you're sorry about the seventh. Too often dieters notice only the times when they fail to stick to their diet (Ferguson, 1975). Depressed people suffer a similar distortion of perception. They fail to notice the pleasant events of life and, as a result, they see their whole lives as disappointing. Recording positive events will help in this situation too (Tharp, Watson, & Kaya, 1974; Kirschenbaum & Karoly, 1977; Fuchs & Rehm, 1977).

Be Sure You Count

It is essential to record the behavior as soon as it occurs. The student who used to insult people worked out a simple recording system that contained the three categories in which he was interested. He divided a 3 × 5 card into three columns: Challenges (for the antecedent event of challenges-to-his-personal-philosophy); Insults; and Reasonable Statements. He carried the card in his pocket. As soon as he had finished talking with a friend or acquaintance and the two of them had gone their separate ways, he stopped and entered checkmarks in the appropriate columns. This system allowed him to answer the following questions immediately after a conversation: "Was my philosophy challenged?" and "How did I respond?" If he had waited until

---

BOX 3-1
Poor Richard's Records

Benjamin Franklin—statesman, scientist, inventor, and author—might well have written this book had he lived long enough. He did, at least, state that he wanted to write a book, called *The Art of Virtue*, on how to achieve goals such as not overeating or overdrinking ("temperance," to use his word), keeping things in order, letting others talk, avoiding waste, being clean, staying calm, and being industrious (Knapp & Shodahl, 1974). He didn't get around to writing the book, but in his personal journals he left records of his own attempts at self-modification, using techniques of self-observation much like those in this book.

Franklin first made a list of the target behaviors, which he called "virtues." He then kept records of his successes and failures for each of the targets. Here is a sample of one of his record sheets.

	Sun	Mon	Tues	Wed	Thurs	Fri	Sat
temperance							
letting others talk	x	x		x		x	
keeping things in order	xx	x	x		x	x	x
meeting goals			x			x	
avoiding waste		x				x	
being clean							
staying calm							
being industrious							

He wrote an X each time he didn't meet his personal goals. He tried to change one set of behaviors at a time. For example, he started working on temperance and let the other behaviors fall as they might. Later he would move to another goal, then to still another one, until he had reached all of them.

Was he successful? He says he was. "I was surprised to find myself so much fuller of faults than I had imagined, but I had the satisfaction of seeing them diminish."

the end of the day, he would have forgotten important details. Also, when he succeeded in not insulting a friend, the immediate recording provided instant self-satisfaction.

If you find yourself saying "I don't need to write it down. Of course I'll remember how much time I spent doing the target behavior!" try to force yourself to keep your frequency count. You will find that, if you don't keep written records, you won't keep any records at all. You might forget; you might rationalize. You should *not* wait until the end of the day and then try to remember how many times and for how long you engaged in the target behavior. If you do, you delude yourself. At best, your count will not be accurate. As soon as the target behavior occurs, stop and record it (Epstein, Webster, & Miller, 1975; Epstein, Miller, & Webster, 1976; Mahoney, 1974).

One of our students reported that, whenever he was working successfully on his diet, he faithfully kept a daily written record of how much he weighed. But then would come that fateful weekend—a dinner party on Saturday night followed by a spaghetti supper on Sunday. Monday morning would dawn, and he knew very well that he gained weight over the weekend. His solution was simple; he wouldn't weigh himself on Monday! Thus he wouldn't have to be confronted with the awful evidence. Not weighing oneself when expecting bad news could easily become a habit, and soon keeping track of one's weight would stop altogether. Then—fat again!

Many smokers report that, because they are disturbed when they realize how many cigarettes they consume each day, they try to avoid keeping a record. Cases like these tell better than any amount of words how important record keeping is to achieving the desired goal.

This requirement means that the recording device has to be truly portable and readily accessible. A smoker may keep a note card inside the cigarette pack. Many people use a 3 × 5 card or some other piece of paper that will fit conveniently in a pocket, bag, or notebook. This, along with a pen or pencil, is all the equipment you need.

Try to fit record keeping into the pattern of your usual habits. Devise a record-keeping system that will remind you of itself. For example:

> for smoking . . . a card inside the cellophane wrap;
> for too much TV watching . . . a chart beside the place where you sit to watch;
> for going to bed too late . . . a chart beside the bed;
> for not studying . . . a record inside your notebook or at the place where you study;
> for eating too much . . . a card beside your place at the table;
> for between-meal snacks . . . a record sheet on the pantry or refrigerator;
> for exercising . . . a chart by the closet where you keep your exercise clothes;
> for socializing . . . a 3 × 5 card that is always in your bag or pocket.

Nancy had a lot of difficulty dealing with one of her coworkers. She made a list of four things she wanted to remember to do when she was with him: listen to him without interrupting, ignore his slightly rude remarks, pause before replying to him, and stop trying to figure out his motives. She made sure that she always had this list in her desk; when she was about to talk with the man, she would take the list out, glance over it, and then hold it while talking to him. Then, as soon as she finished talking, she would check off each item she had successfully performed.

In some cases it helps to use a wrist counter (which is worn like a watch) or a golf counter. This kind of counter helps when the target is something you do very often, like some nervous or verbal habit. For example, Ed wanted to stop swearing and found that it happened about 200 times per day. Taking out a 3 × 5 card and marking it so often would have been tedious, so he used a golf counter. Whatever sort of counter you find convenient, use it. The easier it is to keep records, the more likely you are to keep them.

You should think about recording problems you will meet and figure out ways to deal with them. One of our students wanted to keep track of certain thoughts he had while talking with other people. To make notes on a card while talking would have looked silly; on the other hand, he knew he would forget if he waited until the conversation had ended. So he found another way. Each time he had the thought he wanted to record, he moved a penny from his left to his right pocket. After he had left the other person, he would count the pennies to know how many times the thought had occurred in the course of the conversation.

A woman who wanted to increase the number of times she performed a particular desirable behavior carried toothpicks in her purse and moved one into a special pocket of the purse after each occurrence. A cigarette smoker started out each day with a specific number of cigarettes (30) and, when he got home in the evening, simply counted how many he had left.

Suppose you perform the behavior but discover that your counting device—a 3 × 5 card or whatever—is not there. What do you do? Improvise. A knuckle cracker found a big leaf at the beach and tore a small hole in it each time he cracked his knuckles. Later he transferred this record to his regular chart. A smoker who had left his scoring card at home kept the matches he used to light his cigarettes as a record of how many cigarettes he had smoked.

Written Storage Records

When using 3 × 5 cards, bits of paper, wrist counters, or other devices for keeping records, you need to transfer the information to a more permanent storage record. This storage record may not be exactly the same as the daily (or occasional) record. A woman with the "nervous habit" of pulling off the skin on her feet and legs kept a single count like this:

Pulling off skin													
Day	1	2	3	4	5	6	7	8	9	10	11	12	13	14
Number of times per day	7	9	11	8	4	8	12	7	10	7	9	2	9	2

As a storage record, she made a graph that she kept on the wall of her room.

Our smoker transferred the daily record (illustrated on p. 57) to her storage record. Her record for one week looked like this:

	M	T	W	T	F	S	S	M	T	W	T	F	S	S
E	7													
E	6													
D	2													
O	3													
Total	18													

The young man who kept track of whether he was or was not insulting transferred his daily records to the following chart, which he kept on his room bulletin board.

	Mon	Tues	Wed	Thurs	Fri	Sat	Sun
Challenges	3	4					
Insults	2	3					
Reasonable statements	1	0					

Sometimes you can combine your daily observations with the permanent record. For example, the recorder player kept his chart with his instrument. This way, the chart was always there when he needed it and could serve as both a daily record and a storage record. Record keeping and record storing must be adapted to each person's own behaviors and situations. If you think that the various systems described here don't suit you too well, don't be afraid to improvise or adopt a system not mentioned here.

Summary

Self-observation is the first and vital element of self-direction. Recording your behavior is the basic technique of self-observation. You can count either the amount of time you spend doing something or the number of times you do it. Record positive events as well as negative.

You should make definite plans for how you will carry out your self-observations. Think of what problems may come up and how you will deal with them.

Here are four rules for self-observation:

1. Do the counting when the behavior occurs, not later.
2. Be accurate and strict in your counting. Try to get all instances of the behavior.
3. Keep the recording system as simple as possible. Try to fit it into your usual habits.
4. Keep written records.

RATING SCALES

So far we have presented methods for recording the A-B-Cs of a situation and for recording the frequency or duration of an act. There is another element of the target that you may have to record and that requires an additional technique. Rating scales are appropriate when the intensity of an event is a relevant factor. The pain of a headache, the difficulty in falling asleep (Nelson, Hay, & Hay, 1975), feelings of depression or joy—these are aspects of events that neither frequency nor duration adequately describes. Each can be more or less intense, and it is the intensity itself that is important to your goal.

Intensities can be "measured" by assigning each event a number according to a prearranged scale in which each number has a precise meaning. For example, the goal of a young woman was to increase her feelings of happiness and make her depression less intense (Tharp, Watson, & Kaya, 1974). She invented a 9-point rating scale, in which the points had these meanings:

+4	superhappy
+3	happy
+2	good feeling
+1	some positive feeling
0	neutral
−1	some negative feeling
−2	bad feeling
−3	sad
−4	superdepressed

This is how she kept her record. She briefly described each unit of her day's activities and then evaluated the intensity of her feelings about it. Here is a typical day's record.

talked to Jean	−2
in class	−1
took test	0
saw Dean	−2
had lunch with Jean & Judy	+1
talked to Bill	+3
went home on bus	−3
talked to Jean on phone	−3
studied	0

She made an average of each day's ratings and recorded them on a graph. Notice that this method of recording contains not only the rating of the feeling but also the situation in which the feeling occurs—"with Jean," "in class."

Rating scales are particularly appropriate to record emotions and feelings, because intensity is the crucial issue. Fears, depression, sexual arousal, jealousy, pain, joy, happiness, self-satisfaction, love, and affection have all been recorded with rating scales. Your goals with regard to these emotions and feelings can be expressed as increases or decreases on the scale.

When your goal is to change some emotional state, you won't go immediately from discomfort to total comfort. By rating your comfort, you will be able to see that you are making progress—an important thing to know, for it would be a shame to drop a self-change plan that is working.

A young man was working on his feelings of jealousy toward his girlfriend. This is the rating scale he used to assess the degree of jealousy he felt in various situations:

1   no jealousy at all
2   slight jealousy and irritation
3   moderate jealousy and some real discomfort
4   strong jealousy and discomfort
5   overwhelming jealousy and discomfort

Using this system, he was able to see that he became particularly upset at parties, when his average rating approached 5. By using certain techniques that we will explain later, he made some progress. He saw that at the last two parties he had rated about 3.5—still jealous, but progressing.

How many points should your scale contain? Most of our students choose 5, 7, or 9. For example:

1   perfectly calm
2   a little tense
3   somewhat tense
4   very tense
5   panic

Too small a scale does not allow for the subtle differences you will want to record. Too large a scale will produce sloppy records. Expand or contract your scale to allow for the distinctions that are important to your particular goal. For example, a man whose goal was to overcome nervousness about speaking in front of a group started with the scale above. After rating a few experiences, he noted that he often wanted to assign a number in between the five on his first scale, so he expanded it to a 10-point scale. "In class giving a speech" was about 9; "having a speech assigned" was around 3; "preparing the speech" was 5; "waiting to give it" was 8.

Rating scales can produce better self-understanding, because they help put events into full perspective. For example, the depressed woman whose rating scale we discussed above reported that, after recording the intensity of her feelings for several weeks, she came to realize that "depression is a part of life" and that she had been overreacting to her depression. When she saw the large number of pleasant events that filled her routine days, she gained a new perspective about her life.

The importance of not losing one's sense of proportion is perhaps the essence of the advice that Don Juan, the Yaqui Indian sorcerer, gives to Carlos Castaneda: when you face a crisis, "take death as your advisor" (Castaneda, 1972). If your death is rated as 100, how serious is the discomfort you are suffering at this moment? The use of a rating scale will force you to put events in their true relations to one another and can lead to greater wisdom.

The Daily Log

A system for combining the advantages of rating scales, frequency counts, and recordings of specific situations has been devised by W. Scott MacDonald (1977). His daily log (Figure 3-1) is an easily drawn form, which becomes your recording sheet. It is useful in the stage of the structured diary and can be used to record ratings and events throughout the self-change project.

The column to the left contains an emotion-rating scale. The person notes in the log whatever events are important and, by placing them at the appropriate point in the log, assigns them a degree of emotional intensity. The entries can then be connected with a line; the resulting graph depicts the emotional fluctuations of a day.

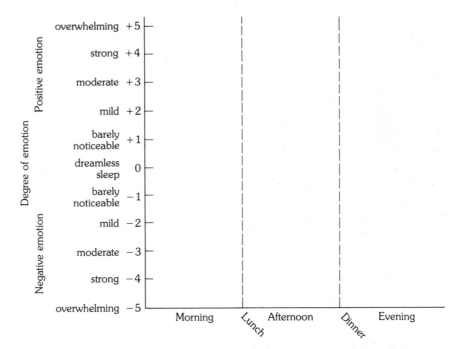

Figure 3-1.   Daily log for recording emotions and their causes. (From *Emotional Life of College Students,* by W. S. MacDonald. Book in preparation, 1977. Reprinted by permission of the author.)

The time of each entry is also noted in the log, and a line is drawn to connect the points. This line shows the transition from one emotional state to another and can be smooth or abrupt, according to how smooth or abrupt you think your emotional shift was. The situation that gave rise to the emotion is also noted in the log.

Figure 3-2 shows a typical daily log kept by a young man in our class. On another day the student's log looked like the one in Figure 3-3. Note how sharply the line falls from "wake up" to test taking on both the first and the second day. The form that such a line takes allows the student to see whether the change was smooth or abrupt. The wavy line from 6:30 to 9:00 P.M. in Figure 3-3 indicates quite effectively rapid swings of feeling. The jump after the "good dessert" is also very expressive.

The choice of events to record is based on their apparent importance. These records may vary from 5 or 6 entries per day to as many as 20.

You don't *have* to use the rating scale given in the left column; if you prefer, you can devise your own. Your scale may have, for example, three points above and below "neutral." You can use the log to record any type of positive or negative feeling—depression, anxiety, love, or joy. Remember: here, too, it is important that you record as quickly after the event as possible, just as in any other technique.

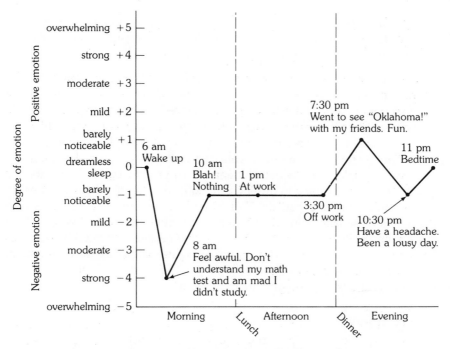

Figure 3-2. Daily log: Sample day 1. (From *Emotional Life of College Students,* by W. S. MacDonald. Book in preparation, 1977. Reprinted by permission of the author.)

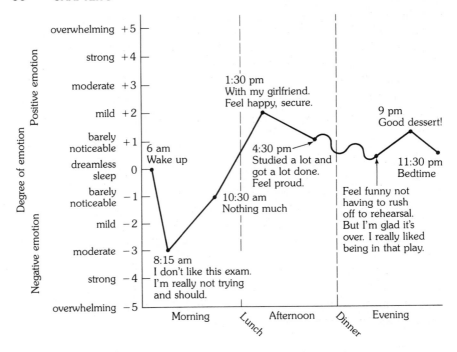

Figure 3-3. Daily log: Sample day 2. (From *Emotional Life of College Students,* by W. S. MacDonald. Book in preparation, 1977. Reprinted by permission of the author.)

A caution: The use of rating scales shouldn't lead you away from the behavioral goal of your self-change efforts. Although rating scales can tell you whether your emotions are shifting in the desired direction (do you feel more joy? are you less depressed?), actual behavioral changes are needed to produce the goal. To have a complete picture of how your plan is working, you may combine the use of a rating scale with counts of observed behaviors.

For example, one of our students was trying to avoid depression by fighting off her tendency to dwell on thoughts that people didn't like her. To achieve this goal, she had decided to replace her negative thoughts with memories of situations in which people had obviously liked her. She kept track of her feelings with a rating scale but also counted "the number of times each day that I successfully switch from thoughts that people don't like me to memories of nice times I've had with people." Thus she counted instances of behavior and rated the accompanying feelings as well.

Summary

Rating scales allow you to gauge the intensity of an event. Therefore, they are particularly good for recording feelings and emotions. You use the daily log to rate intensity of feeling and to record the time and the event that stimulated each feeling. A good technique is that of combining the use of rating scales with counts of actual behaviors.

THE REACTIVE EFFECTS OF SELF-OBSERVATION

Think of what it's like to have someone closely observe your behavior. When your track coach or dance teacher or lab instructor says "I'm going to watch you very carefully now," don't you perform in quite a different way than you do when no one is observing you? You feel self-conscious; you take greater care. In other words, when a behavior is being observed, it may change.

These changes are of different kinds. Perhaps the behavior will become less smooth or automatic; or it may improve, just as an actor's performance can be enhanced by the presence of an audience. These effects are produced also when you are your own observer (Kazdin, 1974c). Behavior "reacts" to the observation, and the effects are known in psychological science as *reactivity*.

When we teach our students how to modify their behavior, of necessity we put a great deal of stress on the importance of working out a good plan for change. Occasionally, a worried-looking student will approach us after a lecture and say "I'm sorry, but I cannot work out a plan."

"Why not?" we ask.

"My problem is that my problem has gone away! I started to gather the data and was doing it regularly, just as you said, but then I just quit the undesirable behavior I was counting. Will that lower my grade?"

This, of course, is the happiest form of reactivity. And, in self-direction, it is the most common. Undesirable behavior tends to diminish, and desired behavior tends to increase solely because you are observing and recording them.

The most important factor in reactivity is your own values. If you are recording some behavior about which you don't really care, that behavior will not be much affected by your recording it (Fixen, Phillips, & Wolf, 1972; Ciminero, 1974). For example, we have counted the number of steps it takes students to walk from a stairway to the classroom door. Then we have asked students themselves to count their own steps. Almost no reactivity was rated; it takes the same number of steps whether one counts them or not. But not many students are overly concerned with the length of their average footstep.

On the other hand, there is much evidence that, when a person cares about a behavior—that is, assigns a value to the behavior—self-recording will change that behavior in the direction of the value (Kazdin, 1974e; Lipinski, Black, Nelson, & Ciminero, 1975; Gottman & McFall, 1972; McFall, 1970; Nelson, Lipinski, & Black, 1976; Johnson & White, 1971; Sieck & McFall, 1976; Komaki & Dore-Boyce, 1978). Dieters who want to lose weight will reduce calories simply because they count them (Romanczyk, 1974); smokers will reduce smoking (McFall, 1970); worriers will stop worrying (Frederiksen, 1975); quieter students will speak up more often in class (Komaki & Dore-Boyce, 1978). Phobic individuals can come to tolerate their feared situations, whether of closed spaces (Leitenberg, Agras, Thompson, & Wright, 1968) or of the open street (Emmelkamp, 1974; Emmelkamp & Ultee, 1974) or of animals (Rutner, 1973). Simply recording the occurrences has reduced the frequencies of tics, such as squinting, arm jerking, and making odd noises with the nose (Thomas, Abrams, & Johnson, 1971; Billings, 1978).

Self-recording can be discouraging, as well as encouraging, particularly if the information tells you that your progress is very slow. Dieters who weigh themselves too often experience these feelings (Mahoney, 1977a). In the first two or three days of a diet, the person's weight may drop several pounds— a loss that offers plenty of encouragement to continue the diet. But after those first few days, when much of the weight loss is only water loss that will be replaced as soon as the dieter resumes normal eating, the amount of daily weight lost is pretty small—often as little as one quarter of a pound. A bathroom scale won't even pick it up. Thus, dieters who weigh themselves every morning will soon begin to feel that such small weight loss is hardly worth all the sacrifices the diet requires. The solution to this problem, of course, is to weigh oneself less frequently, perhaps once per week, so that a real weight loss can be registered. In the meantime, dieters should be recording each day whether they actually followed the diet and how many calories they ate.

Self-recording can also be discouraging if you record only the unwanted things you do. For example, a lengthy daily record of all the times you were depressed or had negative thoughts about yourself might lead you to think even more negatively of yourself. Earlier we mentioned the need to record positive things, such as nice thoughts about yourself and periods of feeling good, because these are things you want to increase, and they may be the result of your recording them.

This is not to say that self-recording is sufficient to change all behaviors. It is not. Our estimate is that in over 15% of self-change projects the goal is achieved by the use of self-recording alone. In many other cases, record keeping represents, if not a "cure," certainly a help. It should also be noted that some researchers have cautioned that reactive effects may be only temporary (Kanfer, 1975; Mahoney, 1977b). For all these reasons, self-recording is best considered as one element in a self-direction program, an element that will allow you to achieve self-understanding, to devise a sensible plan for change, and to measure the success of that plan.

The reactive effects of self-recording can be turned to advantage, and they should be. For example, if you discover that your target behavior is improved or altogether eliminated by self-recording, by all means continue the recording. You can be certain that, if self-recording is the only thing you have done in an effort to change, stopping the recording will stop the improvement (Maletzky, 1974).

Some of our students have found that, even though recording by itself is not enough to bring about some desired change, once you have achieved that change, continued recording makes it easier to *maintain* the change.

A woman who had become a long-distance runner (using self-reward techniques, explained in Chapter 7) reported to us that she no longer needed to use self-reward but that she did need to continue to keep records of her running, or she would begin to slack off.

Using Reactivity to Your Advantage

Since some problems do improve because of self-observation, you can take advantage of this reactive effect to move toward your goal.

A student reports: "For some time I've felt guilty for not helping my wife clean the bathroom. But I always seemed to have something else to do, and cleaning the bathroom was not exactly appealing, so I just continued to do nothing about it and felt guilty. Then I put a chart in the bathroom. Each time my wife cleaned it she made an entry, and each time I cleaned it I made an entry. It took only one week to get me working. Now I check the chart often, making sure that I do my share."

Another student wrote: "I enjoy reading, and for a long time I wished I did more of it. But I'd come home from work tired and mindlessly switch on the TV. I then bought a little notebook and began to keep a list of all the books or articles I read. I got very interested in how my list was growing. I enjoyed finishing reading something and making an entry in my notebook. I'd get it out and skim over it to see how I was progressing. I'm sure I read more now than I did before, because keeping track of my reading is meaningful to me. It actually makes me feel good."

If you are a smoker, try to keep long-term records of how many cigarettes you smoke per day. If you are overweight, try to keep long-term records of your caloric intake (Romanczyk, 1974). As we said before, reactivity alone cannot be guaranteed to be sufficient, but in all likelihood it will be helpful.

You can also increase reactivity by the timing of recording (Rozensky, 1974). For example, you can record calories before you eat or after. Does it make any difference? It turns out that it does. In an experiment some subjects first ate and then marked down the calories contained in their meal, while others reversed the order. The experiment showed that those who recorded *before* eating ate less (Bellack, Rozensky, & Schwartz, 1974). This means that you can use prerecording to control behavior. During the initial stages of estimating your problematic behavior, you may want to record *after* you do the act, to provide a more "natural" record. Then, when you try to control the undesired behavior, you should record before you perform. Obviously, this technique is appropriate only for behaviors you want to reduce. But it can be useful for more than dieting and reducing smoking.

Another researcher (Kazdin, 1974f) suggests that recording early in a chain of behaviors may suppress the unwanted link. The father who used to blow up at his children and spank them began to record "anger" *before*, rather than after, he struck. This had the desired effect. The recording itself broke the automatic chain of anger-striking, and the man was then able to use a less severe form of disciplining his children.

Displaying your records publicly can increase positive reactivity (McKenzie & Rushall, 1974). There's nothing like having a friend check each day to see if you have bitten your nails to keep your hands out of your mouth. A storekeeper wanted to lose weight. He decided to keep a list of all the food he ate displayed in a prominent place in his store, so that his employees would be able to see all he had eaten the day before. Others have simply required themselves to report to someone else, perhaps a small group, about their progress. It is a two-pronged approach, in which you gain positive social rewards if you are succeeding but social punishment if you begin to slip.

Of course, if you falsify your records, public record keeping won't help. People sometimes do this. A chronic nailbiter reported: "Once I realized that I was watching TV and biting my nails and that it felt relaxing. I was chuckling to myself 'I won't tell Joe [her husband] about this,' as though I were fooling him, when of course it was myself I really wanted to fool."

Summary

Observing what you do may change what you do. This can work positively—so that you perform wanted behaviors more and unwanted behaviors less—or negatively, in which case you become discouraged by the bad news. You should try to use the reactivity of self-recording to your advantage. Sometimes the very act of recording is enough to produce change; more often it helps a bit. When you record—before or after—you help yourself control your behavior. Public display of your records can also be helpful.

DEALING WITH PROBLEMS IN GETTING RECORDS

Behaviors Performed Absentmindedly

Certain target behaviors are hard to keep records of, because you don't pay close attention to the behavior. For example, you might absentmindedly pick your face while watching TV or reading. Other behaviors, like talking too loudly or overeating, may be so well practiced that you simply don't notice them any more. Or your thoughts may flit away almost unremembered. Under such circumstances it is hard to get accurate records; this, in turn, will make it even harder to work out a plan for change.

When you are performing an undesirable behavior without paying attention, your first step is to deliberately practice performing the behavior while consciously attending to it. This technique is called *negative practice*. The reason for it is simple. You want your attention to be readily switched on when you begin to perform the undesirable behavior. To achieve this goal, you take the same approach you would take for any other behavior that is not occurring. You practice it. In this case, you need to practice paying attention while you are performing the target behavior.

A young man who habitually cracked his knuckles spent five minutes each morning and five minutes each evening deliberately cracking his knuckles while paying close attention to every aspect of the behavior. If he had allowed his attention to wander, the purpose of the practice (associating the target behavior with paying attention) would have been lost.

A sophomore had developed the habit (over 20 years!) of scratching her arms while sleeping. It had become so bad that some mornings she would wake up to find herself bleeding. "How can I pay attention while I sleep?" she asked. We suggested that each night, when she went to bed, she deliberately scratch her arms for several minutes while paying close attention to what she was doing. Being awake, she was not in danger of scratching until she bled. The reason for suggesting that she do it just before going to sleep, instead of some other time during the day, was that a situation very similar to actually being asleep would generalize most easily. It worked. After a few nights' practice, the young woman was not scratching in her sleep any more (Watson, Tharp, & Krisberg, 1972).

Once you have learned to pay attention to the habitual target behavior, you can begin some plan to eliminate it. The woman above worked out a plan so that she gradually replaced scratching first with rubbing, then with patting, and then with just touching.[1]

Another way to deal with "unconsciously" performed behaviors is to ask others, usually friends, to point out instances of the target behavior. One of us had developed the habit of saying "Okay?" every time he mentioned a difficult point in a lecture. What he meant was something like "I know I just mentioned a difficult point. Do all of you understand it? If not, please let me know, and I'll explain." Somehow this had been shortened to "Okay?" His average, believe it or not, was nine times in every five minutes. (That's what one of his irritated students recorded, at any rate.) The solution was to ask one of the friendly students in the first row to waggle her finger every time the word *Okay* popped out.

Using other people will supply a cue for you to notice when you are performing the target behavior. Another student, bright and excitable, had developed the habit of talking much too loudly—not all the time, but regularly when she was enthused. It was so habitual that she would start raising her voice and keep shouting for several minutes before becoming aware of it. To get a count, she asked her friends to tell her when she was talking too loudly. In another case, an overweight student had his wife remind him whenever he appeared to be overeating.

The situation here is similar to that of using others to remind you of goals; here too, don't allow the reminder to be punishing. Whenever you feel punished, change the system that the other person is using to notify you. The student whose wife reminded him of his overeating reported that at the beginning he used to get very irritated when she said "Ed, you're overeating." That was too bald a statement. They changed her comment to "Ed, dear, aren't you . . . ?" after which she dropped the subject. This incomplete, tactful way of reminding him was not frustrating.

Never allow yourself to be punished for noticing or recording your behaviors. This, after all, would make recording a less frequent behavior, which is exactly the opposite of what you want.

---

[1]We followed up this case first after 18 months and then after 7 years. In the first 18 months the woman had two relapses and used self-modification both times to correct the problem. After 7 years she had had no more relapses and remained free of night-time scratching.

Behaviors That Occur While a Lot
of Other Things Are Going On

Sometimes you are too busy doing something to make a record of a problem behavior just when it occurs. Or perhaps other people are present, and you would be embarrassed to haul out your record notes and make an entry. To cope with this problem, you can use *interval recording*—that is, making entries at specified time periods.

For example, a man who was too self-critical required himself to make an entry in his notes every half hour:

Time	Self-putdown
8:00 P.M.	Studying, having a hard time; told myself I was probably dumb.
8:30 P.M.	Wanted to call Jean, but thought she wouldn't want me to call.
9:00 P.M.	None
9:30 P.M.	Talking with Jean; she said she was glad I called; I told myself she said that just to be polite.

This man could have made a record of his self-criticisms while he was studying but not while he was chatting with Jean on the phone. His system allowed him to pick up this information later.

The disadvantage to such a system is that you may forget. In the rush of chatting with Jean, our man might have forgotten that he had put himself down in his thoughts when she had expressed pleasure at his call. Some students have devised systems to remind themselves that a recordable event has occurred, so that later they are cued to remember. For example, realizing that he had just put himself down in his thoughts, the man above checked a mark on a piece of paper, so that, when he hung up after his talk with Jean, the mark would remind him that he had something to record.

You may have more than one thing to record in your interval. For example:

Time	Self-putdown
9:30 P.M.	Jean said she was glad I called; I told myself she was just being polite.
	Went back to studying; imagined being unable to learn and flunking out of school.

One can use interval-recording systems for all kinds of problems: nail biting, studying, emotional states. Larger intervals can also be used, when timing isn't as important and when you're not likely to forget.

Devising a Plan for Record Keeping

Suppose that the very act of making observations is punishing to you. You don't keep records because you can't stand the news. It is not unusual that a person has difficulty keeping records because she or he doesn't like what the records say. Finding out from your record of cigarettes smoked that you are killing yourself is not, after all, a pleasant experience. So, since keeping records can be painful or tedious, you may be tempted to stop.

It is possible to use self-direction strategies to develop record keeping. Chapters 5, 6, and 7 discuss in detail these strategies in the broader context of setting up plans for change; here we point out only three techniques that you can use to deal with problems in keeping records.

First, you can develop record keeping one piece at a time. The woman who was having difficulty getting along with one of her coworkers realized that she needed to keep track of four different aspects of her relationship with him. At first this seemed impossibly complex. So she required herself to record only one aspect—that of ignoring his unfriendly remarks. After she had practiced this for a few days, she added a second record—keeping track of listening carefully to him. After several more days she was able to record both. She then added the third, and then the fourth. When keeping the records seems too hard, try adding just one item at a time (Nelson et al., 1975).

A second tactic is to reward yourself for keeping records (Stuart & Davis, 1972). A young woman wanted to know how many times per week she was failing to be as assertive as she would like to be. She had great difficulty keeping good records. Finally, she worked out a plan of self-reward in which she gave herself $1 to spend on whatever she liked for each day of accurate record keeping. Her records did improve, and later she switched to rewarding herself for assertiveness itself.

A third system is to ask someone else to check whether you are indeed keeping records. If what you are recording embarrasses you, you don't have to show the actual records to the other person; just indicate that you are keeping the records. For example, a young man who wanted to cut down on his drinking was upset when his records showed that he was drinking an average of nine beers per day. His first reaction was to stop keeping the records. But he wanted to cut down, so he asked several of his friends to inquire each morning if he had kept records for the previous day. You can also use ideas from Chapter 2 to build commitment to record keeping.

Self-recording is a behavior, and it follows the same principles of other behaviors. If you are failing in this step, you should view your failure simply as another goal for self-improvement and work out a system to increase that particular behavior. In other words, make accurate record keeping your first goal.

Summary

If you perform the problem behavior absentmindedly, practice performing it while paying close attention, so that your attention is switched on whenever the behavior occurs. You can also ask others to point out instances of the target behavior. For behaviors that occur while so much is going on that it would be difficult for you to record them immediately, you can use interval recording, in which you record after a specified time period. (Make sure you don't forget!) If for any reason you are failing to self-observe, your first plan for change should be to work out a system to increase accurate self-observation. You can develop record keeping one step at a time, reward yourself for keeping your records, and have others check on your record keeping. Build your commitment to keeping records, because commitment is the basis of all that follows.

SELF-RECORDED DATA AND PLANNING FOR CHANGE

The most obvious reason for getting self-recorded data is to produce better self-understanding. You may see patterns in your structured diary that alert you to certain recurring connections between your thoughts and behaviors and specific situations. You may see regular rhythms in the emotional shifts shown in your daily log. Noting your storage records of frequency counts will enable you to assess your distance from your goal. In Chapters 5, 6, 7, and 8 we will discuss ways of using this information to design a plan for self-directed change. Only careful records of your behaviors and situations will enable you to select and design the best plan possible.

There is also another use for these records—one that is not so obvious but of vital importance. These data will serve as a standard against which you can judge your future progress.

The phase in which you are now—that of self-recording prior to instituting a plan for change—is known technically as the *baseline period*. The baseline period is a time when you make self-observations but don't engage in other efforts to change. This means that your present records constitute a baseline against which future changes can be evaluated. As you will see, the records you collect and analyze for a baseline period are very important to the success of your plan.

The organization of this book is designed to provide you with an adequate baseline. You should be able to begin self-observation after completing this chapter and continue recording while you digest the information contained in the next four chapters. At that point, you will have learned enough to be ready to design an effective plan.[2]

Getting an Adequate Baseline Record

For how long should you gather baseline data? That is, for how long should you just observe yourself before trying techniques to change?

---

[2]For many forms of self-observation you'll want to know how your behavior changes from day to day or from week to week. In other words, you want to evaluate the data in relation to the passage of time. A graph is a useful device for this purpose. Chapter 9 presents detailed instructions for reading and constructing graphs; if you are unfamiliar with graphing, you may wish to read now the section entitled "Making a Graph" in Chapter 9. In summary, it is conventional to measure units of time on the horizontal axis and units of behavior on the vertical axis.

The answer is a simple one: the baseline period should be continued until the graph line is stable—that is, until it shows a clear pattern. Of course there will always be daily fluctuation; but, when you see a basic trend underlying the variations, the baseline can be said to be stable.

Figure 3-4 gives an example of a rather stable baseline. In the figure you can see that, on the first few days, this cigarette smoker showed some degree of variation in the number of cigarettes he smoked, but by the end of the 11th day his daily average was about 25. After 11 days of baseline, this smoker was ready to begin an intervention plan.

The question we are dealing with here is "For how many days would this cigarette smoker have to gather baseline data before he could feel that he had an adequate estimate?" Our rule of thumb is: if the behavior occurs every day, always gather the baseline for at least one week. If, by that time, your record shows only small swings up and down, you have a usable estimate.

Figure 3-5 shows the number of hours a college student studied each night. You can see that, at the end of the first week, she could have had only the roughest idea of her weekly study time, because within that week her schedule had varied so much. This suggests a second rule: when the graph shows large swings from one day to the next, it is best to gather the baseline for at least two weeks.

The general answer to the question "How long should you gather baseline data?" is: long enough to have a good estimate of how often the target behavior occurs. We said "general answer" because there is no absolute rule for predetermining how adequate a baseline record is going to be, and there is no absolute rule for deciding ahead of time how long you should collect data before you begin your intervention plan. After all, the purpose of the

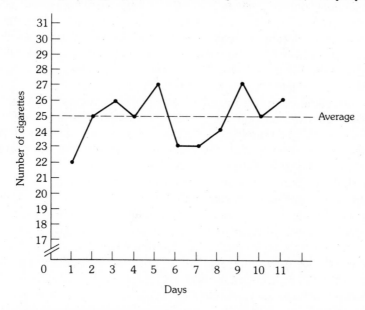

Figure 3-4.   Cigarettes smoked daily.

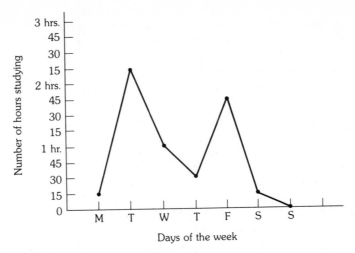

Figure 3-5.   Number of hours studied daily.

baseline is to establish how often the behavior occurs. You end the baseline period when you have some confidence that you understand the actual pattern of your behavior. Some behaviors seem never to show a stable baseline; complaining, for example, or outbursts of anger may be quite variable, because they depend somewhat on how provoking other people's behavior happens to be. Even in such cases, although the graph line may be very irregular, you can still come to understand the pattern.

If your graph shows large swings in some behavior, your definition of that behavior may not be consistent or clear enough to you. Let's say, for example, that on day 1 you count as assertion any time you said something (no matter what) to another person, but on day 2 you record as assertion only those instances in which you spoke up when your rights were violated. In this case your graph will of course show large swings, which are due entirely to the lack of a clear definition of the behavior you are recording.

There are some considerations that can offer help in deciding whether you have kept your record long enough to have a stable baseline. First, it is unlikely that you will get a stable baseline in less than a week. Daily activities vary somewhat from day to day, and, even for behaviors that occur quite frequently, it will take several days to notice any consistency.

Second, the greater the variation from day to day, the longer it will take to get a stable estimate. A good rule of thumb is: if, after three weeks, you still have a lot of up-and-down swings on your graph, use a simple average.

Third, ask yourself whether the period of days or weeks during which you have been gathering the baseline is representative of your usual life. If, for example, you were counting number of hours spent studying and last week was midterm time, then last week couldn't be considered a typical week and shouldn't be used to make an estimate. If you smoke more at parties and in the last five days you went to an unusual number of parties, you couldn't use that period as a good basis for estimating how much you smoke. Every day has something unusual about it, which necessitates gathering the data for at least a week. But what we are suggesting here is that you look for special occurrences that can artificially inflate or deflate your estimate of the frequency of a target behavior. In general, then, always run the baseline period for at least one "normal" week and, as a rule, don't go beyond three or four weeks.

Are the Baseline Data Reliable?

Reliability, in science, refers to a particular kind of accuracy of recording. Data are reliable when two or more observations of the same event result in the same recording. In the self-recording of behavior, you must ask yourself "Am I really recording each occurrence, and am I recording the same events in the same way each time they occur?"

In psychological research we usually try to use two or more observers, who practice recording together until they reach an acceptable level of agreement (usually 85–95%). But in self-modification you are your only observer, and this can lead to some difficulties.

A young man was determined to improve his housekeeping behavior. Two sets of roommates had already thrown him out because he was very sloppy—left his clothes all over the place, never washed dishes, never cleaned the bathroom, and so on. He started keeping records of his behavior and established a category called "acts of good housekeeping." The baseline, after two weeks, was very irregular, so he asked for advice. It turned out that his definition of "acts of good housekeeping" changed from day to day. Sometimes putting his empty beer glass in the sink would earn a checkmark for good behavior, whereas on other days he would count as instances of good behavior only "major acts," such as making his bed or taking out the garbage. The category definition drifted from day to day, and thus his records were hopelessly unreliable.

Here is a brief summary of the most common reasons why a person may have a difficult time making reliable observations and establishing a meaningful baseline. All of these reasons have been discussed earlier in greater detail.

1. You may not have defined your target behavior in terms of behavior-in-a-situation. In short, you may not have been specific enough.
2. The behavior may be just a habit—that is, a behavior you perform without paying attention to it.
3. Perhaps engaging in the behavior is so upsetting to you that you'd rather forget about it than record it.
4. You may not have developed a record-keeping system that is simple enough. As a consequence, you may not be keeping a record of all the instances of the target behavior.

You can reduce each of these problems by consulting the sections of this chapter that discuss them and by following the recommended procedures.

If your doubts about the accuracy of your data persist, you may ask another person to help you by recording along with you, each of you keeping separate records (Kazdin, 1974f). Keep in mind that this procedure may bring problems of its own, since observers also make errors. Nevertheless, the percentage of agreement can be calculated, and, if you get 80% or more, you may consider it acceptable. A simple and widely used formula for calculating percentage of agreement is

$$\% = \frac{\text{number of agreements}}{\text{number of agreements} + \text{number of disagreements}}.$$

Another way of using someone else's help is simply to ask that person to check you now and then to see if you are recording accurately. The young woman who wanted to be more assertive told two of her close friends about her plan. She asked them to question her from time to time to find out if she had indeed recorded specific situations in which they had seen her perform the target behavior. A man who wanted to record all the sweets he ate asked his wife to check with him each time she saw him eating a sweet, to make sure that he was keeping a record of it. People tend to be more accurate if they expect others to check on them (Lipinski & Nelson, 1974; Zegiob, Arnold, & Forehand, 1975).

You should expect your self-observations to be somewhat unreliable (Lipinski & Nelson, 1974; Worthington, 1979). You're too busy leading your daily life to notice *every* instance of a target behavior (Epstein et al., 1975). Thus you must be particularly careful to use techniques that maximize reliability. Use (1) *specifically defined categories* of (2) *behaviors-in-situations* recorded on a (3) *device always present* at the occurrence, with a (4) *simple system* that is (5) *not punishing* and that may even be (6) *positively rewarding,* and do not hesitate to (7) *get others to help you.*

Omitting the Baseline Period

Is there ever a time when you can go directly to the stage of trying to change your behavior, without going through a baseline period? If you are asking whether there is ever a time when you can skip self-observation, the answer is an emphatic *no*. If, instead, you are asking whether you can begin self-observation and, at the same time, start trying to change your behavior, the answer is different.

If a target behavior never occurs, then there is obviously little point in trying to count its nonexistent frequency. For example, if you never study and your target is to develop studying, you already have a baseline count—zero. Even in this situation, there is value in doing some self-observation to see what is the cause of this lack of desirable behavior. A short period of self-observation in which you ask "What are my opportunities to study?" or "What am I doing instead of studying?" can be valuable in formulating a plan for change. In general, whenever you are in doubt, it is best to make some self-observations *before* trying to change. The advantages gained with more self-understanding outweigh the disadvantage of a short delay.

There are some kinds of behavior that occur only at certain times but then occur with a high frequency. Studying during exam periods is a good example. You may not want to study very much throughout the semester but wish that you did study more when exam time comes around. Or you might have a date very rarely, but, when you do, you seem to always act stupidly. What should you do about establishing a baseline?

In these kinds of situations, you cannot gather the baseline until the occasion arises. If it arises quite irregularly, as in the case of exams coming only once each semester, you can do two things. First, be prepared to gather the information *when* the situation does occur. Second, practice ways of dealing with the situation. If you know that you have problems studying enough during exam week, you can begin practicing studying *before* exam week. You can do several things in that connection. You can contrive an exam-like period and let this serve as a baseline phase. You can mock up a two- or three-day period during which you resolve to study at least five hours daily. And you can make observations on daydreaming, desk avoiding, and actual studying that can serve at a later date as baseline data for the actual intervention.

The baseline should be omitted when the behavior is very harmful either to yourself or to others. But particularly in these situations it is important to make structured-diary observations when the unwanted behaviors do occur, so that you can detect the A-B-C patterns. Discovering the antecedents that lead to the unwanted behavior or the consequences that encourage it can be very helpful in devising a successful plan for change.

Summary

Data recorded before beginning a plan can serve as a baseline against which future progress is measured. This baseline, charted on a graph, should be continued until the pattern is stable. This almost always requires at least a week. The data should be as reliable as possible; that is, you should make every effort to use the same standards and judgments each time you consider your behavior. Reliability is increased by specific definitions, careful attention, and simple recording procedures. Other procedures for improving reliability may include the help of someone else and self-reward for good recording. As a general rule, a plan for self-change should not begin until after a stable, reliable baseline is achieved, because only then will you really know the extent of the problem and its exact nature.

YOUR OWN SELF-DIRECTION PROJECT: STEP THREE

You should now begin self-observation for the behavior-in-a-situation you have chosen in step two. For your self-observation you can use a structured diary, a frequency count, or a rating scale.

In order to be successful, you should make record keeping easy and build it into your life pattern. Don't go directly into an attempt to change; first observe the target behavior as it is now occurring.

You should get baseline records for at least one week; as a rule, you won't need more than three. Try to get stable baselines of the target behavior. Be as accurate as you can, because an accurate estimate of the problem will make decision making about plans for change much easier. While gathering data, go on to read the next five chapters, which deal with the principles of behavior and the techniques of change. When you have adequate self-observations, you will be ready to begin your plan for change.

TIPS FOR TYPICAL TOPICS

Certain topics will require especially careful observation of antecedents, of behaviors, or of consequences. Each is discussed in a separate chapter. After reading further, you may want to revise your self-observation procedures to reflect your increased sophistication.

For example, Chapter 5 details the role of thoughts as antecedents; after reading it, you may be better able to detect certain thoughts that you'll want to record.

The Other Sex.   Antecedents are vital in understanding shyness. Be sure to record the details of each event that produces such feelings; also be sure to note your own thoughts or self-statements when you begin to feel uncomfortable. For example, do you tell yourself you won't succeed or magnify your fears? Do you avoid opportunities to interact with the other sex? If you do, what are the cues to your avoidance? Be sure to notice what you are doing *instead* of interacting when you shyly avoid the opportunity.

If your problem is not shyness but awkwardness, gathering antecedents will help you get an accurate understanding of your behaviors. Successful daters have reported receiving more feedback, especially from peers, about how they were behaving in the dating situations (Perri & Richards, 1977). Arrange to get feedback from others—those who are at the same parties, who ride in the same car, or who hear your telephone conversations.

Depression.   The daily log is appropriate here for recording mood and the things that affect it. Be sure to record the positive events and feelings as well as the negative ones; a reason for being depressed is the failure to even notice pleasant events (Fuchs & Rehm, 1977). Also take note of your self-denigrating thoughts (self-putdowns).

Assertion.   Record situations in which you might have been assertive but were not. Record what you expected to happen if you had been assertive; and record what you did instead, along with its consequences. Of course be sure to include instances of assertion as well, together with the consequences.

Specific Fears.   What situations make you anxious? Notice physical situations, such as having to take a test or give a speech, and also your thoughts and worries in those situations. Rate your anxiety in various situations.

Family, Friends, Lovers, and Coworkers.   Try to notice sequences: what do you do that leads to the irritating problem behavior? For example, do you sulk, then want to go home early from a party, and finally say things that betray your jealousy? Record these sequences fully, as in keeping a diary. Be sure to include your behaviors as well as your thoughts.

Smoking, Drinking, and Drug Use.   Careful recording of antecedents will be most helpful. When do you smoke or drink too much? What are you saying to yourself just before you smoke or drink? What are the consequences—what do you get out of it? There is no apparent difference in effectiveness between recording number of urges resisted and number of cigarettes actually smoked (Kantorowitz, Walters, & Pezdek, 1978).

Overeating.   Effective weight loss requires observation of several kinds. As with all recording, be sure to include the antecedents of eating— both problem eating and normal eating. Does feeling full feel terribly good— that is, is it an important consequence? When you begin a weight-loss plan, it is vital that you record what you ate and the situation in which you ate it. The situation can be a feeling, a social occasion, or a physical situation. This kind of observation should be done even before you attempt any self-control, because the self-knowledge you gain will reveal the nature of your overeating problem. Eventually you will need to count calories (Romanczyk, 1974; Green, 1978).

Recording food intake by caloric count will help you learn the calorie value of what you eat. Regular weight records, perhaps weekly, are desirable. When do urges to overeat occur? Careful records are vital to weight loss, because self-deception is characteristic of dieters (Schachter, 1971) and careful recording helps overcome deception.

Studying and Time Management.   Before establishing a full time-management schedule, you'll need to know your current pattern of how you use time. Prepare a daily log, and mark the beginning and ending time for each type of change of activity. You can buy a small daily appointment book for this purpose, or you can make your own daily sheets. Each time, mark when an activity begins and when it ends. For example:

7:00 A.M.   Got ready to go to school.
7:42 A.M.   Turned on television.
8:15 A.M.   Left the house.

And so forth, throughout the day. For studying, record how much of the time you were in a position to study and how much you were actually studying. Record also the consequences of *not* studying. What do you actually do when you study? read and underline? make notes? Be precise.

CHAPTER 4

Behavior/Environment Relationships

You have selected a goal, you have identified the behaviors that need to be
changed, and you have begun to keep records of your present behavior. But
what do your self-observations tell you? What relationships do you see between your behavior and the situations in which it occurs—that is, its environment? What are the principles that describe those relationships? In order
to understand yourself and in order to be able to devise a plan for change,
you must understand the principles that relate behavior to its situational setting—to its environment.

The situations in which your behavior occurs can be analyzed in terms
of the effects that antecedents and consequences have on your behavior. You
may be stimulated to do something by an antecedent and then be further
stimulated by the consequence of what you do. In order to understand yourself, you need to understand the effects of both on your behavior.

You also need to understand the relationship that connects behavior to
language and thinking. It is to that issue that we turn first.

LANGUAGE, THINKING, AND BEHAVIOR

Try to recall how it was when you were learning to drive an automobile. Your
instructor is beside you. The traffic is moderately heavy as you approach an
intersection, and you are concentrating on staying in your lane, at a safe
distance from the car ahead. Twenty yards from the intersection, the traffic
light snaps from green to amber. "Stop!" your instructor says. "There won't
be enough time to get through!" You stop slowly and safely.

The next intersection you approach will find you watching the traffic light
more closely. When it changes to amber, it is likely that you'll say to yourself
"Stop!" and do so. You may have spoken to yourself aloud; more likely, it
was a "mental" message—what is called in psychology *subvocal speech*. In

either case, your saying "Stop!" served as an instruction to yourself. The self-instruction was an antecedent to your behavior of stepping on the brake. It was an antecedent that made you stop this time, just as your teacher's instruction caused you to stop the first time.

This simple instance illustrates principles that operate even in the most complex behavior; but, perhaps because these principles are so pervasive, they often go unnoticed. This chapter discusses these principles. Some will seem absurdly obvious; others, surprising. All are vital to an understanding of how self-direction develops.

The first principle illustrated is both obvious and surprising: the most common method of controlling behavior is through language. We give orders: "Platoon, halt!" or "Take out your driver's license, please!" We make requests: "Pass the salt, please." We give hints: "I suppose it's a good movie, but I'm so tired tonight . . ." We coach: "Good, good; a little more to the right; that's better . . ." Hundreds of examples occur in everyone's daily life. Of all forms of antecedents, the language of others (both spoken and written) may well have the strongest and most immediate effect on our behavior. Of course, we do not always comply. We may refuse, ignore, argue, resent, or laugh. But the effects are there, and language is a pervasive and inescapable influence on our reactions.

In charting chains of events, you will find that the language of other people represents the immediate antecedent of many of your behaviors, desirable as well as problematic. The human environment is in many ways a language environment, and the environment controls behavior largely through language.

So much for your stepping on the brake when your instructor said "Stop!" The more interesting part of the example, however, is the second time you come to a halt because you heard "Stop!" That was you talking to yourself.

Self-Direction through Language

"Talking to oneself," or self-directed speech, is often considered comical, if not aberrant. It conjures up a picture of an old man muttering to himself down a city street or even someone in a mental hospital. (Incidentally, the phenomenon is common enough on college campuses, where professors seem to walk across campus talking to themselves almost as an occupational hazard.) But, as this section will show, self-directed speech is common, useful, often highly adaptive, and, during certain periods of life, routine and normal. For most adults, however, self-directed speech is subvocal. To fully understand this process, we must understand the relationship between talking to oneself aloud and talking to oneself subvocally (that is, silently, covertly, or "mentally"—thinking in words). As we will see, the effects of these two forms of self-speech antecedents are virtually identical.

As very young children develop, a first task of their parents is to bring them into the language community. Children must learn to heed language and to use it. Psychologists Luria (1961) and Vygotsky (1965, 1978) have studied this developmental process in detail and found a regular sequence that is roughly linked to the age of the child. For our purposes, we can illustrate some aspects of this sequence with this example.

"Don't kick over the wastebasket!" the father shouts to the 2- or 3-year old. Too late; the trash is on the floor. The father rights it and says again, this time more gently, "Don't kick over the wastebasket now." Next day, the child approaches the basket, draws back the foot for a happy kick—and stops in midstride. "Don't kick over the basket!" the child says, and walks on by. The sight of the wastebasket may for some time cause the child to mutter the instruction aloud. For a while longer the lips of the child may be seen moving, in a silent self-instruction; eventually all traces of speech disappear, and the child merely walks by, leaving the basket unmolested, as do the adults of the house. No external evidence of self-speech remains. In all likelihood, subvocal speech itself drops out, and the behavior becomes "automatic." Later in this chapter, we will discuss the processes of this "automatization"; for the moment, let's attend closely to the processes by which the child established verbal self-control.

Very young children imitate and incorporate adult speech. First the father says "Don't kick!"; then the child says the same thing, often imitating emphasis and inflection. Control of the child's behavior is passed from father to child. But notice this: the control by language instruction is maintained. Regardless of who says it, the antecedent "Don't kick!" affects the child's behavior. It is normal for young children to use imitated, spoken-aloud self-instructions for self-control (Vygotsky, 1965, 1978; Roberts & Tharp, 1980).

At a certain point, around the age of 5, this self-controlling speech "goes underground," in Vygotsky's (1965) nice phrase. That is, the use of self-controlling language typically becomes subvocal—steadily more silent, rapid, and shorthand. Many psychologists would argue that this is when thinking begins, because thinking can be seen largely as subvocal speech. During earlier stages, before language "goes underground," self-instructing aloud helps children perform even simple tasks more efficiently (Luria, 1961). But the going underground produces a different relationship between behavior and its verbal antecedents.

Our own research indicates that 5- to 8-year-old children, when working with simple button-pushing tasks, perform the task less accurately if they have to say "push," "stop," or the like before the actual behavior (Higa, Tharp, & Calkins, 1978). But verbal instructions don't always interfere; whether they do depends on the difficulty of the task, as well as on the child's age. These same 5- to 8-year-olds, when doing schoolwork, say rules aloud to themselves more often on harder than on easier tasks (Roberts & Tharp, in press).

Even in adulthood, however, the power of self-directed speech as an antecedent is not lost; it is merely not used as often. Donald Meichenbaum (1977) has demonstrated in a long line of research and theoretical development that verbal self-control can be reinstituted, for older children and adults, when new skills are being learned, when self-control deficiencies are present, or in problematic situations. In the next chapter, specific techniques using self-speech will be described. Here, in this theoretical discussion, it need be noted only that self-directed speech (vocal or subvocal) is a powerful controlling antecedent of behavior. It is particularly useful and natural in new or stressful situations.

It was useful and natural for you to say "Stop!" to yourself when you were learning to drive. You probably no longer do so. But the next time you are driving in a strange city, when the caution light stays on a much longer or shorter time than you are accustomed to, you may very well need to talk to yourself again. When the smooth flow of well-learned behaviors is some-how disrupted, conscious self-control comes into play (Kanfer & Karoly, 1972). Difficult situations make us more likely to use self-speech.

Thus you are probably talking to yourself in precisely those situations that you find most fearful, most depressing, or most difficult to cope with. This self-speech is likely to be "underground"—probably no more than a mutter, and even more probably only a quick "speech in the mind." Regardless of the form it takes, this self-speech antecedent has powerful influence over your responses to difficulties. Have you ever said to yourself "This is another of those situations where I make a fool of myself. Get out!" and walked away, lonely and depressed?

In conducting your self-observation program, observe yourself carefully as your problem situation begins to unfold. Try to detect the things you are saying to yourself: they act as instructions.

Principle 1: From early life to adulthood, verbal instructions (from others and from the self) act as powerful guides to behavior, particularly in difficult situations.

Let's now turn to the consequences of your actions.

CONSEQUENCES

A group of people are bothered by the high cost of food. They band together to form a co-op. This requires a lot of effort: making and revising plans, getting food, allocating work schedules, and so on. But when the work is done, each participant is rewarded by a 25% reduction in his or her food bill; all the planning and effort result in a considerable saving for each person. The efforts of these people have had a positive consequence.

Operant Behaviors

Behaviors that are affected by their consequences are called *operant behaviors.* An operant behavior is anything you do that has an effect on your environment. In the example above, the people meet together, plan, and work, and the effect is that they get cheaper food.

The dictionary defines *to operate* as "to perform an act, to function, to produce an effect." Through operant behaviors we function, act, and produce effects on ourselves and on our environment. We operate in and on the world.

Much of our behavior falls into this category. Operant behavior includes all of the complex things we do as we weave the fabric of our daily lives. Our bad habits are operant behaviors we want to eliminate. The things we don't do but wish we did are operant behaviors we want to develop.

We develop operant behaviors—that is, we learn them—through the consequences of our actions. Learning means a change in behavior due to interaction with the environment. Operant behaviors are changed—learned or unlearned—as a result of their consequences.

Principle 2: Operant behavior is a function of its consequences.

Operant behaviors are strengthened or weakened by what follows them. The co-op member calls up a vegetable wholesaler and asks "Will you sell us ten bushels of apples?" The wholesaler says "No, I sell only by the carload." The co-op member doesn't call that wholesaler back.

No matter what we are learning to do—kiss, type, speak, write, study, eat, or compose a string quartet—our behaviors will be strengthened or weakened by the events that follow them. A child learning to speak, for example, will become more verbal if praised than if scolded for talking. A composer will be more or less likely to write a second quartet depending on the events that follow his first one.

Consequences That Strengthen Behavior

The *strength* of behavior, as we are using the term here, refers to the chances that a particular behavior will be performed. Behavior is "stronger" if it is more probable. A man with no weight problem, for example, might be said to have a "strong" resistance to fattening food. Translated into psychological terms, this means that the chances of his resisting fattening food are high. The overweight man, on the other hand, might have a "weak" resistance, which means that the chances of his resisting fattening food are low.

The best practical index for gauging the probability of behavior is its frequency. In behavior analysis, we usually infer the strength of a behavior from its frequency; that is, we count how often the behavior occurs. This is why the chapter on self-observation placed so much emphasis on counting behavior.

Reinforcers

If a consequence strengthens a behavior, it is called a *reinforcer*. How reinforcers strengthen behavior depends on the nature of the consequence.

Principle 3: A positive reinforcer is a consequence that strengthens behavior by its added presence.

Positive reinforcers may be anything—kisses or food or money or praise or the chance to ride a motorcycle. What is a positive reinforcer for one person is not necessarily a positive reinforcer for another. The list is inexhaustible and highly individualized.

A little boy goes to his father and shows him a picture he has drawn. "That's lovely, son" the father praises him. "I really like it. Hey, what's this part?" he asks, giving the child attention. The father's praise and attention are probably positive reinforcers for the child. They increase the chance that in the future the child will show things to his father.

A positive reinforcer is anything that, when added to the situation, makes the behavior that preceded it more likely to recur. The composer is more likely to attempt a second quartet if his or her first composing behavior is positively reinforced. This positive reinforcement might consist of one or more consequences: applause from the audience, the pleasure of hearing his or her own works performed, the sense of satisfaction in knowing that the work meets high standards.

It is important to note that praise, critical and personal, will also have positive reinforcing effects. Thus language acts as a reinforcing consequence, as well as an antecedent.

Principle 4: A negative reinforcer is an unpleasant consequence that strengthens the behavior by being removed from the situation.

If you are standing outside and it begins to rain hard, you might put up your umbrella to keep the rain from falling on your head. The act of putting up the umbrella is thus negatively reinforced by the removal of the unpleasant consequence of getting wet. The act that took away the unpleasant situation is reinforced—that is, made more likely to happen again.

Picture a person talking to a friend. The friend seems bored. The more the person talks on a particular topic, the more bored the friend seems to be. So the talker changes to a new topic. Immediately the friend appears less bored. The act of changing topics is negatively reinforced by the fact that the friend is no longer bored. In other words, changing topics has removed the unpleasant consequence of the friend's boredom.

Just as with positive reinforcers, what is a negative reinforcer for one person is not necessarily so for another. The saying "One person's meat is another's poison" expresses in simple terms this concept; the same thing or event can be positive for one person and negative for another.

Escape and Avoidance

The principle of negative reinforcement explains how we learn to escape or avoid unpleasant consequences. Suppose a mother says to a child who is in a rebellious mood "Come here, please." The child does not come. The mother reaches over and swats the child. The child does not come. The mother raises her hand again. The child comes. The mother drops her hand. By complying, the child has escaped or avoided a second swat.

Technically, *escape learning* refers to behaviors that terminate the unpleasant consequence. The mother keeps spanking until the child submits and comes along. *Avoidance learning,* on the other hand, refers to behaviors that remove the possibility of an unpleasant consequence. The next time the mother says "Come here," the child obeys, thus avoiding a spanking like the one he got in the past. In escape learning the unpleasant consequence is actually delivered, but in avoidance learning it is avoided.

When you begin to analyze your own behavior, you may discover that you do things for which you get no apparent reward. People sometimes think of these behaviors as being "unmotivated," but they are often avoidance behaviors. For example, you may tend to go off by yourself rather than to places frequented by your friends, even though being by yourself is not reinforcing. You might ask "What am I responding to?" The answer may lie in your learning history; that is, you may have learned an avoidance behavior. An important characteristic of avoidance behaviors is that often they are performed in an unemotional, even blasé, way. Such behaviors are evidently not motivated by anxiety. Until someone calls it to your attention, you may be totally unaware that some of your behaviors are based on the avoidance of discomfort.

Reinforcing Consequences

You can see why an analysis of consequences is an important part of a plan for changing. You may find that you are *not* in fact positively reinforced for the behavior you want to perform. You may even find that you are being positively reinforced for some action that makes the desired behavior difficult or impossible. For example, one student wrote in a self-analysis: "I would like to be nicer to my roommate and be able to solve our little difficulties in a friendly way. But I usually fly off the handle and shout at him. The terrible thing is that I get reinforced for that; he gives in!"

By understanding how reinforcing consequences work—positive or negative—you can form better plans for changing your behavior. In self-change you sometimes learn new behaviors—for example, an overeater learns to deal with hunger in some new way instead of eating—and sometimes you simply arrange to be reinforced for acts you already know how to perform—for example, a nail biter is reinforced for not biting his nails.

Reinforcements are important for both learning and simple performance of actions. Theoretical psychologists are still arguing whether, strictly speaking, reinforcement is necessary for learning. But it is clear that your *performance* of behavior is affected by the reinforcement you get. You do what you are reinforced for doing. We are emphasizing behavior and reinforcement for that reason. The principles of behavior here are really principles of performance.

Summary

Operant behaviors are strengthened or weakened by what follows them. Behavior is said to be "stronger" if it is more likely to occur in a particular situation.

A positive reinforcer is a consequence that strengthens behavior by its added presence. A negative reinforcer is an unpleasant consequence that strengthens behavior by being removed from the situation. You learn to escape or avoid unpleasant consequences. What is a reinforcer—positive or negative—for one person is not necessarily so for another and not necessarily so at all times. Some people dislike pastrami; even those who like it would not find a pastrami sandwich reinforcing immediately after a Thanksgiving feast.

Punishment

Principle 5: Behavior that is punished will occur less often.

Psychologists distinguish two kinds of punishment. In the first kind, after a behavior has been performed, some unpleasant event occurs. For example, a child says a naughty word and is immediately reprimanded by her parents. An adult says something rude and immediately receives disapproval from friends. If the reprimand is unpleasant enough and if the disapproval is unpleasant enough, the behaviors that led to that event are less likely to happen in the future. They have been punished.

In the second kind of punishment, after a behavior has been performed, something pleasant is taken away. For example, a child who is playing with her parents says a naughty word and is put in her room by herself. An adult says something rude, and the people he is with go away. In both cases, it is the *loss* of something pleasant—playing with the parents, being with friends— that punishes the behavior that led up to it.

What is the difference between punishment and negative reinforcement? In negative reinforcement an act that allows the person to escape or avoid some event is reinforced by *removing* the event. In punishment, behavior probabilities are reduced in one of two ways: (1) an unpleasant event follows a behavior, or (2) a pleasant event is withdrawn following a behavior.

This chart summarizes the difference between negative reinforcement and punishment.

Negative reinforcement
Your behavior .... escapes or avoids a (usually unpleasant) consequence; this .... strengthens the behavior.

Punishment, type 1
Your behavior .... leads to some upleasant event; this .... makes the behavior less probable.

Punishment, type 2
Your behavior .... leads to the loss of something pleasant; this ... makes the behavior less probable.

Extinction

Suppose you first learn to do some act because you are reinforced for it, but then, on later performances, no reward follows. What was once reinforced no longer is. As a consequence, your act begins to lose some of its strength. This is called *extinction.*

Principle 6: An act that was reinforced but no longer is will begin to weaken.

Two people have been going together for several months but are beginning to fall out of love. He calls her up, she's not home, he leaves a message, but she doesn't call back. Or she drops by to see him, and he doesn't seem very interested. Life, alas, changes, and acts that were once reinforced may no longer be. He will be less likely to call in the future. She will be less likely to drop by.

Extinction occurs all around us, continuously. It is the process by which we adjust our behavior to a changing world. If the woman never returned the man's calls, he wouldn't want to keep calling back forever, nor would the woman want to keep on dropping by to see an uninterested man. Behaviors that are no longer productive are gradually dropped.

Extinction and punishment are not the same, incidentally. In punishment some unpleasant consequence is added or some pleasant event is taken away following your behavior. In extinction nothing happens. If the woman said "Don't call me any more. I don't want to talk to you," that would punish the act of calling. If she simply didn't return calls—that is, she did nothing—that would extinguish the act of calling.

When you are developing any new behavior, it is possible that the behavior will extinguish if there isn't a sufficient amount of reinforcement to build up the strength of the behavior.

Do all acts extinguish equally? No.

Principle 7: Intermittent reinforcement increases resistance to extinction.

Reinforcement that follows each instance of a behavior is said to be *continuous reinforcement.* This could be described as a 100% schedule of reinforcement. But most behaviors in the real world are not reinforced for each instance; sometimes they are reinforced, sometimes they are not. This is called *intermittent reinforcement.*

As you might expect, continuous reinforcement provides for more rapid new learning. But intermittent reinforcement has a most interesting effect: *it makes behaviors more resistant to extinction.* The behaviors weaken more gradually. A behavior that has been reinforced randomly, but on the average of every other time (a 50% schedule), will persist longer when reinforcement is withdrawn than if it had been reinforced continuously.

Let's go back to the example of the spurned lover. Suppose she has been careless about returning his calls and he has been reinforced about half the time for calling her. Finally, she loses interest in him entirely and no longer responds at all to his telephoned messages. (These are called *extinction trials.*)

The intermittent reinforcement schedule he was on before (when she returned about half his calls) means that it will take *longer* for the man to extinguish his calling behavior than if he had been reinforced 100% of the time. If her nonreinforcement continues, of course, extinction will eventually occur. But the number of trials to extinction is affected by the previous reinforcement schedule.

Schedules that are intermittent, and especially those that are unpredictable, are particularly effective in producing resistance to extinction. Some reinforcement schedules are quite thin—for example, if the person is reinforced only once in 25 times. This kind of schedule would produce a great deal of resistance to extinction. After all, the person was reinforced only once in 25 times *before* the extinction trials began, so it is not surprising that the behavior is very resistant to extinction.

BOX 4-1
Freedom and Determinism

The reading of this chapter is almost certain to stir up an issue that has been debated since the beginning of time and that is argued again and again in the mind of every thinking person: freedom versus determinism. Who does in fact control us? the gods, the world, the soul, the self? Are we free to choose our own acts and destinies, or is the feeling of freedom an illusion of beings whose lives are determined by external forces?

Each religion, each philosopher sooner or later has reached the same general conclusion, although the details certainly vary: humankind is both free *and* determined. It is only the degrees of freedom and determinism that can be argued. Each person must live the drama of the conflict between submitting to deterministic forces and achieving available freedom. Religion teaches that we must submit to the will of God, but only by an act of free choice. Science—as exemplified by this book—argues that the environment determines behavior; yet it also argues that you can drastically increase those aspects of your life that you yourself control.

Neither religion nor humanistic philosophy argues that humankind's basic freedom means that natural law is invalid. This chapter presents those principles of natural law that determine behavior. The balance of the book presents schemes for using those principles to increase your freedom. By assuming that your acts are determined and by finding what determines them, you can seek to control the controlling forces, thus gaining freedom. So the old debate about freedom versus determinism is present in this book too. Some readers of our earlier editions have written to say "You speak of self-this and self-that; but if behavior is determined by the environment, how can one be self-directed? You are self-contradictory." These readers are very discerning, but it is not quite a matter of contradiction, for contradiction could arise only if either freedom or determinism alone governed our lives. But our lives take their form in the space between these two abstractions, neither of which fully describes their course.

This effect of intermittent reinforcement is significant for self-change because it helps to explain the persistence of maladaptive behaviors. Why do you do things you are apparently not reinforced for or things you don't even want to do? You may not see the rare reinforcement—such as one in 50 or 100 times—that is keeping your behavior going. Or you may have been intermittently reinforced for maladaptive acts in the past, so that now they are very resistant to extinction. A casual observer might label such behavior "stubborn" or "foolish," not realizing the effect of intermittent reinforcement. Many maladjusted behaviors that you see in yourself or other people persist because they are reinforced on intermittent schedules.

Summary

Behavior that is punished will occur less often in the future. Punishment means either taking away a positive event following a behavior or adding a negative event following a behavior. Both kinds of punishment decrease the likelihood of the behavior.

An act that is no longer reinforced, either positively or negatively, will weaken. This is called extinction. In this process, the behavior has no reinforcing consequence and therefore weakens.

Intermittent reinforcement, however, increases the resistance of a behavior to extinction.

ANTECEDENTS

We now turn to a general consideration of *antecedents* and how antecedent control of behavior develops. Regardless of the power of consequences, your behavior can never be stimulated by its consequences alone. Consequences, after all, occur after a behavior is completed. Antecedents, as we said in Chapter 1, are the setting events for your behavior. As such, they control your behavior.

Antecedents and Positive Reinforcement

Throughout our lives most of our actions are controlled by *cues* (signals). For example, when the bell rings or the lecturer says "That's all for today," students get out of their seats and move toward the door. Each student knows perfectly well how to leave a classroom, but ordinarily no one does so until the cue is given.

Principle 8: Most operant behavior is eventually guided by antecedent stimuli or cues.

The interesting question, especially from the point of view of behavior modification, is "How do we learn the cues?" In any hour of our lives, thousands of cues are provided by the environment. The world is rich with stimuli—conversations, sounds, sights, events, smells—and our behaviors are orchestrated into this complexity.

Cues that evoke a particular action are called *discriminative stimuli*. This technical term is useful because it helps us understand how a cue works. A cue identifies the conditions in which an action will be reinforced or not reinforced. It is a cue that helps us discriminate between appropriate and inappropriate conditions for an action. *Appropriate,* in this context, means that the behavior will be followed by reinforcement. *Inappropriate* means that the behavior will not be followed by reinforcement. In college you soon learn that, when the lecturer says "That's all," it is appropriate to leave. You also learn that, in the absence of that statement, leaving may not be so appropriate.

An antecedent, or stimulus, becomes a cue to a behavior when the behavior is reinforced in the presence of that stimulus and not reinforced in the absence of the stimulus. When a stimulus and a behavior occur and the behavior is reinforced *only* when stimulus and behavior occur together, the stimulus will become a cue for that behavior.

In the laboratory, this process may be studied by reinforcing with food a hungry mouse for pressing a lever when a light is on and by not reinforcing it for pressing the lever when the light is off. The mouse will learn to press the lever only in the presence of the light. In our everyday lives, this process occurs continually. For example, couples who date regularly can "tell" when it is time to leave a party. Each has learned that, when the other gives certain cues—perhaps getting quieter or acting edgy—he or she will be reinforced for preparing to leave. In the absence of that cue, neither is nearly so likely to be reinforced for leaving.

Role of Antecedents in Avoidance Behavior and Extinction

In order to avoid an unpleasant outcome, you obviously have to know that such an outcome is about to occur. You avoid a situation when you get a cue that an unpleasant outcome is imminent. This means that your avoidance behavior is guided by the antecedents—the cues—you get from your environment. If your avoidance behavior is successful, the unpleasant event does not occur.

You can see that, just as consequences affect the behavior that took place before them, antecedents affect the behavior that will take place after them. Later in this chapter, we shall discuss other kinds of antecedents. Here, we are focusing on antecedents that determine avoidance behavior.

Principle 9: An antecedent can be a cue or signal that an unpleasant event may be imminent, and it is likely to result in avoidance behavior.

Suppose that, when you were in your early teens, you weren't very adept at social niceties and often made a poor impression on others. This may have led to unpleasant experiences, and you might have gradually learned to avoid certain social situations. You learned to be shy. Now, several years later, you are much more adept at social behaviors. But you continue to avoid particular kinds of social events—parties, for example, or public dancing—and other situations that in the past would have been unpleasant. You continue to respond to the antecedent as a cue to avoidance, even though the actual unpleasant event doesn't take place anymore. Why?

Avoidance learning is highly resistant to extinction, because the antecedent stimulus evokes the avoidance behavior and the person who has learned the avoidance response will not have an opportunity to learn that the old unpleasant outcome is no longer there.

A common occurrence in our society suggests another example. Children and teenagers are often punished for their sexual behavior, and this punishment is likely to produce various kinds of avoidance behavior. Some will simply learn to avoid being caught, but others may learn to avoid sex altogether. As children grow older and marry, the situation changes. Parents are obviously unlikely to punish their married children's sexual behavior. What was formerly punishable behavior is now permissible. And yet, the person who has learned to avoid making love as a way of avoiding punishment may continue to avoid, even though the situation has changed and the punishment is no longer a threat.

This is how much "neurotic" or maladjusted behavior is learned. Because you were once punished—in childhood, for example—in the presence of a particular stimulus, you continue to engage in old habits of avoidance that to someone else might seem quite "foolish." You may avoid situations that could be pleasant for you, because the signals that control your avoidance behavior continue to operate. One of the techniques of self-modification is to gradually make yourself engage in previously avoided behaviors and situations that now seem to be desirable. Only then can you know whether you will still be punished for the behavior.

Stimulus Control and "Automatic" Behaviors

Now we are in a position to return to our earlier discussion of the ways in which, even in young children, language control of behavior is replaced by nonverbal, environmental-cue control.

When an antecedent has consistently been associated with a behavior that is reinforced, it gains what is called *stimulus control* over the behavior in a seemingly "automatic" way. As an experienced automobile driver, you no longer go through traffic lights yelling "Stop!" to yourself or even saying it subvocally. You slow down and brake when the amber light appears even though you are singing, listening to the radio, or thinking about last night's movie. Because of its previous association with a variety of reinforcements, the amber light has stimulus control over your stopping the car. After all, coming to a halt at the amber light has repeatedly allowed you to avoid collisions, escape fear, earn the praise of your driving instructor, and even elicit your own self-congratulation. In the normal processes of performance, language control is dropped, because immediate recognition-and-response to specific situations is much more efficient. In most situations excessive self-speech is undesirable, since it can actually interfere with our performance; like Hamlet, we become "sicklied o'er with the pale cast of thought." In other words, it is better that we run on the automatic pilot of stimulus control.

Better, that is, when we are running well. Unfortunately, those undesirable behaviors that you now wish to change are very likely under stimulus control, and that stimulus control must be broken and rebuilt. For some people the stimulus control is so strong that it seems almost irresistible, in spite of the fact that it evokes an undesired behavior. One of our students wrote: "I have been losing some weight, but there is one situation I just can't resist. That's when the people who work in my office bring in donuts from King's Bakery. They are too much. When I get to work, as soon as I see that King's Bakery box, I know I'm in trouble!" Her problem was too much stimulus control over her eating. Many overweight people have this same kind of problem; the sight of certain foods almost automatically stimulates them to eat, whether they are hungry or not. Their task is therefore to reduce the control of certain stimuli.

For others, there may be too little stimulus control. Another student wrote: "My problem is that I never write home to my parents. I get the paper out and am all set up. But immediately I start to think of about ten other things I could be doing, and pretty soon I start doing one, so I never get much written to them." Some self-change plans will have to increase the control certain antecedents have over behavior. For insomnia, Bootzin (1972) recommends narrowing the stimulus control of the bed. With the exception of sex, nothing but sleeping should be done there—no reading, no television watching, or conversation. When tossing and turning, the insomniac should get up, maybe stretch on the couch, and return to bed only when sleepy and relaxed.

One way of gaining self-control is to deliberately set up certain antecedents to stimulate a desired behavior. Then, when you want to perform that behavior, you seek out those antecedents. One of our students, for example, wanted to be efficient. She wrote: "I always do my planning as soon as I get off the bus that takes me to school. This puts the planning under the control of that antecedent. I go straight from the bus to an empty classroom and spend a few minutes planning the day, then reinforce myself for the planning." For this student, getting off the bus had gained some stimulus control over the act of planning.

A most important way to increase self-direction is to insert self-speech antecedents, which can interrupt existing stimulus control, and to build new habits. As Chapter 5 details, a problem behavior chain that runs off smoothly may be disrupted by a new antecedent of self-instructions. This is especially useful if your problem behavior is automatic and occurs without your really being conscious of it. For behaviors that are excessively under the control of antecedent self-speech, the appropriate strategy is to substitute new self-instructions—for example, to stop saying to yourself "You're stupid. Quit!" and say instead "You can do it. Hang in there!"

Summary

Eventually, most behavior is guided by antecedents. These guiding antecedents, called discriminative stimuli or cues, come to control behavior that has been reinforced only when the cues are present. Many cues signal that danger is imminent; escaping from those cues is reinforced by a reduction in anxiety, and we learn to avoid those cues. Avoidance behavior is highly resistant to extinction; thus many problem behaviors continue even after real danger has disappeared, because the cue causes us to act as though something we used to fear were still a threat. (This is a description of many "neurotic" behaviors.)

Control of behavior by antecedents (stimulus control) may be either excessive or insufficient. Too little stimulus control is present when the ordinary, available cues don't control behavior—for example, when being in a quiet library with book open does *not* produce studying. Too much stimulus control is illustrated by the person who eats any time food is present, whether or not he is hungry.

Much behavior is controlled by self-speech antecedents, or self-instructions. These self-instructions can be modified to evoke different behaviors. Self-instructions can also be used in the case of "automatic" behavior chains to disrupt them and prevent the resulting undesirable behavior.

RESPONDENT BEHAVIOR

Not all learning is based on the reinforcement of operant behavior. Some behaviors are automatically controlled by antecedent stimuli through a different process than that just discussed. That is because some behaviors have built-in, nonlearned triggers. For example, when the knee tendon is struck lightly, the behavior of leg extension follows automatically. The antecedent stimulus of striking has control over this reaction. A fleck on the eyeball is the controlling stimulus for eye blinking. Milk in the mouth produces salivation automatically from the earliest hours of birth. Behaviors for which there are original, controlling, antecedent stimuli are sometimes called *reflexes*. Humans have fewer of these automatic behaviors than do organisms with less complicated nervous systems, but we do have reflexes, and they are important.

Here is a small experiment that will illustrate one of your reflexive responses. Have someone agree to surprise you with a sudden loud noise. For example, ask a friend to slam a book onto a table sometime when you seem to expect it least. Observe your reactions: you will tense, whip around, and blink. This is a reflexive response; the stimulus is sufficient to cause it. Only repeated familiarity with the stimulus will allow the behavior to fade. But notice, too, that there is an *emotional* component to your reaction—a feeling of arousal and emotional fullness, a discomfort that is much like a small fear reaction that reaches its peak a second or two after the stimulus and then gradually subsides.

This experiment illustrates the control that the antecedent stimulus has over emotional reactions. Indeed, the class of behaviors we are now discussing—the automatic behaviors that are controlled by antecedents—include many emotional reactions. The behaviors in this class have certain properties; for example, they are largely controlled by the autonomic nervous system, they involve smooth muscles, and they are highly similar among individuals of the same species. These behaviors are sometimes called *respondent* behaviors because they occur originally in response to the antecedent stimulus.

The most important characteristic of all respondent behaviors is that the antecedent stimuli are adequate to produce the behavior. This kind of antecedent control over reactions is important because, through this basic process, many emotional reactions become associated with particular antecedents, so that the antecedent comes to elicit them.

A person who is very shy may experience considerable anxiety when meeting strangers. Some people become very upset if they have to stay in an enclosed place. Others are extremely afraid of heights, or airplanes, or snakes. How do these stimuli come to gain control of the person's reaction, so that an emotion like anxiety is elicited? The best answer we have at present is that antecedent stimuli gain control of a person's reactions through the process of *respondent conditioning.*

Respondent Conditioning

Respondent conditioning involves pairing a stimulus that elicits some response with one that does not, in such a way that the two stimuli occur together. The individual reacts automatically to the original stimulus in the presence of the new (or *conditioned*) stimulus.

After a number of such pairings, the person will react to the new conditioned stimulus by itself and in nearly the same way he or she reacted to the original stimulus. In this way, automatic reactions can be transferred to what was a neutral antecedent (that is, an antecedent with no stimulus control over a reaction). This means that what was a neutral stimulus becomes a conditioned stimulus—a stimulus that has control over a reaction—by being associated with an antecedent that already has stimulus control. A new stimulus control is developed.

Schematically, first you have an antecedent—call it A_1—that elicits a response. If A_1 is always preceded by another antecedent—call it A_2—then, after a few such associations, A_2 will develop the same stimulus control over the response that A_1 has. If the response is some emotional reaction, through this process of respondent conditioning the new antecedent (A_2) will develop the capacity to elicit the emotional reaction, even if A_1 does not occur.

This conditioned stimulus (A_2) can then be paired with a new, neutral stimulus (A_3), and A_3 will then come to elicit that emotional reaction. This pairing of A_2 with A_3 (and A_3 with A_4, and A_4 with A_5, and so on) is called *higher-order conditioning.*

The chart below summarizes respondent conditioning processes and explains how we develop emotional reactions to so many antecedent stimuli.

Reflex	A_1 $\longrightarrow$	Response	Automatic, unlearned, triggered response.
Respondent conditioning	$\begin{cases} A_1 \\ A_2 \end{cases}$ $\longrightarrow$	Response	Pairing the "trigger" stimulus with some new, neutral stimulus.
Conditioned response	A_2 $\longrightarrow$	Response	In the absence of A_1, A_2 produces the response.
Higher-order conditioning	$\begin{cases} A_2 \\ A_3 \end{cases}$ $\longrightarrow$	Response	A_2 (conditioned stimulus) is now paired with a new, neutral stimulus.
Higher-order conditioned response	A_3 $\longrightarrow$	Response	Now A_1, A_2, and A_3 can all elicit the response, frequently an emotion.

Emotional Conditioning

A number of years ago, John Watson and Rosalie Rayner (1920) demonstrated how an emotional reaction can be conditioned so that it comes to be elicited by an antecedent that was previously neutral. From the earliest days of our lives, a sudden loud noise is an adequate stimulus for a fear reaction. To associate that stimulus with one that was neutral, Watson and Rayner followed this procedure. A baby was presented several times with a white rat, and he showed no signs of fear. Then he was presented with the rat, and, a few seconds afterward, a very loud, unexpected noise was made behind him. The baby reacted automatically to the startling noise with fear. After several experiences in which the rat was presented just before the frightening noise—so that fear was experienced while seeing the rat—the rat became a conditioned stimulus. By itself, it became sufficient to elicit the fear, even if the noise did not occur. Thus, what had been a neutral stimulus became a frightening one.

In a similar way, emotional reactions can be transferred to many new stimuli in your life. As you have new experiences, you may undergo new associations between conditioned emotional reactions and new stimuli, so that the new stimuli will come to elicit the original emotional reaction.

As we said earlier, once a conditioned reaction is established, a new stimulus may be associated with the conditioned stimulus, so that the new antecedent also acquires stimulus control over the emotional responses (higher-order conditioning).

Principle 10: Through conditioning, antecedents come to elicit automatic reactions that are often emotional.

In most everyday situations, conditioning and operant learning are going on at the same time. For example, a student who is trying to study but hates it and is not reinforced for it not only suffers the effects of not being reinforced but may also develop a conditioned boredom reaction to studying (Watson, 1978).

In real life the distinction between operant and respondent behaviors is not quite as clear as we hope to have made it here (Miller, 1969; DiCara, 1970; Staats, 1968). Most chains of events contain both behavioral and emotional components. For example, think of a person who, having failed a driver's test once, goes back for a second trial. The person is, at the same time, walking into the testing station (the observable behavior) *and* experiencing feelings of anxiety or tension. Many environmental circumstances produce *both a behavioral reaction and an emotional one;* that is, antecedents have an effect on both your behavior and your feelings.

Respondent Conditioning and Language

Many, if not most, conditioned stimuli are words. Parents deliberately try to condition emotional reactions to language, as they teach their children that the street is "Dangerous!" or that the burner is "Hot! Hurt you!" As explained earlier, a behavioral as well as an emotional reaction come to be cued by the same stimulus: the child both withdraws from the dangerous situation and develops an emotional response not only to the stimulus but also to the word for it. For adults, too, emotional reactions are often conditioned to words. If we are told that a spider or snake is "poisonous," we have a different emotional response to it than if we are told that it is "harmless."

This same effect is present when we use language to ourselves. A situation that we tell ourselves is dangerous or depressing can produce fear or depression even before we actually experience it. Therefore, many situations affect us not so much because of their consequences but because of the way we define the situations to ourselves. Staats (1975) has provided an elegant theoretical explanation of the interrelationships among behaviors, language cues, and emotions. Goldfried (1979) has recently developed strategies for restructuring self-statements to produce more adaptive emotional reactions as well as more effective coping with problems.

Summary

Respondent behavior refers to those behaviors that are controlled by antecedent stimuli. In respondent conditioning, a neutral antecedent is associated with a stimulus that can elicit an automatic reaction, and, after a series of associations, the once neutral stimulus becomes itself capable of eliciting the reaction. In higher-order conditioning, another neutral event is paired with the eliciting antecedent, and it, too, acquires the capacity to elicit some reaction.

This process is important because many emotional reactions may be conditioned to particular antecedents in this way. Various emotional reactions, such as joy or depression, may come under the control of antecedent stimuli, so that just encountering the antecedent elicits that reaction. Normally, both operant learning and respondent conditioning are going on at the same time.

Conditioned stimuli are frequently words; thus, language produces emotional reactions—even language we address to ourselves. Because operant and respondent processes are both present when language is antecedent to behavior, what we say to ourselves affects both behaviors and emotions. Many self-change programs require a change in our self-speech.

MODELING

Much human learning occurs by simply observing what others do. This is called *learning through modeling*.

Principle 11: Many behaviors are learned by observing someone else (a model) perform the actions, which are then imitated.

Golf, dancing, chess, and bridge; expressions of love and of anger; even fears—all are learned through modeling. By simply observing a model, you learn behaviors. This kind of learning allows you to develop wholly new behaviors and to modify old ones.

You learn both desirable and undesirable acts this way. For example, you may have grown up with hard-working and ambitious parents. Now you realize that you too have these characteristics. Your parents may also have been rather irritable and inclined to blow up when frustrated. To your chagrin, you see that this description fits you as well. Of course, in your life there have been hundreds of people setting different kinds of examples for you. Your present behavior is not a carbon copy of any one person; rather, you have borrowed a bit of this from one, a bit of that from another, and blended them together to make the unique you.

Learning through observation follows the same principles as direct learning; that is, the consequences of your model's behavior will determine whether you will imitate the behavior. Reinforced model behavior is strengthened *in you;* punished model behavior is weakened *in you.* We learn cues and signals from models. We can even gain emotional conditioning from seeing models frightened by stimuli such as snakes or spiders. And there is evidence that we can learn to be calm, at least to a certain degree, by watching models behave calmly before stimuli of which we are afraid.

In your own self-change project, you can deliberately use your ability to learn through modeling to develop new behaviors. For example, a young man who wasn't very sure of himself on dates asked a friend if they could double-date, so he could see how his friend handled himself. A woman who had an unreasonable fear of birds accompanied a friend who didn't have that problem, to see how her friend dealt with birds.

YOUR OWN SELF-DIRECTION PROJECT: STEP FOUR

This chapter has presented background material that you need in order to embark on a successful attempt at self-change. It's important, therefore, that by now you have a good grasp of the principles that govern your behavior. To make sure, try to answer these questions.

1. What is a positive reinforcer?
2. What is a negative reinforcer?
3. What is avoidance behavior?
4. What effect does punishment have on the frequency of a behavior?
5. What are the two kinds of punishment?
6. What is extinction?
7. What is the effect of intermittent reinforcement on extinction?
8. What guides avoidance behavior—that is, what does the person respond to?
9. What is the role played by the cue, or antecedent, in all operant behavior?
10. What is stimulus control?
11. What is respondent behavior?
12. How does emotional conditioning occur?
13. After a reaction has been conditioned, what effect does the stimulus, or antecedent, have?
14. How does language affect behavior?
15. What is modeling?

If you can answer these questions, you can feel confident that you have a good grasp of the principles that explain your behavior and that you are ready to apply these principles toward self-understanding. If you cannot, re-read the chapter. Find the answers, and write them down. Then take this quiz again.

Now think about your behaviors that you have been observing, get out your observation notes, and answer the following questions about your own target behaviors.

First, about the antecedents of your behavior:

1. What stimuli seem to control the behavior? In what situations does the behavior occur?
2. Do you have either of the following problems: too much stimulus control or too little?
3. Do you react to some cue with an unwanted emotion? What is the conditioned stimulus for it?
4. What are you saying to yourself before the behavior?

Second, about the behavior itself:

5. Is it strong and quite frequent, or is it weak and not very frequent? What does this tell you about what you can do to change it?

6. Is any element of your problem due to something you are avoiding, perhaps unnecessarily?
7. Are you aware of models in your past whose behavior (or, perhaps, some aspects of it) you might have copied?
8. Does any part of your goal involve changing behaviors that are resistant to extinction either because they are intermittently reinforced or because they are avoidance behaviors?

Third, about the consequences of the behavior:

9. Are your desired behaviors positively reinforced?
10. As for actions that make the desired behavior difficult—are they reinforced?
11. Is it possible that the desired behavior is being punished?
12. Is your own self-speech rewarding or punishing your behavior?

Answer these questions carefully. The next four chapters discuss various ways to move toward self-change by using techniques that solve different problems. Some techniques are for the person who is not being reinforced for a desired act; others, for the person who needs to develop stimulus control for a desired act; still others, for the person who already has too much stimulus control over undesired acts. Some are for those who are showing conditioned emotional responses. Your answers to the questions above will tell you which kinds of techniques you should use in your own plan for self-change.

CHAPTER 5

Antecedents

GOAL:

To explain the role of the antecedents of behavior in a plan for self-direction.

OUTLINE:

An introduction to Chapters 5, 6, 7, and 8
Antecedent control
Identifying antecedents
Avoiding antecedents
Changing chains
Arranging new antecedents
Building new stimulus control: The physical and social environments
Your own self-direction project: Step five
Tips for typical topics

AN INTRODUCTION TO CHAPTERS 5, 6, 7, AND 8

We now turn to the actual process of designing a program for changing your behavior, thus moving toward the achievement of your goal. If you have followed us so far, you should have a clear understanding of the principles that govern your behavior and should have gathered meaningful data about your behaviors and the situations in which they occur. These antecedents-behaviors-consequences (A-B-C) data can now be organized in terms of the principles of behavior.

This organization process is discussed in three chapters, one for each of the A-B-C components. The present chapter discusses the A issues—ways of arranging antecedents so that desired behaviors become more likely. Chapter 6 treats the B issues—how behaviors themselves can be changed, replaced, shaped, and originated. Chapter 7 is devoted to the C issues—ways of rearranging the consequences of behavior to gain better self-direction. And Chapter 8 discusses ways of organizing and incorporating all these ideas into an effective plan.

The separation of these topics is unfortunate but unavoidable. We have separated them only because it is not possible to present them simultaneously on the same printed page. But remember: you cannot design a full self-direction plan until you have read *all* the material in these four chapters. A and B and C units are all required for full analysis and planning, although each person may emphasize one or the other somewhat differently. When you rearrange a situation, you simultaneously adjust all three elements. Therefore, a self-change plan is based on all three.

You should continue to work at your self-direction project as you read these chapters. The material is organized so that each chapter allows some planning and analysis, but keep in mind that a full plan will require all elements.

105

ANTECEDENT CONTROL

In Chapter 3, a simple chart was suggested as a scheme for organizing your self-observations:

Antecedents (A)	Behaviors (B)	Consequences (C)
When did it happen? Where were you? Whom were you with? What were you doing? What were you saying to yourself?	Actions, thoughts, feelings	What happened as a result? pleasant or unpleasant?

A complete program of self-direction will require attention to all elements—A, B, and C. In this chapter we focus on A—antecedents. As you consider the principles discussed in the preceding chapter, notice that all behavior/environment relationships eventually evolve into antecedent control: punishment produces cues for avoidance, reward produces cues for proceeding, conditioning produces cues for emotional reactions. For this reason, we are confident in suggesting that you can understand your behavior, and be in a position to control it, if you have fully discovered its antecedents.

This chapter discusses plans for self-direction through three basic forms of antecedent control: (1) by *avoiding* problematic antecedents, (2) by using *new* antecedents, and (3) by *rearranging* chains of antecedents. Each of these three ways will be discussed in turn. However, any effective plan for self-improvement will depend on the accurate discovery of your current system of cues. Discovering antecedents is the first task; we begin with a discussion of that issue.

IDENTIFYING ANTECEDENTS

A married couple had been quarreling. In the past, they had been able to have constructive arguments in which they tried to solve their differences. Lately the man found himself flying off the handle in the middle of an argument, calling his wife names, and swearing. We suggested that he keep a record of what happened just before he lost his temper. He thought about what had happened in the past and made observations for several days. As a result, he reported a consistent antecedent of his anger: "It's a particular expression on her face. I think of it as her holier-than-thou expression, and it makes me angry."

In this case, the unwanted behavior was cued by a single stimulus; for other behaviors there may be a number of antecedents that have stimulus control. When any one of them occurs, so does the problem behavior. "Hurt feelings" was the concern of a young woman, who discovered all these antecedents: "(a) her mother or brother questioning specific decisions or behaviors, (b) her roommate asking her not to be around for a while, (c) her ex-husband questioning her dating or implying that the separation was her fault, and (d) her boyfriend failing to meet her as planned or flaunting the fact that he dated her acquaintances" (Zimmerman, 1975, p. 8).

It may take some time to discover the antecedents that control an unwanted behavior, whether there is a single cue or many. In either case the discovery is vital, because accurate understanding of antecedents can quickly guide you to an effective self-direction program.

If you are not satisfied with your understanding of your own problematic antecedents, reconsider the recommendations and examples in Chapter 3. In our experience there are three likely points of difficulty. The first is simple: have you been recording fully and accurately? Not doing so is the most common (and most self-defeating) error. Many fine students have told us, in effect, "You can't seriously mean that I'm supposed to write all that stuff down. I know what the problem is, and I do notice the situations. Writing them down is just making up exercises for a course." But we are very serious. Only the most experienced self-analyzer can do without written records. Written records will force you to keep your attention on problem situations, when perceptions tend to rush by and become blurred. Cues to problem behavior are often the ones that make you anxious, the ones you don't like to notice and remember. Establishing a rule for written records is itself a powerful technique for increasing self-control.

The second most likely difficulty is not beginning early enough in your chain-of-events analysis. If you begin recording at the moment your problem is clear and overt, you can be nearly certain that you have not begun early enough in the chain. This point is illustrated by our student who became alarmed at his increasing amount of beer drinking. "It happens at night" he said. "I stay home, cook a little something, turn on the TV. I'm bored, get depressed, start popping the beer cans. The antecedent seems to be that I feel lonely." Recognizing his feelings of loneliness was a giant step forward, but that was clearly not the first link in the chain. We suggested that he work further backward: what chain of events produced the loneliness? "I've had three disastrous love affairs in the last year" he wrote. "Self-confidence—zero. Every time I meet a woman, I tell myself not to bother. I've been staying home. Twice last week I could have gone out, once to an auto show and once on a blind date. I declined. The next time a chance like that comes up, I'll try to notice what I'm saying to myself; it's probably some self-putdown."

Self-criticisms made during a telephone conversation may seem far removed from a problem with drinking, but this student saw the long chain that linked last week's refusal of a date to this week's lonely drunkenness. Discovering this distant antecedent allowed him to design a self-improvement plan for a more stimulating social life.

The third most likely difficulty with discovering antecedents is that of identifying self-statements, and it will require a lengthier discussion.

Identifying Self-Statements

As explained in Chapter 4, self-directed messages and thoughts are among the most powerful of influences on subsequent behavior. To help you identify self-speech, we'll divide it into three types: (1) self-instructions, (2) classifications, and (3) beliefs.

Self-Instructions.   Self-statements of this type are the most obvious. "Get out of here!"; "I've got to study tonight!"; "I go three blocks and turn left"; "I can't; I've just had a cigarette" are just a few examples. Self-instructions are difficult to identify because they often occur in a "still, small voice"; instructions are thoughts, so swift that only careful attention can reveal them. Both in discovering antecedents and in using corrective self-statements, the task is to amplify the words until they are loud and clear. It's rather like bringing self-directions back from the underground, so that they can be consciously controlled. Once this principle is understood, most self-instructions *can* be detected. All that is needed is careful attention during antecedent conditions.

When these self-instructions are discovered to be cueing problem behavior, new self-instructions can be substituted. If your problem behavior is so smooth and automated that self-instructions are not in fact present, self-instructions can be added to your chain. But the first task is to discover whether or not self-instructions are the antecedents of your problem behavior now. To

---

BOX 5-1
A Concert Performance in Self-Direction

Not all self-instructions need to be in words. If you are a concert pianist, they can even be in music; that is, they may consist of "hearing" in imagination what you want to actually play on the instrument.

Self-instructions can also be in the form of *visual* imagery. One typical form of self-instruction is to rehearse in imagination your behavior immediately before entering a situation. As a young pianist preparing for a first recital, you see yourself stopping briefly at the door of the concert hall, then slowly walking toward the piano, taking a deep bow to answer the audience's applause, and finally sitting down on the piano bench, ready to play. If done vividly and in detail, such imagery guides your actual behavior as you are about to move across the room.

John Cage, a powerful influence on modern art, is famous for piano concerts of his "random" and improvised music. This interchange took place during a discussion period following one of his performances.

Question from the audience: When you were up there on stage writing down something on some paper, or looking at your watch as if it meant something, or turning to the piano and playing a few octaves apparently at random, or just sitting idle, what were you really doing?
Cage: I was giving myself instructions and then following them.
[Applause and laughter from the audience]

make that discovery, turn up the amplifier of your still, small voice. Hear yourself thinking.

Classifications.   The second type of self-speech, *classifications,* contains less obvious but equally compelling cues. Do you recall saying to yourself "Here comes another one!" or "This is one of those parties where I don't know anybody!" When classification cues are operating, self-instructions are frequently absent, because the classification itself shorthands a whole script that you then perform. For example, when you label a party as one-of-those-where-I-don't-know-a-soul, you do whatever you always do at such parties— sit in a corner, leave early, feel bad. The labeling itself is a cue to self-defeating behavior.

Two strategies for change are available when classification controls your behavior. You may either change the label (say to yourself "Here is one of those parties where I can meet new people") or add full self-instructions ("Introduce yourself, quickly!"). To discover your current classifications and labels, you apply the same techniques you use for other self-speech: attend carefully, amplify your self-speech, and listen to yourself talking.

Beliefs.   The third type of self-speech, *beliefs,* is the most difficult to discover. In fact, belief statements may occur so rarely that they are not directly observable. You must infer them through logical analysis of your self-observations. By *beliefs,* we mean the underlying assumptions on which your self-speech and other behaviors rest.

Recall the example of the young woman with "hurt feelings" we presented earlier in the chapter. All the instances in which she felt hurt—whether by mother, brother, roommate, ex-husband, or boyfriend—presented a common theme. If she had discussed her records with us, we would have asked her "What is common to all these situations? Why does each of these events hurt you? What belief can you see operating here?" We hope that she would have answered "It seems I want approval from everyone all of the time. I suppose I believe that I must be loved by everyone and that each disapproval means that I'm not loved." The conversation might have continued as follows:

"Do you really believe that?"

"I suppose so; it's the way I behave."

"Is it logical?"

"Not really. People can disapprove of some things their loved ones do."

"Must everyone love you, constantly?"

"No. That's absurd."

"What would be a preferable belief?"

"That it is acceptable to be disapproved sometimes, even by those one loves."

Albert Ellis (1962) has theorized extensively about the role that such self-defeating, "irrational" beliefs play in self-speech and behavior. Marvin Gold-fried (1979) and his associates have conducted extensive research on "cognitive restructuring," indicating that the changing of beliefs, in and of itself, can often lead to widespread benefits, emotionally and behaviorally. These writers conclude that there are two "irrational" beliefs that occur most frequently. The first we have just discussed—the belief that constant love and approval from everybody is a necessity. The second is that all our undertakings must be performed with perfection.

In examining your self-observations for problematic antecedents, don't overlook the possibility that a self-defeating belief may be contributing to the cue structure. Because detecting such a belief may be difficult, systematic procedures are advisable. Consider each instance of your problem. Search for some common theme, some assumption that underlies all these instances. Write out that theme, as precisely as possible, and examine it. Is it rational? Do you really believe it, now that it is explicit? In our experience, many people find that they can then readily accept a quite different belief. One doesn't have to be always perfect. One can do very well with some disapproval. By accepting a more reasonable belief, you change a controlling antecedent and begin a new pattern of self-direction (Thorpe, Amatu, Blakey, & Burns, 1976).

Not all antecedents of your problem or goal behaviors are verbal. The variety of cues to behavior and emotions is infinite—from caution lights to facial expressions. The first task of self-direction is to use the power of cues to reach goals. The strategies you can employ to accomplish this task will be discussed under three headings: avoiding antecedents, changing chains, and arranging new antecedents.

Summary

The identification of current antecedents requires careful record keeping. Be sure to trace back the chain of antecedents to its logical beginning. The task of discovering self-instructional antecedents involves carefully observing and amplifying the quiet thoughts that instruct you. Self-defeating beliefs can be discovered by writing out all instances of your problem behavior and identifying their common theme. The illogical nature of these beliefs can then be observed.

AVOIDING ANTECEDENTS

One of the reasons stricter diets work—those in which every particle of food to be put on the plate is determined beforehand—is that the dieter avoids the antecedents of overeating. If all you have in front of you is two pieces of celery and a bowl of soup, you have avoided the antecedents of overeating, such as the sight of a plate of spaghetti or a slice of cake. Chronic alcoholics who successfully stay away from drinking accomplish this by never confronting the crucial antecedent of overdrinking—the first drink. Most people who stay off cigarettes also follow a policy of not having the first one.

These examples illustrate the strategy of *avoiding antecedents,* a wise first step for certain kinds of problems. It is only a first step, but it is a particularly important one for the class of behaviors known as *consummatory responses*—such as overeating, drinking, and smoking—which produce automatically their own reinforcement. For example, overeating is reinforced by the food (in addition to other things); excessive beer drinking is reinforced by the beer; pot smoking, by the effect of marijuana; cigarette smoking, by inhaling the smoke; and so on. Thus every instance of the behavior is automatically reinforced, and the behavior grows stronger and stronger. As we will see in Chapter 7, "Consequences," one logical strategy for changing behavior is to change its consequences; but in consummatory responses the reinforcer cannot be changed because it is part of the behavior itself.

Problem sexual behaviors also resist change in the same way. A young man was concerned with what he felt was "excessive" masturbation, an activity in which he indulged three times a day. The reinforcer was fairly obvious here—the sexual pleasure itself—although, by masturbating, the young man also gained some temporary relief from social anxieties. Since the reinforcing consequences couldn't be separated from the activity, the young man found it necessary to control the antecedent—the place in which he observed that masturbation usually occurred. He began to use a less private campus restroom.

If you are a habitual overeater or smoker or drug user, almost nothing is as reinforcing as your "habit." For such consummatory behaviors, perhaps the most promising type of self-modification plan is one in which you *avoid* the antecedents that set the time and place for your consummatory behavior. The smoker avoids cigarettes, the drinker avoids drinks, and the overeater avoids fattening foods. They all know that, if they are exposed to those stimuli, they will very likely perform the undesired behavior again. Therefore, people with this kind of problem can work out self-direction plans in which they avoid the antecedent.

A middle-aged, overweight man wanted to diet but reported that progress was always followed by disaster. So he began to record the antecedents of his eating binges and realized that, although he normally stayed on his diet quite regularly, there was one situation in which he always ate too much. This was when he and his wife were invited to someone else's house for dinner, something that occurred fairly often. Most of their friends were good cooks, and the result was that the man always overate. He solved his problem by setting a simple rule, to which his wife agreed. Until he had lost 20 pounds, they wouldn't accept any dinner invitations. When someone called to invite them for dinner, he would explain that he had to lose weight and that, because his would-be host or hostess was such an excellent cook and he couldn't possibly resist the food, he must regretfully decline.

That same strategy is available for the smoker who cannot resist a cigarette with morning coffee; she may simply switch to tea and avoid the coffee cue, which so strongly impels her to smoke. The pot smoker can easily list the places where not smoking seems impossible; they too can be avoided.

We recommend this strategy as a first step since it is a strategy that you may begin immediately. During the few weeks of the plan, you will have an opportunity to develop a variety of other tactics. Your self-confidence will improve as you become more acquainted with the patterns of temptation and competence. By the end of Chapter 8 you will be able to design a full-scale plan, which we call "the two-stage process for control of consummatory behaviors." As will be explained later, you will eventually want to develop new, alternative responses to excessive consummatory behaviors. If you only avoid cues, a problem will develop: when you do expose yourself again to those cues, you are likely to find yourself performing the same old behavior. After all, you can't avoid parties all your life. Therefore, we recommend avoiding the antecedents of consummatory responses as a first step that will allow self-control behaviors to be strengthened before they are tested in situations of maximum temptation. By the time you return to the parties, you will know when you must say no and how to do it.

Narrowing Antecedents

A few cases have been reported in which an undesired behavior was deliberately linked to a gradually narrower range of antecedents. The idea is to narrow the range of situations that control the behaviors down to a point where the behavior is unlikely to occur at all.

Nolan (1968) reports the case of a smoker whose self-agreement allowed her to smoke only in her "smoking chair" at home. The chair was placed so that no reinforcement other than the smoking itself was provided; it faced away from the TV set, was not comfortable, and so forth. Once the woman had established the habit of smoking only in that chair, she moved it to the cellar! As can be expected, under this plan her smoking decreased markedly. Similar strategies for achieving stimulus control over nail biting and hair pulling are advocated by Kanfer and Phillips (1970). Goldiamond (1965) reported narrowing sulking behavior in a client so that it would occur only on a particular "sulking stool." Learning to eat properly requires a gradual narrowing of the originally wide range of antecedents that control overeating, until only very few still have stimulus control.

Summary

The first strategy for achieving antecedent control is to avoid the antecedent for the problem behavior. This is particularly appropriate for consummatory behaviors—such as overindulgence in food, drugs, or sex—because they automatically strengthen themselves on each performance by producing their own reinforcements. Because many antecedents cannot be avoided permanently, avoidance is only a first step for establishing self-control. The second step will be discussed later; for now, it is important to avoid antecedents that automatically cue the undesired acts.

CHANGING CHAINS

Another strategy that can be used to control antecedents is to change the chain of events that produces the undesired behavior. Many behaviors are the result of a fairly long chain of events. An antecedent produces some behavior, which leads to a particular consequence, which is itself the antecedent of yet another behavior, and so on. Therefore, the end behavior, which may be an undesired act, is the result of a long series of antecedent-behavior/new antecedent-new behavior. By the time you reach the end of the chain of events, the impulse to perform the final, undesirable behavior is so strong that it is very difficult to restrain. This is particularly true for consummatory behaviors, in which the end of the chain is represented by the behavior that, being automatically reinforced each time, is very strongly established. In some cases, a good strategy may be to interrupt the chain of events *early* (Ferster, Nurnberger, & Levitt, 1962; Bergin, 1969).

In this kind of situation, the final behavior in the chain is usually the one that you recognize as the problem behavior. For example, you may say to yourself "The problem is that I drink too much." But the act of drinking is embedded in a sequence of behaviors, which involves getting the alcohol, making some kind of drink, perhaps sitting down, and then drinking. Sometimes, by analyzing the chain of events that culminates in the final behavior, it is possible to identify an early, weak link in the chain. An interruption there can prevent the occurrence of the final behavior.

Annon (1975) reports the case of a problem drinker who used a complex "scrambling" of previous chain links to stop drinking. This person had consumed up to a pint of vodka before bedtime each night for several years and could no longer sleep without it. He analyzed the components of the usual chain of events that led to drinking—coming home, turning on the TV, going to the refrigerator, putting ice in the glass, pouring a drink, going to the bathroom, undressing, showering, going to bed, pouring another drink, and so on. The man reorganized this chain into a different order. For example, he moved showering to immediately after coming home, delayed going to the refrigerator until after undressing, and substituted cola for vodka in the glass. This scrambling had the effect of decreasing the vodka-drinking probabilities, since it broke up much of the antecedent control.

Building In Pauses

Several tactics for changing the chains of events are available. Perhaps the simplest is to build in a pause. When a chain is well established, you may find yourself responding without thinking, whether the antecedent is a rude statement or a plateful of food. A helpful technique for dealing with this automatic quality of chained antecedents is to pause before responding.

A man had developed the undesired habit of becoming aggressive when others said something he thought was foolish. He worked out a scheme to reinforce himself for pausing a few seconds before responding aggressively. Often those few seconds were enough for him to think of a more appropriate response than a rude remark. Some dieters have improved their diet by requiring themselves to pause after every bite, lay the spoon or fork down, and just sit for a few seconds before resuming eating. Also, having no prepared foods in the house builds a pause between the impulse to eat and the act of eating (Stuart, 1967). And, of course, you can reinforce yourself for pausing.

This technique for controlling antecedents is greatly helped by careful observations. Recall the young man who used to tell off people who made statements contrary to his personal philosophy. Once the young man had identified the antecedent of his rude behavior, he was able to do something about it. One of the things he did was to notice each occurrence of the antecedent. Then he used his noticing the antecedent to provide a pause and think of an alternative behavior. For example, when someone contradicted his philosophy, this young man would say to himself "Now, that's an example of the disagreement-with-my-personal-philosophy antecedent that usually leads to my telling the other person off . . . I'd better pause a moment." The pause itself is a new behavior that can become the antecedent of a more desirable link in the chain of events.

What you do during the pause makes a difference, of course. The man who was upset because he often spanked his children said: "I know that I hit them when they disobey me—particularly when they bicker with each other and I tell them to stop and they don't. So I tried just pausing for a second before spanking them. Sometimes that worked, but sometimes it didn't. I just waited a second and then hit the child anyway. So I started saying to myself 'Now, think. Don't just stand here being angry and then hit. Think. What should I do right now to get the children to behave?'" What that man did during his pause was to give himself instructions. We shall return to the topic of self-instructions in greater detail later in the chapter.

Pausing to Make a Record

Keeping a record of certain events can be used to create a pause in the chain—a pause that may allow you to change the direction of the chain of events (Stuart, 1967). Recall that in Chapter 3 we said that recording an unwanted behavior *before* you do it will reduce its frequency. This probably happens because stopping to record interrupts the chain of events that up to now has inevitably led to the unwanted behavior, giving you a chance to veer off in another direction. If you require yourself to make a record early in the chain of events, you get greater control over later events than if you wait until the last links in the chain (Kazdin, 1974e). For example, as you feel the first signs of panic coming over you, stop and make a rating of the degree of panic you feel. That gives you time to realize that your reaction is (probably) out of proportion to the actual event and that there are ways you can cope.

In general, the earlier in the chain of events you make the interruption, the more effective your plan is. A couple who had developed a destructive pattern of arguing learned to recognize the first signs of such a pattern and arranged to stop immediately to make entries in their structured diaries. Usually this pause was sufficient to break the chain of their destructive arguing.

Unlinking the Chain of Events

A young woman had a problem with excessively frequent urination. She reported that she went to the bathroom an average of 13 times per day. Understandably so, she was upset at this personally and sometimes socially embarrassing situation. She had seen a physician, who had assured her that there was no medical problem.

In gathering the baseline data, she realized that two separate antecedents led to urination. First, she almost never went into a bathroom (for example, to wash her face or comb her hair) without using the toilet. Second, she went to the toilet at the first hint of bladder pressure. To break up the control of the first antecedent (entering a bathroom), she used this simple plan. She would go into a bathroom, perform some behavior that didn't involve using the toilet, and then walk out. For example, she would enter, wash her hands, and leave. Or she might comb her hair or put on lipstick and then leave. In this way, she broke up the inevitable relationship between going into a bathroom (the antecedent) and using the toilet (the behavior).

To break up the control of the second antecedent (the initial hint of bladder pressure), she used the pause technique. Upon feeling the first hint of pressure, she required herself to pause for five minutes before urinating. This simple technique was sufficient, because the passage of five minutes usually found her engaged in some other behavior.

This woman, then, determined two separate antecedent controls over her problem behavior and instituted separate interventions for each. In this kind of intervention strategy, the crucial step is being able to analyze the chain of events leading to the final, undesired behavior.

Suppose your problem is that you eat too many between-meal snacks. The term *between-meal snacks* defines the target behavior as well as the situation—consuming food between meals. What is the chain that leads to this final step? First, you may feel slightly bored or have nothing to do for a couple of minutes. Second, you start moving toward the kitchen. Third, you open the refrigerator or pantry and search for food. Last, you eat the food. If this is your chain, you may interrupt it by having an intervention plan that calls for performing at step 2 some behavior other than moving toward the kitchen. It can be *any* behavior—for example, making a phone call.

Since you can't always avoid being bored or having nothing to do, you cannot reasonably expect to eliminate the last antecedent. Therefore, you should try to break the chain at step 2. If you smoke when you feel tense, it is unlikely that you can eliminate all sources of tension in your life, but you can change what you begin to do as soon as you feel the state of tension building up; for example, you can use relaxation in place of lighting a cigarette, as we will discuss in the next chapter.

This strategy is necessary whenever problematic antecedents cannot be avoided. The old antecedent must lead to a new, desired behavior instead of the old, undesired act. The next case illustrates an unusual use of this strategy.

A depressed young woman discovered through her A-B-C analysis that her "down" feelings were preceded by interactions with other people that made her feel uninteresting, ignored, and even rejected. These feelings would quickly turn into almost obsessive thoughts about her worthlessness, and a deep depression would set in. The chain looked like this:

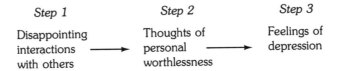

Step 1	Step 2	Step 3
Disappointing interactions with others ⟶	Thoughts of personal worthlessness ⟶	Feelings of depression

She reasoned that not every interaction with others could turn out perfectly for her. Her plan called for changing the second link of the chain. Whenever she felt an interaction to be disappointing, she would, as quickly as she got home, begin to sew. This was an entirely new activity for her, and she began with no previous interest or skill at dressmaking.

She said "I never thought of sewing as something good, but I've discovered that those simple things can have a lot of meaning. And now I'm much less dependent on other people." At the end of her program, she felt much more mature, and her depressions were no longer a problem (Tharp, Watson, & Kaya, 1974).

There is good reason to believe that long chains can best be altered by intervening at both ends. The research and theory supporting this position have been presented by Frankel (1975), who also reports the case study in Box 5-2. As you read this case, notice three features in particular. First, the antecedents were changed both at the beginning and at the end of the chain. Second, the father had to learn a new behavior to be inserted in the chain. Third, the outcome of the new chain had to be reinforced. (Learning new behaviors is the topic of Chapter 6, techniques for reinforcement are discussed in Chapter 7.) This case, too, illustrates that a well-developed plan will often require a combination of strategies.

Summary

Chains of behavior develop as one act becomes the cue for the next; this, in turn, becomes the cue for the next, and so forth, with the entire chain being reinforced by the final reinforcement. Although it is the final act that is likely to be seen as the problem, the entire chain is implicated. Changing the chain can interrupt the automatic, "uncontrollable" nature of the problem. A

BOX 5-2

A Family's Chain

Chains of events are often composed of the behaviors of several people. This case illustrates a chain of family behaviors, which produced unhappiness for all three members.

The Chain

1. Mother asks Bobby to do something at home (when Father asks him, there is usually immediate compliance).
2. Bobby refuses.
3. Mother gets very irritated, screams, and/or hits Bobby.
4. Bobby screams back and rarely complies.
5. When no compliance, either Mother goes and gets Father or Father hears incident occurring and barges in.
6. Father and Bobby yell at each other; usually Father hits Bobby or physically forces him to get moving on task. In any case, Bobby eventually complies.

Specific incidents lasted from a few minutes to several hours, ending when the father, on coming home, was told about the incident and forced compliance. The incidents didn't always go all the way through the chain above. When Bobby complied with his mother's demands or when she didn't tell her husband about an incident, the incident stopped at those points.

The Plan

It seemed that Bobby had learned to use one of his parents to get to the other one. A simple analysis might have stopped after step 3, when Mother screams and/or hits Bobby. The time lag between steps 3 and 6 was sometimes hours, and the whole behavior chain didn't always occur, being intermittently completed by Father. To get modification in the home, Mother was instructed to extinguish her behavior in response to Bobby's noncompliance (step 3). She contracted to either remain calm or leave the room until she could respond to Bobby calmly. In no case was she to call Father or was he to come in. Father also contracted to spend three hours a week with Bobby doing something of Bobby's choosing. At the 3-month follow-up, the parents reported that Bobby's incidents of aggression and noncompliance in the home had been reduced to a level not considered a problem. They rated Bobby's aggression at a raw score of 65 (compared to 80 initially). At the 1-year follow-up, the parents reported that Bobby's behavior at home was still not a problem.

In the old chain Bobby was receiving a strong reward for his misbehaviors—interaction with Father, even though it was an aggressive kind of interaction. It turned out that Father had never learned to play with his little boy. In the new chain, the three hours a week of play with Dad were strongly rewarding to both Bobby and his father. But, before the plan could be instituted, Father had to learn to play, which required another intervention of advice, self-observation, and practice.

Adapted from "Beyond the Simple Functional Analysis—The Chain: A Conceptual Framework for Assessment with a Case Study Example," by A. J. Frankel, *Behavior Therapy*, 1975, *6*, 254–260. Copyright © 1975 by Academic Press, Inc. Reprinted by permission of the author and Academic Press.

chain can be scrambled, interrupted by pauses or record keeping, or changed by substituting one or more links. For long chains it is advisable to change elements both at the beginning and at the end of the chain.

ARRANGING NEW ANTECEDENTS

Thus far we have spoken of avoiding, narrowing, or rearranging antecedents, but the critical problem is often creating *new* antecedents that will cue desirable outcomes. Even our examples of changing chains have usually involved inserting some new behavior or situation, so that a different response can be induced. New antecedents can be inserted at the beginning of a chain or at any point throughout it. In this discussion we will first treat verbal antecedents (self-instructions) and then other forms of stimulus control.

Self-Instructions

Self-instructions are powerful. This power can be used to promote self-direction by developing new self-speech in problematic situations. As you discover the role of self-speech antecedents in your problem situations, it is very likely that one of two conditions is present. Either you are giving yourself instructions and assigning labels that cue undesired reactions, or your problem behavior is "automated" and you can't identify any self-statements. In either event, the same strategy is called for. *Insert into the chain of events new self-instructions that will guide the desired behavior.* On the basis of both logic and research evidence (Meichenbaum, 1977), it can be argued that every self-direction plan should include the use of some new self-instructions.

Fortunately, designing a plan of self-instruction is very simple. The strategy is merely to substitute new instructions for the self-defeating ones you now use. Don't tell yourself anymore "I can't do this!" Say, instead, "I can" (and tell yourself how). If your speech includes self-defeating categorizations, use new labels.

In some early work on study habits, Fox (1966) invented a technique that one of our students used in an interesting manner. The student's goal was to become a professional writer. She knew that she would have to practice a lot to make this a reasonable goal. But, she lamented, she often ran into difficult periods in her writing, when the words just wouldn't come out and she would get discouraged and quit. "I know all writers must have this kind of problem" she said, "but I think the difference between the pros and me is that I quit when things get tough. That's the opposite of what I should do. I should try all the harder then." What she meant was that things-getting-tough should have been an antecedent for working hard, not quitting. At our suggestion, the woman followed this procedure: "When I hit a tough time, I will say 'This is the kind of opportunity I need to practice being a professional. I must write at least one more paragraph before quitting.'" Relabelling these tough times now cued *more* writing.

The form for new self-instruction is very simple. Decide what you want to do, and tell yourself to do it. The only rule is that the instruction should be brief, incisive, and clear. In a study by Harris and McReynolds (1977), the simple self-instruction "Don't bite your nails!" said aloud each time nail biters found their fingers touching their mouths, brought about a long-term reduction of the nail-biting habit.

Here are the self-instructions that a shy man used to talk himself through approaching a new acquaintance: "Go up to her and say hello. Don't forget to smile. Look into her eyes. Face her directly. Be open." If you are explicit, giving yourself instructions can guide you through a new and unfamiliar behavior by reminding you of some steps you might forget in the stress or excitement of the novel situation.

Couldn't you get all these benefits by just "remembering" what you do, without actually saying the words? Perhaps, but, unless you say the words, your "remembering" may be too vague to be useful. Actually saying the words, in your mind or imagination or even aloud, brings up self-speech from the underground and allows it to exercise full power. In our experience, beginning students most often fail to harness the power of self-instructions because they don't truly self-instruct. They "figure it out," decide that saying the words is "silly," and skip over the crucial behavior—actually saying the words in the critical situation.

Self-instructions can be rehearsed, even in imagination, as a problem situation is anticipated—a practice that can be quite useful. Other forms of practice may also be used, such as writing out the intended self-instructions and rereading them just before the event. For example, a man who wanted to appear less brusque to his employees read to himself these instructions from a typed card just before an employee came in for an interview: "Now take about two extra minutes, go slowly, be polite, stop doing other things, and give your full attention. It will pay off." But eventually, to be effective, self-instructions must be used in the actual situation.

Here is an example of a more complex use of self-instructions. The principal of an elementary school found it extremely difficult to express any negative reaction to her teachers. She could praise them, of course, but not give them suggestions for improvement. If she wanted to say "This is not an adequate lesson plan; you must prepare it in more detail," she became embarrassed and often wound up speaking in such generalities that the teacher didn't understand what she was trying to say.

The first thing the principal tried was to "psych herself up" before these interviews—saying to herself "You can do this. Be firm. You're supposed to be the boss." But it didn't help.

She then prepared a small "script" of what she wanted to say to the teacher—short, precise, and to the point, like "Your being late this week has inconvenienced your team members." She rehearsed this sentence in imagination several times just before the interview. Then she talked herself through the actual situation as follows: "Be pleasant. Be patient. That's right. Now.

Here's a pause. Say it." Then she said aloud "By the way, your being late this week has inconvenienced your team members. Can that be corrected?" Four such interviews were all she needed to gain the necessary confidence to be able to comfortably give negative feedback. But she maintained the habit of preparing a short "script" in advance and repeating it to herself just before an interview.

In each of the instances above, we have urged that self-instructions be clear, concise, and directly related to the desired behavior. More general statements may also be of some benefit, but they shouldn't be substituted for precise self-instructions. For example, if you are attempting to alter belief statements, it can be very useful to state your new belief aloud as a reminder before you enter a difficult situation (Kanter & Goldfried, 1979). Or state the old belief and tell yourself that you no longer believe it. A young student, who had just moved into her own apartment (against her parents' wishes), reminded herself while driving back home on Saturdays "Remember, I can

---

BOX 5-3
Self-Instructions in the Wilderness

Audrey Sutherland is famous in Hawaii for her daring solo trips into the wilderness of the northern shore of Moloka'i, an inaccessible area of narrow jungle valleys surrounded by the highest cliffs in the world, fronting on the deep ocean. Several times in her book of adventures she tells how she dealt with the dangerous situations she encountered during her explorations. For example:

> I came now to the end of the space where I could walk. . . . It was only a hundred feet before the rocky shore began again beyond the precipice, but in the pounding surf there was no way to inch around the face of the cliff, floating and clinging to handholds. I would have to swim out beyond the breakers, pass the cliff face, and then return to shore.
> I gave myself instructions. Take off the jeans, the shirt, the shoes and socks. Pack them inside the bag. . . . Cinch the box onto the pack frame again. Put on the nylon tank suit, the fins. Lash a line to the mask and snorkel from a shoulder strap [pp. 27–28].

And later:

> Now past the cliff face, I waited offshore just seaward of the breakers for a lull. Where was I in the continuous sequence of larger and smaller waves? It is harder to judge from the back side of the waves where your view is only four inches above sea level.
> Give the mental orders: Wait. Watch. Now, swim . . . You're sloppy; coordinate! [p. 29].

From *Paddling My Own Canoe*, by Audrey Sutherland. Copyright © 1978 by The University Press of Hawaii. Reprinted by permission.

tolerate their disapproval. They continue to love me. I have made the right decision. I don't need to have approval constantly." Even during a problem situation, statements of belief or judgment can guide your reactions. When the topic of living alone comes up once more, this student can say to herself "I'm overreacting; I don't need to feel upset" and then add a precise self-instruction: "Relax now. Try to change the subject."

Belief statements about the self can also be rehearsed immediately before the event—for example, "I can stay calm. I can make interesting conversation. I can handle it." Reminding yourself of your good qualities and competence can be useful, because these self-statements can cue behaviors of competence. But, obviously, to make absurd statements to yourself or to tell yourself things you cannot believe would be of little use. Telling yourself "I am the most brilliant woman in the state of Illinois!" will not affect your behavior much, unless you believe it—or unless it's true!

Self-instructions can also remind you of your long-range goals. The shy man above said to himself, before approaching the woman, "Remember, this is important to me. I've got to learn how to talk to women or I'll die a hermit." This kind of self-statement will bring your long-range goal forward in your mind and increase your incentive to perform the next new behavior.

Eliminating Negative Self-Instructions

You may have learned through your self-observations that, as you begin to perform some self-defeating behavior, you are actually instructing yourself to do it. For example, a young woman who didn't seem to be able to relax when she was with men reported that, as soon as a man started talking with her, she would say to herself things like "He's not going to like me" or "I'm going to be shy" or "I'm not going to make a good impression." These "self-instructions" made her tense and probably made her act in a less attractive manner.

A middle-aged man who wanted to become a jogger but found it difficult reported that, as he jogged, he would say to himself "This is probably killing me. I'm going to have a heart attack." Or he would actually visualize a scene in which he had a heart attack, staggered, and fell dead in his jogging clothes. (The fact that his doctor had assured him that it was perfectly all right for him to jog didn't seem to make any difference.) Needless to say, this kind of thinking discouraged his jogging; so he tried to eliminate such thoughts.

A man whose job was less than perfect said that, while at work, he would say things to himself—such as "This is so boring. How depressing! This is awful!"—that made him like his job even less. A dieter confided in us that, when she got a bit hungry, she would say to herself "I'm starving" or "I *must* have something to eat" and then rush off to eat as if she were really starving.

Our advice in all these kinds of situations is to *substitute the self-defeating thoughts with incompatible ones, preferably thoughts that contain self-instructions.* For example, when the shy young woman realized that she was thinking

"He's not going to like me; I'm going to be shy," she was to say to herself "No, not this time. Now, remember: smile, make eye contact, stay calm, listen carefully to what he is saying." That is, she was instructed to substitute "self-coaching" for the unwanted self-defeating thoughts.

The jogger substituted the following thoughts for his negative ones: "If I go slowly, there is no danger. There is no better way to spend my time than getting into good shape." The dieter who said "I'm starving" corrected herself by saying "No, I'm not. I'm just a bit hungry, and that's good, because it means I'm losing weight." The man who didn't like his job substituted thoughts like "It's not so bad. I need the money, and it's an easy job."

Many people treat thoughts or self-statements like those that we have just discussed as unimportant, so unimportant that they don't pay attention to them. Saying to yourself "I'm starving" seems a trivial event. Yet, these very words often guide your actions. They are antecedents you produce for your own behavior. Thus, it is important that you notice them and change them to desirable self-instructions.

Thought Stopping

A variation of self-instructions, called *thought stopping,* has been developed to eliminate unpleasant or self-defeating thoughts (Wolpe, 1958). In their extreme form, such intrusive thoughts are called *obsessions,* and can be on almost any subject—sex, aggression, self-criticism. They can even be nonsense phrases. But in their milder forms, these self-degrading and self-defeating thoughts—such as "I'm no good," "Ugly, ugly, ugly," or "I'm stupid"—are quite common and apparently uncontrollable. The thoughts may be visual as well as verbal—imagining some unpleasant scene that, much like a persistent tune, will not get out of your mind.

Thought stopping, like all self-instructions, is a simple technique. As soon as the unwanted thought occurs, say to yourself "Stop!" Say it sharply, and, if not aloud, say it clearly in your mind. As in the case of other self-instructions, it is vital that you actually verbalize "Stop!" The verbalization brings back from the underground the directing power of language. (It may also be seen as a chain-breaking technique.)

To be effective, thought stopping must include a second step, which is to substitute another thought immediately. This substitute thought should be the opposite of the unpleasant one. If, for example, you imagine a scene in which you are humiliated, say "Stop!" and immediately imagine a scene in which you encounter success. One of our students suffered from embarrassing and repeated sexual fantasies. Using thought stopping, she substituted images of being alone, on a beach, in deep relaxation.

If the intrusive thoughts are verbal, replace them with opposite statements. Cease your negative train of thought and substitute for it something positive about yourself (Hays & Waddell, 1976). For example, as you are waiting for the bus, you go over your performance on some recent tests. Your old, unwanted thought begins to intrude: "I'm dumb, I'm no good." As soon as you notice this thought, say "Stop!" and think instead "I made B on two of those tests and no lower than C on any of the others. Not too bad."

Thought stopping should be combined with the technique of substituting positive self-instructions for self-degrading ones. For example, the shy person is introduced to a new person and thinks "I'm such a turkey, she'll never like me." Immediately, he says to himself "Stop! Be calm, relax. Smile, look her in the eyes. Learn her name. Find out what she is interested in."

One gets better at thought stopping by practicing it. Don't expect immediate total relief, but with practice you can expect the frequency of unwanted thoughts to diminish.

Summary

The most effective way to arrange new antecedents is through self-instructions. Prior to the occasion for a wanted behavior, instruct yourself clearly and incisively. These instructions can pertain to actions or to beliefs; that is,

---

BOX 5-4
Victorian Thought Stopping

In 1875 D. Lewis reported treating a man who was preoccupied with thoughts of nude women and sexual intercourse. For Victorian morality, with its emphasis on chastity, this was a serious problem indeed. Lewis instructed the patient as follows:

> Fix it in your mind that a sensual idea is dangerous and harmful; then the instant one comes it will startle you. By an effort you change the subject immediately. . . . If there is a moment's doubt, spring up and engage in some active exercise of the body. Each effort will be easier, until after a week or two you will have, in this particular, complete control of your thoughts [p. 30].

Two months later Lewis received this letter:

> My dear friend, I do not know in what terms to express my gratitude that all this is past. I found it difficult to control my thoughts at first, but as you advised, I soon fixed the thought of danger in my mind, so that when a lascivious fancy appeared, it startled me, and immediately I took out of my pocket the card you suggested, on which I had written ten words, each suggestive of a subject in which I am interested. Looking over this card, I had no difficulty in changing the subject at once. . . . I can now meet my lady friends and converse with them with real pleasure. My thoughts are not more lecherous and unclean than they would be in the presence of sisters [p. 32].

This gem was reported by Gerald M. Rosen and Herbert A. Orenstein in "A Historical Note on Thought Stopping," *Journal of Consulting and Clinical Psychology*, 1976, *44*, 1016–1017. (Originally published by D. Lewis in *Chastity: Our Secret Sins*. Philadelphia: Maclean, 1875.)

BOX 5-5

Falling Out of Love through Thought Stopping

Mary, a mother of two young children, was "hopelessly" in love with Dan. But Dan had proven to be dishonest, as well as a liar and an exploiter, and to have no intention of going back to her. Mary wrote: "I feel desperate. I know he was just using me, but I still love him. I think about him all the time; I spend half my day crying, and I can't sleep at night. Everything reminds me of him—presents he gave me, TV shows he liked. I find myself doing things like driving past his house or cooking the meals he liked to eat. I ring him up all the time, yet I know there is absolutely no hope of our ever being together again. I don't even think I want to be with him really. I just want to be able to forget him."

When Mary was asked to describe the content of her thoughts about Dan, it became obvious that these were always positive. She thought about the good times they had had and about the qualities she admired in him. She almost never thought of his selfishness, arrogance, or meanness.

Mary's first step toward solving her problem was to make a list of all of Dan's bad points and of all the unfair things he had done to her: "Those days after his wife came back—waiting all day for the phone to ring and then realizing that he'd just forgotten. The way he was using me as a housekeeper."

She also listed the advantages of not being in love with him. For example:

I will not feel so depressed and worthless.
I will be nicer to my children.
I will not be such a drag on my friends.
I will be able to cope with the nursery school committee and the PTA again.

These lists were written on a card that Mary kept with her at all times. She also made a tape recording of them. She read the lists or played the tape at least a dozen times a day and tried to recreate in her mind the scene that was being described, with all its details and emotions. Whenever she found herself thinking something positive about Dan, she would think "Stop!" and substitute an item from the "bad Dan" list.

She also used another form of antecedent control—avoiding things that triggered thoughts of Dan. She threw away his presents and stopped watching his favorite TV programs and cooking his favorite foods. She no longer drove past his house or rang him up. She kept herself very busy doing other things, so her thoughts would be on them rather than on Dan.

In order to tell whether these methods were working, Mary kept a record of her daily moods. She imagined a scale of 0–10, where 0 equaled "as bad as I have ever felt" and 10 equaled "like my old self again." Each evening she looked back at the day and tried to decide what her mood rating had been that day. She also kept a record of the number of positive thoughts she had about Dan.

In the beginning, Mary's mood ratings were around 1 or 2, and her positive thoughts about Dan were almost constant, too many to count. Then things started to improve. Some days were bad, but each week the average mood rating was higher and the average number of positive thoughts about Dan was lower.

(Box 5-5 continues)

BOX 5-5 *(continued)*

After seven weeks, none of Mary's thoughts of Dan was positive, and her mood ratings averaged 7. She stopped listening to her tape and reading her lists. "I really don't want to be reminded of him at all now."

One month later, as she was going to bed, she reached for her notebook, recorded a 10, and realized she hadn't thought of Dan all day.

Reprinted by permission of Gail Tregerthan, University of Hawaii.

you can instruct yourself about the details of the action you plan to take, or you can instruct yourself about your own good qualities and competence.

Self-defeating or unpleasant self-statements can be replaced with more positive ones. Particularly stubborn self-statements can be reduced by using the technique of thought stopping, but the key to success is to add new, adaptive self-statements. Self-instructions should actually be said, aloud or subvocally, as clearly as possible and as close in time as possible to the moment of the actual behavior.

BUILDING NEW STIMULUS CONTROL: THE PHYSICAL AND SOCIAL ENVIRONMENTS

You can also arrange new physical antecedents (or cues) to make your desired behavior more likely. Recall that an antecedent comes to have stimulus control over some behavior if the stimulus is present when the behavior is reinforced and not present when the behavior is not reinforced. Suppose you want to increase your concentration while writing. If you are to increase the control of some antecedent over the behavior of concentrating, you must arrange a special "writing" situation so that (1) whenever you are in that situation, you are concentrating and gaining reinforcement for it and (2) while you are in that situation, you must not perform any other behavior that may be reinforced.

This second feature is very important. Otherwise, the same stimulus could become a cue for more than one behavior, and the competing behaviors could interfere with the target behavior. Thus, you may begin by learning to concentrate-while-writing at a certain place in which you *never* do anything else but write and leaving that situation whenever you are not concentrating. When you are writing at a particular desk and realize that you are not concentrating, you should leave the desk until you can come back to it and concentrate once more.

If you don't have a place that you can reserve for one behavior, you can still make one particular *arrangement* of cues. One man had only one desk, which he used for all kinds of things, such as writing letters, watching TV, and eating. But, when he wanted to concentrate, he always pulled his desk away from the wall and sat on the other side of it. That way, sitting on the other side of his desk (an antecedent) was associated only with concentrated intellectual work.

A dieter used a similar procedure. At first she had found it impossible to go through all the steps we had recommended for breaking up the chain of behaviors that resulted in her overeating. So she began by requiring herself to sit at a particular place for one meal each day. During the meal, she concentrated on performing all the acts necessary for learning new eating habits. In this way, sitting at that particular place acquired antecedent stimulus control over her behaviors of learning new ways of eating.

These are all examples of deliberately establishing antecedent stimulus control, so that you can perform a desired target behavior in response to at least one situation. For some goals, only one such situation is necessary; for others, you may want to be able to perform the desired behavior in more than one situation. For example, Fo (1975) found that students are better off if they can study in many situations, whenever there is an opportunity. This means that in some cases it is desirable to broaden the range of effective antecedents of a desired target behavior.

Stimulus Generalization

Of course, you don't want to spend the rest of your life being able to perform some desired behavior only when you are in the presence of some particular set of antecedents. You may want to be able to concentrate in several kinds of situations, eat properly whenever you are eating, or use social skills with different people. In short, you want your newly learned behaviors to generalize from one situation to a variety of situations. *Stimulus generalization* is the process by which a behavior that has been learned in the presence of one antecedent is performed in the presence of other, similar antecedents.

The more similar the new situation is to the original situation, the easier it is to generalize your newly learned behavior. Therefore, you will want to think about the similarity between other situations and the one in which you can perform the desired behavior. You should begin generalization by performing the target behavior in the situation that is most similar to the original one.

A middle-aged woman suffered from a very strong fear of speaking in front of groups. Using some of the procedures we will recommend in Chapter 6, she developed the ability to speak to a group of three or four friends. Having accomplished that, she tried to generalize the newly acquired ability to new groups. She decided that it would be easier if the "new" group contained at least a couple of friends from the old one, because the new situation would then be very similar to the one in which she first practiced. She arranged things so that such an opportunity would come up. When it did, she performed the target behavior and then reinforced it.

Once you have developed a behavior that you can perform in certain situations, you should gradually take steps into similar situations and, in the process, use self-instructions. A great strength of self-instructions is that they can be used in many situations, creating a bridge from familiar to unfamiliar circumstances. Self-instructions are portable cues; they can be taken with you from party to party, from tennis court to library. Thus self-instructions enhance the development of stimulus generalization.

Precommitment and Programming of the Social Environment

The basic idea in precommitment is to arrange in advance for helpful antecedents to occur. This arrangement can be made when some problem situation is anticipated, especially for those moments of maximum temptation.

A smoker had been off cigarettes for about two months. In the past, he had stopped several times but each time had gone back to smoking. He had been successful this last time because he had identified those situations in which he had lapsed in the past and taken steps to deal with them. One of the problem situations was being at a party. The drinks, the party atmosphere, and the feeling of relaxation represented an irresistible temptation to "smoke just a few," although in the past this had usually led to a return to regular smoking. One night, as the man and his wife were getting ready to go out to a party, he said "You know, I am really going to be tempted to smoke there. Will you do me a favor? If you see me bumming a cigarette from someone, remind me of the kids and that I really don't want to go back to smoking." (One of the reasons he wanted to quit was because he knew he set a bad example for his children.)

What this man did was to arrange in advance to be reminded. He pre-committed himself to facing the knowledge that he would end up smoking again if he tried to have just a few, and he made this precommitment at a time when he was not strongly tempted—*before* going to the party.

This intelligent strategy was possible because he had profited from previous mistakes. Each time a smoker returns to smoking, it is a lapse but it is also a source of *information* about what kind of situations are most tempting (Hunt & Matarazzo, 1973). The man used this information to cope better with the problem situation by enlisting the help of his wife.

Asking other people to cue or remind you can be an effective way of arranging antecedents. You are not asking to be nagged, of course, but simply reminded of what you wanted to do back when you were not being so sorely tempted.

You can teach family and friends how they can help you achieve self-direction. You want to teach them to support, by providing cues and reinforcers, the behaviors you wish to develop and not to support undesired behaviors (Stuart, 1967). Other people represent some of the strongest cues to which we adapt our behavior. Getting them to change their own behavior with regard to you can greatly help you change yours. Most people will be helpful, if they believe you're sincere: "Do you really want me to stop offering you a drink when you come home?" But perhaps the other is losing something by no longer offering temptation: "It was always so pleasant to sit down and

have a drink together when you came home. I guess I hate to give it up."
Other elements may come into play to complicate the situation even further.
For example, two friends or a married couple may thwart each other's attempts
to quit smoking, because each knows that, if the other one quits, he or she
will feel more pressure to quit too.

Precommitment, in the form of reminders, can also be arranged without
the help of others. Setting an alarm clock is one obvious way of doing it.
Preparing a daily or weekly schedule of obligations is another.

Now, at the end of this chapter, we have come full circle back to the issue
of commitment, which we discussed in Chapter 2. Building and maintaining
commitment is a matter of arranging antecedents.

Summary

The physical environment can be rearranged to increase stimulus control
over desired behavior. The technique is to restrict the desired behavior to a
certain situation. Eventually, most behaviors are desirable in several situations,
so that techniques of stimulus generalization are recommended. Desirable
behaviors should gradually be extended to similar situations, thus broadening
the range of controlling antecedents.

When we speak of moments of maximum temptation, we are referring
to those situations that are most likely to result in undesired behaviors because
they contain powerful antecedent control. Precommitment will enable you to
ensure that countercues will also be there waiting, thus making your desired
behaviors more likely. When you know that the old cues are going to be
present, arrange for a countercue to be there too—reminders from others,
the ring of an alarm clock, or self-reminders of your goals.

YOUR OWN SELF-DIRECTION PROJECT: STEP FIVE

By examining your structured diary and/or your self-recording, identify the
antecedents of any problematic behavior relevant to your goals. Devise a
plan, using any two procedures discussed in this chapter, for either increasing
or decreasing antecedent stimulus control. As one procedure, use new self-
instructions.

Write this plan out, just as you have done for the previous two steps.
Don't implement it yet. Chapters 6 and 7 are likely to contain ideas that you'll
want to incorporate in your final plan.

TIPS FOR TYPICAL TOPICS

Overeating, Smoking, Drinking, and Drug Use. The chain of
events that leads to overeating begins at least as far back as shopping. You
can interrupt the overeating chain at several early points—for example, by
shopping when you are *not* hungry (to prevent overbuying), by not *buying*
fattening foods, by not even walking down the cookie-and-cracker aisle, and

by not allowing yourself to become so hungry that you will gorge (Stuart & Davis, 1972). Overeating is likely to have multiple antecedents—many chains all leading to excessive eating. You may eat when bored, sad, angry, or happy. You may always eat what is offered to you even if you are not hungry. You may eat because the food is there or because you want to relax. Learning to eat properly requires careful observation of all those antecedents—emotional, social, and physical (Stuart & Davis, 1972; Leon, 1979).

Interfering at the end of the chain—right at the moment of the overwhelming urge to eat—can often be done by a recommitment strategy. Require yourself to write out an answer to these three questions before giving in to the urge (Youdin & Hemmes, 1978):

1. Why do I want to eat this food, when I have started a program to stop overeating?
2. Whom am I fooling by eating this food?
3. Do I want to be overweight?

The same principles apply to smoking and drug use. Interfere early in the chain by reducing or eliminating the supply of cigarettes, by rationing them if you are cutting down, or by not buying and carrying cigarettes if you are stopping. Interfere late in the chain, right at the moment of the strongest urge, by asking goal questions:

1. Why do I want to smoke this cigarette (or joint), when I have started a program to quit smoking (or using pot)?
2. Whom am I fooling by smoking this cigarette (or joint)?
3. Do I want to keep on being a smoker (or a drug user)?

And ask this question:

4. Am I telling myself that the urge is too strong—that I can't resist it? Do I want to let this urge run my life?

Studying and Time Management.   Three specific forms of antecedent control have proven effective: (1) written planned schedules, kept as reminders in some obvious place; (2) the habit of studying while isolated from other people (Hefferman & Richards, 1979); and (3) self-reminders of goals and values. The third form of control can be accomplished by asking several times a day "Is this the best use of my time right now? If it's not, what would be?" (Lakein, 1973). Revise the written planned schedule according to your answers to this regular questioning.

Assertion.   Distinguish between assertion and aggression; one is appropriate, the other is not. Many nonassertive people get very angry before they speak up, so that, when they do act, they are more likely to be aggressive—verbally—than if they had asserted themselves earlier (Linehan, 1979).

Therefore it is desirable to act assertively early in the chain of events. Early intervention in the chain can be approached through *beliefs* and/or through *self-instructions*. Goldfried (1979) and his associates have shown that timid people often have "beliefs" that they are willing to abandon as soon as the beliefs come under scrutiny—for instance, the belief that others will reject or punish them for the slightest bit of standing up for themselves. Search out such beliefs; they may well be irrational, because more respect is usually accorded those who respect themselves. Changing such beliefs can lead rapidly to changed behavior. *Self-instructions* are particularly useful in coaching yourself through unfamiliar behavior: "Remember, be firm. That's right, you needn't be unpleasant. Just state your position firmly. Good."

   Family, Friends, Lovers, and Coworkers.   Self-instructions are especially useful as antecedent control in strained relationships. If relationships are severely distressed, you may wish to use avoidance, for a time, by limiting interaction to certain situations. Such a case is discussed in detail in Chapter 8 ("Problems in Social Interaction").

   Depression.   When you notice a change in your mood, try to discover what thoughts have led to it. Thoughts such as "I'm a loser" or "I never do anything right" will certainly depress your mood and should be replaced by more positive self-statements. Use thought stopping if necessary. Rehearse positive self-statements, so that you can use them immediately as replacements. This is especially important if you are depressed, because you will tend to criticize yourself for criticizing yourself: "I just thought that I'm a loser. What a stupid thing to think" (Hollon & Beck, 1979). Have a replacement thought ready: "I'm a lo—— Stop! I'm a loyal and sensitive friend."
   The second major tactic for antecedent control of depression is the scheduling of pleasant activities (Hollon & Beck, 1979)—a powerful antecedent of good mood, which is not often used by depressed people (Fuchs & Rehm, 1977). The type of activity—entertainment, socializing, exercise, fantasizing, handicrafts—is not crucial, so long as it is pleasant for you. Schedule these activities regularly and frequently, and stick to the schedule.

   Specific Fears.   Undoubtedly you are avoiding the frightening situations when you can. What are the antecedents to which you react? tension or fear? Note the worrisome things you tell yourself. Are they true? For example, "I'm failing this test. This is a catastrophe!" First, are you actually failing? Second, is it a catastrophe? compared to an earthquake? Can you identify irrational beliefs such as "Anything less than perfect is failure?"

   The Other Sex.   The causes of problems in making friends and dating are of two basic types: shyness and awkwardness. Although the two feed each other, they require two different approaches—and perhaps both approaches simultaneously. If shyness is the main issue, attend closely to the chain of events necessary to produce your goal. Discover where you are breaking off that chain by avoiding social interaction. Then do what you would do in any case of specific anxiety: (1) discover any self-defeating beliefs; (2) use self-instructions to coach yourself through interactions with members of the other sex; (3) develop new antecedents by putting yourself in situations where you can meet and interact with eligible others.

If the problem is awkwardness or ineffectual behavior or overwhelming fear, the problem had best be approached after reading the next chapter.

CHAPTER **6**

Developing
New Behaviors

GOAL:
To teach how to develop new behaviors.

OUTLINE:
Shaping: The method of successive approximations
Incompatible behaviors
Coping with anxiety and tension
Relaxation
Developing new behaviors through practice
Developing new behaviors through modeling
Mastery in the real world
Your own self-direction project: Step six
Tips for typical topics

Any plan for self-change involves developing some new behavior. Four principal techniques for developing new behaviors have been studied and will be discussed in this chapter. They are (1) shaping, (2) the use of incompatible behaviors, including relaxation, (3) rehearsal, and (4) modeling.

These processes have been studied by psychologists and developed into specific techniques for self-direction. These techniques are merely the conscious application of principles that govern learning in natural settings.

SHAPING: THE METHOD OF SUCCESSIVE APPROXIMATIONS

You can't expect yourself to produce a behavior that you don't know how to perform. All the encouragement in the world wouldn't enable a person to successfully pilot a jumbo jet on the first try. Similarly, all the reinforcement in the world wouldn't enable you to suddenly produce desired social skills that you have never had. A behavior that is not yet part of your repertoire, a behavior that you cannot perform, must be learned.

New, complex behaviors rarely emerge spontaneously. Therefore, instead of waiting for some new, desired behavior to emerge, magically full blown, you should begin teaching yourself the new behavior. Start from the point in your store of behaviors that is the closest approximation to the new behavior you want to develop. If approximations are practiced, they will become the basis from which each next, improved step can be taken. This process of successive approximations is known as *shaping*.

When using shaping techniques, begin at whatever level you presently find yourself, and slowly but surely move toward the ultimate goal, reinforcing yourself as you progress. In Chapter 7 you will learn how to use self-reinforcement. Here you will learn how to develop a behavior by successive approximations.

133

How Shaping Works in Self-Directed Behavior

You can now see another good reason for gathering accurate observational data. The baseline tells you your *current* level of performance. And that—or just beyond it—is where the shaping process should begin.

There are two simple rules for shaping: (1) you can never begin too low, and (2) the steps upward can never be too small. Whenever you are in doubt, begin at a lower level or reduce the size of the steps. This has the effect of making it simple to perform the desired behavior, because you feel that your movement upward is easy. And this is very important, for it increases your chances of success.

One of the most common reasons for failure in self-directed projects is the lack of shaping. Some students resist using shaping because they believe that they "should" perform at certain levels and don't "deserve" to be reinforced for performance that is below that level. This is an unfortunate belief (as discussed in Chapter 5), because it makes learning impossible. Shaping increases your ability to do what you believe you should do. If you find shaping at a very low level embarrassing, keep it a secret, but do reinforce yourself heavily for starting.

Here is an example of the shaping schedule of a student who wanted to attain the goal of many hours of studying per week.

Baseline: I am now actually studying an average of 40 minutes per day.
Level 1: I will begin my reinforcement for studying 45 minutes per day, five days a week. This should be easy to do, since I have done it several times in the past.
Level 2: I will require myself to study 60 minutes per day to get the reinforcer.
Level 3: One hour, 15 minutes.
Level 4: One hour, 30 minutes.
Level 5: Two hours.

Notice how carefully the student followed the two rules for shaping: start low and keep the steps small. This allowed her to move, slowly but inevitably, toward her goal.

Notice also that the first steps were smaller than later steps. This is generally a good idea, because very small initial steps will ensure that some progress is made, whereas later it may be possible to make progress more quickly.

When you are following a shaping schedule, you must remain flexible. *Be ready to change your schedule.* You may have to do it, for example, if some of the projected steps turn out to be too large. What you plan on paper may not work out in practice, thus you may have to reduce the size of the steps. You may have to stay at the same level for several time periods, or you may have to return to an earlier level if some setback occurs. The basic rule for these and all other problems in shaping is: don't move up a step until you have mastered the previous one. Notice that the above student's plan is not tied to specific dates for changing levels.

Although it is often useful to make a tentative time schedule as an additional motivator, these arbitrary calendar plans can in fact retard your progress. We have seen students who can advance more rapidly than they had originally estimated. And we have seen others who, in order to meet their prearranged time plans, move to higher levels before the lower ones are mastered. Eventually, they stumble. These potential problems can be overcome simply by remembering that you advance a step when the previous step is secure—then and only then.

The Continuum along Which You Shape

We have been speaking of situations in which you shape your behavior by increasing the amount of time that you perform some desired behavior. Actually, shaping can be used in any situation in which you can gradually increase the criterion—whatever that may be—for the behavior required.

Alan, a young man whose goal was to have more dates, had followed chain-of-events reasoning and decided that the chain he needed to follow was (1) go where women are, (2) smile at them, (3) talk with them, and so on. Step 3 could be broken down into talking with women about "safe" subjects like school or the weather and then progressing to more adventurous conversational topics. After achieving the first steps in the chain, Alan decided to shape his behavior according to the degree of controversy he would bring into the conversation. He chose this dimension because he was made very uncomfortable by conversational disagreements.

Alan's baseline showed that he did very little talking with women on any subject whatsoever. He reasoned that it would be a mistake to move immediately into conversations on controversial issues. Therefore, for level 1 he chose to increase only talking about school. After he could comfortably perform at level 1, he would raise his sights and try a foray into more exciting but (for him) dangerous topics, such as whether a movie was funny or not. That was level 2. Level 3 was at an even higher level of potential controversy—university politics. Level 4 was interpersonal relationships and sex, and level 5 was the most difficult of all for him—national politics, personal philosophy, and the like.

Shaping in this fashion has two advantages. First, as with all shaping procedures, you can perform at a level that allows you to succeed. Second, it encourages analysis of the component parts of a situation—analysis that can result, for example, in seeing that there are levels of difficulty in handling a conversation or that being attractive is the result of several different behaviors. You can work on one part at a time instead of trying to deal with all levels of difficulty at once.

Here are some other examples of shaping. A young woman who wanted to be a writer remarked that she could write only a few paragraphs at a time. She would then "clutch up," unable to go on. She kept records of how many paragraphs she wrote on the average and started off requiring herself to do *one* more than that. Then she raised it to two more, three more, and so on.

A man wanted to cut down on the amount of food he ate, particularly at supper. First, he counted how many bites he took per meal. The average was 52. He then began to follow the rule "No more than 50 bites per meal." Later he cut this to 48 and then to 44. A man who wanted to be able to fast one full day began by requiring himself to go without food till 11:00 A.M. Then he changed to 12:00 noon, then to 1:00 P.M., and so on, and in this way he gradually increased the time he went without eating until he was able to go through a full day of fasting.

A very withdrawn woman who felt she needed to become assertive "in about seven or eight different kinds of situations" started by requiring herself to practice assertiveness in two of the easiest situations and then added the others one at a time.

Problems in Shaping

You can't expect the course of learning to be smooth all the time; this seems to be everyone's experience. The important thing is to keep trying— staying within a shaping program—even if it is the 39th revision of the original schedule.

Encountering Plateaus.   When you follow a shaping schedule, you are likely to encounter plateaus. You may make excellent progress week after week and then suddenly stop. Moving up all those previous steps seemed so easy, when, all of a sudden, a new step—the same size as all the others— seems very difficult. The easiest way to continue upward when you reach a plateau is to reduce the size of the steps. If that is not possible, continue the plan for a week or so. The plateau experience is so common that it should be expected and "ridden out." On the other hand, if in spite of your efforts movement still doesn't occur, it may be that you are at a comfortable upper limit and should think about terminating your plan.

Losing "Willpower."   You now know enough about the principles that govern behavior/environment relationships to also know that there are many reasons why you don't perform a given behavior. In our experience, the loss of self-control in the middle of intervention is most often due to some failure in the shaping program.

For example, a student will say "To hell with it. I can't do it. I want to get in that library and stay there, but I just can't make myself do it. I haven't got enough willpower. And, besides, this whole idea of self-change is ridiculous, because the whole problem is really whether I myself have got the willpower to improve myself. I don't, so I quit."

In our terms, this may be a shaping problem. For example, two hours in the library may be much too severe an increase over current performance. Instead of two hours, this student should have set his first approximation at only 30 minutes. For some students with a near-zero baseline, we have suggested, as a first approximation, merely walking to the library and going up the steps, then returning home to get their reinforcer. But most self-modifiers are simply too embarrassed to perform such elementary steps. They then increase the step to a "respectable" level, which is often outside their performance capacity, and finally quit altogether in a huff of "willpower" failure.

You may experience this failure of self-control in two ways. First, you simply may not get started on a self-modification project; you would like to achieve the final goal but somehow cannot get around to starting toward that goal. This is a shaping problem, and you need to start with a very low step. Remember, if it's embarrassingly low—"Yes, I jog around my living room three times every day"—then just don't tell anyone but do it. Second, you may have started but find that you are not making progress. This may also be a shaping problem, and you need to use smaller steps.

The whole point of shaping is to make it as easy as possible to start and to continue; therefore, you require yourself to do so little more than you can presently do that it is easy to perform the target behavior. Then, after practicing a bit, it becomes easy to move up one more short step.

Not Knowing How to Begin.   By referring to the baseline, you can determine your capability for certain tasks. For others, however, you may not know how to begin; that is, you may not know exactly which acts do come first in a chain-of-events sequence. In this case, you may want to use someone else as a model to get an idea of a starting point.

A young woman chose as her model another woman who was effective in getting acquainted with new people. The model's first behavior was merely to smile responsively. So our young woman used "smiling responsively" as the first step in her shaping plan. As this example illustrates, observing models is especially appropriate when you are uncertain about the exact behaviors you should choose to develop.

Mark Twain knew about shaping, although he didn't use that word. In *Pudd'nhead Wilson's Calendar,* he wrote "Habit is habit, and not to be flung out of the window by any man, but coaxed downstairs a step at a time." Coax yourself.

Summary

Most self-direction plans, particularly those that call for developing some desired behavior, require shaping. Shaping means that, instead of requiring yourself to perform the complete new behavior, you require yourself to perform only a part. Then, in a series of successive approximations to the final goal, you gradually increase the size of your steps. The two main rules of shaping are: (1) you can never begin too low, and (2) the steps can never be too small. You can shape your behavior along any desired continuum.

Common problems in shaping are plateaus—progress stops and you find it hard to go on—and lack of willpower—you are either requiring yourself to start too high or using steps that are too large.

In the next chapter, which discusses self-reinforcement, you will learn methods for rewarding each step along the way.

INCOMPATIBLE BEHAVIORS

Sometimes it is hard to shape down a bad habit. Generally you need something to take its place. It is easier to eliminate an unwanted behavior—or thought—by choosing a desirable replacement and deliberately practicing it. By increasing the new, you automatically decrease the old. This is a better way of getting rid of an unwanted behavior than, for example, trying to punish yourself for your bad habit.

Andrea, a young woman who was bothered by too-frequent arguments with her father, began to observe her own behavior. She discovered the following chain of events. Her father would make some comment about some aspect of her behavior that seemed to bother him (for example, he disapproved of her career goals). Usually Andrea would respond with a frown and the comment that he should mind his own business. This would enrage him, and they would be off to another bitter argument. Andrea knew that her father basically loved her and that he was simply having a difficult time adjusting to the fact that she was now an adult and was behaving like one. She reasoned that, if she substituted kind remarks and a smile when he opened up some topic about her behavior, they might be able to discuss it in a more friendly fashion. Instead of setting out to *decrease* frowning and unkind comments, she set out to *increase* smiling and kind comments.

Thereafter, when he made some remark about her behavior or goals, Andrea would smile at him and strive to disagree as pleasantly as possible. (Of course, she kept a record of her responses and also used other techniques to maintain them.) Increasing the desirable behavior had, in fact, the effect of calming her father, and they progressed through a series of amicable conversations to a new understanding.

Notice that in Andrea's case the goal was to ultimately change not her own behavior but the behavior of another person. The young woman reasoned that (1) she wanted her father to stop treating her as if she were a child and (2) she wanted him to stop arguing with her. But she took the important step of realizing that the best way to effect these changes was to change her own behavior first.

The approach of increasing some incompatible behavior is better than attacking an undesired behavior by trying to extinguish or punish it. Consider a young woman who always gets nervous when she has to talk with men. She feels shy and tends to withdraw from conversations. She could set out to decrease "withdrawing from conversations"—since she considers this to be an undesirable behavior—and she might conclude that she will have to punish herself for withdrawing. Doing so would be a serious mistake. Even if it were possible to punish herself for withdrawing, the punishment would have an unfortunate effect on her emotional problem. She would still feel nervous, shy, and tongue-tied when men were around, and she wouldn't learn any of the new social skills required to reach her goal. Such results would increase the likelihood that she would be punished by rejection and disappointment in her interactions with men. This punishment, coupled with her own self-inflicted punishment, would increase her problem by strengthening the negative emotional conditioning to such situations.

For this young woman, the use of incompatible responses would involve rewarding herself for staying and talking. The staying and talking itself should be shaped, of course, in small steps that could provide success experiences.

Selecting an Incompatible Response

What exactly is an "incompatible response"? *An incompatible response is a behavior that prevents the occurrence of some other behavior.* Smiling is incompatible with frowning, simply because you have only one face and it can do only one thing at a time. Sitting is incompatible with running. Going swimming is incompatible with staying in your room. Being courteous is incompatible with being rude. As you can easily see, for many undesired behaviors there may be several incompatible ones available. When this is the case, you have the opportunity to choose among several alternatives the new acts that you would most like to develop.

A male student was active in campus politics and had been elected to the Council of the Associated Students. In the meetings, he found that he was talking too much and losing his effectiveness because he was irritating the other members. He felt the impulse to talk, he said, with "the force of a compulsion." He first tried simply not talking so much. He did have some success, but, after considering the use of incompatible responses, he reasoned that he could do better by choosing a more active and positive alternative behavior. So he began by "listening." This was a genuinely new act, not merely the suppression of an old one. It resulted in less talking, which he wanted, and also in greater listening, which he came to value more and more.

Sometimes there is no incompatible response one would really like to develop. Even then it may be useful to choose an incompatible behavior, although it is of no particular value in itself. A man who wanted to stop cracking his knuckles all the time decided that, whenever he felt like cracking his knuckles, he would *instead* make a fist. His target behavior was to make a fist instead of cracking his knuckles. A man who habitually bit his nails first set out to shape the behavior of bringing his finger to his mouth but without biting his nails. The young woman who sometimes scratched her skin until it bled substituted patting for scratching.

Figure 6-1 illustrates the competing (incompatible) exercises developed by Azrin and Nunn (1973) to reduce nervous habits.

In the case of nervous habits, won't you simply turn the new behavior into a "nervous" habit? Usually not, because the undesirable "nervous" habit is something that you have been practicing for years and that you probably learned under unusual conditions (perhaps aversive). Therefore, you will need

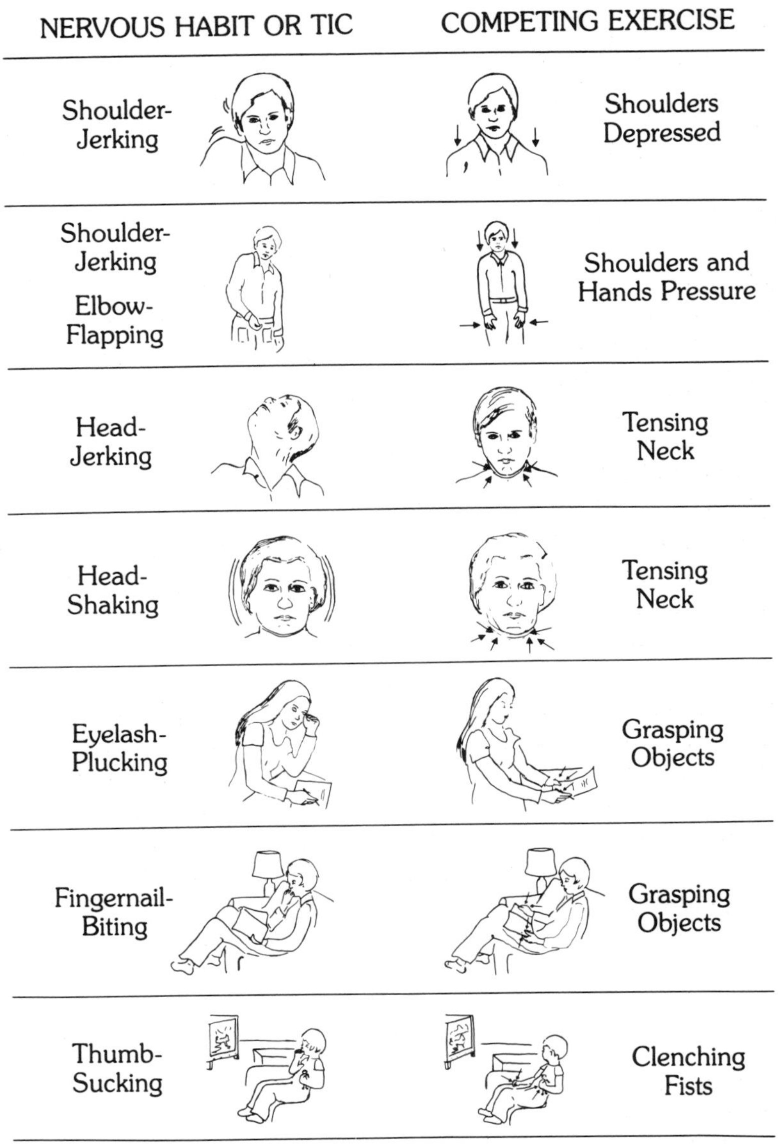

NERVOUS HABIT OR TIC		COMPETING EXERCISE
Shoulder-Jerking		Shoulders Depressed
Shoulder-Jerking Elbow-Flapping		Shoulders and Hands Pressure
Head-Jerking		Tensing Neck
Head-Shaking		Tensing Neck
Eyelash-Plucking		Grasping Objects
Fingernail-Biting		Grasping Objects
Thumb-Sucking		Clenching Fists

Figure 6-1. A pictorial representation of the various types of nervous tics or habits. The left-hand column illustrates the different tics or habits. The adjacent illustration in the right-hand column illustrates the type of competing exercise used for that nervous tic or habit. The arrows in each of the Competing Exercise illustrations show the direction of isometric muscle contraction being exerted by the client. (From "Habit Reversal: A Method of Eliminating Nervous Habits and Tics," by N. H. Azrin and R. G. Nunn, *Behaviour Research and Therapy,* 1973, *11,* 619–628. Copyright 1973 by Pergamon Press, Ltd. Reprinted by permission.)

to practice the new, alternative behavior only long enough to get rid of the problem.

As with shaping, incompatible behaviors may be strengthened with the self-reinforcement techniques discussed in Chapter 7.

Keeping Records. When you select an incompatible behavior you want to increase at the expense of some unwanted act, be sure you keep a record of how often you do the one instead of the other. It's a good idea to select an incompatible behavior as soon as possible and begin to count it, even if you are still doing a baseline count on the unwanted target behavior. Keeping a record of the incompatible behavior will encourage you to perform it (Kazdin, 1974f). Also, it will provide information you can use in gradually shaping the incompatible act while coaxing the bad habit downstairs and out the door.

Summary and Conclusions

Whenever possible, when you want to eliminate an undesired behavior, try to select an opposite, incompatible behavior that you can increase at the expense of the undesirable behavior.

BOX 6-1

Relieving Depression with Incompatible Thoughts

"My problem is that I get depressed, and then I think about death and suicide, and this frightens me. Sometimes I just don't care what happens." This young woman tried a plan of listening to music or talking to friends when depression began, thinking that they would produce feelings incompatible with depression. Although she kept this plan for 48 days, no real improvement occurred.

Then, "I thought why not fight fire with fire—use good-feeling-thoughts to combat depression thoughts. This would be an incompatible behavior (in the mind)."

She selected a fantasy, which she called "my good dream." Whenever a depressed thought or feeling began, she immediately substituted her "good dream" and held the dream in her mind until her feelings moved "back up at least to neutral."

Here is a typical entry from her journal, which she kept along with her frequency counts and mood ratings.

"The bus driver was in a foul mood and, just as I was going out the first door, shouted 'Go to the back!' This made me feel like a fool and really started my depression. Ten minutes had gone by when I reached my job, and by then I was really starting to sink. So I took 15 minutes to try and counter my depression with my good dream. I went in 15 minutes late, but it worked."

It worked remarkably well, as her graph shows (see p. 142). Her depressions dropped from three hours a day to virtually zero. We never found out what her "good dream" was.

(Box 6-1 continues)

BOX 6-1 *(continued)*

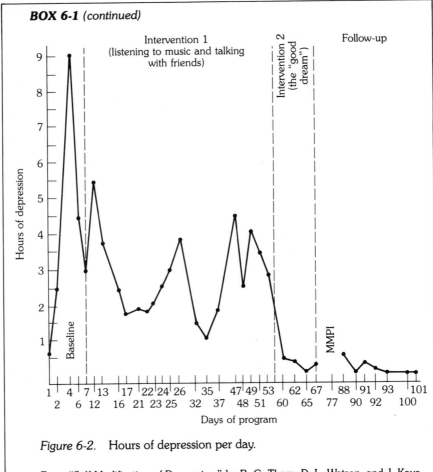

Figure 6-2.   Hours of depression per day.

From "Self-Modification of Depression," by R. G. Tharp, D. L. Watson, and J. Kaya, *Journal of Consulting and Clinical Psychology*, 1974, *42*, 624. Copyright 1974 by the American Psychological Association. Reprinted by permission. (Condensed from the Extended Report, University of Hawaii, 1974.)

To select the incompatible behavior, ask yourself these questions:

1. Is there some directly opposite behavior that I would actually like to increase while decreasing the undesired behavior?
2. What behaviors would make it impossible for me to perform the undesired behavior?
3. If there is no desired, incompatible behavior available, is there any basically meaningless act that I could substitute for the undesired behavior? Would it fit into the formula "I will do _____(the substitute behavior) instead of _____(the undesired behavior)"?

COPING WITH ANXIETY AND TENSION

A young married woman complained: "I don't see how this system will work for me. I really don't need to learn anything new. I just need to get rid of my fears. When my husband wants to make love, I want to make love too, very much; but when the crucial moment comes, I get so nervous that I can't carry on." This is an example in which the desired behavior is available but is inhibited by fear.

A goal common to most plans for self-directed change is to achieve mastery over fears, anxiety, nervousness, or tension. These unpleasant feelings may have been recorded in your A-B-C analysis. If so, you may be able to inspect the Antecedents column and find that your anxieties are present in one or more specific situations. The strategy for change is to produce some other behavior, incompatible with anxiety, for that situation. That behavior should then be reinforced and strengthened, like any other incompatible behavior. It should be noted also that simply reducing the anxiety is ordinarily very rewarding, so that the process reinforces itself.

Phobias, Fears, and Avoidance Behaviors

Some people are so afraid of cats that they will not enter a house until assured that there are no cats there. Others fear heights so much that they are unwilling to go up elevators in tall buildings. Some fear sex to the extent that they don't respond with pleasure even when it would be natural for them to do so. These are all examples of *phobias*—strong fears that most people consider irrational and that interfere with the life of the person who suffers from them.

But there are many milder, and often quite common, fears and anxieties that cause people to lose opportunities for learning and reinforcement. Whenever you have to take a test, for example, you may experience nervousness. Many people try to deal with these unpleasant emotional reactions by avoiding the circumstances that elicit the reactions. They may try all sorts of ways to avoid taking tests—even to the extent of dropping out of school. A man who has fear reactions to women may simply choose to avoid women.

It is likely that the person who has developed some kind of avoidance behavior will decide that such a behavior doesn't make for the most harmonious relationship with the environment. One way of dealing with the problem is to force oneself into the feared situation. As a result, if the fear is actually unreasonable—as it usually is—it will gradually extinguish, and the avoidance behavior will then diminish (Greist, Marks, Berlin, Gournay, & Noshirvani, 1980). But coping with the unreasonable fear by both reducing tension and extinguishing the avoidance behavior seems easier, and is in fact more effective than forcing oneself into the feared situation (Goldfried, 1977). The best way to cope with anxiety in this kind of situation is to develop a new behavior that you can perform in the tension-producing situation and that is incompatible with anxiety.

From Sex to Kung Fu: Ways to Cope with Tension

There are many tactics to produce behaviors that are incompatible with anxiety. Kanfer (1975) has reported the use of *distractors* to reduce anxiety in avoidance situations—that is, the use of activities that distract the person from the anxiety-causing situation. For example, he has suggested that an extremely withdrawn person go to a drugstore for a cup of coffee and specifically record for 15 minutes the number and types of interactions of people sitting at the counter. A shy and insecure woman might feel less anxious at parties if she made a point of making notes about the occupational background of a certain number of guests. In other words, if you are attending to the task of recording and interviewing, you will be less influenced by the anxiety-provoking aspects of the situation. This also allows the natural reinforcement of social gatherings to take effect.

Sexual arousal, too, can be used to combat anxiety, because the two are incompatible. Obviously, there are limits to the use of this "distractor," but, when feasible, it can be helpful. Gary Brown (1978) reported a case in which a client had extreme anxiety whenever he had to drive past a cemetery at night. Usually he avoided driving at night, but, if he did have to drive past a cemetery, he had "an overwhelming compulsion to stop the car, turn the inside light on, and look at the back seat." The client was instructed to practice driving past a cemetery near his home while imagining scenes of sexual activity with his wife. He began the imagined scenes when he was far enough from the cemetery that anxiety would not interfere and arranged to be maximally aroused just as the tombstones appeared. He did this 30 minutes each day for several days. His anxiety at the cemetery dropped to zero, and after a few days he was able to drive past without sexual arousal and without fear.

Another condition that can result in responses incompatible with anxiety is *intellectual curiosity.* Here is an example. A young law student suffered from an abnormally strong fear of "diseased organisms." To overcome his fear, he took some courses in anatomy and obstetrics, thus replacing the response of anxiety with the competing response of intellectual curiosity. In his own words, he enrolled in these courses with the "double view of becoming acquainted with all conditions and of freeing myself from all apprehensions as to repulsive things . . . while I satisfied my thirst for knowledge" (Bringman, Kirchev, & Balance, 1969).

This student was the German author Johann Wolfgang von Goethe, and his plan was carried out during his stay at the University of Strassburg in 1770–1771. Although in describing his plan for self-direction Goethe did not use the language of behavior modification, his plan was indeed a self-modification program and a remarkably successful one, as his later extensive writings on anatomy attest.

Gershman and Stedman (1971) have reported cases in which Oriental defense exercises were used as behaviors incompatible with anxiety. Their "Mr. P." feared closed places—elevators, locked rooms, trains, and others—

and had begun to feel anxiety when wearing tight clothes and even his wedding ring. Their plan had Mr. P. go into a closet and, as soon as the door closed, engage in *kung fu exercises* (at which he was already adept). His anxiety disappeared after no more than 20 seconds. After several such trials, he was able to stay in the closet for up to an hour without doing his exercises or feeling any anxiety. He then began to practice in elevators, and it took him only two sessions to feel comfortable there too. All his anxieties disappeared, and a six-month follow-up showed no signs of recurrence. These same investigators reported similar results for Mr. R. who used *karate exercises* to inhibit his anxieties.

Transcendental meditation can also be used to cope with stress. In a popular book, Benson (1975) argues that meditation leads to "the relaxation response" and teaches his clients to meditate once or twice each day for 15 or 20 minutes. There is a theory that meditating somehow "inoculates" the person against tension. Whether this actually occurs or not is unclear, for the research evidence is conflicting. Marlatt and Marques (1977) found that meditating did lead to less alcohol drinking, perhaps because of relaxation, but Wedding (1976) found no "inoculation" effect of meditation. It seems likely that meditation used at the actual time when a fear-producing or tension-producing situation occurs is most likely to lead to relaxation. Meditating is not so much an inoculation against tension as a way of coping with stress by interfering early in a chain of events that usually leads to tension.

Boudreau (1972, pp. 97–98) reported the case of a college student who "expressed fears of enclosed places, elevators, being alone, and examinations. His avoidance behavior to these situations was extreme, having started when he was 13. The physiological sensations he experienced gave him the additional fear of mental illness." The man, who was adept at transcendental meditation, was instructed to practice meditation after imagining some fear-inducing scenes for half an hour every day and *also at the actual appearance of fear-evoking situations.* "Marked improvement followed," says Boudreau. "Within one month, the avoidance behavior to enclosed places, being alone, and elevators had all disappeared. Once his tension level had decreased, he did not experience abnormal physiological sensations, and this reassured him as to his physical and mental state."

People who are often tense or whose nervousness seems to occur in a number of situations may find that meditating at the beginning of the day and again at midday, for ten minutes or more, will relax them, so that chains of nervousness don't get started.

Summary

You can reduce fears and anxieties by (1) identifying carefully the situations in which you are uncomfortable, (2) choosing a behavior that is incompatible with anxiety, and (3) practicing the behavior in the situation that produces anxiety. Several behaviors that are incompatible with anxiety have been studied and used to eliminate anxiety. They include record keeping, sexual arousal, martial-arts exercises, meditation, and intellectual analysis. The most reliable incompatible behavior, however, is systematic relaxation, to be discussed next.

RELAXATION

Relaxation is of particular interest because it is a reliable, easily learned behavior that can be used to cope with a wide variety of problem situations. According to the dictionary, relaxation is "the casting off of nervous tension

---

BOX 6-2
How to Meditate

There are several ways to meditate. Here's one.

Sit in a comfortable chair in a quiet room away from noise and interruptions. Pay no attention to the world outside your body. It is easiest to do this if you have something to focus on in your mind. For example, concentrate on your breathing or use a mantra, a word you say softly over and over to yourself. Here are three different mantras: *mahing, shiam,* and *wen.* Choose one. Don't say the mantra out loud, but think it, silently and gently.

When you first sit down and begin to relax, you will notice thoughts coming into your mind. After a minute or two, begin to say the mantra in your mind. Do this slowly, in a passive way. As you say the mantra to yourself, other thoughts will come into your mind. As a matter of fact, after a while you may realize that you've been so busy with these thoughts that you haven't said your mantra in several minutes. When you become aware of this, just return gently to the mantra. Don't fight to keep thoughts out of your mind; instead, let them drift through. This is not a time for working out solutions to problems or thinking things over. Try to keep your mind open, so that, as thoughts other than the mantra drift in, they drift out again, smoothly as the flowing of a river. The mantra will return, and you will relax with it.

It is important to make this a gentle process, a relaxing time. Don't fight to keep thoughts out of your mind. Don't get upset if you are distracted. Merely let the mantra return.

It is best to meditate in preparation for activity—for example, before you go to work—rather than after you are already tensed up. If used as soon as you begin to be tense, it is a good coping reaction. For example, one man meditates for ten minutes as soon as he wakes up, for he begins to grow tense quickly, and then repeats as necessary throughout the day.

People often nod off to sleep while meditating. Don't try to use meditation as a substitute for sleep. If you do go to sleep, usually you will find that five minutes of meditation afterwards will make you quite awake. Some people notice that meditating makes them feel very awake—so much so that, if they meditate before bedtime, they can't get to sleep.

Adapted from *Psychology: What It Is, How to Use It,* by David L. Watson. Copyright © 1978 by Harper & Row Publishers, Inc. Reprinted by permission.

and anxiety." It is both a mental and a physical response—a feeling of calmness and serenity and a state of muscular release and passivity.

Relaxation can be induced in many ways—among them, meditation, which we have already discussed, and yoga. Many psychologists teach their clients these techniques as well as others. The method used is not important (Barrios & Shigetomi, 1979; Lewis, Biglan, & Steinbock, 1978; Miller & Bornstein, 1977); the relaxation is. A reliable method for learning to relax is to use deep muscular relaxation. As you read this sentence, try relaxing your hand and arm or your jaw muscles. If you can do so, you will quickly realize how much energy you tie up in excess muscular tension. You can also experience subtle mental changes as your muscles "cast off their tensions" (Evans, 1976).

In this chapter we present a particular way of inducing deep muscle relaxation called the *tension-release* method. It is a method that has been carefully studied in self-directed strategies. You can easily learn it by yourself and employ it quickly in real-life situations. If you are already adept at some other technique for inducing relaxation, there is no reason for not using your own. Any form of relaxation will do, as long as you can produce it quickly, thoroughly, and at your own instructions.

Don't use alcohol, drugs, tobacco, or any other substance to achieve relaxation. If you do, you won't learn the independent self-direction of relaxation you need to overcome real-life anxieties. We have known students who required almost no practice to achieve relaxation. Once they understood the principle of telling themselves to "relax," they were able to do so almost immediately. If you can already do that, you may not need this next section. But we do advise that you go through the tension-release exercises to check your own ability. And, if you do need to learn, you will find the process very pleasant.

Once you have learned relaxation, you will use it to replace anxiety responses in situations in which you are now uncomfortable or that you now avoid. Later, we will discuss how you can gradually achieve this goal by using shaping, modeling, and other methods to develop the skill. The basic idea is to learn to produce relaxation *at the first sign of tension*. That is the reason for the tension-release method, which calls for *tensing* muscles and then *releasing* them. You will learn to recognize the signs of tension, so that, when you feel them later in real-life situations, you can quickly produce the release that is relaxation. In this way, you can use the first signs of tension (for example, while taking tests or talking to strangers) as the cue to relax and interrupt the tension process early in its sequence. This method of recognizing tension and producing relaxation is a very effective strategy for coping with any form of anxiety (Goldfried, 1971, 1977; Goldfried & Trier, 1974; Snyder & Deffenbacher, 1977).

How to Use the Relaxation Instructions

The tension-release instructions (Box 6-3) are like a set of exercises, one for each group of muscles. The final goal is to relax all groups simultaneously

---

BOX 6-3
Relaxation Instructions

Muscle groups	Tension exercises
1. the dominant hand 2. the other hand	make a tight fist
3. the dominant arm 4. the other arm	curl your arm up; tighten the bicep
5. upper face and scalp	raise eyebrows as high as possible
6. center face	squint eyes and wrinkle nose
7. lower face	smile in a false, exaggerated way; clench teeth
8. neck	a. pull head slightly forward, then relax b. pull head slightly back, then relax
9. chest and shoulders	a. pull shoulders back till the blades almost touch, then relax b. pull shoulders forward all the way, then relax
10. abdomen	make abdomen tight and hard
11. buttocks	tighten together
12. upper right leg 13. upper left leg	stretch leg out from you, tensing both upper and lower muscles
14. lower right leg 15. lower left leg	pull toes up toward you
16. right foot 17. left foot	curl toes down and away from you

(Box 6-3 continues)

---

to achieve total body relaxation. But each muscle group can be relaxed separately. Relaxation, like many complex goals, cannot be achieved all at once, so you should follow a gradual procedure in learning it. First, you learn to relax your arms; then your facial area, neck, shoulders, and upper back; then your chest, stomach, and lower back; then your hips, thighs, and calves; and finally your whole body.

The general idea is to first tense a set of muscles and then relax them, so that they will relax more deeply than before they were tensed. You should focus your attention on each muscle system as you work through the various muscle groups. This will give you a good sense of what each set feels like

BOX 6-3 (continued)

First for each muscle group	*Then for the whole body*
Tense the muscles and hold for 5 seconds.	Now tense all the muscles together and hold for 5 seconds.
Feel the tension. Notice it carefully.	Feel the tension, notice it carefully, then release. Let all tension slide away.
Now release. Let the tension slide away, all away.	
	Notice any remaining tension. Release it.
Feel the difference.	Take a deep breath. Say softly to yourself "relax," as you breathe out slowly.
Notice the pleasant warmth of relaxation.	
Now repeat the sequences with the same group.	Remain totally relaxed.
Repeat again. Do the sequence three times for each group of muscles.	Repeat breathing in and then out slowly, saying "relax," staying perfectly relaxed.
Tense. Release. Learn the difference. Feel the warmth of relaxation.	Do this three times.
	The exercise has ended. Enjoy the relaxation.

In your daily life,
in many situations
Notice your body's tension.
Identify the tense muscle groups.
Say softly to yourself "relax."
Relax the tense group.
Feel the relaxation and enjoy it.

Adapted from *Insight vs. Desensitization in Psychotherapy*, by G. L. Paul. Copyright 1966 by Stanford University Press. Reprinted by permission.

when it is well relaxed and when it is tense. The exercises may require 20 to 30 minutes at first; but, as you learn, you will need less and less time.

The process for achieving deep relaxation is as follows: Choose a private place, quiet and free of interruptions and distracting stimuli. Sit comfortably, well supported by the chair, so that you don't have to use your muscles to support yourself. You may want to close your eyes. Some people prefer to lie down while practicing. You may find it especially pleasant to practice before going to sleep.

As you can see from the instructions in Box 6-3, the basic procedure for each muscle group is the same: *tense* the muscle, *release* the muscle, and *feel* the relaxation. This process can be easily memorized. You may also want to memorize the specific muscle groups and the exercises for each; for example, the hands are exercised by making a fist and the forehead by raising the eyebrows. Memorizing is useful because, in the early stages of practice, holding the book up to read the instructions interferes with the exercises.

For this same reason, some people make a tape recording of the instructions, so that they can rest quietly, listening to the instructions and following them. You can do the tape recording yourself, by slowly and clearly reading the instructions into an inexpensive cassette recorder. If you don't like the recorded sound of your own voice, ask someone to do it for you. But choose your "instructor" with care. Be sure that his or her voice is soothing and relaxing to you. If, for any reason, the voice makes you tense, it will interfere with learning. Should this happen, find another, more suitable voice.

A recording is not necessary, though, and is useful only in the earliest stages of learning. Very soon, you will want to know the instructions by heart, so that you can relax whenever you want, quickly and at any time or place. Whether you are using the written or the recorded instructions, you should stop using them as soon as you can remember the process.

The goal is to produce relaxation at your own self-instructions. At the first sign of tension in real situations, tell yourself to relax. This is the reason for the final exercise—saying "relax" slowly and softly as you breathe out while totally relaxed. You can then transfer this self-instruction into your natural environment. Whether it is a crucial tennis match, a quarrel with a neighbor, or a final exam, you will be able to breathe the word "relax" and produce relaxation instead of anxiety.

How to Practice Relaxation

As soon as you have practiced enough to tense and relax some muscle groups, it's time to begin the exercises in other situations. You can practice tension release of some muscle groups while driving, riding the bus, attending lectures or concerts, sunbathing at the beach, sitting at your desk, or washing dishes. Relax whatever muscles are not needed for the activity you are engaged in at the moment. Choose a wide variety of situations. It is best not to begin with a situation that represents a particular problem for you.

It's not necessary to use all muscle groups during this practice. Exercise those groups that you've learned to control in your private sessions. If you detect tension in one group—your face or your thighs, for example—practice relaxing that group.

This phase of practice has three purposes. First, you learn to detect specific tensions. You will discover that you are prone to tension in particular muscle groups. For some people it's the shoulders and neck that tense up most often; for others, the arms or the face. Relaxing these specific groups will decrease your overall tension.

Second, you learn to regulate the *depth* of relaxation. Whereas it is crucial to learn total, deep muscle relaxation—even to the point of physical limpness—it is not necessary or desirable to use this full response to combat all tensions. Relaxation is a physical skill, just as weight lifting is. The strong man does not use his full strength to hold eggs, although he has it available for moving pianos. As we will discuss shortly, you can use *deep* relaxation as a response incompatible with anxiety in specific situations that you find problematic. But *graduated* relaxation is a general self-directed tactic, useful in many circumstances.

For example, one of us uses the "relax" self-instruction between points in tournament handball to produce more suppleness and control of the muscles of the upper body. One of our students, Valerie Lloyd, conducted a study in which relaxation was used to combat muscle cramping while rock climbing. She found it effective for both beginners and expert climbers. Although she conducted the study while the climbers were simply standing on the edge of a step, the skills transferred and were effective on the sheer face of rock cliffs (Lloyd, 1976). Total, limp relaxation is not what you want in situations of this kind. But the graduated relaxation of certain muscle groups is a highly valuable skill, and you can begin to learn it by practicing both shallow and deep relaxation.

The third purpose of this phase of practice is to learn to relax in as many situations as possible. Even if you may set out to combat a specific anxiety in a specific situation, the odds are high that you will find additional situations in which relaxation is useful (Goldfried, 1971; Zemore, 1975; Goldfried & Goldfried, 1977). Sherman and Plummer (1973) trained 21 students in relaxation as a general self-direction skill. All but one reported at least one way in which they had benefited from the training; the average was 2.1 per person. The most common situations in which they used relaxation were social situations, sleep problems, test anxiety, handling of interviews, and efforts to increase energy and alertness. Sherman (1975) reported that, two years after training, the students still used the strategy.

Practicing relaxation in many situations, even in your early stages of learning, will prepare you to use it as a general skill for self-direction.

If your goal is total, deep muscle relaxation, you should continue to develop the basic skills in private sessions. You will be fully skilled when you can totally relax without using the tension technique. Tensing the muscles before relaxing them is only a training method, and it should be dropped as soon as you can relax without it. Then, just saying "relax" to yourself or simply deciding to relax will produce the relaxation at the depth you want.

Using Relaxation as an Incompatible Response

In this section we discuss how to use relaxation, as you would any other incompatible response, in order to achieve a specific goal.

Weil and Goldfried (1973) report a simple illustration. The person they were counseling was an 11-year-old girl who suffered from insomnia. She became tense when she tried to go to sleep and spent the night tossing and turning. The girl was given recorded relaxation instructions to use at bedtime. She practiced until she had learned to relax deeply; then she stopped using the recording and placed herself into deep relaxation without the instructions. With several weeks of self-administered relaxation, she eliminated the insomnia.

The case of Susan in Box 6-3 is a good example of the use of relaxation as a response incompatible with test anxiety. Susan followed exactly the same procedures we have suggested for you, except that she had some assistance from her counselors in the initial stages of her relaxation training. But, basically, her counselors gave her the advice we are giving you. Susan's success is by no means unique. Research has indicated that her "cue-controlled relaxation" is particularly helpful to test-anxious students (Russell, Miller, & June, 1975).

As a general rule, you should use relaxation just before the time you expect your anxiety to begin—just before the plane takes off; while you are waiting to walk to the front of the room to give your talk; during the earliest

---

BOX 6-4
Learning to Relax

Susan, an 18-year-old freshman, was extremely nervous while taking tests. She studied long and effectively but made only Ds and Es on examinations, even though she could answer the questions after the exam was over. She came from a small rural high school, where the teachers overlooked her poor exam performances, because she was one of their brightest students and excelled in projects and reports. In the large university she lost this personal understanding and support.

Susan's counselor first gave her some brief paper-and-pencil tests to measure her anxiety and also three subtests of a well-known IQ measure. She then had four training sessions, one per week, to learn how to relax. The method she followed was the same one you are learning in this book. She first practiced at home and then extended her practice into real-life situations in which she was reasonably comfortable. After her fifth session, she had to take a number of course examinations. Using her cue word "calm" (like our "relax"), she relaxed during the examinations and performed remarkably well. Before her relaxation training, her average test score was 1.0 (on a 4-point system). After relaxing, her scores averaged 3.5. She completed the term with a 2.88 grade point average.

Her counselor then gave her again the anxiety and IQ tests he had given her before relaxation training. When compared to her first scores, the tests indicated that her specific examination anxieties were reduced and that her general level of tension was also lower. She even improved on two of the IQ measures. Obviously, relaxation cannot improve "intelligence," but replacing anxiety with relaxation allowed Susan to perform closer to her real potential.

Adapted from "Treatment of Test Anxiety by Cue-Controlled Relaxation," by R. K. Russell and J. F. Sipich, *Behavior Therapy*, 1974, 5, 673–676. Copyright © 1974 by Academic Press, Inc. Reprinted by permission of the authors and Academic Press.

stages of sexual foreplay; immediately before you go in for an interview or an exam; or while you sit in the dentist's waiting room.

You may be thinking right now "But I can't always predict exactly when tension will begin." Right! And this is why you must learn the tension phase of the relaxation program. You will then be able to recognize the beginning stages of tension and use that information as the cue to relax. And, of course, you will be able to use the word "relax" to cue yourself whenever you feel anxiety mounting.

Relaxation has been used to interfere with many problem behaviors, such as insomnia (Nicassio & Bootzin, 1974), and even to reduce pain (Levendusky & Pankratz, 1975). Ernst (1973) reports a case in which relaxation was used to stop "self-mutilation"—more specifically, the case of a woman who repeatedly bit the insides of her lips and mouth, causing tissue damage and pain. She learned deep muscle relaxation during a baseline period in which she recorded with a golf counter the frequency of her self-biting. Then she began to relax, using the golf-counter click as the cue. She paid particular attention to relaxing the muscles of the jaw and lower face. As Figure 6-3 indicates, she almost totally stopped her self-mutilating behavior.

One of our students reported: "I want to reduce spacing out in class, that is, I want to increase the number of times my attention is on what the lecturer is saying. My mind wanders to all sorts of things, such as feelings I've been having about people or escape fantasies—you know, like backpacking or

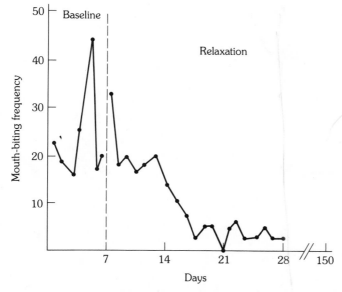

Figure 6-3.   Daily self-recorded mouth-biting frequencies. (From "Self-Recording and Counterconditioning of a Self-Mutilative Compulsion," by F. A. Ernst, *Behavior Therapy*, 1973, 4, 144–146. Copyright 1973 by Academic Press, Inc. Reprinted by permission.)

getting 20 acres of land and living on it with my friends. Another way I have of not being there is one I learned in grammar school, where I felt the teachers were powering me around. I'd find something ridiculous in what they said and laugh to myself about it or tell the person next to me. My plan is to use deep muscle relaxation to feel easy, instead of using my old tricks. That way my mind will wander less. I'll come in to the lecture hall five minutes early, relax good, and try to listen to what's going on." This student's plan was very successful, as demonstrated by Figure 6-4.

You may notice that both the spaced-out student and the mouth-biting woman used two forms of behavior incompatible with their problem behavior—self-recording and relaxation—which may account for their success.

Combining New Self-Instructions with Relaxation

John is getting ready to take a final exam and, as usual, is getting very nervous. His palms are sweaty, his muscles are tense, his stomach is sour. Also, he is worrying: "Suppose I fail? Suppose I can't remember anything? Suppose I panic?" Theorists differ on what is causing what here: is it the thoughts that lead to the anxiety, or is it the anxiety that leads to the thoughts, or is it both, in a vicious circle? What is clear is that John needs to get rid of both reactions. He needs to relax, and he needs to eliminate those self-defeating thoughts (Goldfried, 1977).

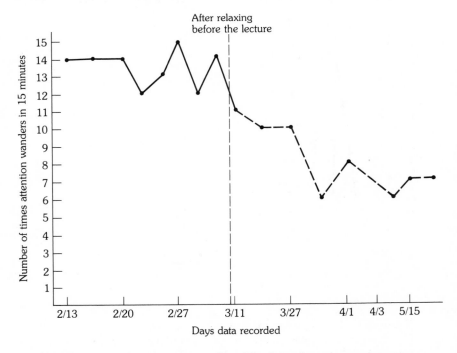

Figure 6-4. Paying attention in class: Number of times attention wandered.

John begins a two-sided self-change project, in which he practices relaxation before taking tests and stops his self-defeating thoughts, following the procedure suggested in Chapter 5. Ten minutes before an important test finds John telling himself to relax, using tension-release exercises, thought-stopping his panicky thoughts, and reminding himself that he is adequately prepared for the test.

This two-sided effort will be necessary whenever your anxiety is accompanied by thoughts that support the tension. Besides test anxiety, two other common situations are speech anxiety and social anxiety. Before giving a speech, you may be physically tense and at the same time thinking "I won't do it right." Both the tension and the thought need to be dealt with.

If you only stopped the tension, for example, but continued the self-defeating thinking, the tension would be back. If you got rid of the thoughts but let the tension continue, the tension might lead to more self-defeating thoughts.

Relaxation and the Method of Approximations

Often relaxation techniques require the use of approximations—a strategy very similar to shaping. Remember, shaping is changing or increasing a behavior gradually, step by step. With relaxation, too, you may need to use this technique; that is, you may need to gradually increase your mastery of a behavior-in-a-situation.

For example, some of our students have been unable to move directly into exams and relax, as Susan in the above example did. So they have used graduated steps, such as going into the examination room two or three days before the test and practicing relaxation in the empty hall.

In designing your plan, you may want to use a detailed schedule of steps. The following case may be helpful.

Linda, a college senior, wrote: "I am really very afraid of birds, under almost any conditions. This sometimes makes me look like a fool—for example, I won't go to the zoo because there are so many birds around, loose as well as in cages—and often causes me unnecessary fear and trepidation. My life would be more pleasant with fewer fears!"

Here is Linda's hierarchy:

A. When *one or two birds* are 15 yards away:
   1. Turn and face the birds.
   2. Take one step toward the birds.
   3. Take two steps toward the birds.
   4. Continue until I have walked a total of 5 yards toward the birds.
   5. Begin step B.
B. When *more than two birds* are 15 yards away:
   1. Turn and face the birds.
   2. Take two steps toward them.
   3. Take four steps toward them.
   4. Continue until I have walked a total of 5 yards toward the birds.

She then repeated the procedures, beginning at a 10-yard distance, first from a single bird and then from a group of birds. Next, she repeated the procedure, beginning at 5 yards. In the last stages, she would begin at 3 yards from the birds and move to within 3 feet of them, then gradually increase the amount of time, in seconds, that she spent close to them.

At first, Linda had difficulty, but she reported that, by getting her boyfriend to hold her hand, her anxiety was considerably lessened. This worked well until, perhaps out of boredom, the boyfriend gave her a "playful push" and she found herself frighteningly close to the birds, which set her back about three weeks. (It also set their romance back a bit.)

Using friends, as Linda did, is a good idea (Moss & Arend, 1977). Be sure to tell them not to give you a playful push. Having a friend around when you are coping with nervousness in a social situation would be particularly appropriate, so long as the helper is serious in his or her desire to be helpful.

Summary

Incompatible behaviors prevent the occurrence of undesired ones. Whenever you want to get rid of an undesired behavior, choose an alternative behavior for that same situation. When emotional reactions are the problem, relaxation is a useful incompatible response.

At the beginning, relaxation should be practiced privately, then quickly employed in many real-life situations. As soon as relaxation is a well-developed skill, it should be practiced in those situations that produce anxiety. Ideally, relaxation should be practiced immediately before the time when anxiety usually begins. You may need to combine relaxation with positive self-instructions, and you may need to develop relaxation through shaping.

DEVELOPING NEW BEHAVIORS THROUGH PRACTICE

Simply rehearsing a behavior, over and over, in the situations in which you want it to occur is the fundamental way of mastering that behavior. All the other methods that this book teaches are merely ways of making that rehearsal more likely to take place. Practice does make perfect. In order to get the practice, however, you often need to analyze sequences, shape carefully, reinforce, and so on, because you must discard old behaviors and feelings before you can rehearse the new ones. But you shouldn't forget that actually performing the behaviors—that is, rehearsing them—is the final technique for attaining the goal. You will know that the new behavior has become a habit when you don't need any special techniques to keep it occurring.

It is likely that you will have some difficulty arranging actual rehearsals. You can't practice relaxing in the presence of snakes, because (fortunately) snakes are not always around. You may not be able to practice overcoming test anxiety, simply because there may be no examinations for several weeks. An even more important problem may be that you cannot arrange small enough real-life steps for practicing relaxation. And, without these preparatory steps, the final steps may overwhelm your attempts to relax when you are dealing with the old anxieties.

Imagined rehearsal may solve these problems.

Imagined Rehearsal

Rehearsing behavior in imagination is called *imagined* (or *covert*) rehearsal. There is convincing evidence that imagined rehearsal can improve many physical skills—for example, shooting free throws in basketball (Richardson, 1967). In behavior analysis, behavior therapy, and self-directed behavior change, there is good reason to think that many techniques rely on imagined rehearsal for their effects.

Research evidence points to the fact that, in reaching your goals, actual events and actual behaviors are much more effective than imagined ones. Therefore, actual practice and performance are the final strategies. However, since imagined events and behaviors can influence actual behavior, using imagined events has many advantages. Imagined events and behaviors can be practiced quickly and easily. Most important, they can be controlled: imagined pigeons are less likely to fly suddenly toward you than real ones.

For that reason, imagined rehearsal can be used to provide *extra* rehearsals, to provide *preliminary* rehearsals, and to provide rehearsals that *emphasize* certain features of a behavior or situation. Thus, imagined rehearsal can often speed up your journey toward your goal. It is a form of visual self-instruction. For example, in 1976 the U.S. Olympic ski team, before making difficult downhill runs, would rehearse the entire run in their imagination, thinking of each bump and turn and how they would cope with it. They turned in better runs than they had before, and the United States got some surprising medals (Suinn, 1976).

BOX 6-5
Classical Practice

Whatever you would make habitual, practice it.
EPICTETUS (c. 50–c.138)

Practice is everything.
PERIANDER (d. 585 B.C.)

For the things we have to learn before we can do them,
we learn by doing them.
ARISTOTLE (384–322 B.C.)

Practice is the best of all instructors.
PUBLILIUS SYRUS (1st century B.C.)

Practice makes perfect.
ANONYMOUS

To use imaginary practice, try to imagine your behavior and the situation in complete, minute detail. For example, if you imagine an introduction to a stranger, you should think about the way the imaginary person looks, the expression on his or her face, what he or she says, how you react, and all the other details of the physical situation. You may have to imagine the situation in its component parts in order to concentrate separately on imagined sounds, textures, and other elements.

It is important that you attain a vivid picture. It doesn't have to be as clear as if you were watching a movie, but it should be as clear as a very vivid memory. Sometimes your imaginary scenes become more vivid with practice. A good way to check the vividness of these imagined behaviors-in-situations is to compare it with that of some scene you recreate in your imagination, a scene you know and can visualize very well—for example, what it looks, feels, smells, and sounds like to be lying on your bed in your room. First, visualize the scene of your room. Then compare the visualized behavior-in-a-situation with the scene of your room. The two should be nearly equally vivid.

You can increase your success with imaginal methods by making your images more vivid (Wisocki, 1973; Paul, 1966). Also, you should be able to start and stop an image at will.

Imagined Rehearsal and Relaxation

One of the best uses of imagined rehearsal is in the practice of relaxation. In this technique, you imagine yourself remaining calm and relaxed in different situations. But you carry out the imagined rehearsal while being actually in a state of deep muscle relaxation.

Earlier we pointed out that you may find it necessary to approach feared situations gradually, maintaining your state of calm relaxation. Suppose that you become tense when you take tests. You know, of course, that there are different kinds of tests, some worse than others, ranging from unimportant simple quizzes to make-you-or-break-you final exams. In a case like this, you might write down behaviors-in-situations in hierarchical order. For example,

> taking a test that doesn't count for very much
> taking a test when I am not prepared
> taking a surprise test
> taking a test when the professor watches me all the time
> taking a midterm exam
> taking a test that determines my grade in the course

It would be most unusual if these situations happened to come along in exactly that order. In imagination, though, you can rehearse them in any order and as many times as you wish.

Liza, one of our students, used the list above with imagined rehearsal plus relaxation. Since her courses had only midterms and finals, she wanted to prepare in advance for those situations and to proceed gradually. After learning deep muscle relaxation, she lay on her couch with a pillow, just as she had done when practicing relaxation. While deeply relaxed, Liza imagined the first item in the list—taking a minor test—while being just as relaxed as she was at that moment. She held that scene for a minute or two, imagining all sorts of details—feeling the hardness of the desk at which she sat, putting the pencil in her mouth while thinking of an answer, going back over each answer—and all the while remaining perfectly calm. Then she cleared her mind, checked herself for any signs of tension, relaxed again, and went on to the next item. She tried to do one of these sessions each day.

Liza spent about 10 to 15 minutes on the exercise, although the length of time varied with her mood and ability to deeply relax. In general, she went down her list in order—from least to most difficult. But she moved around some, too, occasionally trying to begin with a difficult situation. If she couldn't visualize it and stay calm, she relaxed again and moved back to an easier level.

About five weeks into the semester, Liza learned that she would have to take a quiz, entirely unannounced, in her geology section. She was so surprised that she nearly panicked; but she was able to induce relaxation by going through a rather hasty tension-release exercise. She relaxed enough to do well on the quiz, although she barely finished in time.

This incident illustrates the only error Liza made in her plan. During the same weeks in which she was using covert rehearsal, she should have been practicing the relaxation response in many outside situations. Then she would have been better prepared to relax in the geology lecture hall.

The pop quiz motivated her to continue the imagined rehearsal. By the time midterm exams arrived, Liza had been able to imagine being relaxed throughout her entire hierarchy and had used relaxation several times in her actual lecture halls. Both steps were probably important. Imaginary rehearsal with relaxation gave her some practice in situations before they came up. Actual rehearsal of relaxation in various physical surroundings gave her practice in the situations in which she would later face the tension-producing tests.

The technique of imagined practice with relaxation is similar to the clinical technique of desensitization (Paul, 1966). In the latter it has been traditional to work out carefully graded hierarchies, going from the least fear-producing to the most and exposing the client to each one in turn, increasing the fearfulness of the situation as the client learns to imagine being in the situation while remaining relaxed. In self-controlled relaxation training, this hierarchical approach is probably not necessary (Goldfried & Goldfried, 1977). Just exposing yourself to a tension-producing situation will slightly reduce your tension in it (Goldfried & Goldfried, 1977; Greist et al., 1980). But you will achieve better results if you can relax in the situation. Thus, imagining yourself in tension-producing situations and becoming relaxed is a good way to get ready to cope with those situations.

Summary

Rehearsing a behavior, over and over, in the actual situation is the best way of mastering that behavior. When rehearsals are difficult to arrange in real life, imagined rehearsal may be used in the initial stages. Imagined rehearsals must be vivid and include both situation and behavior. When imagining behaviors in feared situations, use relaxation. But imagined rehearsal is only a prelude, a bridge to actual rehearsal in real-life situations. Your ultimate plan must include actual performance in actual situations.

DEVELOPING NEW BEHAVIORS THROUGH MODELING

Observation of others who have skills you lack and want to develop can be useful in all learning situations. Learning through observation of models seems to be one of the basic processes by which learning occurs—for the infant as well as for the old person.

If you find someone who has the very skills you want, don't hesitate to try straight imitation. None of us mind using imitation when we are learning tennis or driving, but we are often embarrassed to think of imitating others' social or personal behaviors. As we counseled our student who watched how his friend dealt with women, "If you decide to smile when you meet someone, as he does, you will be smiling your own smile, not his. You will be answering with your own comments, not his. You will do everything in your own style. You'll be yourself, but yourself smiling and answering."

Imagined Modeling

In using imagined rehearsal, some people have difficulty imagining themselves doing acts they cannot perform in real life. For instance, imagining that you are sending your overcooked steak back may seem so unrealistic that you lose the scene or you end up imagining instead yourself eating the steak anyway. If this happens, you might use the technique of imagined modeling. This process is similar to imagined rehearsal, except that you imagine someone else, instead of yourself, performing the behavior, being reinforced for it, and so forth. In general, this technique has been found effective (Cautela, 1976; Kazdin, 1974a, b, c, d).

When you use others as imagined models, you don't have to use real persons who are known to you, although you may do so. Here are some recommended procedures for imagined modeling.

1. Imagine a model who is similar to you in age and sex (Kazdin, 1974b).
2. Imagine different models in each situation, rather than one person only (Kazdin, 1974d, 1976b).
3. Imagine a model who begins with the same difficulties you have—one who must cope with the problem rather than one who has already mastered the problem (Meichenbaum, 1971; Kazdin, 1973a). In other words, your model should also be afraid of the pigeons, although he or she successfully approaches them; your model is also tempted by fattening food; and he or she has to muster up some courage to send the steak back.

4. Imagine your model being reinforced for successful coping, preferably with desired natural outcomes (Kazdin, 1974d, 1975b, 1976a, 1976b).

Imagined modeling can be used as a first step in preparing yourself for imagined rehearsal. But increase the degree of *your* imagined performance, not that of someone else. If you imagine only others as models, the technique is not likely to be effective (Gallagher & Arkowitz, 1978). There is no need to use imagined modeling if you are able to effectively use rehearsal, either actual or imagined. If you can successfully imagine yourself rehearsing behaviors, it is probably better to use yourself as your own "model."

MASTERY IN THE REAL WORLD

We cannot emphasize too much that, no matter how valuable all the imagined techniques are, they are only bridges to performance in the real world. Imagined rehearsal and all its supporting tactics can help you prepare for real-life situations. *But you must rehearse your developing behaviors in the actual situations in which you want them to occur.* Therefore, no plan is complete without tactics for transferring your behavior from imagined rehearsal into real life.

For example, Gershman and Stedman (1971) had one of their clients use karate exercises as the incompatible behavior for anxiety about his flying lessons. He constructed a hierarchy of such items as "gaining altitude," "saying to myself 'How high *am* I?'" "passing over tree tops too low," and so on. He went through the various items while vigorously engaged in his karate exercises, until he was able to consider them without anxiety. Then he began to transfer the plan into real life. He rehearsed before going to the flying field and, again, in the men's room before reporting to his instructor. He developed confidence and eventually became able to fly without anxiety.

Whether you have used imagined relaxation rehearsal for dieting or being assertive, for test anxiety or fear of birds, the next step is planning to transfer these behaviors into real life, according to the principles discussed earlier in this chapter. You may wish to review the sections on shaping and incompatible responses, which describe those strategies. Often we do need to begin in imagination, but the real-life situation is far more effective as a learning arena than its imagined substitute (Sherman, 1972; Flannery, 1972; Goldstein & Kanfer, 1979). It is certainly reasonable to believe that when one learns new responses, even from models, it is the rehearsal in the actual situation that brings about long-lasting change (Bandura, Jeffery, & Gajdos, 1975; Blanchard, 1970; Thase & Moss, 1976).

YOUR OWN SELF-DIRECTION PROJECT: STEP SIX

You should now be able to draw up another version of your plan for self-directed change, taking into account the methods for developing new behaviors that we have just discussed. Consider your own goals and write plans for using each of the four methods for developing new behaviors that we have discussed—shaping, incompatible behaviors, rehearsal, and modeling. Later, you will want to choose the most effective total package, but for now you should specify ways in which you might use each of the methods.

Don't implement the plan yet. The next chapter discusses methods of self-direction through control of consequences. Your final plan will include elements of antecedent control as well as elements of consequence control.

TIPS FOR TYPICAL TOPICS

Overeating, Smoking, Drinking, and Drug Use.   There has been a great deal of controversy on the best way to stop smoking, especially on whether it is better to quit cold turkey or to cut down gradually (Bernard & Efran, 1972; Flaxman, 1978). A recent review of the research literature (Pechacek & Danaher, 1979), however, concludes that the best way is a fairly rapid cessation. Abrupt quitting should be delayed for two weeks or so (Flaxman, 1978), until self-directional skills have been organized and practiced. You can, for example, set a date two weeks away, and use the period for conducting self-observation, designing the plan, thinking how you will cope with urges to smoke, and practicing your plan.

This is a good principle to follow with dieting as well. Choose a moderate level of calories, and for two weeks or so practice the general skills of self-control. Then, fairly rapidly, cut the calorie level to your actual goal.

For all consummatory behaviors, the development of alternative responses is crucial. In weight control, there is an assortment of new behaviors that you can resort to. Definitely increase exercising. It is easier to lose weight if you do so, and you are more likely to keep it off (Leon, 1979; Cohen, Gelfand, Dodd, Jensen, & Turner, 1980). Learn to substitute less caloric foods; for example, eat fruit instead of dessert, or drink water instead of soft drinks or beer. Learn alternative things you can do instead of eating, as you react to many different situations. Find alternative things to do at times when you could be tempted to overeat.

Relaxation is an extremely valuable alternative behavior. Tension or anxiety often leads to overconsumption—of food, alcohol, tobacco, or dope. Include relaxation in your plan; learn to relax, and apply relaxation at the first cue that you are tense. Apply it automatically at the first sign of your craving.

Assertion.   You need not wait to practice new assertive skills until real opportunities occur. Research results encourage the use of imagined rehearsal as a first stage in developing assertive behavior. When imagining the scenes, use relaxation as a prelude (Shelton, 1979); also, use multiple models (Kazdin, 1976b); and be sure to imagine the full scene, including a favorable outcome (Kazdin, 1976b).

Specific Fears.   Expect to use the full range of suggestions offered in this chapter. Develop a plan that includes (1) practicing an incompatible behavior and probably relaxation; (2) gradually approaching the feared situation, first in (3) imagined rehearsal, then in (4) the actual situation. Your plan for change should rely heavily on this chapter.

The Other Sex.   If social anxiety prevents you from making friends, develop a full plan as discussed for specific anxieties. Relaxation is the incompatible behavior to choose. There are two stages in developing new behaviors that are smooth and pleasing to others: selecting the behaviors and rehearsing them. If you don't know what to do, ask someone who is successful, or watch carefully. If these behaviors seem alien or difficult, use imagined rehearsal with relaxation as a preliminary stage.

Family, Friends, Lovers, and Coworkers.   The crucial task in improving strained relationships is selecting the specific behavior that will produce the long-range goal. Gottman and his coworkers (Gottman, Notarius, Gonso, & Markman, 1976) found that married people are ruder to each other than they are to complete strangers. Gottman's group set up rules for coping with quarrelsome relationships with others: be polite; really listen to the other, without assuming that you know what she or he will say; be willing to compromise; express your feelings and expect the other to do the same.

Any or all of these rules would make excellent goals for improving strained relationships.

Depression.   The new behaviors needed to combat depression are those that lead to pleasant activities. Your plan should be aimed at increasing pleasant activities drastically. Do not overlook small pleasures. Fuchs and Rehm (1977), who have developed a very effective self-control program for depression, encourage depressed people to set three subgoal activities for each major goal and to make those activities personally pleasant, no matter how modest they are—calling a friend for a chat or going to the library to get a book. Our students have used an enormous range of activities: engaging in the "good dream" (see Box 6-1), embroidering or sewing (see "Unlinking the Chain of Events" in Chapter 5), reading travel folders, cactus-gardening, or browsing in the gourmet section of the market.

Studying and Time Management.   Three specific new behaviors should be developed for studying more effectively: (1) Make *written outlines* or summaries to organize the material; (2) *rehearse* these outlines or summaries by repeating them aloud (without looking at your notes); (3) *practice for tests* by asking yourself questions and answering them (Robinson, 1970). What you do within a scheduled block of study time does make a difference.

For other scheduled blocks (housecleaning, cooking, writing letters, or doing volunteer work) you may know well enough how to perform the behavior. For your self-change goal, the issue is actually sticking to the schedule. Thus, motivation is crucial, and the next chapter will address that problem.

CHAPTER 7

Consequences

GOAL:
To teach how to use reinforcement to encourage desired behaviors.

OUTLINE:
Discovering and selecting reinforcers
How to use reinforcement
Extinction
Self-punishment
Reinforcement in plans for self-direction
Theory and research in self-directed consequences
Your own self-direction project: Step seven
Tips for typical topics

One of the basic formulas for self-direction is to arrange reward for desired behaviors. "Self-reinforcement" is one of the essential and most frequently used elements in self-directed plans—and one of the simplest.

How do we use positive reinforcement in self-direction? *The basic principle is that a positive reinforcer is made contingent on the desired behavior.* The idea of *contingency* is very important. A contingent reinforcer is one that is delivered after, and only after, a certain desirable response. Even a pleasant stimulus acts as a reinforcer only if it is made contingent on an improved response. If you gain a positive reinforcer whether or not you perform some desirable behavior, that reinforcer will not affect the behavior. If, instead, you can gain the reinforcer only by performing some behavior, that behavior will be strengthened; that is, it will be more likely to occur again. It is the contingent relationship that is important, not the positive reinforcer alone.

The use of self-reinforcement was one of the first techniques studied systematically in the field of self-directed behavior. A decade ago, in the first edition of this book, self-reinforcement was the cornerstone of all self-change plans, because it was the best understood of techniques. As our understanding of self-control processes has deepened, many new procedures have emerged, which often seem more sophisticated than simple self-reward. And many writers seem ready to put old self-reward out to pasture.

This would be regrettable, however, because the arrangement of consequences is still one of the three best horses in the stable of self-direction. The research evidence continues to support its use. For instance, in studies of naturally occurring examples of self-control, successful self-controllers, regardless of the problem area—overeating, studying, dating, or smoking—were three times more likely to use self-reward procedures (real or imagined) than were unsuccessful self-controllers (Perri & Richards, 1977; Perri, Richards

& Schultheis, 1977). In formal self-control programs, the addition of self-reinforcement to self-monitoring increased weight loss for dieters (Bellack, 1976). The only negative evidence for self-reinforcement comes from plans that already have some external reinforcement operating. Later in the chapter we will discuss when to self-reinforce and when not to self-reinforce. But in order to decide when self-reinforcement is useful and design intelligent self-reward interventions, the principles and procedures for arranging consequences need to be treated first.

DISCOVERING AND SELECTING REINFORCERS

A simple formula for self-change is to rearrange the contingencies so that reinforcement follows desirable behavior. To do so, you need to know what reinforcers you have available for rearrangement. Therefore, during the observation period, you should be searching for reinforcers. This section discusses ways of discovering and cataloging reinforcers, so that you'll be able to select reinforcers you can use.

Direct Observation of Reinforcing Consequences: Possibilities and Problems

Behavior analysis maintains that most habitual behaviors—including undesirable ones—are maintained by some form of reinforcement. Occasionally you can readily discover these reinforcing consequences. Here are two examples.

A male student kept careful baseline records of his studying behavior. He recorded the situations and opportunities for studying (for example, "at library, 42 min."). He also recorded his actual study time ("4 min.," "15 min.," and so on). The baseline rate of actual study time was very low—less than 20% of the time he was in an appropriate study situation. What was the reinforcer for all this inattention-while-in-study-situation? He was able to report it instantly: instead of reading, he spent his time talking with friends sitting near his usual table.

This reinforcer, incidentally, was not only clear but very available for rearrangement. Our student designed an intervention plan that required him to spend at least 60 minutes studying in his room, a behavior he would then reinforce with a trip to the library, where he could converse with single-minded devotion. He reported that his plan increased both his study time and his socializing.

A colleague of ours reported that he had developed the bad habit of bluntly telling others when he thought they weren't acting very intelligently. "What do you think reinforces this behavior?" we asked him. "I guess it's the feeling I have that I am intelligent," he answered. "When I show others that they are dumb, I also show myself that I'm not. The trouble is, of course, that it makes them angry."

We suggested that he do an A-B-C analysis and pay particular attention to his thoughts and images after the behavior of pointing out other people's stupidity. The analysis was clear; a theme of intellectual superiority was present in the C column of his baseline records. We suggested that he could gain the same reinforcer (feeling intelligent) by intelligently choosing a positive statement instead of making some deprecating remark. These two examples illustrate how an easily discovered reinforcer can be rearranged to support new, alternative behaviors. The same reinforcer is gained but for a different behavior.

It is likely that, in this kind of situation, you will have discovered the reinforcer for your undesirable behavior while observing yourself. The easiest kind of intervention plan is simply to rearrange the reinforcers that you are already getting, so that they are used to reinforce some desirable behavior rather than some undesirable behavior.

Of course, situations are not always so simple. There are cases in which the reinforcers, although evident, cannot be so easily detached from the problem behavior, as in *consummatory responses,* discussed in the preceding chapter. There, the discovery of the reinforcers is not an issue, since, although easy to identify, the reinforcers cannot be detached from the behavior and rearranged into an intervention plan.

Problems can also arise when the reinforcing consequences of behavior are not so obvious. Sometimes the most careful observer can't discover what they are. Two conditions that commonly obscure reinforcers are *intermittent reinforcement schedules* and *avoidance behaviors,* both of which were first discussed in Chapter 4.

Intermittent Reinforcement Schedules.   Some habitual behaviors are reinforced only intermittently. If each instance of your problem behavior were followed by reinforcement, careful observation could reveal the reinforcer in question. But some of your more persistent actions are followed by reinforcement only some of the time. Remember that intermittent reinforcement leads to greater resistance to extinction. Thus, you might expect to find that an intermittent reinforcement schedule is responsible for maintaining especially persistent problem behaviors.

Suppose, for example, that some problem behavior receives reinforcement on an average of only once every 25 times. If this behavior occurred five times per week, it would take five weeks of observation to detect the *first* instance of reinforcement. Before you could establish that a 1-to-25 ratio was the intermittent schedule, you would need hundreds of observations, and the baseline period would necessarily extend for a year or two. This kind of observation might be interesting scientifically, but it wouldn't be appealing at all to the individual who wanted to change his or her behavior.

Avoidance Behaviors.   Avoidance behavior creates even worse problems for the person trying to discover reinforcers, because the aversive consequence may not occur at all. When you have been punished for a behavior in the presence of a cue, that cue will come to elicit avoidance of the behavior. Thus, if you are successful, you will not be punished again and will not be able to observe the negative reinforcer, simply because it will not occur. Although avoidance learning probably accounts for many problems, you might keep observing forever and not detect the specific punishment you are avoiding.

Bill, a sophomore, wanted to go out for his dormitory's intramural basketball team. He had not played competitively in high school and had not even played many pick-up games since he was about 14, although he enjoyed shooting baskets alone. Bill told us that he really had a baseline. During three semesters of college in which he wanted to go out for a team, he just couldn't make himself do it. He wanted to know how he could discover the reinforcer for not-going-out. Of course, he couldn't discover such a reinforcer, and neither could a professional. It didn't appear that any alternative behavior was particularly attractive to Bill; he did not, for instance, prefer swimming to practicing with a team. In a case like this, we can suspect a pattern of avoidance learning. During high school, some unpleasant consequence probably followed Bill's efforts to participate in organized basketball. That consequence might well be lost in his history of learning. Even if Bill had been able to remember the punishment he once received, he would have needed new positive reinforcers to strengthen the behavior he now wanted—joining the dormitory team.

In summary, if you can discover the reinforcers that are supporting some undesirable behavior, you may be able to rearrange them so that they will reinforce some desirable behavior. Three conditions can interfere with the process. The behavior may be inalterably attached to the reinforcer. The problem behavior may be on an impossible-to-detect intermittent reinforcement schedule. You may be engaging in avoidance behavior. In these three conditions, the reinforcers may not be discoverable or controllable. Your strategy, then, must be to discover reinforcers that are controllable. The reinforcers don't need to be those that are actually maintaining your problems. You can use *any* reinforcer, as long as it increases the frequency of your desired behavior.

Positive Reinforcers

If you cannot rearrange or even discover the reinforcers for a particular behavior, you can still modify your behavior by selecting some reinforcer that presently is not supporting the desirable target behavior but that can be arranged to do so.

A positive reinforcer is anything that will increase the occurrence of the behavior it follows. Reinforcers can be things, people, or activities. A "thing" reinforcer might be a doughnut, a $5 bill, a new dress, a fancy shirt, a stereo record—anything you want or would like to have. A "people" reinforcer might be going on a date with your girlfriend or talking with your boyfriend on the phone—spending time with someone you enjoy. An "activity" reinforcer is any event that you enjoy—playing a game, going to a movie, or having dinner out. Even "doing nothing"—talking with friends or loafing—can be a reinforcer. Usually these kinds of potential reinforcers are not limited to any one behavior or situation. You may just feel like going out for a beer or a pizza. Any kind of special occasion like that can be used as a reinforcer. *The task is simply to connect contingently the occurrence of the reinforcer with the target behavior.*

The most important reinforcers are those that will eventually maintain your new behavior, once it is solidly in place. Those reinforcers can be used to support the steps along your way. For example, one of our students aspired toward membership in the scholarly society Phi Beta Kappa. That meant harder work, with the reward of higher grades. She used the reinforcer of "grades awarded" to increase her studying time, except that she awarded the grades herself. She entered an A for excellent, a B for good, and so forth beside each entry in her study record. Another student wanted to increase her range of friends. She reinforced making friendly overtures to new people with the reward of phone chats with her best friend.

Using these "logical" reinforcers—logical because they use the same rewards you are striving toward—is highly desirable. But if you cannot arrange logical reinforcers, any pleasant event can reinforce behavior, and the range of reinforcers is potentially as wide as the range of objects in the world—as wide as the range of human activities. Just as an example of this variety, here is a partial list of the reinforcers used by our students:

praising oneself
taking bubble baths
making love
going to a movie or a play
going to the beach
mountain climbing
smoking pot
smoking cigarettes
spending time at a favorite hobby
spending money
playing records
listening to the radio
eating favorite foods
going out "on the town"
playing sports
getting to "be the boss" with a girlfriend or boyfriend
spending extra time with a friend
"pampering" oneself
reading pornography
reading mystery stories
taking long breaks from work

putting on makeup
not going to work
"doing anything I want to do"
going to parties
being alone
"doing only the things I want to do, all day long"
"not doing my duty sometimes"
goofing off
watching TV
gardening
engaging in soft, relaxing daydreams
engaging in fantasies of sex
engaging in fantasies of success

Given the tremendous scope of any list of possible reinforcers for any one individual, how can you decide which are the potentially effective reinforcers for yourself? Answering the following questions may help you.

1. What will be the rewards of achieving your goal?
2. What kind of praise do you like to receive, from yourself or from others?
3. What kinds of things do you like to have?
4. What are your major interests?
5. What are your hobbies?
6. What people do you like to be with?
7. What do you like to do with those people?
8. What do you do for fun?
9. What do you do to relax?
10. What do you do to get away from it all?
11. What makes you feel good?
12. What would be a nice present to receive?
13. What kinds of things are important to you?
14. What would you buy if you had an extra $20? $50? $100?
15. On what do you spend your money each week?
16. What behaviors do you perform every day? (Don't overlook the obvious or the commonplace.)
17. Are there any behaviors that you usually perform instead of the target behavior?
18. What would you hate to lose?
19. Of the things you do every day, which would you hate to give up?
20. What are your favorite daydreams and fantasies?
21. What are the most relaxing scenes you can imagine?

Wherever you are in your own self-direction project, stop at this point and take a few minutes to think about the questions above. You should be able to give several specific answers to each. If you can, you will have a good-sized catalog of possible reinforcers.

When No Reinforcers Seem to Be Available

At times you will feel that there are just no reinforcers available that you can manipulate. This happens most often when you are locked into a rigid and demanding schedule. Marsha, a 19-year-old student, was struggling to stay in school. She had registered for morning classes only (starting at 7:30), because at 2:00 each weekday she had to be at the bakery where she worked as a salesperson. When she finished at 10:00 in the evening, she frequently had papers to write, exams to study for, and other numerous demands on her time. She lived with her mother, who was partially disabled; so house-work, laundry, and shopping occupied most of her weekend. She dated only occasionally, and Sundays she slept. Marsha's goal was to increase the amount of time she spent in pleasant activities.

Each reinforcer she cataloged seemed to require time for its enjoyment, and there never seemed to be any time. For example, Marsha wanted new clothes, but she had no time to really enjoy wearing them. She thought she wanted a new FM stereo receiver, but what she really wanted was time to listen to music. She had a rich catalog of things she wanted, but she could not manipulate them.

Another situation in which selecting a reinforcer is a problem is one in which nothing seems to be a reinforcer, simply because nothing seems to be any good. Observe yourself the next time you feel depressed. One of the components of your depression is the feeling that nothing is desirable or worth doing; as the language of behavior modification would express it, stimuli lose their reinforcing function. Things no longer matter. Depressed students often report that their reinforcer catalogs are blank.

Another problem—that of not being able to specify an available reinfor-cer—occurs when everything in your reinforcer catalog costs more than you can afford. A male student turned in a reinforcer catalog that looked like this:

1. guitar
2. new amplifier
3. new boots
4. trip to Alaska next summer
5. quitting school for a year and doing *nothing*

This student was self-supporting and currently living on his previous summer's earnings, but his budget was so narrow that the first four items were out of the question. He was having so much academic trouble that a part-time job seemed unwise. The fifth reinforcer was also unrealistic for financial reasons.

These are unhappy cases. However, the opposite can also be a prob-lem—that is, already receiving all the major reinforcements. This situation may not be so unhappy, but, as far as choice of reinforcer is concerned, it has exactly the same effect as the situation in which no reinforcers seem to be available. Specifying a reinforcer that will help you change your behavior is very difficult. What can you do when, for any of the reasons we have discussed, no practical reinforcer seems to be available? To answer this question, we turn to a discussion of three possible solutions—the Premack principle, the use of verbal self-reinforcement, and the use of imagined reinforcement.

The Premack Principle

Named after the psychologist who studied the phenomenon most systematically, the Premack principle states, in effect, that, if behavior B is more likely to occur than behavior A, the likelihood of behavior A can be increased by making behavior B contingent on it. Here is an example from an experiment conducted by Homme, deBaca, Devine, Steinhorst, and Rickert (1963) with nursery school children. Small children are very likely to run around and make noise and less likely to sit quietly in their seats. If you wanted to increase the probability of their sitting quietly in their seats, you could do so by arranging events so that, *if* the children sat quietly, *then* they could run about freely. Sitting quietly is behavior A; running around is behavior B. Initially, B is frequent but A is not. The Premack effect works like this. First the children sit quietly for a few minutes. Then, and only then, they are given the opportunity to run around and make noise. In subsequent trials, sitting quietly will increase in frequency, as long as it is a necessary step to the behavior that was already very frequent—running around.

Notice that in the description of this kind of reinforcer there is no mention of fun or pleasure or feeling good. The point of the Premack effect is that an activity does not have to "feel good" in order to be useful as a reinforcer. *Any behavior that you perform frequently can be used to reinforce any behavior that you perform less frequently.*

Can you see the usefulness of this principle? Suppose that you have defined your goal in terms of a behavior-in-a-situation that you would like to increase. You try to think of some pleasurable reinforcer you can connect to the target behavior, but nothing seems available. The Premack principle tells you that you can use any one of certain behaviors that you engage in every day—such as taking a bath, going to work or school, eating, watching TV, or talking to friends on the phone—to reinforce the target behavior by connecting its occurrence to the goal behavior. The design of the plan is to require yourself to perform the goal behavior *before* you perform the behavior that occurs frequently.

A young woman wanted to increase her exercise time to 15 minutes each day. Taking a shower was one of her frequent behaviors. Following the Premack principle, she simply arranged that she wouldn't take a shower until she had done her exercises.

Of course, you must be cautious in selecting high-frequency behaviors as reinforcers, because there are some behaviors that you engage in frequently but that you would stop immediately if you only could. It is best not to choose such behaviors as Premack-type reinforcers, for they are usually aversive and will transfer their aversive characteristics to the target behavior by emotional conditioning (Danaher, 1974). For example, a young man had developed a strong fear of riding in automobiles and consequently walked everywhere, although he didn't like it. He asked if he should use this distasteful walking as a reinforcer. We advised against it; to do so would be punishing himself for the target behavior, which is not the point at all.

Select for a Premack-type reinforcer some behavior that is not aversive. The behavior can be simply neutral: for example, although not many people find brushing their teeth wildly pleasurable, very few probably find it really unpleasant. The point is to select a behavior that is (or can be) frequent in free-choice conditions. Thus you might also select an activity that is not as frequent as you would like it to be. For example, one student chose "dreaming about my trip to Europe" as a reinforcer, in spite of the fact that this day-dreaming generally occurred less than once a day. She liked to lie quietly and picture the different routes she might take on her trip, the hostels in which she might stay, and the different museums she might visit. But this activity required quiet, a relaxed atmosphere, and time enough to get thoroughly into the fantasy. She reasoned that this was a good Premack-type reinforcer, be-cause, if given the opportunity, it would be very frequent.

Hers was a correct and sophisticated analysis, because a Premack rein-forcer, like all behavior, varies with the situation. The woman arranged the quiet time in which she could enjoy her daydream, thus making it an even more powerful reinforcer.

A studious young man wanted to spend a few minutes, just before going to sleep, reviewing the material he had learned that day. The trouble was, he reported, that when he lay down to sleep, he started having random fantasies and, before he knew it, he was asleep. "It's like my brain started showing me movies of the day's events. Should I get rid of these fantasies?" he asked. "Don't get rid of them" he was advised. "Take advantage of the fact that they always occur." So he put them on contingency. Just before he lay down to watch the movies his brain had in store for him, he would go over the lessons he wanted to review. Then he could have his fantasies. Having the fantasies reinforced his reviewing.

Another example reported by Goldiamond (1965) is that of a married couple who wanted to increase the frequency of their lovemaking. They used their highly regular and frequent visits to the barber and beauty shop as reinforcers for their less probable sexual activities.

A good strategy is that of employing the behavior that you usually per-form *instead* of the target behavior as the *reinforcer* for that target behavior. For example, a man who wanted to spend some time in the evening reading "cultural" materials spent instead all of his time reading whodunits. This was a very frequent behavior, and it obviously interfered with his reading the cultural material. So he used the whodunit reading as a Premack-type rein-forcer. If he spent a certain amount of time reading cultural material, then he would reinforce that behavior by allowing himself the more frequent activity—reading mystery stories.

The possibility of using this strategy is the reason for including the question "Are there any behaviors you perform instead of the target behavior?" in the list of questions we asked you to answer when cataloging reinforcers. Since we all have certain activities we often engage in, the Premack principle can be used as a resource even when reinforcers seem discouragingly scarce.

Brushing your teeth in the morning, using a pillow to sleep on, taking a coffee break, eating lunch, taking a nap after lunch, calling a friend, going to the union to play bridge—all of these behaviors can be used to reinforce less frequent behaviors. And this is why one of the questions we suggested for cataloging reinforcers was "What behaviors do you perform every day? (Don't overlook the obvious or the commonplace.)"

Examples of Premack-type activities used in published cases of self-directed behavior change include eating, continuing to drive after stopping in traffic, urinating (Johnson, 1971), sitting on a particular chair (Horan & Johnson, 1971), smoking, making telephone calls (Todd, 1972), and opening daily mail at the office (Spinelli & Packard, 1975).

Now let's return to a case we discussed above—that of Marsha, the young woman who had no time for reinforcers. Yet there were many things she did every day—perhaps too many. She decided that her target should be to do three things she wanted to do but never had time for: visiting a favorite aunt, practicing yoga, and attending a sensitivity group. She was a fastidious housekeeper, so she selected one of the duties that she regularly performed (cleaning the bathroom) and allowed herself to do it only *after* she had done any one of the three target activities. Thus she used the Premack principle to increase the amount of time she spent doing things she wanted to do.

Verbal Self-Reinforcement

Praise is one of the fundamental methods of control in all human society. Parents, teachers, coaches, politicians, and lovers all encourage behavior by praising it. "Verbal reinforcement" is only a technical description of praise and an acknowledgement that praise is a most powerful reinforcer. Later in this chapter we will discuss techniques for arranging the praise of others so that it will reinforce your behavior.

Here we discuss verbal *self*-reinforcement—that is, self-encouragement following desired behavior. Recall the discussion of the power of bringing self-directions up from the underground. That same technique can be used to increase the reinforcing power of self-speech as well. Every individual experiences pleasure at meeting a goal and at behaving according to his or her own standards. But if that pleasure can be made verbal, brought up from the underground, it can take on stronger reinforcing properties.

The technique is merely to tell yourself "Good. You did it." Say it either covertly or aloud, but say it clearly. Say it after each instance of your desired behavior.

This reinforcer is always available. In our experience, you are likely to omit self-praise from your plan for two reasons. First, you may think it sounds silly or is absurd. It is not; don't underestimate the power of language. Second, you may think that self-praise will result in conceit or a sense of self-importance. That is also incorrect, because self-reinforcement should be used only on contingency, following behavior that meets your own standards. This is very different from puffing yourself up without reason. Verbal self-reinforcement is a way of marking off your successes justly, privately, and realistically.

Imagined (Covert) Reinforcement

Just as Premack-type activities provide potential reinforcers when none seem to be available, so do *imagined* reinforcers. Imagined reinforcers have been traditionally called "covert" reinforcers by behavior analysts. *Covert,* which means hidden or secret, expresses the notion that mental events—thoughts, images, subvocal speech, fantasies, and so on—are indeed hidden from someone who observes you. But they are *not* hidden from you, the self-observer, so we prefer to refer to them as "imagined."

We have already illustrated with an example two instances of thoughts used as reinforcers—feelings of intellectual superiority and daydreams about travel. There is some research evidence that, if things, people, or activities act as reinforcers, imagining them may also be reinforcing (Epstein & Peterson, 1973a, 1973b; Ascher, 1973; Wisocki, 1973; Krop, Calhoon, & Verrier, 1971; Blanchard & Draper, 1973; Cautela, 1970, 1971a, 1972; Marshall, Boutilier, & Minnes, 1974).

In all likelihood, imagined reinforcers are not as powerful as their actual counterparts. But imagined reinforcers have the advantage of being completely portable and easily accessible. Although you may be unable to travel or go skin-diving during the winter, you can imagine doing so. Imagining pleasant and relaxing scenes, such as a lazy swim on a hot day (Cautela, 1973), can be used to reward yourself for performing a desired behavior. Imagined reinforcement is used the same way as any other kind of reinforcement; it is arranged to follow a desirable behavior.

To discover potential imagined reinforcers, you can record the frequencies of your thoughts and fantasies and select the reinforcers in the same way you would other Premack reinforcers. Or you can consider imagining any of the reinforcers you have discovered when you answered the 21 questions in the section on positive reinforcers.

One of the most powerful forms of imagined reinforcement is the anticipation of future outcomes. For example, dieters can use images of themselves after losing weight—slim, attractive, athletic, dressed fashionably, or whatever image of themselves that reflects the wish they want to fulfill by losing weight (Horan, Baker, Hoffman, & Shute, 1975)—to reinforce their dieting (Cautela, 1972).

Many problem behaviors are continued because of imagined outcomes, and these outcomes are frequently unrealistic. Goldfried (1977) offers an excellent example. A group of unassertive people came to see that they let themselves be mistreated by waiters, cashiers, and even friends because of illogical imagined outcomes. They believed that standing up for themselves would be followed by disapproval and embarrassment. Once they began to anticipate different outcomes (greater respect and comfort), their assertiveness increased.

Beliefs about behaviors always involve anticipated consequences. In all likelihood, the very best imagined reinforcement is an anticipation of realistic outcomes. Not only will reinforcement benefits be present, but long-range goals will be brought to mind, and thus commitment will be strengthened again. So there are decided advantages to using reinforcers that are "logical," in the sense of being connected to the chain of events you want to forge. The depressed person can use anticipation of feeling good to reinforce efforts to overcome low moods; the smoker can imagine better health and breath to reinforce efforts to stop smoking; the test-anxious person can imagine being able to take tests calmly.

Choosing the Reinforcer

When choosing a reinforcer, you should keep in mind a few things. One is that the reinforcer you select must be accessible to you. There is little point in choosing a new car as a reinforcer if you don't have the money to pay for it.

Second, you should choose potent reinforcers. The stronger the reinforcer is—that is, the more you want it—the more it will make the work of changing, and therefore obtaining the reinforcer, worthwhile. Ask yourself "Do I really think I'll stop performing the undesired behavior (or start the desired behavior) just because I will get X (the reinforcer)?" A young woman intended to use a morning bubble bath to reinforce her new behavior of coming in by midnight. But, she decided, that reinforcer wasn't really strong enough. Staying out late (her problem) was probably more pleasurable than bubbling her bath. So she chose another reinforcer—listening to the radio when she dressed in the morning. This new reinforcer was accessible, could be put on contingency, and was potent, because music and news were an important part of this young woman's morning ritual.

But the reinforcer must not be too valuable to you. For example, would you really give up a visit to your boyfriend or girlfriend if you didn't perform the target behavior? You must be prepared to do so if you choose that as the reinforcer, because the reinforcer *must be put on contingency.* You have to give it up if you don't perform the target behavior. Anything you find indispensable is not a good choice for a reinforcer, because every reinforcer must be *manipulatable.* Of course, if you could occasionally give up something that you find very very valuable in exchange for the control that gives you over yourself, then it, too, might be a good reinforcer. In choosing the reinforcer, then, you should make sure that it is potent, accessible, and manipulatable.

Imagined, or covert, reinforcement is often the technique of choice because imagined reinforcers are accessible and manipulatable. The choice among several imagined reinforcers usually comes down to these questions: Is it really necessary that you choose a "logical" imagined reinforcer? Are there some circumstances in which "arbitrary" and disconnected covert reinforcers, such as imagining relaxing scenes, are preferable? Psychologists don't agree on this subject. Many argue that logical consequences are always preferable. Others recommend the use of any imagined scene, if it is pleasant and relaxing. (We will present examples of both in the later section on the covert reinforcement of imagined rehearsal.) After all, the *potency* of a reinforcer must be considered, and if a nonlogical reinforcer is more powerful, it may be preferable.

Consider the case of taking tests with the help of newly learned behaviors such as relaxation and self-instructions. You can at the same time use logical imagined reinforcers—getting back the paper with an A, for example. This kind of reinforcer has the advantage of being realistic and logical and of representing a bridge to the world of actual contingencies. Or you can imagine unrelated reinforcers, such as some favorite scenes of extreme pleasantness. Particularly in anxiety-producing situations, this kind of unrelated reinforcer may have some advantage if the imagined scene helps to produce relaxation. Bajtelsmit and Gershman (1976) emphasize that such a relaxation can produce a respondent conditioning effect, thus increasing relaxation in the test-taking situation.

Our recommendations here are the same for covert as for tangible reinforcers. Logical reinforcers are preferable, but there are conditions in which a more powerful, unrelated reinforcer can be profitably used to bridge the time when natural reinforcers seem far away and hard to imagine.

Although there are many advantages to using imagined reinforcement, a few words of caution are in order. To be effective, the images must be vivid (Wisocki, 1973). But, since not everyone can produce vivid, lifelike images, it is necessary that you practice the imagined reinforcement until you can almost feel the water, almost touch the clothes, or hear the music almost as clearly as if you were at the concert. If you cannot produce images that vivid, you should not rely on imagined reinforcement.

This is another argument for using anticipated outcomes as reinforcement. Presumably, you would not have chosen your goal unless you clearly imagined its long-term outcome. Thus you can take even the early steps of your self-improvement plan with the covert reinforcement of a vision of your realized goals, which will allow you to achieve both reinforcement and recommitment.

Finally, the use of verbal self-reinforcement is always advisable. Praising yourself, silently or aloud, for desirable new behavior is easy, accessible, and manipulatable. We recommend that it be included in every plan. The only reservation we have is its potency; therefore we also recommend that another form of reinforcement also be included in your self-direction plan.

How can you tell whether you have chosen the right kind of reinforcer? Remember that you will continue to observe yourself as you strive to change. Your own data will tell you if you are having an effect by placing some reinforcer on contingency. If not, then of course you'll have to change the reinforcer.

Summary

The simplest formula for self-change is to rearrange contingencies, so that reinforcement follows desired behavior. Your A-B-C records will often reveal the contingencies that maintain your current problem behavior; perhaps you can arrange for these contingencies to follow instead your new steps toward your goals.

In cases of consummatory responses, avoidance behaviors, or intermittent reinforcement you may be unable to discover or disconnect the old reinforcement patterns. Thus you will need to construct a catalog of potential reinforcers.

When no reinforcers seem to be available, there are three strategies you can use. First, you may choose an activity reinforcer (also called a Premack reinforcer). This means choosing an activity in which you engage frequently (or would engage in frequently if you had a free choice) and perform this activity only after the target behavior has taken place. Second, you may use verbal self-reinforcement, praising yourself for complying with your plan. Third, you may choose imagined reinforcement; imagining, as vividly as you can, something that you consider reinforcing after you have performed a desired behavior can strengthen that behavior. The most useful imagined reinforcement is imagining the rewards your goal will eventually bring.

Wherever possible, reinforcers should be logically connected to your eventual goals. They should also be potent, accessible, and manipulatable.

HOW TO USE REINFORCEMENT

Prompt Reinforcement

How often should you get reinforcement? The ideal situation is one in which the reinforcement occurs immediately after you perform the desired behavior. The longer a reinforcement is delayed, the less effective it is. And, if it has to compete with some other strong reinforcer that is occurring immediately after the target behavior, it will not be effective at all.

This is a very important thing to keep in mind when you arrange for behavior changes. Remember, whatever your current behavior, it is now being reinforced in some way. Whatever your goal, it will be reinforced at some *later* time, when it is achieved. The dieter is reinforced immediately for overeating. Only weeks from now, when a new image is reflected in the mirror, will he or she be reinforced for *not* eating. At nine o'clock in the morning, shortly after a nice breakfast, a dieter will choose to diet. At noon, walking through the cafeteria line, our same dieter will probably choose not to stick to the diet.

This kind of choice, which depends on how far away in time the reinforcers are, has been studied carefully by psychologists (Ainslee, 1975). Their conclusion is that there are points in time when an immediate reinforcement will be chosen by anyone and that, the closer you draw to immediate reinforcement, the more likely it is that you will choose it. For this reason, self-reinforcement systems are a vital part of self-directed strategies. By providing yourself with extra immediate reinforcement, you can tip the balance and cause yourself to choose long-term goal behaviors. If the dieter arranges the reinforcement of, say, watching an enjoyable TV program immediately after (or even during) self-restraint, dieting is more likely to be observed than if he or she depends entirely on the long-range rewards of being slim someday. In other words, it is the TV program that right now competes with an extra bowl of spaghetti, not the dim dream of slimness in what, at the moment, may appear as a faraway future.

Always try to reinforce quickly after performing the target behavior. You must not only structure your life so that you have opportunities to perform the new target behavior but also arrange things so that you have opportunities to be reinforced for your performance.

One of our students decided to increase her study time. The reinforcement for studying was to have a soda. Before intervention, she had observed that she drank about five or six sodas each day. All she had to do was to make them contingent on studying the required amount of time. If she studied, she got the drink; if she didn't, no drink. She would go to her study place, put in whatever amount of time was required by her schedule, and immediately go for a drink. Thus, she was providing reinforcement very quickly after performing the desired behavior.

Many times the Premack effect can be used to supply a quick reinforcement following a performance of the target behavior. A young man who took a shower every night required himself to exercise 15 minutes before he took the shower. If there is an activity that you engage in daily (a Premack-type reinforcer), you can make it immediately contingent on the performance of the goal behavior by scheduling the desired behavior just before the Premack activity usually occurs.

A married student developed the habit of swearing excessively. His baseline average was more than 150 swear words per eight hours! He had worked out a plan in which he got strong reinforcers from his wife if he reduced his daily average by 10% for one week. Unfortunately, he never made it to the end of the week. After one or two days of good language, he would revert to his old habits. We advised him to reduce the delay of reinforcement. His new contract, agreed to by his wife, called for *daily* reinforcement if he reduced his undesired language by 10%.

Although the general principle is that the reinforcer should be delivered as quickly as reasonable after the desired behavior is performed, in some cases *it is vital that the delay be extremely short.* This is especially true when the undesired behavior consists of consummatory or fear responses. For example, a cigarette in the mouth *right now* is more reinforcing than the thought of cleaner lungs six months from now. A piece of pie in the mouth *right now* feels a lot better than that remote picture of the scales, weeks or even months from now, showing a drop of several pounds. Biting your nails *right now* is more rewarding than the thought of the movies you will go to as a reinforcer Saturday night.

The same kind of problem exists for people who are afraid of some situation, such as talking in front of an audience or going in the water to swim. It feels much better to avoid the feared situation *right now* than to think about how nice it will feel when you get a reinforcer at the end of a week.

Whenever the target behavior has to do with very strong habits or feared objects, you should try to provide yourself with positive reinforcement immediately after performing the desired behavior. For example, a smoker asked his wife to praise him immediately each time he resisted the impulse to light a cigarette.

Imagined (covert) reinforcement has the apparent advantage that you can think of it instantly. But some reinforcements are easier to conjure up than others. Our students have generally found verbal statements easier to produce than imagined scenes. Getting in the right frame of mind is often necessary to produce idyllic, relaxed fantasies and can't be done rapidly enough for on-the-spot reinforcement. But self-reinforcement statements can—"Good! You passed up that joint!" "All right! You're a terrific dieter!"—and they are rapid and effective.

Tokens

If your reinforcer is something that you can carry around with you, such as candy, or if it is something that you commonly do, such as talk with a friend, you can supply quick rewards for the target behavior. The same is true of self-praise.

But suppose your reinforcement is not portable or is not some easily arranged activity. In these cases you may be unable to deliver the reinforcement immediately after performing the desired target behavior. When, for any reason, you cannot have the reinforcer quickly after the behavior, *token reinforcers* may be appropriate.

A token is a symbolic reinforcer—symbolic because it can be converted into real reinforcement. Money, for example, is a token reinforcer, for it is the things that money can buy that make money attractive and therefore represent the real reinforcements. Such devices as poker chips, gold stars, checkmarks, ticket punches, and dollar bills have all been used as tokens.

Many people choose a *point system* of token reinforcement to modify their behaviors. In a point system the performance of the desired behavior results in gaining a specified number of "points." These points can then be "spent" for reinforcement. The cost—so many points per reinforcer—is also specified in the contract that people who use a point system draw up with themselves.

The main function of tokens, whether they are objects or points, is to bridge the delay between the time when you perform the desired behavior and the time when you can partake of the reinforcer. For many people, the chosen reinforcer is something they are going to do at the day's end. They may use a particularly nice supper, or the opportunity to watch TV, or a talk with friends in the evening as a reinforcer contingent on their having performed the target behavior earlier in the day. For all of these delayed reinforcers, tokens can be used during the day to provide the necessary immediacy.

A man who wanted to substitute being-nice-to-friends for being-rude-to-friends selected watching TV in the evening as his reinforcer. Since he couldn't be sure when the opportunity to be nice to his friends would arise during the day and couldn't rush off to watch TV as soon as he had performed his target behavior, he decided to use a token system. He carried a 3 × 5 card in his pocket and made a check on it when he performed the target behavior. Then, later in the evening, he would allow himself to watch TV if he had earned the number of points his shaping schedule required for that day. He used his tokens cumulatively; that is, the more points he earned during the day, the more TV he could watch at night. His "menu" looked like this:

1 token	30 minutes of TV watching
2 tokens	60 minutes
3 tokens	90 minutes
4 tokens	as much as I want

Using a token menu like this has the advantage of making it possible to employ a great variety of reinforcers instead of just one or two. Very few activities, such as watching TV, are equally appealing (reinforcing) every day. One night you might want to watch TV, but another night you might want to go to a movie, and on a third night you might want to go to a party. A young woman used a menu like this to deal with a situation that employed several reinforcers:

1 point	can watch TV up to one hour
2 points	can watch TV as much as I want
3 points	can watch TV as much as I want or can go to a movie
4 points	can do any of those things, plus can read any kind of book or story I want
5 points	can do any of those things, plus can go out with friends if they ask
6 points	can do all that, plus can ask friends to go out with me

An even broader net was cast by a student whose last menu item was "Every Saturday morning *anything* I want to do requires 4 points." This kind of system works if you can create opportunities for the desired behavior but does not work if you have to wait for the opportunities to come to you. For example, if you earn points for studying, you can always finish the required amount of studying on Saturday morning; but if you earn points for being nice to friends, you may not have the opportunity to perform the target behavior, because your friends may not be around.

A token system makes it easy to increase a behavior gradually. For example, over time you can gradually require more and more performances of the target behavior in order to earn a token. You might start a music practice program, for instance, by getting 1 point for every 15 minutes you spend practicing; after a few days, you get 1 point for every 20 minutes, and so forth.

Reinforcement for Thoughts and Feelings

There is experimental evidence that using reinforcement can influence your thoughts and feelings (Mahoney, Thoresen, & Danaher, 1972). Several case studies have been reported that illustrate the use of this technique.

For example, a graduate student suffered from persistent depression. She believed that she would be far less depressed if she could be honest with herself and others. Thus her target behavior was to increase the number of "honest, authentic statements made to myself and other people."

Examples of "honest, authentic statements" included:

"That made me angry!"
"Even if she is my sister, I don't like what she is doing."
"I just put on an act—a good act, but totally phony."
"I don't agree. Pro football is brutal."

Figure 7-1 shows the frequencies of this student's honest statements. After 20 days of *baseline* self-observation, she began her first intervention plan; she called it "autosuggestion" and required herself each morning to "*will* myself to feel better, psych myself up, just not indulge my black morning moods." For about three weeks, the plan worked; her number of honest statements climbed, and so did her mood. Then both quickly tumbled. At that point she began the following full program of tokenized reinforcement.

"For each verbal expression of feeling or opinion (talking to myself included), I will award myself 1 point, to be redeemed on the following schedule: for each 5 points I'll have 15 minutes of free time to do anything I choose; or each point will be paid in money at the rate of 1¢ per point, and this money can be spent on 'luxury' things I usually wouldn't buy. Bonus for attaining a new high will be rewarded by a special event of equal value. Also, for each time my morning autosuggestion works, I will get 5 points. My morning coffee will also be contingent on getting myself into a better mood."

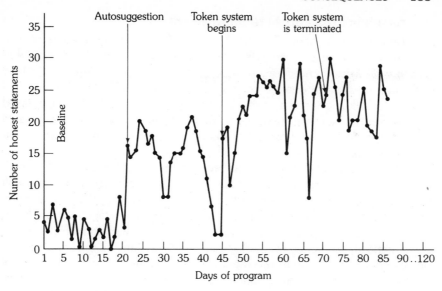

Figure 7-1.   Number of honest statements per day.

Her honest statements jumped quickly to over 30 a day. There were ups and downs, but the average stabilized at over 20. She terminated the plan after about a month and a half. Psychological tests, and her own report, showed that her depression was remarkably improved (Tharp, Watson, & Kaya, 1974).

Vigorous debate surrounds the question "Is it possible to affect thoughts by reinforcement?" (Rachlin, 1977a, 1977b; Ellis, 1977; Mahoney, 1977a). Our own position is that *verbal statements* (overt and covert) are affected by consequences, whether or not one calls them thoughts. A man suffered from frequent self-deprecating thoughts. He believed that he was so odd that he might be brain damaged and felt persecuted by others. To increase positive self-thoughts, he put four small index cards into his packet of cigarettes. One card was blank. On the other three he wrote positive statements about himself that were among the very few he believed—something like "I'm proud of being a loyal friend," for example. When he took out his pack, he read the top card to himself, put it on the bottom of the stack, and then smoked a cigarette as a reinforcement. When the blank card came up, he had to think of some new positive statement about himself (Mahoney, 1971). This plan involved using a Premack-type activity as a cue *and* as a reinforcement for performing the desired behavior.

Positive self-statements can be made more frequent by reinforcement, both overt and imagined (Krop et al., 1971; Krop, Perez, & Beaudoin, 1973). Giving yourself reminders (cues) to make positive self-statements and then following the statements with some form of reward is an effective procedure (Epstein & Hersen, 1974).

Avoiding Problems in Reinforcement

An ideal intervention plan should *increase* the total amount of reinforcement you receive; that is, *the gross amount of reinforcement should be higher during self-directed change than it was before.* This principle is particularly important in cases of depression (Fuchs & Rehm, 1977). The student who wanted to make honest statements used this principle, and the plan increased her free time as well as the luxury articles she allowed herself. Any plan should increase the total amount of reinforcement you receive, but particularly if you are depressed.

One of our colleagues was an avid stamp collector. His goal in self-direction was to increase the amount of time he spent writing professional material. During baseline he recorded not only his writing time but also the amount of money he spent on his stamp collection. It averaged about $5 per week. His self-change plan called for reinforcing his writing with money to buy stamps. If he reached his weekly goal of writing time, he rewarded himself on Saturday with $10 in stamp money. Thus, increasing the total amount of reinforcement gave him an additional incentive for continuing self-direction. It also bridged the time gap until he would be rewarded for his professional writings.

A second problem to be avoided is "wearing out" reinforcers. If your intervention plan requires that you reinforce yourself very frequently for some behavior—particularly if the reinforcement is a daily one—you should select several different reinforcers. If you don't, you may satiate on a particular reinforcer. To say that you *satiate* means that the reinforcer has lost its reinforcing quality through repeated presentation. For example, think what would happen if you used chocolate candy as a reinforcer. For a couple of days, eating chocolate would be enjoyable. But anyone, even someone with the sweetest tooth, will eventually get enough candy. So, after a few days, the chocolate candy wouldn't do the job anymore. A stimulus for which the person is satiated is no longer an *effective* reinforcer.

If you are going to need daily reinforcement (and many plans call for just that), use a variety of reinforcers. Of course, a way of getting around the problem of satiation is to use the token system, which can easily allow for a menu of reinforcement, like the following one.

1 point .... one chocolate bar *or*
one carbonated drink *or*
one beer *or*
one pack of chewing gum *or*
one piece of fruit

A third problem you should avoid is selecting a reinforcer that will punish someone else. For example, if you want to pay yourself $10 per week as a reinforcer and you are married, you should get your spouse to agree to the payment. Otherwise the money in your pocket might be money out of your spouse's pocket. This situation could cause arguments that would be punishing, not reinforcing. Thus, if your reinforcer involves any inconvenience to other people, be sure that they agree with your plan.

A fourth problem can be avoided if you use independent reinforcers for each plan. Suppose that you decide to start two plans simultaneously. In one, you are going to lose weight by eating less; in the other, you are going to increase your study time. Suppose also that you pick one single powerful reinforcer to apply to both. If you perform the desired behavior during the week, then you can do anything you want on Saturday and Sunday.

Let's say that you do very well on the study plan and succeed in putting in the required number of hours. But you don't do so well on the weight-loss plan; you give in to temptation and eat too much. What should you do on Saturday—get the reinforcement or not? If you do take the reinforcement (arguing that, after all, you did perform the required study behavior), then you will also be reinforcing your *not* sticking to your diet, which is clearly a mistake. On the other hand, not giving yourself the reinforcer would be a failure to reward studying. The conclusion this example suggests is clear: if there is more than one plan, use different reinforcers, so that, if you fail on one plan, you still get reinforced for the successful one.

Sharing Reinforcers

Sometimes the reinforcers that you select are shared with other people or affect them as much as they affect you. Even in such a case, it is *your* behavior that establishes the contingency. For example, a young woman chose going to the movies with her boyfriend as a reinforcer. She needed his cooperation in her intervention plan because, if she failed to perform the target behavior, she would have to miss seeing the movie with him. But if she did miss the movie, *so would he.* The pleasurable experiences we have with other people—being together, doing favorite things, loving—are often very powerful reinforcers and thus are ideal choices for an intervention plan. But, if you want to use them, you must have the cooperation of the other person.

Many times one person will decide to modify a particular aspect of his or her behavior because a friend or lover is concerned about it. A man might smoke, for example, and his friend might disapprove. It is often possible to use the other person who is not changing his or her behavior as a partner in the process of change. This is particularly true if you are trying to get rid of some behavior that the other person doesn't approve of or if you are trying to increase some behavior that the other person wants you to increase. The change in your behavior becomes the reinforcer for the partner's behavior of cooperation. Or the partner may simply care enough to be willing to share a reinforcer. We know of a wife who agreed with her student husband not to talk with him until he had spent so many minutes on a paper he was writing.

Using activities with others as reinforcers is effective not only because the reinforcer is a powerful one but also because it brings another force to bear in your intervention plan. The other person, who may stand to lose if you fail to perform the target behavior, will put pressure on you to do it. If your determination begins to lag, your friend may say to you "You better do it! I want to see that movie!"

A special situation arises when a couple undertake the same plan together. Before deciding on such a course, both partners should make sure that they are equally committed to the plan and goals. When two partners both try to lose weight, for example, and one or both subtly influence or sabotage the other's efforts, they may be less successful than if only one were trying (Zitter & Fremouw, 1978).

Using Others to Dispense Reinforcers

If you have complete control over a reinforcer, it may be possible for you to give this control to another person. People who dispense reinforcement to someone else are called *mediators* (Tharp & Wetzel, 1969). If your reinforcer is something tangible, like money, you may give it to another person and explain what you must do in order to get it back. Or, if the reinforcer is some activity in which you normally engage in the presence of the other person, you can structure the situation so that you must have permission to engage in the reinforcing activity and get that permission by performing the target behavior.

Reinforcement by significant mediators, such as spouses, can have its own positive effects. Israel and Saccone (1979) found that using a monetary reinforcer for improved eating habits increased weight loss. But when the reinforcers were dispensed by the dieters' spouses, the long-range effectiveness of the program was even greater. This point is vividly dramatized by the cases described in Box 7-1 (Matson, 1977) and in Box 7-2 (Kau & Fischer, 1974).

BOX 7-1
Self-Modification of Exercise Behavior

A need for regular physical exercise led to the selection of this problem. While regular physical exercise itself can be reinforcing to some persons, for [this woman] it was not. In order to establish and maintain an exercise habit, an attempt at self-directed behavior change seemed appropriate.

Method

A prior attempt to establish an exercise routine using the Premack principle (tooth brushing at night contingent upon the completion of a series of calisthenics) had not been successful, for the contingency was ignored. Therefore, the present plan placed control of the reinforcers in the hands of another person. The husband was the logical choice, and the intervention plan was put into a written contract that he and she signed. The plan had the following features:

(Box 7-1 continues)

BOX 7-1 *(continued)*

1. The form of exercise was jogging.
2. Money and social activities of the [woman's] choice (for example, going to a movie or eating at a restaurant) were the reinforcers. [She] received 25¢ immediately after jogging. At the end of each week, if she had jogged every day (and earned $1.75), she could select and engage in one of several possible social activities with her husband. Otherwise, none of the social activities was permitted.
3. The husband dispensed the reinforcers and tabulated points.
4. In addition, points were earned for jogging. The long-term goal was set at 40 points per week . . . where four points could be earned by jogging 1 mile within 9.59 min. and . . . more earned by increasing the distance . . . and reducing the time. This was approached through a series of intermediate steps. The plan was to begin with the jogging of 1 mile, with gradual increments of 0.25 miles.

Results

The results of the intervention plan can be seen in Figure 7-2. At the end of the first week of intervention, 20 points were earned, representing a sharp increase in exercise activity from a baseline of zero. After this initial spurt, progress slowed but increased to 23 points in the second week. Jogging had occurred on only 4 days, but, because of the increased distance run, more points were earned. The third week showed a drop in total number of points to 19. Jogging occurred on 4 days, during the fourth week of intervention, and again occurred on only 4 days of week 4. Up to this point, the activity reinforcer had not been given,

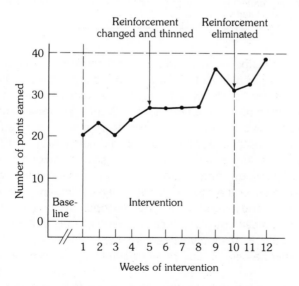

Figure 7-2. Number of points earned by exercising.

(Box 7-1 continues)

BOX 7-1 *(continued)*

because jogging had not occurred daily during any of the 4 weeks. A change in the program was adopted at the start of the fifth week; the activity reinforcer was made available after earning 25 or more points per week (rather than running every day), and the 25¢ payment was eliminated. This was followed by an increase in total points to 27 for the fifth week. The 12th week showed the highest level of activity, with 38½ points earned—only 1½ points short of the long-term goal, even though the activity reinforcer had been eliminated at the beginning of the 10th week.

Formal reinforcement was terminated before the long-term goal (40 points per week) was reached, for two reasons. First, the subject had become satiated with the activity reinforcer. For 2 weeks prior to its elimination, she had earned enough points to gain the reinforcer but had not bothered to "collect" it. Second, the natural positive results of regular physical exercise were being noticed. She felt better and more energetic than when she began the program. She had lost several pounds without any change in eating habits. With these natural reinforcements, the long-term goal was soon reached. As the natural environment had taken over and begun to maintain the desired behavior, the program was judged to have been successful.

The key to the success may have been the placement of control of the program with another person. The controlling person, the husband, was firm in his commitment to the plan and the rules agreed upon. The contingency between the behavior and the reinforcers was maintained rigorously.

From "Self-Modification of Exercise Behavior," by M. L. Kau and J. Fischer, *Journal of Behavior Therapy and Experimental Psychiatry*, 1974, 5, 213–214. Copyright 1974 by Pergamon Press, Ltd. Reprinted by permission.

A smoking "clinic" experiment provided recent ex-smokers with a special telephone number they could call to hear a recorded tape praising them for continuing not to smoke. A significantly higher number of these smokers stayed off cigarettes than of those not provided with the telephone-reinforcing service. Arranging to have the praise of others is apparently very effective, even when it comes from the recorded voice of strangers (Dubren, 1977).

For some college students, parents may be logical mediators. If you are receiving money, clothes, use of an automobile, or any other potential reinforcer from your parents, you may include them in a contingency plan in the service of your goals. Many parents are willing to cooperate with their children in a contingency reinforcement plan, because many of their children's goals are likely to be similar to their own goals for the children—good grades, steady progress toward a degree, and perhaps even writing home more regularly.

Whenever you use another as your mediator, it is important that the person understand exactly what he or she is supposed to do—namely, that

BOX 7-2

Social Reinforcement by the Spouse in Weight Control: A Case Study

The subject, Mrs. L., was a 44-yr-old female, 5 ft 6 in. tall and weighing 174 lb. She had made numerous unsuccessful attempts to lose weight over the past ten years employing treatments ranging from "do it yourself remedies" to an assortment of fad diets and then drug therapy administered under a physician's care. Also, her husband had tried a treatment of verbal abuse during which he routinely made statements such as "You are so fat I am ashamed to be seen with you." He also offered to buy Mrs. L. a new wardrobe if she would lose 30 lb. The most weight ever lost was 12 lb. in six weeks with drugs. She remained at the new weight for 12 weeks of treatment, and gained the weight back within one month when medication was discontinued. With all treatments a consistent pattern was weight loss for a few weeks followed by a return to old eating habits and weight gain again. Mrs. L. frequently snacked while cooking or shopping, remarking that she did not have the necessary willpower to lose weight.

During an initial phase of self-observation and the arrangement of new antecedents, she lost less than one-half pound per week. Then a plan involving social reinforcement was added. The subject stated that Mr. L.'s verbal abuse of her weight was highly aversive. Therefore, the frequency of these comments was made contingent on weight loss. If Mrs. L. lost 2 lb. a week, Mr. L. was to compliment his wife two or more times each evening for progress being made on her diet. No derogatory comments about her figure were allowed. If the weekly criterion was not reached. Mr. L. was to use verbal abuse of Mrs. L.'s figure as frequently as desired. A contract was signed by both persons with each spouse serving as a reliability check for the other. Mr. L. was to assure accurate weighins and Mrs. L. made sure no verbal abuse of her weight was used inappropriately. When the contract was violated the offended spouse used a verbal reminder such asd "you just called me a fat hog; this violates the contract we made."

Greatest weight losses were reported during the social reinforcement phase (39 lb.). Mrs. L. attributed her success to self confidence created primarily by praise she received from her husband. She indicated that maintaining weight at or below the goal (135 lb.) during follow-up was due to praise and gradual weight loss resulting in altered eating habits (i.e., eating at the dining table and consuming smaller portions). During self-monitoring and environmental restructuring, little weight loss resulted. Mrs. L. reported that snacking was eliminated but her calorie intake increased at mealtime.

Mr. and Mrs. L. stated that social reinforcement resulted in better social interactions at home. Both were pleased with the weight loss and increased positive affect shown toward each other. They indicated that positive behavior learned during treatment would be a continued emphasis in other aspects of their relationship.

he or she is supposed to reinforce contingently and is not supposed to punish you. If you fail to perform the target behavior and he or she withholds the reinforcer, that is unpleasant enough. You don't need further punishment, such as scolding, which may even cause you to discontinue intervention altogether.

A student wrote: "I *have* to be wearing my contact lenses by the time I go home this summer. If I don't, my mother will say I'm wasting money. Besides, I don't like the way I look." The reinforcer she chose was an unusual one. "If I meet my goal for each day, my roommate (the mediator) will let me use her fountain pen to doodle and write with for 15 minutes. I like that fountain pen because it writes without smudging and because of the sound it makes on the paper. I will ask my roommate to dispense the reinforcer and to check with me each day how many hours I've worn my contacts. And when I'm up to 10 hours a day, I'll buy my own pen!" By the end of 42 days, she was wearing the lenses 12 hours a day, with perfect comfort.

You can use others, then, as sources of reinforcement or to check up on your performance of the target behavior. If you are having difficulty making yourself do the target behavior before taking a reinforcer, it is helpful to ask a friend to check up on you. If you find yourself being too lenient, use another to spot-check you (Kazdin, 1974f).

Summary

Specify exactly what you must do in order to get the reinforcement you have selected—first, specify the behavior, then the reinforcer. In selecting reinforcers, try very hard to minimize the delay of reinforcement—the time between actual performance of the target behavior and reinforcement for the performance. The prompter the reinforcer, the more effective. Verbal self-reinforcement is especially useful because it can be used instantly. When using material or activity reinforcers, a good method to bridge any unavoidable delay between performance and reinforcement is the use of a token system, in which you gain points, or tokens, as soon as you have performed the target behaviors; these tokens can later be turned in for real reinforcers. In the ideal reinforcement system, by performing the target behavior you actually *increase* the positive reinforcers you have been getting.

There are a few things you need to keep in mind. If you overuse a reinforcer, you may become satiated with it. You shouldn't use a reinforcer that will punish someone else, and you should use a separate reinforcer for each intervention plan.

Some of the most effective reinforcers are activities you engage in with other people. If these people will cooperate—and you can reinforce them for cooperating—you can use those activities as reinforcers. Or you can transfer control of certain reinforcers to others so that they'll give you the reinforcer if you perform the target behavior. This is a highly desirable system if the mediators are firmly committed to your goals.

EXTINCTION

As you will recall from Chapter 4, extinction is the weakening of a behavior by withdrawing reinforcement from it. This is a simple strategy when used in the laboratory. If an experimental animal is no longer given food pellets, it will eventually quit pressing the bar. In self-direction, however, extinction is more complicated. When real-life reinforcers are withdrawn, other reinforcers automatically rush in to fill the vacuum. When used alone, extinction is very rarely an effective self-directing strategy.

The following case illustrates the point. A student wanted to reduce the frequency of cutting his trigonometry class. His midterm grade was D, and it was obvious that poor attendance was the reason. His A-B-C analysis clearly showed that class cutting was being reinforced by shooting pool and playing pinball, because he was going to the Billiard Palace instead of the classroom. His plan called for withdrawing this reinforcer; when he cut class, he would go home immediately. But this plan didn't result in less class cutting, since he found himself listening to the stereo in his room instead. The correct procedure here would have been to reinforce class attendance, perhaps by making the Billiard Palace contingent on it. When you withdraw reinforcement from an undesired behavior, you should simultaneously increase reinforcement for the alternative, desired behavior.

However, there is one use of extinction that may be helpful—*imagined extinction* as advocated by Cautela and his associates (Cautela, 1971b; Ascher & Cautela, 1974). This procedure is used when you wish to reduce a behavior but cannot remove the reinforcement. Removing the reinforcement may be impossible for two reasons. First, reinforcement may be attached to the behavior itself, as in consummatory responses. Overeating is reinforced by the food itself; sexual behaviors are reinforced by the sexual pleasure; and so on. Second, some behaviors are reinforced by other people, and often you cannot control their responses to your behavior. For example, you may wish to stop your behavior of sulking, but your spouse reinforces it by being upset or oversolicitous or by indulging you in some way.

Imagined extinction, like reinforcement, takes place entirely in your own imagination. The advantage of using imagination is that all things are possible there, even removing reinforcement. For example, Ascher and Cautela (1974) counseled an obese man who wanted to give up eating an especially tasty and fattening food as follows:

> [He] was asked to imagine that he was seated in a delicatessen and that the waitress had brought two bagels stuffed with cream cheese and Nova Scotia lox (the troublesome food). His mouth was watering; he could not wait to devour them. He took the first bite but was somewhat disappointed because the food did not seem to have the usual amount of flavor. He opened the bagel, looked at the lox, smelled it, but everything seemed to be normal. He put some salt on it and took a second bite. He experienced even less flavor than before. With each successive mouthful there was less and less flavor, until, when the first bagel

was finished, he did not bother to eat the second one. [He] was instructed to imagine this several times each day, and especially before [going out to eat bagels and lox]. After two sessions during which [imagined extinction] was extensively employed, he no longer desired bagels and lox; for 3 months following, he avoided this food [pp. 233–234].*

The basic technique is to imagine as vividly as possible all elements of your undesired behavior and also imagine that the usual reinforcement does not occur. Each scene should be imagined about 15 times daily (Cautela, 1971b).

Suppose, for example, that you want to decrease your sulking, but your A-B-C analysis indicates that your spouse always follows that behavior by asking "What's the matter, darling?" or by being especially nice to you, until you come around. The imagined scene would include your usual sulking in front of the TV, but this time you would imagine that your spouse makes no response whatsoever and merely ignores you and proceeds with his or her business.

Like all covert procedures, imagined extinction should be used only if you can keep good control over your fantasies. If, for example, the imagined scene we described above drifts off into a quarrel with your spouse, you should terminate the extinction procedure. Cautela warns that extinction is sometimes accompanied by a brief *increase* in the problematic behavior before it begins to decline. He also warns that some people do indeed become actually angry at the people whom they are imagining in the extinction scenes. Generally, these are temporary problems, but if they should appear to be of a more serious nature, imagined extinction should be stopped.

Imagined extinction is a promising technique, but research evidence on its effectiveness is as yet slight. In our own view, the effects are likely to be enhanced if combined with covert modeling. In the bagels-and-lox example, the man finished his imaginary scene by refusing to eat the second portion. We recommend including a covert rehearsal of the desired behavior as a part of any covert extinction.

Summary

Extinction—the weakening of a behavior by withdrawing reinforcement from it—is easier to manage in the laboratory than in real life. It can be an effective technique, however, if it is combined with the additional reinforcement of a desired, alternative behavior. Imagined extinction is an amusing technique, in which the real consequences of problem behaviors are imagined to disappear—for example, imagining the situation of eating some fattening food and finding it somehow tasteless. To be effective, imagined extinction

*From "An Experimental Study of Covert Extinction," by L. M. Ascher and J. R. Cautela, *Journal of Behavior Therapy and Experimental Psychiatry*, 1974, 5, 233–238. Copyright 1974 by Pergamon Press, Ltd. Reprinted by permission.

should probably be coupled with covert rehearsal of a desired alternative behavior.

SELF-PUNISHMENT

So far we have concentrated almost entirely on positive reinforcement. It may have occurred to you that it would be possible to use punishment in a self-modification project. As you recall, we have discussed punishment in detail in Chapter 4.

Why Punishment Alone Is Insufficient

Many plans that rely solely on punishment don't work. There are several reasons why this is so. The first reason is that the undesired behavior may be resistant to mild punishment. Suppose you have decided to eliminate some undesired behavior that makes you feel guilty, depressed, sad, embarrassed, or nervous. In short, the behavior itself is already punishing you. Yet, you continue to practice the behavior. The implication is clear: the performance of the behavior is somewhat resistant to punishment. To use punishment as an intervention technique would require heaping on a large amount of additional punishment, and you are unlikely to do that.

In fact, if you used punishment, you could make things worse. One way behaviors become resistant to punishment is by being first mildly punished and then positively reinforced. If you are somehow being reinforced for the behavior but are unaware of the reinforcer, you might actually increase the behavior's resistance to punishment by supplying a small punishment followed by an (unnoticed) positive reinforcement.

The second reason for avoiding punishment is that punishment alone doesn't teach new behaviors. Punishment suppresses the behavior it follows, but what happens *instead* is determined by the reinforcement that follows the various things you might attempt. Your plan should provide for designating and reinforcing desired alternatives to your problem behaviors. Otherwise the plan is incomplete.

One of our students had three jobs plus a full load at college. Her first plan consisted of punishing herself for *not* performing a desired behavior by depriving herself of one of the few things in her life that she enjoyed. She had somehow managed to keep two hours free every Friday afternoon, and she always used them to go to the beach with a close friend. Her plan proposed to punish excessive eating by giving up this weekly pleasure. We strongly disagreed with this idea. Her life needed enrichment, not a further impoverishment of positive reinforcers. We suggested that she reward dieting by adding another social activity (if necessary, at the expense of her quite adequate study time). To lose her one weekly contact with a friend would have made her even more dependent on her only other real pleasure—food. Besides, her overall happiness required a broader spectrum of pleasant events. Punishment would have restricted her life and would have also made dieting less likely.

The third reason for not including punishment in your plan is that you will thereby be less likely to carry out your plan. In teaching a course in behavioral self-control, Worthington (1979) found that only one-third of the students actually inflicted self-punishment when their plans called for it.

From the preceding discussion, it should be evident that punishment alone is usually an undesirable strategy. This is true for either kind of punishment—adding an aversive stimulus to a situation or removing a positive reinforcer. Even in situations in which punishment seems to be the only alternative, other strategies should be explored.

When you are performing some undesired behavior, you may be able to reinforce positively an incompatible behavior instead of punishing the undesired behavior itself. Therefore, before you decide to use punishment, always search for an incompatible behavior that you can positively reinforce instead. (Recall that incompatible behaviors are discussed in detail in Chapter 6.) In a controlled study of weight loss, for example, dieters were more successful if they used self-reinforcement for losing weight than if they punished themselves by forfeiting a cash deposit (Mahoney, Moura, & Wade, 1973).

Yet there are times when, no matter how many alternatives you explore, punishment still seems the only answer. For example, your target may be an undesired behavior like smoking or overeating that, at the time you do it, is so impelling that no positive reinforcer can compete with it. Or you may already be getting such a good supply of positive reinforcers that you cannot find others to add. In these cases, punishment does indeed seem the only answer. If so, what kind of punishment should you use?

The Loss of Positive Reinforcement as Punishment

When punishment is used, it should involve giving up something pleasant that you usually receive. This is better than using an aversive stimulus as punishment (Kazdin, 1973b). In other words, don't whip yourself and don't pinch yourself.

Here are some examples of punishment in the form of giving up usual pleasures. One person might not allow herself to take a customary bath if she has not studied enough. Another might not allow himself to eat some preferred foods if he has performed some undesired behavior. If you are accustomed to going to a movie on Saturday night, you could punish yourself for your nonperformance of a target behavior by staying home. One of our students followed the plan of dividing the foods he usually ate into really nice ones and so-so ones. If he didn't perform his target behavior, he didn't allow himself to eat the nice ones. Many people use the general category of "things I do for fun" to require themselves to perform some target behavior before they allow themselves to engage in the "fun" activities. Another student, who was in love with a man in another state, used the daily letters she received from him. Each day she handed the unopened letter to a friend. If she performed her target behavior, she got the letter back, unopened. If she did not perform the target behavior, her friend was instructed to open and read the love letter.

Some of our students have had success with such plans, but a better strategy is to combine positive reinforcement with punishment, so that you lose *additional* rewards, not customary ones. A plan to increase studying could call for an extra movie per week if your goal is met, but only if your goal is met.

A token system can be used for a combination program. For example, each time you perform some undesired behavior, you lose one point. The gains and losses don't have to balance each other, of course. One man we know gained one point for each hour he didn't smoke but lost ten points for each cigarette he smoked.

Lutzker and Lutzker (1974) report the program that a woman who wanted to lose weight arranged with her husband. She could earn several reinforcers for losing a half-pound or more each week, but the most effective part of the plan involved a "household duties" punishment. Before beginning the plan, she and her husband divided the household chores into "his" and "hers." The husband took up more chores than he had had before. Each week, after her weigh-in, if she had lost weight or stayed even, he continued doing the chores on his list for the next week. If she had gained weight, she had to do his chores in addition to her own. She lost weight.

Precommitted Punishment

As you may recall, precommitment refers to making some arrangement in advance, so that you will be more likely to make choices of behaviors that are in your long-term best interest. Precommitted punishment, therefore, means arranging in advance that some particular punishing event will take place if you perform a certain undesired act. Precommitted punishment may be appropriate when the undesired behavior is so rewarding that no new reinforcers can be found to counter it. Take smoking, for example. Once you are a steady smoker, almost nothing feels as good as a cigarette after 24 hours without one. Therefore, you may feel that you must resort to some punishments to keep yourself from lighting a cigarette. In cases like this, a technique suggested by Nurnberger and Zimmerman (1970) might work.

In their study on smoking, these researchers had each participant make out a bank check to his or her most hated organization. (For someone whose political leanings are to the right, this might be a Communist organization; for someone who is a firm atheist, it might be some organized church, and so on. Anyone can make a list of organizations he or she really disapproves of, perhaps even hates.) The agreement was that, if the person performed the undesirable behavior, the check would be mailed to the organization by someone else.

Like Odysseus, and like all of us who set alarm clocks, these smokers arranged precommitments at the time when they would choose not to perform a certain act—in their case, smoke. This is a good precommitment strategy.

It is also important that the experimenter (or some other person) is the one who mails the check, and not the smoker. Suppose you planned to punish yourself by tearing up a dollar bill for each cigarette you smoked. In the situation of having just smoked, unless you had arranged for someone else to do it for you, it is unlikely that you would in fact tear up the bill (Hall, Axelrod, Weiss, & Rohrer, 1971).

You can arrange advance control of yourself by giving over some kind of forfeit to a helper. You can require yourself to study for two hours before going to a movie, give a friend $10, and instruct the friend to call you every half hour from 7 to 9 o'clock. If you don't answer the telephone, the friend is to mail the money to your worst enemy (Rachlin, 1974). One of our students wanted to completely eliminate using sugar, no longer adding it to coffee, cereal, and other foods. So she selected a cup from her treasured collection of handmade coffee cups, marked it with a piece of tape on the bottom, and instructed her husband to break it if she used any sugar.

In these precommitment strategies, the trick is to make the penalty so heavy that in fact you never apply it. *Precommitment should work as a deterrent, not as a punishment.* In this way, precommitment is consistent with our general recommendation that you should not in fact punish yourself. In precommitting, you must arrange for penalties that would be so unpleasant that you simply won't incur them.

A heavy forfeit, however, presents problems of its own. The specter of a great loss may create new anxieties; the helper who holds the forfeit may begin to seem less a friend than a menace. A middle-aged man was determined to stop smoking. His wife, who had recently stopped, was willing to cooperate to almost any extent. The husband was an avid collector of cacti and other small succulent plants. During the years, his garden had grown down the wall and into the lawn, and even the kitchen counter often held young plants as a kind of incubator. His precommitment plan arranged that, for every cigarette he smoked, his wife was to destroy one young cactus. The precommitment worked, in the sense that he smoked no cigarettes for seven days. But the threat was intolerable. He prowled the house and garden wondering which plant would be sacrificed if he smoked. And how would they die—drowned in the toilet or crushed under his wife's heel? After one week, he canceled the agreement and felt at ease with his wife once again.

Any form of self-punishment, even when used as a deterrent, brings about problems and should be approached carefully. Precommitted punishment should be used only temporarily and only when you can quickly bring desirable behavior under the control of positive reinforcement or natural rewards (Rachlin, 1974).

Punishment as a Temporary Solution

Punishment can be a temporary and partial tactic for achieving some goals. But, remember, it is only temporary and only partial. Any form of punishment may be useful only as a means to developing the behaviors you want. You just can't say that you have reached your goal unless your desired behavior is being supported by positive means. There is no point in using self-punishment except when it leads to positive reinforcers.

At times the positive reinforcer will be simply the good feeling of having successfully carried out your intervention plan. Maybe you have stopped smoking or biting your nails; maybe you have increased the frequency of some desired behavior. At other times the positive reinforcer will be some pleasurable response from your environment; someone is happy because you have stopped the undesirable behavior, or new positive reinforcers are available because you have acquired some new competence.

If there is some reason to expect that these new reinforcers will develop quickly, a short-term form of self-punishment may be acceptable. The punishment can tide you over until the new positive reinforcement takes effect. But if these new reinforcers can't be expected to develop "naturally," then you had best program some positive reinforcement for alternative behavior.

There is perhaps one form of self-punishment that can be recommended in early stages, and that is the "punishment" of facing up to the unfortunate consequences of a problem behavior. Imagining the real consequences of a sex offense, for example, can be a powerful deterrent: prison, publicity, and the loss of family and friends. Imagining the continued loneliness and frustration of social withdrawal can provide strong motivation to persevere in building social skills. A systematic plan for reminding yourself of these long-range punishments can keep you from drifting from your goals. Youdin and Hemmes (1978) recommend to dieters that they stare at their naked bodies in the mirror for 60 seconds a day while thinking about overeating. Force yourself to read the latest figures on cancer and smoking.

Reminding yourself of the unfortunate consequences of some problem behavior can be considered as yet another way of building and maintaining commitment.

Summary

Self-punishment doesn't necessarily teach any new behaviors. Many intervention plans that rely *solely* on self-punishment don't succeed. There are some situations in which self-punishment may be necessary—if, for example, there are no positive reinforcers available or if the undesired behavior is so strongly reinforcing in itself that a direct, counteracting consequence is required for not performing it. Consummatory behaviors are typical examples of this situation.

If you do decide to use punishment, you should follow these rules:

1. Remove something positive instead of adding something negative. (Always try to figure out a way to increase behavior by adding something positive.)
2. Use punishment only if it leads to more positive reinforcement.

3. Devise a plan that combines punishment with positive reinforcement.
4. You may use precommitted punishment as a deterrent strategy, but only temporarily until the desired behavior can be supported by positive consequences.

The only recommended form of "punishment" is the systematic facing of the negative, long-term consequences of a problem behavior. This helps build commitment.

REINFORCEMENT IN PLANS FOR SELF-DIRECTION

Now we must consider the place of reinforcement in the A-B-C sequence. Powerful as reinforcement effects may be, they must be organized into a total intervention plan that involves antecedents, behaviors, and consequences. As you read this section, bear in mind the preliminary plans you have developed as step five (for antecedents) and step six (for developing new behaviors). By adding reinforcing contingencies to these plans, you will bring them to full potential.

Reinforcement and Antecedent Control

In Chapter 5 we described several methods for achieving antecedent control: avoiding antecedents, narrowing them, and building new ones by performing the desired behavior in new situations. *Each of these tactics involves a behavior change that should also be reinforced.*

For example, avoiding old antecedents was recommended as a first tactic for reducing undesirable consummatory responses. Thus, avoiding the morning cup of coffee can reduce the temptation to smoke; avoiding parties, at least for a while, can help bring overeating, pot smoking, or drinking under control. But this tactic involves a sharp decrease in reinforcement, since the old ones are lost. Therefore, new reinforcement is needed—reinforcement gained for avoiding the old antecedents.

The dieter who refused dinner invitations for a month arranged with his wife that they would go to a movie on the nights when the parties were held. A student who was smoking too much reinforced her avoiding pot parties with a long telephone chat with a friend the next morning. The young man who avoided excessive masturbation by choosing a busier restroom carried a mystery paperback with him and read it only while using the new facility. Each of these plans replaced the lost reinforcement with a new one, made contingent on avoiding an antecedent.

The same principle applies to behaviors performed in the presence of new antecedents: reinforcement should follow. Recall the theoretical discussion of stimulus control in Chapter 4. Cue control of behavior is built by reinforcing behavior in the presence of the cue. Since your eventual goal is to have your new, desired behaviors become habitual and "automatic," you must build this stimulus control through reinforcement in the presence of the new antecedent.

Reinforcement and the Development of New Behaviors

Every new behavior will require some reinforcement. If the behavior itself doesn't carry enough immediate reinforcement automatically, you will need to add additional contingent rewards. For example, we have suggested that the best new behaviors are those that are incompatible with some un-desired behavior. Some smokers have tried the technique of substituting some other behavior for smoking—for example, taking a piece of chewing gum instead of lighting a cigarette. But this technique is rarely effective if the smoker relies solely on the reinforcing quality of the gum, because, compared to a cigarette, gum is a rather weak reinforcer for the person who is addicted to tobacco. It would be better not only to employ the alternative behavior but also to heavily and quickly reinforce the performance of chewing gum instead of smoking. The necessity for reinforcing most new behaviors is a general principle, which we will illustrate further with a discussion of two topics: imag-ined rehearsal and shaping.

Imagined Rehearsal.   As discussed in Chapter 6, *imagined rehearsals* influence real performances according to the usual principles of behavior: reinforcement strengthens, punishment weakens, shaping is useful, incom-patible responses are necessary, and the like. For this reason, in rehearsing a desired behavior in imagination, it is useful to follow it with an imagined reinforcement (Kazdin, 1974d).

Cautela (1972, 1973) gives several examples of imagined reinforcers, such as swimming on a hot day and hearing good music. The following is one of Cautela's (1972) examples. Suppose you are a dieter who wants to practice control of overeating. You imagine, sometime during the day and wherever you happen to be, that you are "sitting at home watching TV. . . . You say to yourself 'I think I'll have a piece of pie.' You get up to go to the pantry. Then you say 'This is stupid. I don't want to be a fat pig.' " You should follow this imagined scene with the imagined reinforcement—the swim or the music. Here is another scene you can rehearse in imagination: "You are at home eating steak. You are just about to reach for your second piece, and you stop and say to yourself 'Who needs it, anyway?' (reinforcement)" (Cautela, 1972, p. 213).

The advantage of this form of imagined event is that the dieter can practice many times a day, in addition to the actual practices at meals and snacks. Also, the dieter is probably more likely to refuse the food in the imagined rehearsals than in real life. Imagined rehearsal can be a way of practicing while temptation is low, especially when your own behaviors are not yet firm enough to earn reinforcement in the real world. Another example from Cautela (1973) illustrates this point. A young man who had almost no experience or skills in approaching young women was taught to imagine the following scene and to self-reinforce it with imagined swimming in a warm river.

> Say to yourself "I think I'll call Jane for a date." As soon as you have this scene clearly, switch quickly to the reinforcement. As soon as you have the reinforcement vividly, hold it for two seconds. Then imagine that you walk to the phone and start to dial (reinforcement). You finish dialing. She answers. You say hello and ask her if she is free Saturday night. You tell her that you would like to go out with her. . . . Now do the whole sequence again. Make sure that the image is vivid. You can see the kitchen, feel the telephone. This time try to imagine that you are comfortable and confident as you call [Cautela, 1973, p. 30].

A similar example, adapted from Kazdin (1974d), is for the person who wants to become more assertive but whose skills are not developed well enough yet to risk them in the real world.

1. Imagine that you are eating in a restaurant with friends. You order a steak and tell the waiter you would like it rare. When the food arrives, you begin to eat and notice that it is overcooked.
2. Imagine that you immediately signal the waiter. When he arrives, you say "I ordered this steak rare, and this one is medium. Please take it back and bring me one that is rare."
3. Imagine that in a few minutes the waiter brings another steak, rare, and says he is very sorry this has happened.*

If you want to develop more general assertiveness, you should imagine several such scenes—saying no when a person asks for a favor you don't really want to do, protesting against being shortchanged, objecting when someone cuts in front of you in a line, or any other scene you can think of that reflects one of your own real-life dissatisfactions. And in each scene, let the positive reinforcement grow naturally out of the rehearsed behavior: you get the steak you want! If you are rehearsing in imagination how to deal with a persistent door-to-door salesperson, you can follow your imagined firmness by imagining the person leaving quickly and your own feeling of competence and self-assurance. Whenever possible, use a desirable "natural outcome" as your reinforcer. The advantage of using brief, independent scenes is that you can reinforce the various stages along the way.

Several psychologists have argued that the use of imagined reinforcement is not so much a use of reinforcement as it is another use of relaxation. In other words, the imagined scene of the lazy, summer river is more relaxing than reinforcing. So, imagined reinforcement should be thought of as a behavior incompatible with anxiety (Ladouceur, 1974; Marshall et al., 1974).

*From "Effects of Covert Modeling and Model Reinforcement on Assertive Behavior," by A. E. Kazdin, *Journal of Abnormal Psychology*, 1974, *83*, 240–252. Copyright 1974 by the American Psychological Association. Reprinted by permission.

But, since relaxation itself is reinforcing, imagined reinforcing scenes have more than one effect. When you imagine getting the steak you want or seeing the salesperson disappear or admiring your own slim body after dieting, not only do you receive reinforcement but you are also reminded of your goal and encouraged to move your imagined rehearsal quickly into real life.

Shaping.   The technique of shaping, which was discussed at length in Chapter 6, also illustrates the necessity of reinforcing all new behaviors. Here, we will complete our discussion by adding the one remaining rule for correct shaping: each step must be reinforced.

The definition of each shaping step is actually a standard or criterion. For example:

Step one: 2,000 calories per day
Step two: 1,800 calories per day
Reinforcer: one hour of television per evening

For step one, the reinforcer is taken only when the standard for that step is met (2000 calories). For step two, the standard becomes 1800 calories daily, and only then will television be watched.

Shaping steps are no different than any other behavior; if their natural consequences are not yet strong enough, they require arranged reinforcement. The case of Linda (Chapter 6), who feared birds, is a good illustration. As she built a schedule of steps closer and closer to the birds she feared, she didn't use at first any extra reinforcement, since she received strong rewards from her pride for mastering the fear; in other words, moving near the birds was "intrinsically" rewarding. But, when her schedule brought her quite close to the birds, she got stuck. She simply couldn't stay relaxed. At this point Linda introduced a token system. For each step up the hierarchy, she earned so many points, which she could turn in at the end of the day to "buy" certain privileges, such as allowing herself extra dates, doing "idiot" reading, and so on. Her goal was to increase her total positive reinforcements so that she would gain something for getting really close to the birds. At last report, although she said that she still didn't like birds, she could approach birds without feeling nervous.

As Linda's example illustrates, reinforcement is often necessary to strengthen the approach toward a feared situation. In Linda's case, two separate forms of reinforcement were employed. One was the formal token system, which Linda used to bolster the last, most difficult stages of approach. But the earlier, less obvious reinforcement was the presence of her boyfriend. The woman originally elected to include him because his presence made her feel more relaxed. But his walking beside her also had reinforcing value for the approach behavior.

Cheating.   Taking the reinforcer without having performed the target behavior is a fairly common occurrence in self-direction. Almost everyone does it sometimes. You should watch yourself very carefully, however, because cheating more than occasionally—say, more than 10% of the time—indicates a shaping problem. Therefore, you should redesign your shaping schedule so that you will be reinforced for performing at some level that you find realistic. As long as you are able to provide a contingent reinforcement, you are building toward the final goal, no matter how small the steps are or how low you begin. If you cheat, don't abandon the project—redesign it.

A young man whose final goal was to save $7 each week began by requiring himself to save 50¢ each day (he put it in a piggy bank), even though he had almost never saved any money before. He used the reinforcer of eating supper only after he had put the money in his piggy bank. After three days, he skipped his saving for one day but went ahead and ate supper anyway. This was the beginning of a two-week period during which he more often skipped than saved but ate his supper. He realized that this kind of cheating was due to a problem in his shaping program. So he wrote a new contract, in which he required himself to save only 25¢ each day—a more realistic place to begin, in his case—in order to gain the reinforcer.

Objections to Self-Reinforcement

If you are encountering the idea of control-through-consequences for the first time, you probably find it peculiar. Many students object. They don't believe that a desired behavior *should* be deliberately self-rewarded; virtue should be its own reward. We agree. The goal is to make your desired behavior so smooth and successful that the natural consequences of daily life will sustain it. When you reach that stage, self-reinforcement (and all the rest of your plan) can go underground; only your skill will be left showing. Self-reinforcement is a temporary strategy, like verbal self-control, to be used only until behaviors become automated into their settings. But, like talking to yourself, reinforcing your behaviors will continue to be a useful, temporary device whenever virtue again fails to reward itself enough.

But some of our students have continued to object. "Even if we grant that point," they say, "you can't learn—really learn—under these conditions of self-bribery. It's all an act, not real behavior." Well, we reply, what is real and what is an act? If you could put on an act of playing tennis well enough to win real matches, would you feel embarrassed because "it's just an act"? Skill is a real thing, however you learn it. But, if you mean that "self-bribed" behavior cannot sustain itself, you have a point. If you are motivated to perform your new behavior only by the "artificial" rewards in your plan, you probably won't continue, once you tire of playing the game. Remember that we cautioned you to select a behavior-change project that you really value. If your changed behavior will bring greater self-respect and a happier life, then these rewarding consequences will sustain you in the long haul. Self-reinforcement is to be used only now, and in future times when a stronger push is needed to get you off-center and rolling.

Summary: When to Include Self-Reinforcement in Your Intervention Plan

Now that we have discussed methods for adding reinforcement to self-change projects for antecedent control and for developing new behaviors, the questions to be answered are: When should self-reinforcement be included in the project? When can it be omitted?

We suggest the following rule-of-thumb answer: during the process of learning, make sure that any new behavior is followed promptly by some reinforcement. Some behaviors will be reinforced naturally and immediately, merely by being performed, and require no contrived reinforcement. For example, the tennis player who coaches herself by self-instructions will be reinforced in the swift consequences of her ongoing play. In social interactions, the social game is also swift, and improved behaviors are likely to produce their own rewards. In such situations, inserting self-reinforcement after each performance of the behavior can be distracting. Indeed, inserting self-reinforcement into a situation that is intrinsically or immediately rewarding can even detract from performance (Kirsch, Heatherington, & Colapietro, 1979; Lepper, Greene, & Nisbett, 1973; Barrera & Rosen, 1977).

But many new behaviors, particularly in their early stages, are not followed by natural reinforcement. Natural reinforcement can be a long time coming for the dieter, the beginning exerciser, the fearful, the shy—indeed, for most who first undertake self-directed improvement. Self-conscious, contrived reinforcement is designed to strengthen behavior until the behavior becomes self-sustaining by producing its own rewards. Therefore, our rule-of-thumb—that new behavior should be followed by some reinforcement—most often means that you should include some form of contrived reinforcement in the early stages of your plan. Not always; but don't exclude reinforcement unless you are confident that the environment itself will provide the necessary immediate reinforcement.

THEORY AND RESEARCH IN SELF-DIRECTED CONSEQUENCES

Can you really achieve your goals by rearranging the consequences of your behavior? The research evidence suggests an unqualified yes. But exactly how this works, from the theoretical point of view, is the subject of lively debate.

The issue is usually broken down into two questions. First, can one learn to self-reinforce? Second, do self-administered consequences really reinforce and punish behavior?

Learning to Self-Reinforce

Children and adults can learn to self-reinforce by imitating others, by following instructions, or by receiving rewards for self-reinforcing (Bandura,

1971; Kanfer, 1970). Bandura and his associates have taught even pigeons, monkeys, and dogs to "self-reinforce"—that is, to not take freely available rewards until after they had performed the desired behavior. These animals were taught by an experimenter who removed the food trays if the animals tried to take the reward before performing. Once learned, self-reinforcing persisted for some time (Bandura & Mahoney, 1974; Mahoney & Bandura, 1972; Mahoney, Bandura, Dirks, & Wright, 1974). Catania (1975) argues that this isn't really self-control, any more than refraining from shoplifting is self-control. If there were no external punishment for shoplifting (or taking the food), everyone would eventually walk out with whatever reinforcers they wanted.

Theoreticians who make this kind of argument point out that there has to be some external reason to self-reinforce and to stick to the planned contingencies. Rachlin (1974) correctly points out that a student would not make moviegoing contingent on studying unless the external reasons for studying—grades and career success—were meaningful.

Of course, in self-directed behavior, the external contingencies are provided by your goals. You choose your goals because achieving them will improve your life. When you are working for goals that you genuinely value, self-rewarding and self-punishing can certainly be carried out; competent self-directors do so all the time.

Is Self-Reward Reinforcing?

Many studies demonstrate that self-administered reward increases behaviors. These studies, which have been reviewed in several articles (Bandura, 1971; Kanfer, 1970; Speidel, 1977), have dealt with the positive effects of self-administered reward on manual work by children, arithmetic problems by college students, schoolwork by elementary school pupils, and accuracy of judgment by adults.

But there is a vigorous debate concerning *why* and *how* self-reward works. Does self-reward work because of reinforcement? Skinner (1953), Bandura (1976), Staats (1968), and many others believe that it does and that it works according to the same principles by which children learn because of their parents' reinforcement or pigeons learn because of the experimenter's food pellets.

Others (Ainslee, 1975; Catania, 1975; Rachlin, 1974) point out that self-reward is a very complicated process, which contains many effective elements. For example, when you reinforce your behavior, you are calling your own attention to it. You are giving yourself clear information, clear feedback (Castro & Rachlin, 1980). You are making the behavior more vivid, even more vivid than in self-recording alone. You are teaching yourself to discriminate between correct and incorrect performances. You are reminding yourself of your long-term goals and of your rules for getting there (Nelson, Sprong, Hayes, & Graham, 1979). You are learning *self-awareness* (Catania, 1975).

Reinforcement is very likely one significant element in self-rewarding. But the other elements are also important and add more support to the strategy of self-reward in achieving self-determination.

YOUR OWN SELF-DIRECTION PROJECT: STEP SEVEN

Review the previous versions of your plan, which included elements of antecedent control and development of new behavior, in light of what you have just learned about rearrangements of consequences. Also plan for following new behaviors with self-reinforcement. Be sure to include verbal self-reinforcement, plus at least one other technique.

The result may well be your final plan. Before implementing it, however, read the next chapter, which will help you combine A, B, and C elements into a comprehensive package.

TIPS FOR TYPICAL TOPICS

Assertion. Most nonassertive people suffer from the unreasonable expectation that some awful consequence will necessarily follow from their attempts to assert themselves—"If I do, he won't be my friend anymore." Use instead imagined positive reinforcement, and anticipate the favorable outcomes. If you assert yourself early, moderately, and politely, the actual consequences are likely to be very pleasant. However, if you realistically expect to be punished by someone for asserting yourself, you can take steps to minimize the effects of that punishment (Shelton, 1979) by practicing being assertive in imagination, by relaxing, and by concentrating on the positive consequences of your behavior.

Use shaping and reinforcement, beginning with assertive behaviors that are likely to produce success. As you risk more, you may feel guilty or hurt after having been assertive. If these feelings persist, they will decrease your chances of maintaining the gains you have made; so try to eliminate those feelings by using thought stopping and by concentrating on the positive consequences of your newly learned assertiveness.

Depression. Use self-reinforcement to increase the frequency of your desired behaviors. Your plan should have this general form: (1) *Schedule* pleasant activities frequently. (2) *Reinforce* yourself for engaging in the activities; be very liberal and reinforce only on contingency, but begin with shaping steps that you can meet (Fuchs & Rehm, 1977). (3) *Replace* denigrating self-speech with realistic self-praise; be sure to include verbal self-reinforcement for each desired behavior.

Specific Fears. As you get closer and closer to the feared situation, you may need self-reinforcement. Add it to your plan at that time. For all plans, include verbal self-reinforcement. Use it at each stage and for each behavior you approve of.

The Other Sex.   Use self-reinforcement to bridge any gaps between where you are now and where you would like to be—more relaxed or skillful. The natural reinforcements offered by the other sex are strong enough to maintain behavior (!), once confidence and skill have been achieved.

Family, Friends, Lovers, and Coworkers.   Reinforce yourself for doing what is needed to improve the relationships, and be sure to reinforce the others: "Hey, that was really nice. We sat and talked about our problem without anyone blowing up. I really appreciate the effort you are making." We don't think this is Machiavellian; it's courteous.

Studying and Time Management.   Reinforcement is highly important in studying and time scheduling—much more important than poor and disorganized students believe. In fact, successful students tend to develop self-reinforcement techniques on their own, without a course or a book like this one (Hefferman & Richards, 1979; Perri & Richards, 1977). Often reinforcement can be obtained by a simple rearrangement. For example, use pleasant occupations (leisure or hobbies) to reinforce the more difficult ones like studying, so that one is directly tied to the other and reinforces it. In drawing up your time-management plan, make sure that a pleasant block of time follows any particularly difficult one, and follow the rule that you must complete the difficult activity before you move to the pleasant one.

Whenever you can't arrange your activities as described above, use other reinforcers, however arbitrary: movies, candy, cash, tokens. Your basic plan should (1) be based on a firm schedule, (2) include enough pleasant activities, and (3) provide for reinforcement for following the schedule.

Overeating, Smoking, Drinking, and Drug Use.   Reinforcement is a vital element in your plan. Reinforce yourself for avoiding the situations that cue excessive consumption.

Use reinforcement to strengthen all the behaviors your self-control requires, such as counting calories, resisting urges, exercising, graphing, and avoiding temptation.

As often as possible, use the natural reinforcement that your long-range self-control will bring. Consider the benefits of your diet: do you feel better, happier, more alive? Consider the benefits of giving up tobacco, three of which you will enjoy as soon as you quit (Pechacek & Danaher, 1979)—immediate clearance of smoke from your lungs, clearance of carbon monoxide from your blood, and reduced risk of sudden death. Remind yourself of these three rewards. Remind yourself of the immediate and long-term benefits of giving up alcohol or drugs. These, too, are quite numerous.

But odds are, you will continue to need other forms of reinforcement to replace the consummatory behaviors. Reinforce alternatives, and arrange for reinforcement from others. Successful weight losers received positive feedback from several external sources, such as parents and peers (Perri & Richards, 1977).

CHAPTER **8**

Planning for Change

GOAL:
To describe the steps involved in putting together a plan for change.

OUTLINE:
Combining A, B, and C elements
The features of a good plan
Formulating the plan
Your own self-direction project: Step eight
Tips for typical topics

An effective plan must combine antecedent, behavior, and consequence (A-B-C) elements. The goal of this chapter is to help you design such a plan. First, we will illustrate some ways of integrating A, B, and C elements, and then we will discuss the principles that characterize a sound plan. So far we have treated each technique and principle in isolation, independently of one another. But an effective plan for change needs to bring together and integrate all these techniques and principles. Therefore, we have chosen two topics that illustrate how the various elements must be combined, just as they must be combined in actual change processes. Any complete intervention plan could be used to illustrate coordination, because every plan must combine and coordinate the many features it involves. The two examples chosen here—the *two-stage process for consummatory behaviors* and *problems in social interaction*—have been selected because they are both common and difficult to implement.

COMBINING A, B, AND C ELEMENTS

A Two-Stage Process for Consummatory Behaviors

In Chapter 5 we suggested that undesired consummatory behaviors can be reduced by avoiding the controlling antecedents—at least as a first step. In Chapter 7 we suggested that heavy reinforcement may be needed to carry out that avoidance successfully. But few such antecedents can be avoided permanently; eventually you'll want to return to dinner parties, be able to walk into a bakery, or go back to the morning cup of coffee. New behaviors must be developed—behaviors that can be performed even in the old, tempting situations. Developing new behaviors has been discussed in Chapter 6. What follows is a two-stage process for changing consummatory behaviors that coordinates all elements.

In stage 1 deliberately avoid the antecedent. For example, don't go to parties where you will be strongly tempted to smoke, or don't confront yourself with high-calorie food. Then, *in stage 2, build new behaviors* so that you can go to parties or eat only a small amount of dessert.

In stage 1 you gain the reinforcer for simply avoiding the tempting antecedent situation. In stage 2 you gain the reinforcer for being able to withstand exposure to the antecedent without performing your old, undesired behavior.

Larry, a man who had unsuccessfully tried to quit smoking several times, did an analysis of the situations in which he had returned to smoking after having "quit" for a few days. He found that one of those situations was taking a coffee break or eating lunch with his colleagues, several of whom smoked. Their cigarettes looked so inviting that he would bum one and then be "hooked" again. In stage 1 of his plan Larry avoided these antecedents for two weeks, carefully explaining to his friends what he was doing and reinforcing himself for successful avoidance. He was not tempted so much on the weekends, because he spent them with his wife, who didn't smoke. After he had been off cigarettes for several weeks, he entered stage 2, in which he gained the reinforcer specifically for not smoking with his friends at lunch. After this had worked for a week, he added coffee breaks to his daily schedule and reinforced himself specifically for not smoking at coffee breaks. Now Larry's task was to remain vigilant for tempting antecedents and to reinforce himself for not smoking when the antecedent occurred. He was able to tell when such an antecedent was present, because he would suddenly realize how much he wanted a cigarette. The morning cup of coffee, a meal, a relaxed period, another smoker, a party—these were the kinds of tempting antecedents that he had to learn to deal with.

Rehearsal in imagination is a good technique for this kind of situation. Several times a day Larry would imagine himself in a situation in which he was tempted to smoke—concentrating on imagining all the details and including his own strong craving for a cigarette—and yet *not* giving in and resisting the temptation.

You may also try to eliminate a situation's stimulus control gradually. If there are a dozen different antecedents of smoking or overeating, you try gaining control over them one at a time. This gives you a feeling of progress, which is a welcome reinforcer. This procedure is a form of shaping, in which you first eliminate the easier antecedents, one at a time, and then move up to the more difficult ones.

The basic idea behind the two-stage process for consummatory behaviors is first to avoid antecedents that cue the unwanted behavior and then to gradually gain control over them. You gain control through techniques like imagined rehearsal, rehearsal in the real world, shaping, reinforcement, using others to help you, and the like.

This seems to be one of the hardest lessons for people with consummatory problems to learn. The idea of stimulus control and, consequently, of eliminating stimulus control over unwanted behaviors is not part of the usual "common-sense psychology." And this may be precisely why people have difficulty gaining control over behaviors such as overeating. They don't see where the control lies in the environment, so they don't know how to go about wresting control away from the antecedents that govern such acts. And, yet, the overeater eats in response to emotion—anger, boredom, or depression—or to the sight of food, time of day, or schedule. These are the antecedents that control his or her overeating. Similarly, the smoker responds to time of day, food, coffee, drink, social occasions, boredom, excitement, and so on.

If you are addicted to overeating, smoking, or other consummatory acts, use the two-stage procedure we have outlined. First, avoid the controlling antecedents, if necessary one at a time. Second, develop a new behavior to be performed in response to the old cue, so that, when you are once again confronted with the antecedents, you won't slip back into automatically performing the consummatory act. Like any new behaviors, this new behavior will have to be rehearsed, shaped, and reinforced.

Problems in Social Interaction

The two-stage technique we have been suggesting is not limited to consummatory behaviors. It can be applied successfully to other kinds of problems—for example, to those related to social interactions. Problems in interacting with other people are often very difficult to solve, because they may seem to be the other person's fault. But such problems, too, will often yield to an intervention plan, if the plan carefully coordinates antecedent, behavior, and consequence elements, as the following case illustrates.

Leslie and Helen worked together, and, over a year's period, their relationship had deteriorated to the point that just seeing each other made them angry. When they did talk to each other, the inevitable results were anger and hurt feelings. The obvious solution—that of avoiding each other—was impossible, since they had to work in the same room day after day. So one of them, Leslie, decided to do something about it; more precisely, she decided to try a two-stage intervention program. The first stage was an effort to control the antecedents for both of them.

Stage 1. Leslie instituted a "cooling-off period," in which she simply didn't talk with Helen except when it was absolutely necessary. When she did talk, she would confine her remarks to business topics and try to be either neutral or mildly pleasant. This was reasonably effective. After a couple of weeks they settled down for two months of occasional, brief, relatively calm interactions. Most important, anger seemed to have disappeared from the picture.

This first stage of Leslie's program is an example of avoiding the controlling antecedent—in this case, talking with the other person—long enough to begin to develop other, more desirable reactions. The importance of developing some new and more desirable behavior cannot be stressed enough. In the case of these two women, for example, if no new behavior had been developed, the "cooling-off period" would have ended in failure. Eventually their work would have required them to have more substantial conversations, and they would have gradually returned to their old behavior of stimulating each other to anger.

Stage 2. Leslie then went into a second stage, in which she (1) did not respond to any "anger-producing" remarks from Helen; (2) positively reinforced Helen for any pleasant remarks (if Helen said "I'm not sure you're doing a good job," Leslie would ignore her; but, if she said "That seemed to work out very well," Leslie would say "Why, thanks very much. It's kind of you to say that"); and (3) praised Helen for her good work and refrained from criticizing her less-than-good work.

When the antecedent of your undesired behavior is the behavior of another person, it is sometimes possible to change the behavior of the other person by reinforcing him or her for another kind of behavior.

Very often interpersonal problems develop because one person begins to punish the other. Receiving punishment often incites people to revenge, so that a vicious circle is established. One punishment leads to the next; this, in turn, leads to more punishment, and so on until the relationship is destroyed. One way of breaking this vicious circle is to realize that you can reinforce yourself for reinforcing someone else. And you reinforce someone else by paying attention or making some statement that is rewarding.

When you are involved in a problematic interpersonal relationship, you can ask yourself "What kinds of antecedents am I providing for the other person? How could I reinforce desired behavior?" Your intervention plan might involve paying attention to the "good" things the other person does and reinforcing the person for them. You then reinforce yourself for reinforcing the other. In a book on how to achieve a good marriage, Knox (1971) suggests keeping records like this:

The husband records: Wife's desirable behavior	Wife's undesirable behavior	Husband's response to wife's behavior
The wife records: Husband's desirable behavior	Husband's undesirable behavior	Wife's response to husband's behavior*

Comparing the two records allows you to see if you are in fact trying to punish your spouse's undesired behavior instead of trying to reward his or her

*From *Marriage Happiness: A Behavioral Approach to Counseling,* by D. Knox. Copyright 1971 by Research Press. Reprinted by permission.

desirable acts. This record can also show how the spouse's behavior represents an antecedent for your own and vice versa. It tells what changes you should ask of your spouse and what changes you should try to make in yourself.

This kind of recording and comparison can be used by any two people who want to improve their relationship. A pair of roommates had developed a pattern of arguing that seemed likely to make their friendship much less rewarding for both. The vicious circle went like this. Anne would do something that Betty thought was arrogant. Betty would then put down Anne. This would anger Anne, who, in turn, would attack Betty. From Anne's point of view, Betty was a "putdown artist." From Betty's point of view, Anne was intolerably arrogant. They came to us, and we thought that both were partially right: Anne was arrogant, and Betty seemed to enjoy putting her down. Deciding who was "right," however, was not the point and wouldn't have helped very much in any case.

The two worked out a mutual agreement whereby Betty would ignore Anne's outbursts of arrogance and Anne would ignore Betty's "putdowns." Each also agreed to tell the other when an act particularly pleased her. Thus they agreed to provide new antecedents and new reinforcers for each other.

Two people working together to improve their relationship can develop specific agreements: you give up this, and I'll give up that; you do this, and I'll do that. Since certain changes in another person to whom you are close can be a powerful incentive for you to change, this kind of mutual agreement is a powerful technique.

Summary

Good plans for change must include elements of antecedent control, the development of new behaviors, and control of consequences. We discussed three examples—one for controlling consummatory behaviors and two for changing irritating interactions with other people.

THE FEATURES OF A GOOD PLAN

If you have been following the steps suggested at the end of each of the preceding chapters, you are already close to a final plan for self-change. At the end of this chapter you will be ready to complete it. It is important that you have confidence in your plan. If you have attended carefully to the principles already discussed, that confidence is likely to be well placed. There is no such thing as a perfect plan for a problem; in fact, you could adopt several different plans for the same goal, any one of which could be successful. Not everyone will develop the same kind of plan for similar goals; but, if the plans are sound, any one of them may succeed. This chapter will discuss the features that characterize a sound plan.

A successful plan cannot be vague. If only vague intentions were needed to change problem behavior, you wouldn't need the full range of techniques you have been reading about. Of course, sometimes you can change your behavior by simply alerting yourself to the need to do so. But, for problem situations, you need more deliberate plans for self-change.

A Theoretical View of a Good Plan

A successful plan will include all these features: (1) rules that state the kinds of techniques for change you will use in specific situations, (2) goals and subgoals, (3) feedback on how you are progressing, derived from your self-observations, and (4) comparison of feedback to goals and subgoals to measure progress.

Rules.   Rules govern much of your life. When we talk of rules with students, they sometimes groan "Rules, rules, rules! What I want is less rules, not more." These comments may be appropriate for rules set by others. Self-directed behavior involves setting rules for oneself in the service of reaching one's goals. Social rewards and punishments influence our personal rules, but the rules we have made for ourselves are the ones that influence our behavior the most (Weiner & Dubanoski, 1975; Lovitt & Curtiss, 1969).

Adopting personal rules doesn't constrict our lives or limit our opportunities. Rules make our behaviors more organized, more economical. Only through clear rules can we realize our values and goals.

If some behavior is *not* a problem for you, you follow your own rules without paying much attention to them. If you have little difficulty asserting yourself, for example, you don't have to state some explicit rule like "I must be sure to speak up for my rights when someone is taking advantage of me." But, when you are *not* meeting some goal, you need to set clear, explicit, specific rules to guide your behavior until that behavior, too, becomes habitual.

When you say "I will reward myself with two points for every time I make an honest statement," you are setting an explicit personal rule. When the rule has been made explicit, you are more likely to make those honest statements. That's the whole purpose of rules—to make the desired behaviors more likely.

In your plan for self-direction, the rules are statements of the techniques you will use in specific situations; they become antecedents or cues to your behavior change. Here are several examples of rules that have been included in self-direction plans.

> Every night, between 7 and 9 o'clock, I will practice relaxation exercises for 20 minutes.
>
> Before leaving for a dinner party, I'll ask my wife to remind me not to overeat.
>
> Whenever I feel the first signs of muscular tension, I will immediately say "relax" to myself.
>
> When I have studied for one hour, I will award myself 2 token points.

The typical plan will have more than one rule. For example:

Each day in my art history class, I will make at least one comment. Each time I make a comment, I will make a checkmark on my record card. When I have accumulated 5 checkmarks, I will allow myself one glass of wine or beer in the evening.

These are three separate rules that describe, respectively, the first shaping step for the student, his record-keeping system, and his token-system plan for contingent reinforcement.

Each element of a plan can be stated in terms of situation-technique rules. The successful plan makes these rules explicit and precise.

Goals and Subgoals.   Making goals and subgoals explicit is vital to the success of any plan (Spates & Kanfer, 1977). Each subgoal has to be formulated precisely enough for you to be able to compare it with your performance and know exactly if you have achieved the subgoal.

In drawing up your plan, you must remember that the long-range standard is not necessarily the immediate standard. Shaping, the method of approximations, requires that we set subgoals along the way. Each subgoal should be exactly specific, becoming the standard by which you can judge success at each stage (Greiner, 1974, discussed in Kanfer, 1975). During the life of your plan you will keep revising standards for yourself. In effect, you will have a series of plans, one for each subgoal.

For each subgoal you make specific rules for yourself to follow. These rules tell you which situations require which techniques. The subgoal for that situation is some specific outcome. For example,

Rules for subgoal 1: Each day I will practice relaxation techniques (at first I'll do this 20 minutes per day), until I can relax without going through all the muscle tension-release steps.

Rules for subgoal 2: Each day I will spend at least 10 minutes rehearsing in my imagination applying for a job, until I can think about it with a tension rating no greater than *mild.*

As each subgoal is met, the next step can begin with new rules and subgoals. The goal for each step is the level of performance needed to advance to the next step.

Feedback Gathering.   Any effective plan must incorporate a system for gathering information about the progress you make. If you are learning to serve in tennis, you don't strike the ball and then close your eyes. You follow the trajectory of the ball carefully, getting information about its speed, twist, and whether it lands in court or not. Your standard is *ball in the court;* if your feedback tells you that it is *out,* you can perform some operation to correct your behavior. If you had no feedback, you couldn't possibly improve.

All goal-oriented behavior is governed by this principle. Without some information about your performance (feedback), you cannot correct yourself, whether your goal is to be a better student, a better lover, or a better tennis player. For this reason your plan must include a system for collecting data. Of course, you are already doing that for baseline purposes, as outlined in Chapter 3. But you must continue to self-record for the whole duration of your plan, so that self-correction can occur.

Thus the person attempting to lower anxiety about a job interview keeps noting from time to time his or her anxiety, to see if changes are occurring. The person counting the number of self-defeating thoughts per week continues to count. The person counting the duration of each marathon swim session continues to record elapsed time.

Comparison of Feedback to Goals and Subgoals.   The next step in your plan follows logically. In fact, most of the time it is quite automatic: feedback is compared to the standard. "How am I doing?" you ask yourself. The answer may be "Terrific!" The ball landed in the court, you studied 15 hours, your mate loves your lovemaking.

But for most of us most of the time, the answer is not likely to be "Terrific!" Things are not quite so perfect, and we see that we are slightly off our ideal standard. We then make some adjustments, and some improvement generally occurs. Whether these adjustments are minor or major, you won't be sure that they are the right ones—or even that they are needed—unless you record your self-observations and compare them to your goal.

When the feedback tells you that you have achieved some subgoal, you move up to the next step. You may continue the same plan if it is working, or you may change it if it is not. Of course, you continue to get feedback, so that you can know if the techniques you use are indeed working.

This comparison process is central to effective self-direction (Kanfer, 1975). It is a process that characterizes successful people in every kind of activity. The writing of novels, for example, might seem dependent on the rush of inspiration and the caprice of the muse. Not so: firm, daily work goals—in terms of number of pages (or even words) written—have been characteristic of novelists as diverse as Anthony Trollope, Arnold Bennett, Ernest Hemingway, and Irving Wallace. Equally important, each of these writers counted his output daily and compared it to his daily goal (Wallace & Pear, 1977). Even author George Sand—the "Notorious Woman" often portrayed as impulsive and passionate—observed a nightly work schedule of 30 written pages, no matter what her condition.

Adjustments in the Plan.   At some point you will advance to a goal that requires new tactics. For example, you may have used relaxation and covert rehearsal until you reached your first standard—comfortably imagining starting a conversation with a stranger. But now you must perform that behavior in the real situation, and that will require some reinforcement and shaping steps. Although your new plan will include different techniques, it will have the same elements that characterize all successful plans: explicit rules, precise goals, feedback gathering, and comparison of feedback to goals.

FORMULATING THE PLAN

As you begin to formulate a complete plan, it is well to review the most important issues presented in the preceding chapters. These issues can be formulated as a series of questions. If you can answer all of them positively, you are ready to combine all you have learned into an effective personal plan.

_____ Have you specified the goal clearly?

_____ Have you made changes in the way you specified the goal as your self-understanding increased?

_____ Have you taken steps to build commitment to do the work of changing?

_____ Have you worked out a self-observation system you can use when the problem behavior occurs?

_____ Do you keep written records?

Here is a checklist of the steps involved in designing intervention:

_____ If your goal is to decrease some unwanted behavior, have you taken steps to discover and eliminate the antecedents of that behavior?

_____ Have you developed a plan to change thoughts that represent the antecedents of the behavior?

_____ Have you examined your beliefs to see whether they are contributing to your problem behavior?

_____ Have you developed a plan to cope with the physical antecedents of the behavior?

_____ Have you worked out a plan to deal with the social antecedents of the behavior?

_____ Have you taken steps to provide antecedents that will encourage your new, desired behavior?

_____ Have you developed some thoughts you can use as antecedents of the new behavior?

_____ Does your plan include specific self-instructions?

_____ Have you planned for physical antecedents to become cues?

_____ Have you asked others to encourage you or structured your social environment to provide helpful antecedents?

You should be able to answer yes to most of the questions above.

_____ As you try to develop new behaviors, do you use some form of shaping?

_____ If your goal is to decrease an unwanted act, are you planning to use some incompatible behavior to substitute for it?

_____ If your problem involves anxiety or tension, are you going to practice relaxation?

_____ Have you made provision to rehearse any new behavior you want to develop?

_____ Does your plan call for imagined rehearsal?
_____ Have you made provision to rehearse in the real world?

Here too, you should be able to say yes to most of these questions.

_____ Have you discovered through self-observation what may be reinforcing your unwanted behaviors? If so, have you developed a plan for using that same reinforcement to strengthen a desired behavior instead?
_____ Have you developed a reinforcement plan in which you are rewarded if you take appropriate steps in your plan for self-change?
_____ Does your plan include a token system?
_____ Does your plan include Premack-type reinforcers?
_____ Does your plan include verbal self-reinforcement? reminders of the reinforcement you will receive if you stick to each step of your plan?
_____ Does your plan include any form of precommitted punishment?
_____ Does your plan include an arrangement ensuring that you'll be reinforced in the real world for any changes you make in your behavior?

Remember, your chances of success increase if you use a variety of techniques. And a solid plan involves antecedents, the behavior itself, and consequences. If you have not yet worked out a plan that includes elements of all three, now is the time to stop and do so.

Brainstorming

Once you have reviewed procedures for each of the A, B, and C elements, your plan is ready for final design. It is here that students often get cold feet. Knowledge of principles is absolutely necessary, but that knowledge doesn't necessarily lead to creative ideas for specific plans. In our experience, students are likely to be more inhibited in formulating plans than is necessary. Any plan you create can be checked for the soundness of principles and for common sense. Often the difficulty is generating that very first idea.

Before settling on a final plan, it is often useful to use once more the technique of *brainstorming* (see "Tactic Seven" in Chapter 2 and Box 2-1). Remember that the goal of brainstorming is to generate as many ideas as possible, quickly, without being critical of them. The four rules are:

1. Try for *quantity* of ideas.
2. *Don't criticize* your ideas; don't even evaluate them. You will do that later.
3. Try to think of *unusual* ideas.
4. Try to *combine* ideas to get new ones.

Here's an example. Jim, who had a bad case of acne when he was in high school, has developed the habit of picking at his face. He wants to stop this habit, because it tends to inflame his sensitive skin, produces infections, and makes him look terrible. But it is an automatic habit, and he is having trouble thinking of ways to stop it. After having gone through the checklist,

Jim tries to brainstorm solutions: "I have to stop. Let's see. I could . . . slap my face every time I do it. No, that's dumb." Long pause, no ideas. "Oh, yeah, I was criticizing the idea. Don't do that now. Just produce a lot of ideas, evaluate them later. OK. So, I could slap my face every time I do it. I could ask Lois to tell me to stop whenever I do it. I could ask my parents to tell me, too. I could rub my face instead of picking it. I could pull out my hair instead. Ha! I could suck my thumb, or——I could pick my nose. Ha! No criticism now! I could say to myself 'I want to stop picking my face, so I won't do it now.' I could do that and rub my face instead of picking. I could remind myself that it might get red or infected. Since I do it when I'm watching TV, I could put a sign on the TV reminding me not to do it. Ditto for studying. Put a sign on my desk. I could report to Lois every day about how much I did it the previous day, and show her that I was cutting down. Ditto my parents. Every day I could cut down a little more over the day before. If I didn't, then I wouldn't get to watch TV that day; but, if I did, I'd put aside some money for something—for some clothes or a record. I could force myself to do it for hours at a time till I got so sick of it I'd never do it again. I could . . ."

That shows how the brainstorming process works. Having written down these ideas, Jim must then select the sensible ones, design a tentative plan, and then examine it to make sure that it is in accord with the principles he has learned.

A Sample Plan

This is the plan of a college student who wanted to reduce her anxiety about speaking to her professors. Her plan is not perfect, and we have chosen it because it demonstrates a plan's strengths as well as weaknesses. Read the plan critically, and try to anticipate our remarks about its different features.

In her report this student wrote: "I almost never talk with my professors. They scare me. Sometimes I have questions; at other times I would just like to talk with them. But I have spoken only to one, Prof. A., all year, and that's only for a few sentences at a time. My goal: increase talking with my professors.

"I will develop my behavior gradually, on a shaping schedule. Each step will represent a new standard. I have to start really low, because my baseline is nearly zero. This is my shaping schedule:

Step 1: Say hello to a professor.
Step 2: Talk with a professor for 15 seconds.
Step 3: Talk with a professor for 30 seconds.
Step 4: Talk for 1 minute.
Step 5: Talk for 2 minutes."

Our analysis: So far, her plan is generally satisfactory, except that she should have specified how many times she would rehearse each step before moving to the next. In other words, her plan lacks specific subgoals for each step.

Collecting feedback: "My wristwatch has a sweep-second hand. If I turn the band, the watch will be on my wrist facing up. I can sort of look down to check the time, without being too obvious. As soon as the conversation is over, I'll write down notes—how many seconds, the professor's name, where we were, and so forth."

Comparing feedback with standards: "On the inside front cover of my notebook I'll write my shaping schedule. It shouldn't be too hard to check whether I met my standards or not."

Our analysis: Perhaps. But it would have been better if she had also used a graph in her notebook. Using the watch that way is a nice idea. Electronic watches are inexpensive these days and very useful for timing behavior.

Techniques: "I decided to use a combination of Premack and food reinforcers. Since I eat lunch every day at school, I set a rule that I wouldn't eat lunch until I had performed whatever step was required by the schedule."

Our analysis: Selecting "lunch" as the reinforcer may seem drastic; but, since her schedule is reasonable and develops slowly, she should never actually have to go without food. At the same time, she gains the reinforcing effect that lunch would have on the target behavior.

There are several other problems with her plan. Other techniques should have been included, principally self-instructions before the conversation and self-praise after it. Notice that she doesn't include any rehearsal in imagination. That is probably all right in this case, because she doesn't seem too uncomfortable about rehearsing in the actual situation. Nevertheless, we would have recommended learning relaxation and relaxing herself before approaching the professor. All in all, this plan sounds too simple.

Results: "This plan didn't work. I could work at steps 1 and 2 OK. But at step 3 I got into trouble because the professor wouldn't quit talking to me, and suddenly I was involved in a complex conversation and became quite nervous. So I worked out a second plan."

Our analysis: Good! Plans are made to be changed if they don't work.

Plan 2: "The reason the first plan failed was that the professor carried me too far up the schedule. Looking back, it seems inevitable that this would happen. I might have gotten up to 3 minutes, or something like that, but at some point some professor would have just continued talking to me, and I'd be in trouble. I decided to enlist the aid of one particular teacher.

"I stopped Prof. A. in the hall and explained the situation to him. I selected Prof. A. because I like him and he was the only one I talked to during my baseline period. I know he is interested in students. I explained that I wanted to use him to practice on. He thought this was kind of funny, but I got my nerve up and explained why the first plan had failed. This conversation was very difficult for me, and I could see that I needed a new schedule. Here it is:

Step 1: Talk with Prof. A. in the hall for 15 seconds.
Step 2: Talk with him for 30 seconds.
Step 3: Talk for 1 minute.
Step 4: Talk for 90 seconds.
Step 5: Increase 30 seconds at a time, up to 5 minutes.

"I was going to do each step three times before going on to the next one. There were two parts to this plan. First, I was going to do the talking in the hall. Then, after I got pretty far up the schedule, I was going to repeat the entire sequence in his office, because it was more scary to talk with him in his office than in the hall. After I got to step 4 for talking in the hall, I started step 1 for talking in the office. Even that was too hard, so I put in some new steps. Step 1a was just sticking my head in and saying hello. Step 1b was talking for 5 seconds in the office. Step 1c was talking for 10 seconds in the office. Then I went back to the old schedule. Prof. A. agreed not to force me to talk longer than I was supposed to. Same reinforcer as before, same feedback and comparison."

Our analysis: The rules are clear. Goals are present, and feedback and record keeping seem adequate. The double shaping plan is complex but intelligent. We still would have preferred to see self-instructions, self-praise, and relaxation in the plan. We would not predict much success with this revision either.

Plan 3: "Plan 2 works pretty well," she continues. "Prof. A. and I are now talking for as much as 3 minutes in the hall and 2 minutes in his office. The trouble is that there are lots of other professors. I need to be able to generalize from Prof. A. to others. I have decided to use Prof. A. again. Here is my new schedule:

Step 1: Go up to Prof. A. while he is talking with another professor and say hello to both of them.
Step 2: Go up and talk to Prof. A. while he is talking with another professor. Say at least a sentence to the other one.
Step 3: Talk with the other one for 5 seconds.
Step 4: Talk with the other one for 10 seconds.
Step 5: For 15 seconds.
Step 6: For 30 seconds, then on up from there by 15-second jumps.

Prof. A. has agreed to cooperate. He'll know where I am in the schedule and will bail me out whenever I complete my time for that particular step. Also, some professors seem unfriendly to me and others are pretty good, so I will go up to Prof. A. only when he is talking with one of the friendly ones."

Our analysis: This is a critical step, for she is building the new behavior so that she can use it in a variety of situations. Also, she realized that an unfriendly professor is a different antecedent stimulus than a friendly one, and she decided to deal with the easier antecedent (the friendly person). Plan

3 was apparently successful. By semester's end, she was able to talk with professors who seemed friendly, which she seemed to consider a significant improvement.

All in all, this student did very well. We were particularly pleased with her readiness to change plans when the comparison process demonstrated that her plans were not working. Her plans were, with one exception, explicit. Her rules were clear. Her goals were well shaped into subgoals, and the standards for advancing were made explicit in plans 2 and 3. Her data collection was careful. These are the reasons why she was successful in spite of the fact that we would have designed a different plan. We spoke with her many months after the course ended. "Why didn't you include self-instructions and self-praise in your plan?" we asked. "Oh" she said, "I talk to myself all the time anyway!" And relaxation? Why hadn't she used it? "I really don't know" she said. "I could always have backed up and used it, if everything had failed. I just didn't want to wait. Besides, I was right, wasn't I?" "How so?" we asked. "Must have been: I'm talking to you."

Success is hard to argue with, and this case illustrates that your self-judgment should be relied on. She *was* right, even though we still think she should have relaxed.

Designing the Final Plan

Here are the steps you need to take:

1. State your goal. If it is a complex goal or one that will take a long time to learn, state the first short-term goal. State your current level of performance; your baseline records provide you with this information, which you can use to set your subgoals. Be specific about your goal, so that it gives you a standard; that is, you know exactly what must be accomplished.

2. State *extremely specific* rules for each subgoal. What behaviors will you have to perform in each situation to achieve the subgoal? Examine the three preliminary plans you prepared in Chapters 5, 6, and 7, and consider various alternatives. You may select features from only one of your preliminary plans or combine elements from all of them. Consider each technique. Which techniques will you use? Which would be interesting to carry out? Which seem powerful? You increase your chances of success if you use several techniques.

3. Be sure that you get accurate self-observations and feedback all along the way.

4. Compare performance to goals. (This step is discussed further in Chapter 9.)

If you have absorbed the material in the book up to now, you should be able to design several plans for any one goal. Whether you are successful will depend less on the specific tactics you adopt than on how well you stick to the strategy and to the overall requirements of a good plan.

Once you have chosen your plan and decided on each of its elements, you should write it out and sign it (Kanfer, Cox, Greiner, & Karoly, 1974). This becomes your contract with yourself. The contract should list your rules as well as your goals and subgoals, and it should tell you how to get your feedback. A formal contract increases your chances of success (Griffin & Watson, 1978; Seidner, 1973). Therefore, you should prepare it with all the seriousness of a formal document.

Display it. Keep it in your notebook or on your mirror. You may even display it publicly if you want the encouragement of others. Make it clear and explicit. When it becomes necessary to change the plan, rewrite the contract. And sign the new one.

YOUR OWN SELF-DIRECTION PROJECT: STEP EIGHT

If you didn't do it before, fill out the checklist about the plan you are considering. Incorporate as many different techniques as you can. Write out your plan in detail, following the steps described above. Sign your contract and begin implementing it.

TIPS FOR TYPICAL TOPICS

Look up your particular goal in the Topic Index, at the back of the book, and read every section of the book in which that kind of goal or problem is discussed. This may give you ideas for your plan or remind you of something you've forgotten.

CHAPTER 9

Is It Working?
Analyzing the Data

GOAL:
To teach how to analyze data and troubleshoot for problems.

OUTLINE:
Making a graph
Analyzing the data
Tinkering and troubleshooting
Your own self-direction project: Step nine

This chapter discusses the processes of gathering feedback information (self-observations) and comparing it with your goals and standards. Only with feedback can you decide whether you should continue with your plan or modify it. Only with feedback can you know whether it is time to advance. The question you can answer by comparing feedback with goals and standards is "Are you achieving your goals?"

This may seem a simple question that calls for a simple yes or no. And sometimes you can answer it clearly and continuously. The person who never smokes again, the man who has a girlfriend for the first time in his life, and the overweight person who quickly drops ten pounds—all these self-managers know they are succeeding, and they don't need elaborate techniques for assessing their progress. They know because there is a clear and rapid change in their situation from the baseline period to the intervention period. They measured the target behavior *before* intervention and also *during* intervention, and the differences indicated that some change had occurred.

More often, though, progress is gradual rather than dramatic. As you shape your responses, as you reach plateaus and go beyond them, as you go through unusual periods in your life, your behaviors gradually change. Often you don't clearly remember from one week to the next exactly how you felt or how often you actually did the things you wanted to do. In fact, most people seriously misjudge their progress, probably because they quickly adapt emotionally to new performance levels. We change our goals as we change our abilities.

When people misjudge the progress they are making, they generally do so by underrating it. Those who don't rely on their frequency recordings are often tempted to discontinue a plan even though it is succeeding, simply because they believe that it is failing. The reverse, of course, may happen, and an ineffective plan may be continued, fruitlessly, because data are not properly collected and examined.

It is crucial that you continue to record your behavior throughout the operation of your plan, because recording provides the evidence you need in order to know whether the plan is having the desired effect.

The best way to organize your data for easy examination is to put them on a graph. Each day or week you gather your observations. At the end of a few weeks, you will have a stack of these pieces of information. By putting them all together on one graph, you can note progress or lack of it. Graphing your data facilitates the comparison between your actual performance and your goals and standards.

MAKING A GRAPH

Marlene wants to increase her studying and for one semester has kept a record of how many hours she studies each week. Here is her record for the semester: 8, 9¼, 9¾, 9½, 9½, 10¼, 10¾, 10¾, 8, 9½, 10¼, 11, 8½, 12¼, 10¼. Confusing, isn't it? That long string of numbers makes it hard to see whether there is an upward progression or not. Perhaps there is: the last number is bigger than the first. But notice that the third from the last is no bigger than the first; so maybe there is no progress. With a graph, none of these problems would exist and Marlene could see quite easily whether there is any appreciable upward movement over the semester.

To make her graph, Marlene first draws the *abscissa*—a horizontal line at the bottom of the page—and divides it with 16 marks, one for each week of the semester. This is also called the *horizontal axis* and is illustrated in Figure 9-1. Then, beginning at the zero point on the abscissa, she draws a vertical line (up) and marks off 14 equally spaced points on it, one for each hour per week she might have studied. This is called the *ordinate,* or *vertical axis.* Figure 9-2 shows the horizontal and vertical axes. It is conventional to indicate the passage of time on the horizontal axis and the goal-behavior on the vertical axis. Notice that the point where the two lines originate is the zero point for each line—zero weeks horizontally and zero hours vertically.

Marlene has kept a record of the total number of hours she studied for each of the 16 weeks. For week 1, the total number of hours was 8. Using a ruler, she traces a light line straight up from week 1 until it is opposite the spot on the vertical line that corresponds to 8 hours. Then she traces another

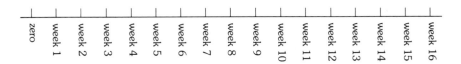

Figure 9-1. The horizontal axis of a graph (abscissa).

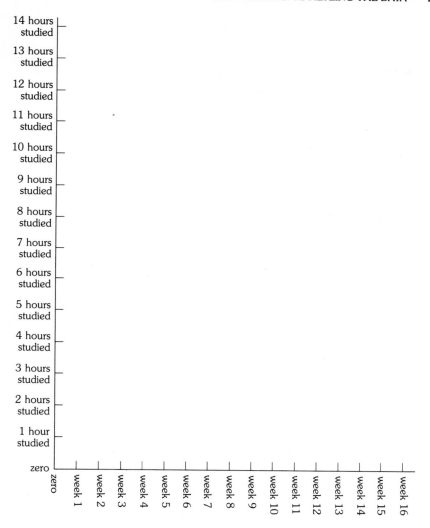

Figure 9-2.   The horizontal and vertical axes of a graph.

light line straight over from 8 hours until it meets the vertical line. At the spot where the two lines cross, she places a dot. Figure 9-3 shows this first data point. She then does this for each pair of numbers—the week and the total hours studied that week. The lines should be erasable. (The simplest method is to use graph paper, which is ruled into small squares especially for this purpose.) She repeats this process for each of the 16 weeks of the semester, each time connecting the week—for example, week number 8—with the total number of hours studied that week—for example, 10¾. At each point of intersection she places a dot. The final product, with all the dots put in, looks like Figure 9-4.

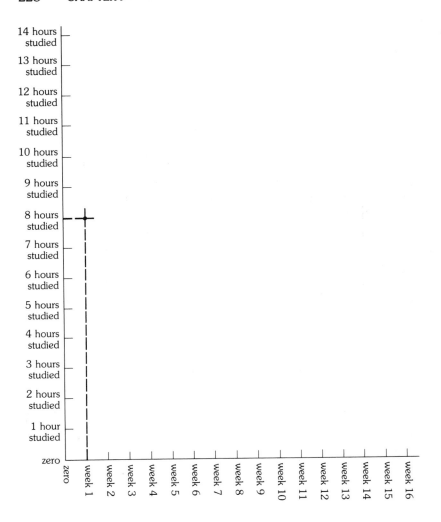

Figure 9-3. The first dot on the graph.

Marlene had recorded study time in quarter- and half-hours. This means that she had to measure off the quarter- and half-hour spaces on the graph's vertical axis and draw the light lines starting at 9¼, 9½, and 9¾ hours.

As you become more experienced with graphs, you will be able to estimate accurately the points of intersection and you won't need to draw the light lines anymore (especially if you use graph paper). This is an advantage, because the purpose of a graph is to create a simple visual display that makes records clear. Most people erase the light lines after inserting the dots, because this procedure leaves the graph uncluttered. Graph paper provides a clear background by using darker lines for the axes.

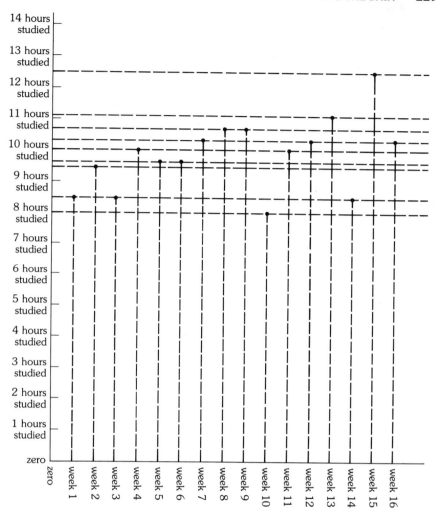

Figure 9-4.   The graph with all the dots in place.

Marlene too erases the light lines after inserting the dots. Then, as a last step, she connects the dots with a line, so that, by just glancing at the graph, she can follow the progress she has made through the weeks.

It is tedious to write "Week 1," "Week 2," "Week 3," and so on and to write "1 hour studied," "2 hours studied," "3 hours studied." So the custom is to write only the numbers along each axis and use labels underneath and at the side to describe what the numbers stand for. Marlene has labeled the vertical axis "Total hours studied" and the horizontal axis "Weeks of the semester." Figure 9-5 shows Marlene's finished product.

Sometimes it is unnecessary to include all the numbers on the vertical

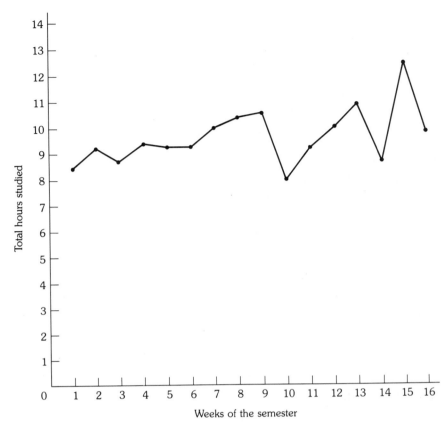

Figure 9-5.   The finished graph.

line. Suppose you were working on losing weight, and your weekly weight was varying between 148 and 135 pounds over a semester. It would be silly to start the vertical line at zero pounds and mark 135 points on it before you got to one you would use in making the graph. You can break the line, usually by making it wavy, to indicate that you are not starting at zero (see Figure 9-6).

By inspecting her graph, Marlene was able to see her data quite clearly. She saw a pattern of general progress, slow and steady, with only minor fluctuations, except for weeks 10 and 14. She reviewed her daily logs for those weeks and found that during both she had been ill for several days. Marlene concluded that her time-management (plus reinforcement) plan was working rather well. She resolved to continue it for the following semester but raised her goals to 18 hours per week. (Her graph was excellent, but her GPA was only C+.)

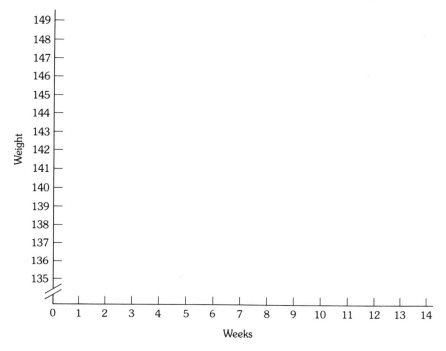

Figure 9-6.   Simplified form of graph.

ANALYZING THE DATA

Tom wanted to increase the number of comments he made in his classes. In his report he wrote that he found it difficult to speak in public because he was afraid that others would think that his comments were silly or trivial. This fear was particularly acute in very large classes, in which he felt that whatever he wanted to say had to be good enough to justify taking the time of so many people. His baseline was zero.

Tom decided to begin by practicing in small classes and then, if that worked, to try it in larger classes. His goal was to speak at least once per day in a class. He used a high-probability behavior as a reinforcer: "My reinforcer was playing in my group. This is a very powerful reinforcer for me in two ways: I really enjoy playing guitar, and, if I didn't show up for a gig, five other guys would wring my neck."

Figure 9-7 is a graph of Tom's data. Notice that, in making his graph, he counted only school days, so each week has only five days in it. This is sensible, because Tom had opportunities to practice his new behavior only during the school week. He always had his notebook with him when he went to class, so it was easy for him to make a simple check on a piece of paper every time he spoke up in a class.

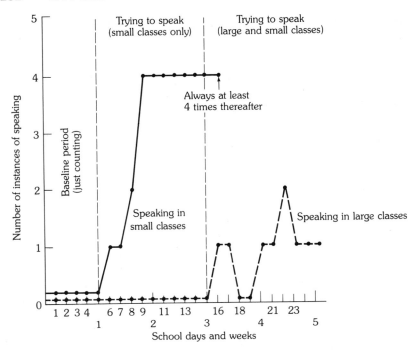

Figure 9-7.   Speaking in class.

Tom's graph shows a very rapid improvement in his speaking behavior in small classes (see Figure 9-7). Beginning on the first day of his plan, he began to make some comments, and within four days he was engaging in what he considered to be constant participation. These are unusually good data. Most people progress at a slower rate, as Tom himself did when he went into the second stage of his plan—speaking in large classes. You can see from the graph that he did make some progress but that his improvements were interspersed with setbacks—days in which he didn't talk at all. This is the kind of situation in which a graph is particularly helpful, for it shows that you are making *some* progress.

Here is another example—the case of a person who didn't make progress for a long time. Vicky, a young woman with a smoking problem, wrote: "For every cigarette smoked, I marked a piece of paper that I kept stuck into the cellophane of the cigarette pack.

"By examining my baseline, I decided to force myself to cut down so that I'd never smoke more than 15 cigarettes per day. I used a token system reinforcer, earning money for whatever I wanted to buy."

Figure 9-8 shows Vicky's graph. Note that she marked a dot on the vertical line for each cigarette she smoked but wrote in only numbers 5, 10, 15, and so on, just to get a neater graph.

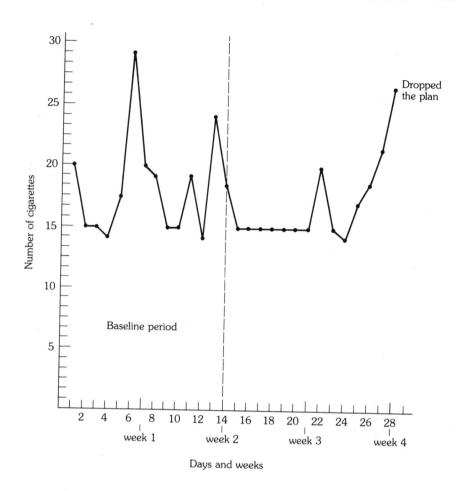

Figure 9-8.   Number of cigarettes smoked (first plan).

At the end of the fourth week, Vicky's graph clearly showed that her plan, although briefly effective, was collapsing. She abandoned recording and also the rule for reinforcement she had set for herself. Cutting down was too hard, she said. "Maybe I don't really want to quit." She talked about all the smoking and drinking in the clubs where she and Greg often danced.

After a period of time, she wrote the following: "One night when we were out, Greg started laughing at me for not being able to quit smoking. He said I had no willpower. He could quit, he said, but wasn't ready yet. This made me angry. He had been chain-smoking the whole night! 'OK,' I said, 'we should both cut down and stick to it.' He smoked a lot more than me, so we cut down proportionately. He got to smoke one pack and I got to smoke

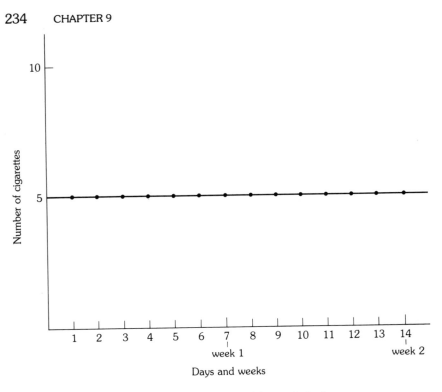

Figure 9-9. Number of cigarettes smoked (second plan).

5 a day. To make things more difficult, we switched brands. We hate each other's cigarettes."

Her second plan, as you can see in Figure 9-9, shows an improvement. It also shows that, under certain circumstances, Vicky could cut down smoking. The plan of cutting down with her boyfriend was a good first step, because they could offer support to each other for *not* smoking. Comparing the data with her goals encouraged Vicky to continue her "competition" with Greg.

We don't know what happened in the long run, but we predict that she went back to her earlier level, unless she adopted a plan for developing control independently of Greg.

Changes in the Target Behavior

During the course of a plan the actual target behavior may change. This shift can be natural and desirable, if the changed goal represents a new level of self-understanding; then, a new target behavior is necessary to describe the new goals.

Sally was very shy and withdrawn, especially in groups. She thought about her problem and came to the conclusion that, if she smiled more, she would appear less withdrawn and would also gain reinforcement from others. Her original goal (plan 1) was to increase smiling behavior by simply making

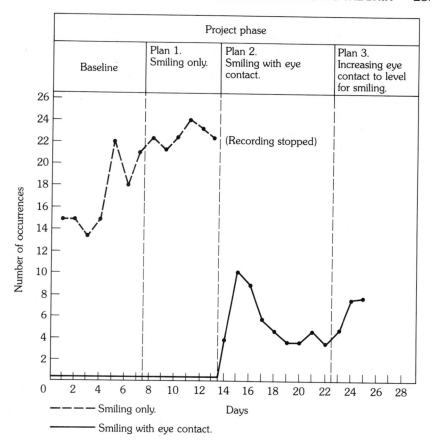

Figure 9-10.   Smiling and eye contact.

a note on a card each time she smiled at someone she didn't know well. After she had established a baseline, she worked out a plan in which she earned tokens, to be applied later to the purchase of elegant clothes, by smiling at people. (She gave herself instructions to smile.) She enlisted the help of her roommates to administer the token system.

Figure 9-10 presents part of her data. Notice several interesting features of that graph. First, Sally seemed to improve just because she was keeping records; her smiles increased even during the baseline period. Her graph shows an increased frequency that really didn't change much after she moved into the intervention period of plan 1. Of course, she was quite pleased.

Around day 11 or 12, she began to rethink the definition of her problem. "I started to realize," she later wrote in her report, "that, although I was smiling more at people, I still appeared withdrawn. This was because I was not looking at them; I was smiling but looking down at the ground. Most people feel that looking into someone's eyes is a sign of interest, so I decided that just smiling at others wasn't enough. I had to smile, *and* I had to make *eye* contact." What Sally had done was to change her definition of the target, to broaden it. In plan 2, she counted not only smiling but also *eye* contacts that lasted several seconds. She began the second part of her plan (plan 2) on day 14. In this revised plan, she gained her tokens for smiling *and* maintaining about 3 seconds of eye contact and gave herself instructions to do both. These revisions reflect her new understanding of the behaviors that are necessary in order to appear interested rather than withdrawn when meeting people.

Plan 3 represents the last phase of Sally's program. In this phase she was to begin shaping eye contact, so that it would occur as often as smiling alone had occurred in plan 1.

She could have avoided this new shift in her plan, of course, by starting out with a definition of her target problem that included both smiling and eye contact. This, as we said earlier, didn't occur because at the beginning of her plan she had not realized how important eye contact was. Only after she had increased her smiling did she realize that she needed to add eye contact to her goal.

As you continue with a plan, your definition of some category of your target behavior may change. This is often desirable, because it indicates that you are learning more about your behavior and you can make more subtle discriminations among various kinds of behavior. Don't stick blindly to your original category of target behavior. If you do change some definition, be sure that you are fully aware of the change, for you will want the increased sophistication to show in your data.

Changing Targets and Establishing a New Baseline

When changing target behaviors, or ways of defining the categories to be observed, it is possible to establish a new baseline. When the changes are substantial and abrupt, a new baseline is advisable. It is like beginning a new plan. For example, you might change your behavior from "smiling at people" to "going to public places." This is a major shift in the behavior to be observed, and it calls for a new baseline.

Sometimes your change will be your *adding* something to an ongoing plan, as Sally did by adding eye contact to smiling. If she hadn't been sure that her baseline for eye contact was zero, she actually should have gathered some baseline data so that she could judge her progress during her plan for change. She could have simply continued reinforcing smiles for a few days while counting how often she also made eye contact. You can get a baseline by simply continuing the first target behavior for a few days while, at the same time, counting how often you perform the new target behavior, which is to be added to the contract. For example, you might have started out with "dieting" as your target and, after a few weeks, decided to add "exercising" to your plan. In that case, you would continue to reinforce dieting for a few days while you get a baseline on exercising.

Even if you decide to skip the baseline period for a new target, under no circumstances should you skip making self-observations. You need to continue to keep records of your new target just as you kept records of your old one. You need to learn how your new target behavior is related to its antecedents and consequences, just as you learned these essential data for the old target behavior. Sally, for example, reported that she found certain kinds of people easier to make eye contact with than others. This knowledge helped her develop her new target behavior.

Lack of Baseline for Incompatible Responses

If your initial problem was an undesired behavior, you probably began by getting baseline data on that behavior. Later, you may have decided to increase an incompatible response at the expense of the undesired behavior. If you have done that, you are likely to find that, while you may have a very good baseline for the undesired target behavior, you don't have a good baseline for the incompatible one. Furthermore, as a plan develops, the incompatible category may change as you develop new understanding and skill. Should new baseline data be recorded?

If the new, incompatible behavior is one that you intend to continue permanently, then you will want to get a separate baseline for it—for example, deciding to increase reading "good" books as a behavior incompatible with "wasting time." You can use the same strategies that you would employ for any shift in categories.

If you don't intend to continue the incompatible behavior—for example, slapping your hand instead of cracking your knuckles—then it is not necessary to get a separate count of the incompatible behavior as long as you are keeping a good record of the undesired target. Any number of shifts can be made in the incompatible behavior without affecting the category to be recorded. However, be sure to indicate on the graph each shift in your strategy, because you need to see what works and what does not.

TINKERING AND TROUBLESHOOTING

It often happens that a simple plan is not enough by itself to change the target behavior. After you begin the plan, you discover something that makes it more difficult to manage than you had anticipated. This happens so often that you should expect it. It is not always possible, however, to know exactly *what* to expect—that is, what form the difficulty will take.

There is a sound strategy for dealing with this problem. Begin a plan. Look for what makes it difficult to carry out, for what interferes with it. Now formulate a more sophisticated revision, which deals with the sources of difficulty.

Here is an example. Rebecca wrote: "There was this person I worked with, Jean, that I really didn't like at all. As a Christian, I know that loving one another is an important command. But I couldn't bring myself to love Jean—not with *agape* [God's love]. She felt the same way, which made it worse." Rebecca decided to work out a self-change plan with the goal of increasing *agape* for Jean.

Her plan was sound. She wrote a detailed contract, which included six shaping steps for talking to Jean in a friendly way.

> Step 1: Smile at Jean at least once a day at work.
> Step 2: Smile and say "Hi."
> Step 3: Go up and ask her "How's everything?"
> Step 4: Compliment her on something.
> Step 5: Talk about upcoming events at work.
> Step 6: Talk about anything else.

Rebecca gathered records carefully on a steno tablet that she always carried at work. Her reinforcement system used candy as an immediate reward for being nice to Jean and tokens to be used to buy favorite things as longer-term reinforcers.

Results: "The first two steps worked out fine, but when I asked Jean 'How's everything?' I caught her off guard, and she began talking so much that I became uncomfortable and wanted to withdraw. While I felt ready to approach her, I wasn't ready for her response. So, I revised my plan."

In the second plan, Rebecca was dealing with a problem that she had not even foreseen when she devised her first plan. She was tinkering with her system for change, getting all the parts to work well together.

"I shared this plan with one of my closest friends. He works with me and knows of my problem. I told him that I would let him know when I was planning to talk with Jean and asked him to give me about two minutes and then call me to his office. That way I had enough time to exchange friendly greetings with Jean, without feeling uncomfortable." The reinforcers were the same, and the record keeping continued.

Results: "The two-minute limit worked really well. If I felt like talking to Jean longer, I'd just ask my friend to please wait until I was finished. Also, I dropped the idea of complimenting Jean so deliberately. I felt this wouldn't be sincere. I decided that, if she did something I felt I could honestly compliment, I would."

After several weeks Rebecca wrote: "I can honestly say that things are now fine between Jean and me. The plan really helped, but in my case all the credit goes to God, who worked in Jean's heart as well as in mine to bring us closer together."

Tinkering helped a bit, too. *The basic idea behind tinkering is this: Start with a simple, sound plan. Find out what interferes with it, and revise your plan to deal with the interference.*

A good way to find out what exactly is interfering with your plan is to use one of the problem-solving tactics described in Chapter 2—defining a problem by listing all its details. You try to think of everything that happens that seems to keep you from carrying out the steps required by your plan for change. Then, of course, you set up a new plan to try to cope with those details. Here's an example.

A 55-year-old man in our class submitted this final report:

"*My goal:* I wanted to build up to running a mile or so every other day.

"At the time I began, I had never run at all, so the baseline was zero.

"*Antecedents:* What I needed was an antecedent that would get me started! I really don't think I refrained from running because I would get painfully winded or anything. It's just that there always seemed to be something else to do, so I didn't start. Going for a run requires all sorts of behaviors—putting on the footwear, shorts, and so on, limbering up a bit, then starting running.

"*Intervention plan:* My first plan was to require myself to run one quarter of a mile every day. I intended to gradually increase my running up to a mile or so. My self-contract was that I would get a dollar to spend on anything I wanted for every time I ran.

"If you look at my graph (Figure 9-11), you'll see that this plan worked for the first three days, but after that I just sort of quit. I just drifted for two weeks and then faced up to the fact that I wasn't running, so I redesigned my program.

"After several days of doing nothing, it became painfully obvious that plan 1 was not working. So I listed all the reasons why it was not working:

I've never run that far and it seems like a long way to run.
I might give myself a heart attack—that's my fear.
I tell myself 'It's too far, and it could be dangerous.'
It seems like a lot of trouble. I find all sorts of excuses for not going running.

"I decided that I probably wouldn't get a heart attack if I ran really slow. I made a mental note to ask my doctor about it next time I have a checkup. I also decided that the main reason I didn't go out was that it just seemed like a long way for a duffer like me to go. I guess the main reason I quit was that I was starting too high. Then I remembered the shaping rule about not starting too high. 'Why should I expect to be able to start that high?' I asked myself. And I redesigned my plan as follows:

Stage 1: Put on footwear and clothes, and walk around the house (30 yards).
Stage 2: Go around the house twice (60 yards).
Stage 3: Go around the house four times (120 yards).
Stage 4: Go around the house six times (180 yards).
Stage 5: Once I get to this point, I will run a quarter of a mile. When I can do that, I will try to increase to half a mile, then three-quarters of a mile, and then finally one mile.

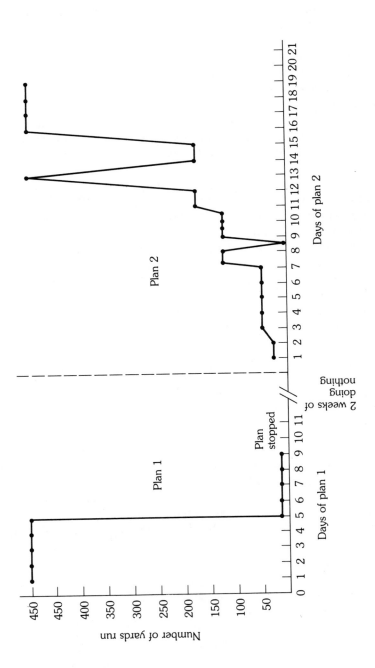

Figure 9-11.   Daily running.

"I have done several things to make sure that I stick to this ridiculously easy shaping schedule. First, I established the rule that I have to do my 'run' before I can have a beer or eat supper. Second, I explained the whole thing to my wife and told her that I really wanted to build up exercising this way. I also precommitted myself to do it by asking her (1) to remind me to do it, (2) to call me on it if she saw me eating or drinking a beer before I had done my exercise, and (3) to check on my progress by examining the chart I keep posted on the kitchen cupboard, on which I record my daily progress. Third, I set aside five minutes each morning to imagine resisting the temptation to have a beer or eat when I come home from school or work. I imagine coming home and saying to myself 'Wow, it's time to relax after another hard day!' I see myself getting a can of beer, and, just as I'm about to pop the top, I practice resisting this urge and saying to myself 'But first, I'll go for a short run.'

"At the time of this writing, I am able to run a quarter of a mile regularly and hope to be able to increase."

The right-hand part of Figure 9-11 shows this man's progress.

In listing the details of your problem, you are looking for whatever is interfering with your plan. It helps if you ask yourself these questions: What makes it difficult or impossible to perform the target behavior? Is it some antecedent (like Rebecca's being startled by Jean's rush of words)? Is it the nonperformance of a behavior (like Sally's lack of eye contact)? Is it some emotional reaction or some pattern of thought that leads me astray? Is it some consequence that reinforces the wrong behavior or does not reinforce the right one?

When you discover that your plan is not succeeding, don't become discouraged and drop self-direction altogether. In our experience, most failures are due to some technical flaw: you haven't made careful observations, you aren't rehearsing enough, or you haven't changed antecedents or consequences. Therefore, if the plan is not working, look for technical flaws. Use the checklist in Chapter 8 to search for things you may not be doing. Identify and analyze your mistakes and keep in mind that successful self-changers use more techniques and for longer periods of time.

Summary

The data you collect through your observations will lead you to make certain decisions about your plan. Your record (often in the form of a graph) may show such clear improvement as to warrant continuing the plan unchanged, as in Figure 9-7. Figure 9-8 illustrates the opposite extreme—data indicating that the plan needs careful reworking. This involves rethinking each aspect of the plan for possible change: specifying a behavioral target, making observations, learning how the behavior is related to its antecedents and consequences, and making a plan for change.

If in the course of your plan you decide to change the target behavior, you may need to establish a new baseline.

When your plan for change proves inadequate, tinkering can be a good strategy to follow: start off with a sound but simple plan and observe what interferes with it. Then revise the plan, taking into consideration the sources of interference. To do this successfully, you have to analyze your mistakes and learn from them.

YOUR OWN SELF-DIRECTION PROJECT: STEP NINE

Make a graph of your data. Remember: you record the *time* on the horizontal axis and the number of *occurrences* of the target behavior on the vertical axis. An accurately made graph will clearly tell you whether or not you are effecting changes in your target behavior. If you are not, analyze your mistakes and start a tinkering strategy.

CHAPTER **10**

Termination

GOAL:
To identify the steps you need to take to ensure that, when you stop the
project, you don't lose what you have gained.

OUTLINE:
Evolving goals
Formal termination: Planning to maintain gains
Dealing with problems
Long-term projects
Your own self-direction project: Step ten

During the course of our lives, we constantly examine and reexamine our goals and often revise them. It is a rare student who as a senior wants exactly the same things that he or she wanted at freshman registration. College itself is designed to foster reevaluation, since it constantly exposes the person to new ideas and opportunities. At other times of life, when one is in a steadier groove, reevaluation is less likely, simply because new situations—with the concomitant changing feelings and changing behaviors—occur less often.

EVOLVING GOALS

When you consciously engage in a program of self-change, you can also expect to be in for a reexamination of your goals. This is because you will see new possibilities in your own behavior as well as in the situations. You do not simply bring your behavior up to some prespecified criterion and then continue contentedly into the sunset.

Actually, ultimate goals (even in a precisely worded self-direction contract) are not only unclear—they may even be unknown. All you can know for sure is that you want to take a step in some general direction. At times, of course, a particular goal is clear from the beginning—to stop smoking, to weigh less, or to stop biting your nails. More often, though, goals must be revised en route, because the information needed for the later decisions doesn't come until some change has already been achieved.

In some cases your target behaviors change as you move toward final goals. A person trying to learn weight-controlling behaviors may change the specific target from jogging to calorie counting to not eating when depressed, and so on. Our experience is that overeaters, when they first begin a self-change plan, don't really believe that all these targets are necessary. But, as they learn more about the conditions under which they overeat, they come to see that they must change each of several target behaviors.

Sometimes one chooses the wrong target behaviors and, after a few days of unsuccessful attempts to reach some goal, realizes that a change has to be made in the target. For example, we have seen students increase their study time through self-change projects but achieve only minor gains in knowledge or grades. After a while they realize that it is not a matter of increasing the time spent studying but, rather, of concentrating better or writing accurate chapter summaries, and these become their new goals.

Sometimes you won't know your ultimate goal until you reach it. Then you realize that you have gone as far as you want to go. This is a normal process. Think of Sally, the young woman who wanted to respond more attractively when she met people. At the beginning of her self-change plan she had little idea of what her ultimate goal should be. She wasn't even aware of the fact that smiling alone wouldn't be enough. In the course of her plan she discovered that she must be able to make eye contact. Only after she had learned this new behavior could she decide how often she should perform it in order to meet her goal.

Even in the simplest situation—one in which you have correctly chosen a simple target behavior and the behavior is indeed leading to your ultimate goal—the desirable amount of performance may not be clear until after you have practiced the new behavior. Imagine two students both of whom start out to increase the amount of time they study each day. At the beginning each is studying very little—an average of half an hour per week. Both succeed in increasing study time to 5 hours per week, and both see their ultimate goals getting closer. At this point, student A may conclude "Well, that's my upper limit. I probably could keep on shaping myself up to higher levels, but I don't really want to. That's a good balance with other activities I value, and improving my grades further is not worth sacrificing my other interests."

Student B, on the other hand, might decide to keep going. Having reached the level of 5 hours per week, this student might say "This is fine, but I want to go further, up to 15 hours per week. I'm still idle a lot, and the satisfactions I get from learning are greater than I thought they would be."

Both of these decisions are based on personal values. But neither of them could have been made until each person had experienced a new level of attainment. The conclusions this suggests are that the decision to terminate a self-change plan is a value decision and that your values shift and evolve as you interact with your environment. It is often unrealistic to decide far in advance on a termination point of your self-change plan.

Informal Termination

What we just said doesn't mean that you cannot reach a point when your data match your goals. You decide that you still don't like cockroaches but, since you no longer hesitate to turn on the light in your own kitchen for fear of seeing a cockroach, you are satisfied that you have reached your goal. When your graphed data are at the level at which you currently place your goal, you can certainly say that you are finished—at least with this, at least for now. This may seem so obvious that it doesn't need discussion. But, in fact, the interesting point about formal termination is that it is so rare. Most successful intervention plans are not officially ended on a particular day. They seem to die a natural, happy death, because the desired behavior continues without the use of formal self-change planning.

When we talk with students some months after they have completed our course, we often ask about their self-direction plans. A quite common reaction is the embarrassed confession that they're not keeping records any longer and they're not using any systematic plan either (Boren & Jagodzinski, 1975). But the problem? Oh no, it's really not of much concern anymore; the studying or the dating or the getting up late in the morning isn't a hassle now; in fact, they haven't thought about it for a long time.

From our point of view, this is an excellent "termination" outcome. We don't advocate formal self-modification as a lifestyle. We see formal self-change plans as a temporary expedient, a device to use when you are trapped in a behavioral-environmental bind that requires particular planning to break. Therefore, the fact that self-controlled planning is no longer necessary means that you have really succeeded—succeeded in achieving an adjustment whereby you and the environment are mutually supporting a pattern that you endorse. Formal self-modification becomes less and less necessary, so you gradually do it less and less. When it is truly unnecessary, you have reached an adjustment of the behavior to its environmental situation.

There is one danger, however. Some people, after they have made some progress toward their goal but haven't reached it, are strongly tempted to slack off in their efforts to change. A man who started out to lose 40 pounds found that after losing 20 he was no longer sticking to his diet or self-change plan. "I think what happened was that I felt pretty good. I had lost those 20 pounds, and I felt better and looked better. But of course I still greatly enjoyed overeating. So I went back to overeating, which made losing any more weight impossible. In fact, I'm not really sure I want to give up overeating entirely. It is enjoyable, and what is life for? Maybe I'll stay 20 pounds overweight; it's not so bad." This may reflect a true change in the man's goals, and he is certainly entitled to his values. If you find yourself in this situation, in which you have petered out before reaching some original goal, try going through the commitment-building procedures described in Chapter 2, this time taking into consideration your new level. Perhaps you will find that you are now content; perhaps the commitment procedures will show you that you still want to change. The danger here is drifting—halfway to some original goal, half-pleased with your progress, half-disappointed with it. The commitment procedures will help you clarify your values, so that you can either be completely pleased with your progress or be prepared to redouble your efforts to change.

It may have occurred to you that the overeating man will probably regain the 20 pounds he lost. Suppose he wants to be sure that this doesn't happen? It is true that some self-change projects just gradually peter out, as the person successfully reaches some new goal. It is also true that some people revert to the old, unwanted behavior or to some undesired level of it. How can you guard against this danger? By formal termination, in which you take deliberate steps to keep this problem from arising.

FORMAL TERMINATION: PLANNING TO MAINTAIN GAINS

When you have developed new behaviors that move you toward your goal, you must keep in mind they *are* new behaviors. As such, not being well practiced, they can be lost and the old, unwanted habits may reappear. At this point you have *two goals: (1) to maintain gains and (2) to make sure that any newly learned behavior transfers to new situations* (Marholin & Touchette, 1979). For example, if at the beginning of your plan you study more than you did before but later note that you are slipping, you have a *maintenance* problem. If you have studied well this semester but find that, when you start your new courses the next term, you don't seem to do as well, you have a *transfer* problem. Either way, of course, you will observe that you are no longer performing the desired behavior.

Evolving Natural Contingencies

What keeps behavior going in the natural world? The contingent relationship between the behavior and its reinforcement. Therefore, it is possible to stop a self-change plan and keep the target behavior at some new, desirable level by arranging for the real world to reinforce the target behavior.

Suppose you have successfully increased your study time and improved your study habits after a lifetime of being a bad student. Where in the natural environment can your studying be reinforced? Not in a relatively advanced course that has several prerequisites, because that course will draw on a background that you may not have. There will be other courses, however, that don't draw on such a background; they let you start from the beginning. In this type of course you are much more likely to be reinforced for new, good study habits than you would be in an advanced course.

The point to remember is that you should *plan for natural environmental situations that will reinforce your new competence* without simultaneously punishing you for skills you still lack.

One of our students, who had learned how to talk comfortably with men, wrote: "I'm still careful in striking up conversations. I look for guys who seem easy to get to know and stay away from the stuck-up ones." In a way, this is a continuation of shaping procedures. But a good plan will move the source of reinforcement gradually away from tokens and contracts into real-life situations.

Here is an example of this process. Jack was assigned, early in the semester, to a small-group team project in one of his courses. The team of six met regularly to complete the project it had been assigned. Jack had always felt awkward in small peer groups—an awkwardness that he expressed by alternating between strained silence and sarcastic remarks. He took the opportunity of being a member of a team to improve himself by reinforcing the frequency of friendly or task-related statements he made in the group. His reinforcement was time spent surfing, and the amount depended on how often he performed the target behavior each week. Jack greatly improved his performance and his comfort.

Because he was still not completely satisfied when the course was over, he regretted the end of the semester. He wanted another situation in which to practice but felt that the reinforcement of surfing was no longer necessary. From among several possibilities, Jack chose to start attending evening meetings of the Writers' Club. This was a good choice because he was very interested in writing and had much to say on the subject. Furthermore, any lapses into his more aggressive behavior wouldn't be punished too severely, since criticism of the members' work was part of the club's functions. In short, this group was one into which he could bring his newly acquired abilities and from which he could expect enjoyment and relative lack of punishment. These natural reinforcements would solidify and increase the kind of participation he valued.

New behaviors, if they really reflect good adjustment, should find natural support and natural reinforcements. In early stages of termination, though, it is often helpful to remind yourself of the chain of events that bolster your behavior. A woman who had succeeded in losing many pounds through self-reinforcement for reduced eating was delighted to discover that other people found her more attractive. As a result, she had many more dates. She stopped the reinforcement but posted a sign on the refrigerator door: "Dieting keeps the telephone ringing!"

When your new target behavior has become well established through your self-intervention plan, you will want to search for opportunities to practice it and gain the reinforcements that the world has to offer for that behavior. *You should make a list of the kinds of situations in which you are likely to be able to perform the behavior and be reinforced for it.*

Thinning: Building In Resistance to Extinction

In the unprogrammed environment you don't get reinforcement *every* time you perform some behavior. In your self-modification plan, instead, you may have been doing just that in order to produce the fastest change. Once you start thinking about transferring to naturally occurring reinforcers, you take certain steps to ensure that your newly gained behaviors are not lost because of extinction. Taking such steps is necessary, because a behavior that has been reinforced continuously is one most likely to extinguish in the natural environment, where reinforcements do not occur every time.

The best way to ensure that extinction does not take place is to place your target behavior on an intermittent reinforcement schedule. This means that you don't stop your self-modification plan abruptly. Once you have established an acceptable upper level for your target behavior, you can cut down the ratio of its reinforcement.

A wife had been working to increase the number of times she communicated warm and affectionate feelings to her husband. He had complained that she seemed cold and disinterested, but she knew that this was a reflection of her overt behavior and not of her feelings. Therefore, she also knew that a self-modification plan could be very helpful. And, in fact, she did achieve a sharp increase of the desired behavior by using a token system.

Every time she performed the desired behavior, she reinforced it by giving herself a point (a token), which at a more convenient time could be turned in for selections from a menu of very desirable foods. A piece of cake, for example, cost one token; a pizza, two; a beer, one; and a glass of champagne, four. However, she reached a desirable upper limit. Her husband would soon tire of a constant stream of "I love you. I love you! You are wonderful!"

At this point, instead of stopping her reinforcement system straight away, she started preparing for the fact that her husband didn't reinforce her new behavior every time. She did so by *thinning* her reinforcement schedule—that is, moving to an intermittent schedule of reinforcement. She began to thin in the most simple way—by not getting a token every time. She cut down so that she got tokens only 75% of the time. She then reduced further, to every other time (50%); then only 25%; and so on. She didn't do this too rapidly, for a slow thinning process guards against extinction. With this procedure, it took her an increasingly large number of statements to gain one token.

In thinning, you must be careful to continue to count the frequency of the target behavior, because there is some danger that it will decline. You might be able to stand some drop from your upper goal, but you'll want to know if there has been a drop and, if so, how much of a drop. If the natural contingencies are slow to evolve, alternating between periods of thinning and 100% reinforcement can keep your frequency at an acceptably high level.

Dealing with Lack of Reinforcement from Others

Rick had taken a short course in how to increase open communication in marriage. He told us that he had always wanted to be able to be more open and had carried out a self-change project toward this goal. But his wife, Roberta, had not taken that course and was irritated and put off by Rick's efforts to change their mode of communication. Obviously he was not going to be reinforced by her for his new behavior. Rick then started a plan in which he would invite Roberta to cooperate and try to get her to discuss why she was opposed to his attempts to improve their communication. He was careful to praise her for any participation in this kind of discussion and also reminded himself not to ask her to change too quickly and to be patient. All the while he continued to reinforce himself and to keep records of his new behavior, because he feared that it would drop away from lack of reinforcement if he did not. He realized that in the long run he might be reinforced for his changes—when Roberta, too, had changed—but also correctly saw that he would have to continue with a careful plan to get this to happen.

As the example of Rick and Roberta illustrates, when you change yourself, you may affect others, and they may not reinforce you for your new behavior. Anyone who learns to be more assertive, for example, will find that others do not always smile broadly at those who stand up for their rights. In these kinds of situations you will have to notice your own gains and benefits and remind yourself of your goals in order to see that you are in fact being reinforced for your new acts, even though others may be slow in reinforcing you.

Finding Social Support for New Behaviors

Real lack of reinforcement from others can have a definite negative effect on your newly developed behaviors. Heller (1979) reports that people are more likely to drop out of psychotherapy if they have no support from others for the changes they begin to make. Just being able to talk with someone else about your plans for continuing to practice your new behaviors can be quite helpful. You can also ask people to reinforce you, to prompt you, or to monitor your self-recording. Ask yourself "Is anyone concerned about or interested in how I have changed?" If not, then your gains are likely to be lost.

Take deliberate steps to get others to help you fight a possible relapse: "If you see me studying, remind me that I wanted to do it, please"; "Hey, let me brag a minute: I've been off cigarettes for two months now. For me, that's great"; "I've lost five pounds. Do I look any different?" Working with a buddy who is also doing a self-change project is helpful in this regard, because you can support each other's efforts to maintain changes. In Karol and Richards' (1978) study, smokers with a "buddy" who was also trying to stop and who could telephone encouragement to the other showed greater reduction of smoking at eight-month follow-up than smokers who had no "buddy." Even if you don't have someone who is also trying to change, you can ask a friend to listen to you a bit, to reinforce you when you've been doing well, and to prompt you to continue.

Programming for Transfer

When a habit first develops, it is tied to a particular set of antecedents, as we discussed in Chapter 4. If a different set of antecedents occur, the habit may not transfer to them. Thus you can lose your gain because of lack of transfer. For example, a man who learned to control his overeating during the fall was surprised to see most of his newly learned good eating habits disappear with the arrival of the Thanksgiving-to-Christmas season—a new set of antecedents. To avoid losing a new habit through lack of transfer, you can program for transfer.

The first step is to keep in mind the general principle that governs transfer (Glogower & Sloop, 1976; Nay, 1979): *habits are set by antecedents, and new antecedents will not necessarily call up habits you have just learned.* In fact, the old, undesired habits may reappear. Thus, each time you are in a new situation, you should expect that a newly learned desirable behavior may not occur (Marholin & Touchette, 1979). Keeping the general principle in mind will help you enhance transfer when it is needed.

You can, for example, use self-instructions: "This is a new situation. I'd better be careful or [the new habit] won't transfer to it. Remember [then give yourself instructions to perform the desired behavior]." A woman who had worked on her strained relationship with a colleague used this kind of reminder when she practiced dealing with other coworkers.

A second step is to test for transfer before stopping the plan. Deliberately seek out new situations. Test yourself. Can you perform the behavior in the new situation?

Summary

Your newly developed behaviors will require some special attention if they are to be *maintained* over time and *transferred* to additional situations. Maintenance and transfer can be strengthened by planning for natural reinforcements to occur—that is, by seeking out situations in which the new behavior will be valued or successful. Simultaneously, resistance to extinction can be increased by thinning self-administered reinforcement to an intermittent schedule.

When natural reinforcement is slow to come, remind yourself of your goals and the reasons for choosing the new behavior. Also, arrange to have others remind and praise you. Self-reminders, self-instructions, and encouragement from others are appropriate also to increase transfer. Each new situation into which you carry your new behavior will present a new challenge; prepare yourself to meet these challenges by using covert rehearsal, self-instructions, and practice.

DEALING WITH PROBLEMS

You should expect some problems in maintaining and transferring newly developed behaviors. This isn't pessimism; it's realism. Anticipating problems allows you to deal with them as soon as they appear, when they are still small, and before your newly developed behavior has begun to disappear. It's like keeping a fire extinguisher around; you can put out the small blazes before you need to call the fire department.

Your belief that you can cope with the problems will affect how hard you try to overcome them, and that in turn will affect your success (Bandura, 1977). If you have had some success in dealing with your target task so far, there is good reason to expect that you will continue to be able to cope with it, even if new problems appear. But old habits of thought may linger, and you may find that you tell yourself "I can't cope with this new problem." For example, a man who had successfully learned to manage his time well and had changed from "disorganized" to "well organized" was transferred to a new job, which presented him with many new kinds of situations. The company itself was not well structured. For two weeks he floundered. He reported: "Then I realized I was telling myself I couldn't cope with this new job. But it wasn't the job that was overwhelming me; I was overwhelming myself. I decided to keep records of my self-defeating instructions and to remind myself that I had managed to cope with the other job. I began to find ways of getting better organized, using time-control techniques again."

When you run into a problem, follow this four-step process (D'Zurilla & Goldfried, 1971): (1) list all the details of the problem; (2) try to think of as many solutions as you can; (3) choose one of the solutions or perhaps combine a few of them; (4) think of ways you can put the solution(s) into operation. This is of course the same procedure we suggested in Chapter 2, when we discussed how to specify the target behavior. Here we are suggesting that you can use these steps to think about problems you encounter in maintaining some newly developed behavior. An example will make our point clearer. A young man reported that his target behavior was to stop drinking so many colas at work. He drank several pints every day. He succeeded in reducing his habit, but then he changed jobs and became a night taxi driver. Within a few weeks he realized that he was back to drinking several pints of cola each night "to keep myself awake."

First he listed all the relevant details of the problem:

It keeps me high.
There are convenient machine outlets on practically every corner.
I tell myself that it helps me stay awake.

Then he listed some possible solutions:

Tell myself "Don't do it, Larry" whenever I approach a pop machine.
Keep a record in the cab and a total record at home.
Stop driving the taxi.
Substitute some less harmful drinks.
Buy the drink, then throw it in the rubbish.
Get fully adjusted to working at night, so I don't have to use the drinks to stay awake [notice that this is also a detail of the problem].
Keep track of all the money I'm spending on it.

Remember that in taking these steps you should expect to go back and forth from listing details to listing possible solutions, as this man did.

Here is the solution he finally chose: "I decided to do three things: (1) tell myself 'Don't do it,' (2) keep a record of the money I spent and of the number of colas I drank each day, and (3) go to small stores where I could buy fruit juice instead of colas or similar drinks.

"Results: it worked very well. I haven't touched a Coke since I started this project. I have become instead an orange-juice freak."

Richards and Perri (1978) trained students who were concerned about academic underachievement to acquire better study skills. They also trained some of the students to use simple problem-solving strategies when they ran into problems. Richards and Perri found a rapid deterioration in the maintenance of the study skills among the students who tried no problem-solving strategies. They also found that those students who used problem-solving techniques were able to keep up their improved study skills up to one year after the completion of their training. In another study (Perri, Richards, & Schultheis, 1977) it was found that ex-smokers who stayed off cigarettes were more likely to have used problem-solving techniques than were those who caved in and went back to smoking.

If your plan involves giving up something you enjoy doing, such as overeating, drinking, or smoking, you should expect problems and relapses. Anticipate the possibility that you will fall off the wagon, and choose now the strategy you will use if that happens. This will lessen your chances of falling off and increase your chances of getting back on if you do indeed fall off. When your first plan falters, notice what parts were successful and for how long. Be sure to keep the successful features in your later plans. Also, beware noticing only the failure; notice your success as well. For example, if you stayed off overeating, smoking, or drinking for six days but then relapsed, don't think of it as a total failure. After all, you succeeded for six days. Could you repeat those six successful days? Maybe you should carry out your plan in six-day stretches or set six days as the first level for a shaping plan of gradual increase.

Finding natural reinforcements, thinning, fading out parts of the plan, programming for transfer, and using problem-solving strategies are all ways of increasing the chances that you will hold your gains after you terminate the plan. As the following section makes clear, it is also important that you make sure that you have had adequate practice before you terminate your plan.

Practice

In general, behaviors are made more probable by providing some optimum number of trials on a reinforcement schedule. At some point a behavior will "take hold." This take-hold point is the result of a complicated system of schedules of reinforcement and antecedents, but it also has something to do with the number of times the behavior is practiced. John Shelton (1979, p. 238) writes: "Regardless of the particular methods chosen to promote transfer, practice is crucial. Recall that individuals lose 50% of what they learn during the day following the learning trial. . . . Practice is the one way to overcome this." The more available a response is to a person, the more likely the transfer is, and the availability of the response is directly affected by practice (Goldstein, Lopez, & Greenleaf, 1979).

Think about learning to drive a car. When you begin, you have to concentrate fully on every aspect of your driving behavior. You dare not take your mind off it for a second. But, after several years' driving experience, you can drive long distances without this concentrated attention.

The need for practice implies that you will not want to terminate your program as soon as you reach your goal. Mandler (1954) trained people at a task until they were able to perform it without error 0, 10, 30, 50, or 100 times. He found that, the more practice his subjects had, the more easily they transferred their training to new situations. Thus, plan to "overlearn." Goldstein and his colleagues (1979, p. 14) write: "The guiding rule should not be practice makes perfect (implying simply practice until one gets it right, and then move on), but practice *of* perfect (implying numerous overlearning trials of correct responses *after* the initial success)."

We can give no specific rule for the precise number of overlearning trials you should use, although it is clear that, the more, the better. A trial of thinning reinforcement will tell you whether you have adequately overlearned. Continue to keep records. If, as soon as you begin to thin the reinforcement, the frequency or strength of your target behavior drops alarmingly, you know that you haven't practiced enough. A second kind of test is to try the target behavior in a new situation. If difficulties arise, go back to practicing with a formal self-change plan. In general the target behavior is more likely to remain strong and transfer to other situations if you have had a lot of practice and if you have practiced in a number of different situations (Goldstein et al., 1979).

It is especially important to practice in those real-life situations that have been a problem. In developing a new behavior, you may have used all sorts of covert techniques. Be sure to transfer this practice to real-life situations and practice it there long enough for the new behavior to take hold. The ultimate path for all self-change techniques is practice in real-life situations.

The Risks Involved in Stopping Too Soon

There doesn't seem to be much of a risk that you will continue the plan too long. The only risk is that you will become bored or just tired of the thing. This is no great problem. It probably means that you are past the time when you could have stopped. On the other hand, there is a risk in stopping too soon, because you may lose your gains.

If you have gradually been increasing some desired behavior and stop too soon, you will find out easily enough: you will fall below the termination level. *For this reason, we recommend continuing systematic self-observation after termination of self-change steps until the behavior has stabilized.* A significant decrease means that you should reinstitute a systematic change program. It's best to be conservative in the matter of termination. Whenever you are in doubt about whether to continue the plan, continue it. Be sure to continue counting until you know that the desired behavior has "taken hold."

Summary

Anticipating the possibility of problems in maintaining and transferring new behaviors will allow you to plan ahead and thus make those problems less likely. If the problems do occur, there are several tactics that you can employ to reduce them. First, become very familiar with the four-stage problem-solving process we have described, and use it. Second, prepare in advance a plan you can use in case your new behaviors should weaken. Third, practice, practice, practice—practice *past* perfection. Fourth, continue to observe yourself even after other formal interventions have been terminated.

LONG-TERM PROJECTS

Some goals can be achieved only through a long-term effort. Once you have been a heavy smoker, for example, you may have to maintain vigilance for years to stay off cigarettes. And you may have to reactivate self-change plans if you slip back into smoking.

It is best to reinstate a self-change project as soon as an old problem reappears. If you once smoked 40 cigarettes per day and succeeded in quitting only to find yourself back to an average of 3 per day five months later, institute a plan immediately. It's better to quit at 3. This applies to any consummatory act and to any behavior that has produced an addiction.

There are several reasons why you can expect old, bad habits like smoking or overeating to reappear. First, you may deceive yourself a bit and say "Now that I have this under control, I can do it just a little bit." So you try smoking just at parties or overeating just on "special" occasions. But because such acts have been heavily developed as habits in the past, they will return easily, and you may soon find yourself smoking in many situations or overeating on many occasions.

Second, in the past such acts have been associated with certain situations. You ate when you were depressed or smoked when you were tense or nervous. As life again brings on depression or tension, you may respond again in your old manner. Third, there may be physical reasons—at times even addictions—that encourage your return to some undesired behavior.

The rule for all these problems is the same: expect the bad habit to return, and reinstate a plan for changing as soon as it does. Also, learn from your mistakes. Suppose you quit smoking but after three months you say to yourself "Well, I can just smoke a couple at this party." Two weeks later you're back to a pack a day. Learn from that. The next time you quit, be prepared to deal with parties. It would be a mistake to conclude "I just have no willpower." Instead, you should conclude that you must attend carefully to the particular situation that tempts you.

Overeaters will encounter similar problems. When self-direction stops, weight control stops (Hall, Hall, Hanson, & Borden, 1974). For example, Thanksgiving dinner is one antecedent situation that leads many people to overeat. The Christmas season is another. By January, you may have regained ten pounds and have to reinstate a plan to lose weight and to control your eating.

Once you have learned techniques for self-change, you can continue to be a personal scientist. You will continue to informally observe your behavior, its antecedents, and its consequences. Occasionally you will decide that some goal needs a systematic self-direction plan. People who continue to try to manage their lives are more likely to be successful. In a research project in Utah (Cohen, Gelfand, Dodd, Jensen, & Turner, 1980), fat children who lost weight and kept it off were compared with fat children who lost weight but regained it. The successful ones exercised more, and they also made more long-term attempts to control their overeating. For example, they themselves managed their overeating behavior instead of having their parents manage it. And those who continued self-management kept their weight down.

One of our students returned after several years and reported: "I'm glad I didn't forget those self-direction techniques. After I left your course, I didn't use them for a long time. Things went well, I got married, and we had a baby boy. But he made me very nervous, and I used self-direction techniques to learn patience in reacting to his crying. I kept records and required myself to pause before reacting. During the pause I thought of the many ways in which the baby would make my life better. Do you remember? That's the same technique I used in your course whenever you frustrated me. I'd pause and try to think of something good about you. And I used the same reward: had a beer."

YOUR OWN SELF-DIRECTION PROJECT: STEP TEN

As you consider termination, there is a series of procedures you should follow:

1. Make a list of opportunities for practicing your newly learned behavior. Rate these opportunities in terms of how likely you are to be naturally reinforced for the new behavior.

2. If you suspect that your new behavior will not be naturally reinforced, continue to reinforce yourself or arrange for reinforcement from others.

3. Program for resistance to extinction by thinning your self-reinforcement.

4. Find social support for the new behavior.

5. Program and test for transfer. We list several ways of programming for transfer. Use more than one; this will increase your chances of successful transfer.

6. Practice using the problem-solving steps to deal with new difficulties.

7. Be sure to practice the new behavior until it is perfect, then practice doing it perfectly. The more you practice after you have reached goal level, the more likely it is that your behavior will persist.

8. In long-term projects, be ready to reinstate a plan as soon as an unwanted behavior begins to appear.

CHAPTER 11

Uses and Limits of Self-Directed Change

GOAL:

To discuss the limits of self-direction and the possible choice of a professional helper; to see how the principles of self-direction can be used to help others and how they can be used again in the future if necessary.

OUTLINE:

The limits of self-directed change
Seeking professional help
Helping others
Self-management as a lifelong practice

Throughout this book, we have described points of potential difficulty in self-change. We have approached these points with optimism and suggested ways to cope with the problems as they arise. There are, however, definite conditions in which self-direction will not be effective. Under those conditions, some kind of help is necessary. After a period of professional help, self-modification can begin and the learning of self-determined behavior can proceed.

THE LIMITS OF SELF-DIRECTED CHANGE

There are at least three conditions that limit the feasibility of a self-directed project. They are: (1) unclear goals, (2) insufficient skill in designing the plan, and (3) not enough control over the natural environment. We will discuss each of these in that order.

Unclear Goals

This limitation is an obvious and logical one. Setting specific goals in terms of behavior-in-a-situation is the first step in the mechanics of goal achievement. It is also the first requirement for an effective plan. You cannot set shaping steps unless they are steps to somewhere. You cannot reward behavior unless there is some criterion for determining when the reward is earned. Think of one of the simplest examples we have discussed—improving study behavior. Very few students are unconcerned about the quality of their academic work. But generally they are concerned not with *how* to increase their studying but with *whether* to make the changes necessary to improve their work. A student may ask "Do I really want to? Maybe I should drop out for a while, maybe forever. On the other hand, my future requires college. But what future? Do I really want that future? What do I need to know? What do I *want* to know?" This kind of questioning can take place any time someone considers some form of self-change, from becoming less socially anxious to becoming an early riser.

So long as you are unable to formulate clear, here-and-now goals, it is useless to undertake a self-modification program. There is nothing particularly wrong with having unclear goals. In fact, times of self-questioning are often very creative times, and the tension is worth feeling because it helps in the task of genuine self-examination.

But for some people, at some times, this uncertainty persists and intensifies. Then the uncertainty can become emotionally upsetting. It may interfere with the things you want to do, and you may be unable to break out of the conflict into a decision. Conflict can produce acute distress and make problem solving difficult. You may truly want to change this situation but be unable to do it. For this problem, personal counseling or psychotherapy is probably the best *first* step—although, as we shall see, not the last one.

Insufficient Skill in Designing a Plan for Change

It is clear that some efforts at self-change work better than others. There are technical differences in strategies that make a real difference in outcome. Self-directedness involves a set of skills and knowledge. If one doesn't have enough skill to formulate a solution to a particular problem, self-change is not very likely to occur. Familiarity with the principles of behavior is one way of facilitating skill building. Study of the techniques discussed in this book is another. But actual performance of self-directed projects is the best. Some people learn the skills without ever considering them abstractly. But, no matter how they are learned, skill and knowledge must be acquired somehow. Without them, self-modification cannot be expected to succeed.

Your competence to deal with a problem is always a function of two things: your skills and the difficulty of the problem. So, "adequate skills" is not an absolute concept. Your skills may be adequate for some problems but not for others. Increasing skills means expanding the range of problems and the degree of difficulty with which you can deal. But even experts in self-modification, who could reasonably be expected to be proficient in these matters, encounter situations in which consulting other professionals is useful. Any individual who is engaged in behavior modification will run across *some* technical problems that challenge his or her immediate capacity to analyze. This is a situation in which help from others is appropriate. Professional help may be particularly appropriate, since professional, technical expertise is often exactly the missing ingredient. Professionals can be useful consultants who assist you back to the route of self-directedness.

Insufficient Control over the Natural Environment

In some circumstances the problems you encounter do not relate to technical analysis. They are, instead, problems that require for their solution situations that simply cannot be arranged. The natural environment is often stubborn and always complex. The small steps required by some self-management programs may not be arrangeable in a bustling and unpredictable world.

We can illustrate this problem by comparing two actual cases, one that was manageable and one that was not. It is interesting that the manageable one was an extremely severe problem, whereas the unmanageable one seemed relatively mild.

A career navy officer was responsible for training naval recruits in beach landings. For several years he had not faltered in the performance of this duty, even though it required truly extraordinary personal courage. This courage was required because the officer had developed a nearly overwhelming fear of water. The history of his fear was easily traceable to a series of terrifying beach landings during earlier combat years. The fear had become conditioned to the surf itself. For days before each new beach-landing exercise, this officer would be in a state of dread, sleeplessness, and shame. His extraordinary courage cannot be overemphasized, as all those who have consistently forced themselves into fearful situations will realize. But courage does not suffice to remove the fear itself.

This officer designed a totally effective self-management program. He correctly outlined a series of gradual relaxed approaches to the surf, starting from a distance of 50 yards and ending by splashing in breakers over his head. He achieved relaxation in two ways. First, he conducted the program in a maximally relaxed atmosphere—on a public beach, on the weekend, on picnics with his family. Second, and most important, he used the relaxed and secure feelings that being with his wife gave him. He made each of his approaches to the water while holding her hand. Because she was a loving and understanding person, she helped by providing rich cues for relaxation—smiling, attentiveness, patience, and affection. In a matter of two months, they were enjoying swimming together, and the man's fear during landing exercises had disappeared.

Although this was a severe problem, it yielded to self-modification because the natural environment of the officer was manageable in two important ways. First, the surf is a relatively stationary thing. When a feared object is stationary, you can regulate your distance from it. If the feared object moves around unpredictably—as birds do, for example—it is much more difficult to carefully regulate approach steps.

Second, the officer could count on his wife's sensitive willingness to cooperate. Recall the opposite situation described in an earlier chapter, when the boyfriend pushed the young woman who feared birds into a flock of pigeons. When a self-modification program requires certain behaviors by other people, you must be able to induce those behaviors.

Our second case illustrates the problem of lack of control over the environment. Marianne, a very shy woman, found herself suffering from increasing loneliness during her second year in college. She had always been very quiet and didn't really mind that, but now she had become almost completely isolated socially. Because she lived at home and took a city bus to her campus each day, she saw her classmates only on campus. A careful analysis revealed that she felt reasonably comfortable talking to just one person at a time but that her discomfort increased sharply when she was in a group. At those times, her rate of speaking fell to almost zero.

Marianne attempted to increase her conversations by carefully shaping the time spent with one other person and by requiring herself to increase the number of sentences exchanged in conversation. The plan was not successful, because her small college had only one main building and the students were always together in a small space. Therefore, the opportunity to talk to one person at a time almost never occurred. The discomfort Marianne felt when others joined her two-person group was too great for her to overcome. The social mixing was too continuous and uncontrolled for her to get the gradual practice opportunities she needed. In this case the natural social environment could not be organized in the way her shaping program required.

We suggested that Marianne use the help of her school counselor, who did provide the initial assistance she needed. After growing more comfortable in her conversations with the counselor, Marianne was enrolled in a counseling group. This small group provided an artificial but well-controlled social environment. She was able to practice many conversational behaviors in that setting, and her anxieties diminished. She was then better equipped to continue her self-improvement program in the more difficult natural environment.

Summary

Three conditions may suggest that the limits of effective self-modification have been reached. (1) Personal goals may not be clear enough to permit the choice of goal behaviors. (2) The technical problems of designing a plan may be greater than the skills that can be acquired by reading this book. (3) The natural environment itself may be too chaotic or unyielding to allow a plan to succeed. Under any of these circumstances, professional advice may be helpful.

SEEKING PROFESSIONAL HELP

If, for whatever reason, your own attempts to manage your feelings or behaviors are not successful, it is reasonable to think about a period of help from a professional. What do professionals do? Although they may take different approaches, they all employ one general strategy: they help establish situations that encourage the development of new behaviors and emotions (Kanfer & Goldstein, 1975; Ullmann & Krasner, 1975; Kanfer & Phillips, 1970).

The principles governing professional help are not different from those by which self-change operates. The helping professions don't force behaviors and experiences on people against their wills. Unless the self-guiding, self-directing functions of the client are engaged in the process, behavioral and emotional changes simply do not occur during psychological treatment. For this reason, counselors and psychotherapists have always warned that their help is effective only when the client is motivated to change.

So the reader who chooses professional help will find himself or herself still engaged in building personal skills of self-direction. What you will find is professional assistance in creating an environment that fosters your own efforts to change. Professionals don't solve the problems; they help you solve them.

Psychological helpers use a variety of techniques to create these new environmental supports. Some procedures have been developed into "schools" of treatment, and there is much dispute among practitioners over preferred methods. Ideally, different methods should be selected for different problems facing different clients.

The criterion for selecting a method should be how well the method may be expected to establish an environment that best fosters the individual's goal. Any one of these environments is not in itself "better" or "worse" than another, but one may certainly be preferred over another for a given goal.

The Intelligent Consumer of Psychological Help

"Comparison shopping is just as logical in choosing a therapist as in buying a dishwasher, and considerably more important" ("A guide to finding the right therapist," 1976).

The purpose of this section is to help you become an intelligent consumer of professional help. Thus, this section is written for the consumer, not the provider, of services. It focuses not on the niceties of theory but on the simple—and crucial—questions that the prospective client of psychological help would ask: "What am I in for?" "Will it help?" "How will it affect my life?" "To whom should I go?" Our discussion is meant to help you answer these questions.

Ralph Nader's approach has come to psychotherapy. In fact, Nader's group has published a booklet on being a consumer of professional help (Adams & Orgel, 1975). It emphasizes several points. First of all, you should shop around for someone with whom you think you can work. You can use the initial interviews with a therapist to make your decision. Should you stick with this person? The Nader booklet says that you should feel confident and comfortable with your counselor and free to talk about your problems. The fact that you do or don't like the person a lot is not all that important. Also, you should do comparison shopping—that is, search for a good price.

Over 30 groups around the country have prepared lists of professional helpers in their communities ("A guide to finding the right therapist," 1976). These lists include the helper's name, age, sex, amount of experience, usual fee, usual length of treatment, procedures used, and other relevant information. You can get a list for your community by getting in touch with local consumer groups or with city or state social-work, psychiatry, and psychology organizations.

Many groups suggest that therapist and client have a written contract specifying the goals and techniques of the process. The contract should detail goals, costs, and time involved. For example, you may feel you want someone with whom you can discuss your uncertainty about career goals or your fears about your upcoming marriage. You should make clear to the prospective therapist that these are your goals, and the therapist should be equally clear about his or her goals for you. If you and the therapist don't come to an understanding about this vital point, you may end up spending a lot of time dealing with things that the therapist thinks are important but in which you have little interest. Of course, the contract should be flexible, since you may change goals in the course of therapy. Those who suggest a contract also stress the fact that a contract will strengthen your commitment to change. The contract system is far from typical, but its principles are highly desirable; its goals may also be achieved by verbal agreement.

An important question you may have in mind as you shop for a professional helper is "What am I in for?" You may ask yourself "What will be done with me?" But neither of these is the right way to ask the question. A better way is "What will the professional do to help me help myself?" A variety of techniques can be used to achieve this goal. Some therapists are eclectic and change their approach according to the needs of the client. But most stick fairly close to one or another theory. Therefore, as an intelligent consumer, you will want to know something about the kind of therapy being offered for sale.

The ideal helper possesses the full range of techniques and can vary them according to your needs. Unfortunately, the ideal helper is a rare product, and you cannot assume that you are going to find it. You can certainly maximize your chances by behaving like an intelligent consumer and carefully evaluating the products offered for your money and time.

Evaluating Professional Helpers

Are professional degrees a reliable proof of competence? They are reliable to some extent, but only to some extent. The Ph.D. is generally the minimum degree required for the independent professional practice of psychology, and the degree should be in the area of practice. The practice of psychiatry requires an M.D. or D.O. and experience as a resident in psychiatry in a mental hospital. Therefore, an M.D. or D.O. degree alone is not enough to qualify someone to practice psychiatry. To practice social work, the person must have at least an M.S.W. This profession, too, like psychology and psychiatry, has many specialties, not all of which equip the social worker to professionally advise on psychological problems. For pastoral, vocational, and educational counselors, the degree requirements are even less standardized.

Is a legal license or certificate to practice a reliable assurance of the helper's competence? Holding such a license or certificate ensures only a minimum of training and experience. Not all licensed individuals are equally competent. Furthermore, few states require licensing or certification for certain helping professions—for example, social work and pastoral counseling. In addition, professionals working in institutions are often excused from legal requirements, so that a lack of licensing in that case does not indicate low qualifications.

Summary

The following steps can help you choose a professional helper. First, get some printed guide to available therapists in your area. Try to have a clear idea of what you are looking for and what you hope to gain from professional help. Then try to match what you think are your needs with what is offered. Shop around. See if there is going to be a contract between you and the professional. Ask the many important questions we have mentioned: "What technique is being used?" "What effects should I expect?" "What are the risks?" Use the first session to evaluate the professional. Change if you think that changing is wise. Take at least as much care as you would if you were buying a washing machine.

In this way, the process of self-determination can proceed during any phase in which professional help is used. The helping professions are just that—*helping*. This word implies a responsibility toward you, the person who's seeking help in the continuing process of achieving self-determination.

HELPING OTHERS

When should you seek professional assistance in your efforts to help someone else? The answer is a simple one: when you have decided to help someone and are unable to do it successfully. This situation is most likely to occur when you are trying to help someone for whom you have responsibility. If you are a parent, you are responsible for your young child. If you are a teacher, you are responsible for your pupils. If you are a resident counselor, you are responsible for the delinquent girls or boys who live in your cottage. Cases like these are clear-cut. If you are unable to help your charges achieve the behavioral goals that have been set for them, it is appropriate for you to seek expert help. Although many helpers—such as psychotherapists and psychodynamically oriented counselors and psychiatrists—may be expected to offer advice, the professional behavior therapist is more likely than other professionals to offer direct advice that will facilitate your task of helping others.

Behavior-change programs are very similar to those for self-modification. The problem must be behaviorally specified, observations and baseline data collected, an intervention plan designed, a contract specified, and reinforcement made contingent on the desired behavior. The principles, too, are the same—avoiding punishment, using immediate reinforcement, shaping carefully, selecting incompatible responses, and so on. The difference between changing oneself and helping others change lies in issues such as who should devise the plan for changing.

If you are the person arranging the plan, you may collect the observations and work out ways to modify certain behaviors by reinforcing, shaping, and, more generally, using the necessary techniques to change behaviors. For example, one of our students wanted to change the behavior of her child, who each night left his bed and went to sleep under his sister's. The mother kept a record of how often the child did this (she put blocks under the child's bed, which had to be moved if the boy was to sleep there). Later she worked out a plan to gradually reduce her son's behavior by rewarding with gold stars his staying in bed. Throughout her plan to help the child, she occasionally consulted with us.

But what if your concern is for a friend, a fiancé, a spouse, or a roommate—more generally, someone for whom you are not responsible? To what extent should you intervene in someone else's life and behavior?

In our society we place high value on self-determination; that is, we believe that each person should as much as possible determine what he or she will do. However, if the person himself or herself requests your help, few would think that it is unethical for you to try. The question then is "When is your help helpful?"

When someone has asked for your assistance in designing an intervention, the primary question you should ask yourself is "Do I know enough to be able to help someone else?" If all that is asked of you is to listen patiently to a distraught friend or to share some of your own experiences in handling a similar crisis, the answer is probably yes. But if your help is supposed to take the form of specifically designing some kind of behavior-modification intervention, the answer is probably no. *If your sole preparation is having read this book, you are not ready to help others design interventions, except perhaps for the simplest kinds of problems.*

This may seem inconsistent with our general encouragement to attempt self-modification in quite complex situations. But, in fact, it is not inconsistent. In *self*-modification, you are required to judge your own feelings, your own reinforcers, your own current behavior capacities, your own relative values, and all the complexities of your personal life. And you are probably the best judge of all of these things. But making these judgments for someone else is just as difficult as it would be for someone else to make them about you.

Of course, the behavioral principles you use when the target is someone else are the same you employ in self-modification. But the effects of a plan on yourself can be judged immediately and sensitively by you. The effects of a plan on someone else are much more difficult to perceive. Emotional effects are especially subtle and difficult to judge in other people. Frequency data on behavior changes are available, of course, and effectiveness can be judged in this way. But the more subtle feeling reactions occur long before frequency data can be evaluated. In self-modification your plan will be continuously guided by your own judgments and emotional reactions. It is difficult to be this sensitive to *other* people's concerns. It is even difficult to be present often enough to try to understand.

That is not to say that these skills cannot be learned. Of course they can be, and that's what professional training for expert consultants is for. Consulting an expert is one way to learn the necessary skills. Also, an increasing number of excellent references are now available. Careful study of these materials will represent a highly desirable preparation and increase your knowledge of how to help others.

For example, if you are thinking of designing a behavior-modification program for your own child, you should master a source such as Patterson and Gullion's *Living with Children* (1968), Becker's *Parents Are Teachers* (1971), or Eimers and Aitchison's *Effective Parents, Responsible Children* (1977).

If you have adequate access to the information you need, there is no reason why you may not attempt to help someone else. In some instances your own study may be sufficient. At other times, for more complex issues, you should seek consultation for yourself in order to become a more effective helper of others. In trying to help, we suggest a conservative estimate of your own skills. Behavioral techniques are powerful ones, and they can go awry, with unfortunate but still powerful results.

SELF-MANAGEMENT AS A LIFELONG PRACTICE

Life *is* trouble. Only death is not.
    ZORBA THE GREEK

Life is just one damned thing after another.
    ANITA LOOS

As you terminate your self-change project, what lies ahead? Blue skies and cloudless days, with no problems to darken the horizon? We wish you well, but we also have to predict that sooner or later something else in your life will benefit from a systematic application of self-change techniques.

We are back to transfer of training. You have learned these techniques by using them on one personal problem, and perhaps you have also taken tests on them. But will you think to use them two years from now, when a new problem comes into your life?

Zorba the Greek and Anita Loos weren't being pessimistic, they were both realistic. Expecting problems means being ready to cope with them when they occur. No one coped better than Zorba. How can you increase the chances that in some future situation you will use techniques you have found effective in the past?

One way is to practice the techniques in more than just one kind of project. That is, if you practice record keeping or positive self-instructions in several different projects, you will be more likely to keep records and to self-instruct in the future when these techniques are needed.

Anticipating problems, and thinking of ways of using self-change techniques in dealing with them, may also increase your chances of remembering them when the time comes. For example, "I know I spend my money un-wisely. So far it hasn't made much difference, but it's just a matter of time till I am completely on my own, and then it's going to matter a lot. When that happens, I could keep records, set rules, and state those rules as self-direc-tions." Or "Everybody says that the job interviews for graduates are very difficult and competitive. Well, I could practice relaxation beforehand." Stop for a minute now and think about problems you will probably encounter in the next two years or so. How will you cope with them?

For all of us self-management is a daily habit. As you were working on your project, you had to proceed step by step to achieve the kind of perfor-mance you wanted. But for many of the areas of your life, self-direction is already something you do without the formal statements of a self-modification plan. You begin to feel a bit blue, so you tell yourself "Cheer up!"; you notice the good things in your life; and you schedule some fun activities. Without thinking about it, you have been doing the kinds of things we recommend for someone who is depressed. You used self-instructions, and you noticed and scheduled rewards. Or, when you realize that you are growing uncomfortably tense in some situations, you can tell yourself "Relax" and release tension from your muscles and begin to cope.

In sum, you will always be using self-management to deal with what Zorba and Anita Loos were talking about. When you run into problems that require thoughtful self-direction, we hope you will remember the techniques in this book.

References

Adams, S., & Orgel, M. *Through the mental health maze.* Washington, D.C.: Health Research Group, 1975.

Ainslee, G. Specious reward: A behavioral theory of impulsiveness and impulse control. *Psychological Bulletin,* 1975, *82,* 463–496.

Annon, J. S. *The behavioral treatment of sexual problems. Vol. 2: Intensive therapy.* Honolulu: Enabling Systems, 1975.

Ascher, L. M. An experimental analog study of covert positive reinforcement. In R. D. Rubin, J. P. Brady, & J. D. Henderson (Eds.), *Advances in behavior therapy* (Vol. 4). New York: Academic Press, 1973.

Ascher, L. M., & Cautela, J. R. An experimental study of covert extinction. *Journal of Behavior Therapy and Experimental Psychiatry,* 1974, *5,* 233–238.

Azrin, N. H., & Nunn, R. G. Habit reversal: A method of eliminating nervous habits and tics. *Behaviour Research and Therapy,* 1973, *11,* 619–628.

Baer, E., Foreyt, J. P., & Wright, S. Self-directed termination of excessive cigarette use among untreated smokers. *Journal of Behavior Therapy and Experimental Psychiatry,* 1977, *8,* 71–74.

Bajtelsmit, J. W., & Gershman, L. Covert positive reinforcement: Efficacy and conceptualization. *Journal of Behavior Therapy and Experimental Psychiatry,* 1976, *7,* 207–212.

Bandura, A. Vicarious and self-reinforcement processes. In R. Glaser (Ed.), *The nature of reinforcement.* New York: Academic Press, 1971.

Bandura, A. *Principles of behavior modification* (2nd ed.). New York: Holt, Rinehart & Winston, 1975.

Bandura, A. Self-reinforcement: Theoretical and methodological considerations. *Behaviorism,* 1976, *4,* 135–155.

Bandura, A. Self-efficacy: Toward a unifying theory of behavioral change. *Psychological Review,* 1977, *84,* 191–215.

Bandura, A., Jeffery, R. W., & Gajdos, E. Generalizing change through participant modeling with self-directed mastery. *Behaviour Research and Therapy,* 1975, *13,* 141–152.

Bandura, A., & Mahoney, M. J. Maintenance and transfer of self-reinforcement functions. *Behaviour Research and Therapy,* 1974, *12,* 89–97.

Barrera, M., & Glasgow, R. Design and evaluation of a personalized instruction course in behavioral self-control. *Teaching of Psychology,* 1976, *3,* 81–83.

Barrera, M., & Rosen, G. M. Detrimental effects of a self-reward contracting program on subjects' involvement in a self-administered desensitization. *Journal of Consulting and Clinical Psychology*, 1977, *45*, 1180–1181.

Barrios, B. A., & Shigetomi, C. C. Coping-skills training for the management of anxiety: A critical review. *Behavior Therapy*, 1979, *10*, 472–490.

Becker, W. *Parents are teachers*. Champaign, Ill.: Research Press, 1971.

Bellack, A. S. A comparison of self-reinforcement and self-monitoring in a weight-reduction program. *Behavior Therapy*, 1976, *7*, 68–75.

Bellack, A. S., Rozensky, R., & Schwartz, J. A comparison of two forms of self-monitoring in a behavioral weight reduction program. *Behavior Therapy*, 1974, *5*, 523–530.

Benson, H. *The relaxation response*. New York: Morrow, 1975.

Berecz, J. Maintenance of non-smoking behavior through self-administered wristband aversion therapy. *Behavior Therapy*, 1979, *10*, 669–675.

Bergin, A. E. A self-regulation technique for impulse control disorders. *Psychotherapy: Theory, Research, and Practice*, 1969, *6*, 113–118.

Bernard, H. S., & Efran, J. S. Eliminating versus reducing smoking using pocket tokens. *Behaviour Research and Therapy*, 1972, *10*, 399–401.

Billings, A. Self-monitoring in the treatment of tics: A single-subject analysis. *Journal of Behavior Therapy and Experimental Psychiatry*, 1978, *9*, 339–342.

Blanchard, E. B. Relative contributions of modeling, informational influences, and physical contact in extinction of phobic behavior. *Journal of Abnormal Psychology*, 1970, *76*, 55–61.

Blanchard, E. B., & Draper, D. O. Treatment of a rodent phobia by covert reinforcement: A single subject experiment. *Behavior Therapy*, 1973, *4*, 559–564.

Blatt, S. Levels of object representation in anaclitic and introjective depression. *The Psychoanalytic Study of the Child*, 1974, *29*, 107–157.

Bootzin, R. R. Stimulus control treatment for insomnia. *Proceedings of the 80th Annual Convention of the American Psychological Association*, 1972, *7*, 395–396.

Boren, J. J., & Jagodzinski, M. G. The impermanence of data-recording behavior. *Journal of Behavior Therapy and Experimental Psychiatry*, 1975, *6*, 359.

Boudreau, L. Transcendental meditation and yoga as reciprocal inhibitors. *Journal of Behavior Therapy and Experimental Psychiatry*, 1972, *3*, 97–98.

Bringman, W. G., Kirchev, A., & Balance, W. *Goethe as behavior therapist*. Paper presented at the meeting of the Southeastern Psychological Association, New Orleans, February-March 1969.

Brown, G. Self-administered desensitization of a cemetery phobia using sexual arousal to inhibit anxiety. *Journal of Behavior Therapy and Experimental Psychiatry*, 1978, *9*, 73–74.

Castaneda, C. *Journey to Ixtlan*. New York: Simon & Schuster, 1972.

Castro, L., & Rachlin, H. Self-reward, self-monitoring, and self-punishment as feedback in weight control. *Behavior Therapy*, 1980, *11*, 38–48.

Catania, A. C. The myth of self-reinforcement. *Behaviorism*, 1975, *3*, 192–199.

Cautela, J. R. Covert sensitization. *Psychological Reports*, 1967, *20*, 459–468.

Cautela, J. R. Covert reinforcement. *Behavior Therapy*, 1970, *1*, 33–50.

Cautela, J. R. Covert conditioning. In A. Jacobs & L. B. Sachs (Eds.), *The psychology of private events: Perspectives on covert response systems*. New York: Academic Press, 1971. (a)

Cautela, J. R. Covert extinction. *Behavior Therapy,* 1971, *2,* 192–200. (b)

Cautela, J. R. The treatment of overeating by covert conditioning. *Psychotherapy: Theory, Research and Practice,* 1972, *9,* 211–216.

Cautela, J. R. Covert processes and behavior modification. *Journal of Nervous and Mental Disease,* 1973, *157,* 27–36.

Cautela, J. R. The present status of covert modeling. *Journal of Behavior Therapy and Experimental Psychiatry,* 1976, *6,* 323–326.

Chambliss, A., & Murray, E. J. Cognitive procedures for smoking reduction: Symptom attribution versus efficacy attribution. *Cognitive Therapy and Research,* 1979, *3,* 91–95. (a)

Chambliss, A., & Murray, E. J. Efficacy attribution, locus of control and weight loss. *Cognitive Therapy and Research,* 1979, *3,* 349–353. (b)

Ciminero, A. R. *The effects of self-monitoring cigarettes as a function of the motivation to quit smoking.* Paper presented at the meeting of the Southeastern Psychological Association, Hollywood, Fla., 1974.

Coates, T. J., & Thoresen, C. E. *How to sleep better.* Englewood Cliffs, N.J.: Prentice-Hall, 1977.

Cohen, E., Gelfand, D., Dodd, D., Jensen, J., & Turner, C. Self-control practices associated with weight loss maintenance in children and adolescents. *Behavior Therapy,* 1980, *11,* 26–37.

Danaher, B. G. Theoretical foundations and clinical applications of the Premack Principle: Review and critique. *Behavior Therapy,* 1974, *5,* 307–324.

Davison, G., & Neale, J. *Abnormal psychology.* New York: Wiley, 1975.

DiCara, L. Learning in the autonomic nervous system. *Scientific American,* 1970, *222,* 30–39.

Dubren, R. Self-reinforcement by recorded telephone messages to maintain non-smoking behavior. *Journal of Consulting and Clinical Psychology,* 1977, *45,* 358–360.

D'Zurilla, T. J., & Goldfried, M. R. Problem solving and behavior modification. *Journal of Abnormal Psychology,* 1971, *78,* 107–126.

Eimers, R., & Aitchison, R. *Effective parents, responsible children.* New York: McGraw-Hill, 1977.

Ellis, A. *Reason and emotion in psychotherapy.* New York: Lyle Stuart, 1962.

Ellis, A. Can we change thoughts by reinforcement? A reply to Howard Rachlin. *Behavior Therapy,* 1977, *8,* 666–672.

Emmelkamp, P. M. G. Self-observation versus flooding in the treatment of agoraphobia. *Behaviour Research and Therapy,* 1974, *12,* 229–237.

Emmelkamp, P. M. G., & Ultee, K. A. A comparison of "successive approximation" and "self-observation" in the treatment of agoraphobia. *Behavior Therapy,* 1974, *5,* 606–613.

Epstein, L. H., & Hersen, M. A multiple baseline analysis of coverant control. *Journal of Behavior Therapy and Experimental Psychiatry,* 1974, *5,* 7–12.

Epstein, L. H., Miller, P. M., & Webster, J. S. The effects of reinforcing concurrent behavior on self-monitoring. *Behavior Therapy,* 1976, *7,* 89–95.

Epstein, L. H., & Peterson, G. L. The control of undesired behavior by self-imposed contingencies. *Behavior Therapy,* 1973, *4,* 91–95. (a)

Epstein, L. H., & Peterson, G. L. Differential conditioning using covert stimuli. *Behavior Therapy,* 1973, *4,* 96–99. (b)

Epstein, L. H., Webster, J. S., & Miller, P. M. Accuracy and controlling effects of self-monitoring as a function of concurrent responding and reinforcement. *Behavior Therapy*, 1975, *6*, 654–666.

Ernst, F. A. Self-recording and counterconditioning of a self-mutilative compulsion. *Behavior Therapy*, 1973, *4*, 144–146.

Evans, I. Personal communication, 1976.

Ferguson, J. M. *Learning to eat*. Palo Alto, Calif.: Bell, 1975.

Ferster, C. B., Nurnberger, J. I., & Levitt, E. G. The control of eating. *Journal of Mathetics*, 1962, *1*, 87–109.

Fixen, D. L., Phillips, E. L., & Wolf, M. M. Achievement place: The reliability of self-reporting and peer-reporting and their effects on behavior. *Journal of Applied Behavior Analysis*, 1972, *5*, 19–30.

Flannery, R. F., Jr. A laboratory analogue of two covert reinforcement procedures. *Journal of Behavior Therapy and Experimental Psychiatry*, 1972, *3*, 171–177.

Flaxman, J. Quitting smoking now or later: Gradual, abrupt, immediate, and delayed quitting. *Behavior Therapy*, 1978, *9*, 260–270.

Fo, W. *Behavioral self-control: Training students in the self-improvement of studying*. Unpublished doctoral dissertation, University of Hawaii, 1975.

Fox, L. Effecting the use of efficient study habits. In R. Ulrich, T. Stachnik, & J. Mabry (Eds.), *Control of human behavior*. Glenview, Ill.: Scott, Foresman, 1966.

Frankel, A. J. Beyond the simple functional analysis—The chain: A conceptual framework for assessment with a case study example. *Behavior Therapy*, 1975, *6*, 254–260.

Frederiksen, L. W. Treatment of ruminative thinking by self-monitoring. *Journal of Behavior Therapy and Experimental Psychiatry*, 1975, *6*, 258–259.

Fuchs, C. Z., & Rehm, L. P. A self-control behavior therapy program for depression. *Journal of Consulting and Clinical Psychology*, 1977, *45*, 206–215.

Gallagher, J. W., & Arkowitz, H. Weak effects of covert modeling treatment of test anxiety. *Journal of Behavior Therapy and Experimental Psychiatry*, 1978, *9*, 23–26.

Gershman, L., & Stedman, J. M. Oriental defense exercises as reciprocal inhibitors of anxiety. *Journal of Behavior Therapy and Experimental Psychiatry*, 1971, *2*, 117–119.

Glasgow, R. E., & Rosen, G. M. Behavioral bibliotherapy: A review of self-help behavior therapy manuals. *Psychological Bulletin*, 1978, *85*, 1–23.

Glogower, F., & Sloop, E. W. Two strategies of group training of parents as effective behavior modifiers. *Behavior Therapy*, 1976, *7*, 177–184.

Goldfried, M. R. Systematic desensitization as training in self-control. *Journal of Consulting and Clinical Psychology*, 1971, *37*, 228–234.

Goldfried, M. R. The use of relaxation and cognitive relabelling as coping skills. In R. Stuart (Ed.), *Behavioral self-management*. New York: Brunner/Mazel, 1977.

Goldfried, M. R. Anxiety reduction through cognitive-behavioral intervention. In P. C. Kendall & S. D. Hollon (Eds.), *Cognitive-behavioral interventions: Theory, research, and procedures*. New York: Academic Press, 1979.

Goldfried, M. R., & Goldfried, A. P. Cognitive change methods. In F. H. Kanfer & A. P. Goldstein (Eds.), *Helping people change*. New York: Pergamon Press, 1975.

Goldfried, M. R., & Goldfried, A. P. Importance of hierarchy content in the self-control of anxiety. *Journal of Consulting and Clinical Psychology*, 1977, *45*, 124–131.

Goldfried, M. R., & Trier, C. S. Effectiveness of relaxation as an active coping skill.

Journal of Abnormal Psychology, 1974, *83,* 348–355.

Goldiamond, I. Self-control procedures in personal behavior problems. *Psychological Reports,* 1965, *17,* 851–868.

Goldstein, A. P., & Kanfer, F. H. (Eds.). *Maximizing treatment gains.* New York: Academic Press, 1979.

Goldstein, A. P., Lopez, N., & Greenleaf, D. Introduction. In A. P. Goldstein & F. H. Kanfer, *Maximizing treatment gains.* New York: Academic Press, 1979.

Gottman, J. M., & McFall, R. M. Self-monitoring effects in a program for potential high school dropouts: A time series analysis. *Journal of Consulting and Clinical Psychology,* 1972, *39,* 273–281.

Gottman, J., Notarius, C., Gonso, J., & Markman, H. *A couple's guide to communication.* Champaign, Ill.: Research Press, 1976.

Graziano, A. M. Futurants, coverants, and operants. *Behavior Therapy,* 1975, *6,* 421–422.

Green, L. Temporal and stimulus factors in self-monitoring by obese persons. *Behavior Therapy,* 1978, *9,* 328–341.

Greiner, J. M. *The effect of self-control training on study-activity and academic performance.* Unpublished doctoral dissertation, University of Cincinnati, 1974.

Greist, J. H., Marks, I. M., Berlin, F., Gournay, K., & Noshirvani, H. Avoidance versus confrontation of fear. *Behavior Therapy,* 1980, *11,* 1–14.

Griffin, D. E., & Watson, D. L. A written, personal commitment from the student encourages better course work. *Teaching of Psychology,* 1978, *5,* 155.

A guide to finding the right therapist. *Psychology Today,* March 1976, p. 96.

Hall, V. R., Axelrod, S., Weiss, L., & Rohrer, S. *Use of self-imposed contingencies to reduce the frequency of smoking behavior.* Paper presented at the meeting of the Association for the Advancement of Behavior Therapy, Washington, D.C., September 5–6, 1971.

Hall, S. M., Hall, R. G., Hanson, R. W., & Borden, B. L. Permanence of two self-managed treatments of overweight in university and community populations. *Journal of Consulting and Clinical Psychology,* 1974, *42,* 781–786.

Hamilton, S. B. Instructionally based training in self-control: Behavior specific and generalized outcomes. *Teaching of Psychology,* in press.

Harris, G. S., & McReynolds, W. T. Semantic cues and response contingencies in self-instructional control. *Journal of Behavior Therapy and Experimental Psychiatry,* 1977, *8,* 15–17.

Hawkins, R. P., & Dobes, R. W. Behavioral definitions in applied behavior analysis. In B. C. Etzel, J. M. Le Blanc, & D. M. Baer (Eds.), *New developments in behavioral research: Theory, methods, and application. In honor of Sidney W. Bijou.* Hillsdale, N.J.: Erlbaum, 1977.

Hay, L., & Hay, W. Self-recording forms. Developed at Duke University Medical School, Durham, N.C., 1975.

Hays, V., & Waddell, K. A self-reinforcing procedure for thought stopping. *Behavior Therapy,* 1976, *7,* 559.

Hefferman, T., & Richards, C. S. *Self-control of study-behavior: Identification and evaluation of natural methods.* Paper presented at the meetings of the Association for the Advancement of Behavior Therapy, San Francisco, December 1979.

Heller, K. The effects of social support: Prevention and treatment implications. In A. P. Goldstein & F. H. Kanfer (Eds.), *Maximizing treatment gains.* New York: Academic Press, 1979.

Higa, W. R., Tharp, R. G., & Calkins, R. P. Developmental verbal control of behavior: Implications for self-instructional training. *Journal of Experimental Child Psychology,* 1978, *26,* 489–497.

Hollon, S. D., & Beck, A. T. Cognitive therapy of depression. In P. C. Kendall & S. D. Hollon, *Cognitive-behavioral interventions.* New York: Academic Press, 1979.

Homme, L. E., deBaca, P. C., Devine, J. V., Steinhorst, R., & Rickert, E. J. Use of the Premack principle in controlling the behavior of nursery school children. *Journal of the Experimental Analysis of Behavior,* 1963, *6,* 544.

Horan, J. J., Baker, S. B., Hoffman, A. M., & Shute, R. E. Weight loss through variations in the coverant control paradigm. *Journal of Consulting and Clinical Psychology,* 1975, *43,* 68–72.

Horan, J. J., & Johnson, R. G. Coverant conditioning through a self-management application of the Premack Principle: Its effect on weight reduction. *Journal of Behavior Therapy and Experimental Psychiatry,* 1971, *2,* 243–249.

Hunt, W. A., & Matarazzo, J. D. Three years later: Recent developments in the experimental modification of smoking behavior. *Journal of Abnormal Psychology,* 1973, *81*(2), 107–114.

Israel, A. C., & Saccone, A. J. Follow-up of effects of choice of mediator and target of reinforcement on weight loss. *Behavior Therapy,* 1979, *10,* 260–265.

Janis, I. L., & Mann, L. *Decision making.* New York: Free Press, 1977.

Johnson, S. M., & White, G. Self-observation as an agent of behavioral change. *Behavior Therapy,* 1971, *2,* 488–497.

Johnson, W. G. Some applications of Homme's coverant control therapy: Two case reports. *Behavior Therapy,* 1971, *2,* 240–248.

Kanfer, F. H. Self-regulation: Research, issues, and speculations. In C. Neuringer & J. L. Michael (Eds.), *Behavior modification in clinical psychology.* New York: Appleton-Century-Crofts, 1970.

Kanfer, F. H. Self-management methods. In F. H. Kanfer & A. P. Goldstein (Eds.), *Helping people change.* New York: Pergamon Press, 1975.

Kanfer, F. H. The many faces of self-control, or behavior modification changes its focus. In Richard B. Stuart (Ed.), *Behavioral self-management: Strategies, techniques, and outcomes.* New York: Bruner/Mazel, 1977.

Kanfer, F. H. Self-management: Strategies and tactics. In A. P. Goldstein & F. H. Kanfer (Eds.), *Maximizing treatment gains.* New York: Academic Press, 1979.

Kanfer, F. H., Cox, L. E., Greiner, J. M., & Karoly, P. Contracts, demand characteristics, and self-control. *Journal of Personality and Social Psychology,* 1974, *30,* 605–619.

Kanfer, F. H., & Goldstein, A. P. (Eds.). *Helping people change.* New York: Pergamon Press, 1975.

Kanfer, F. H., & Karoly, P. Self-control: A behavioristic excursion into the lion's den. *Behavior Therapy,* 1972, *3,* 398–416.

Kanfer, F. H., & Phillips, J. S. *Learning foundations of behavior therapy.* New York: Wiley, 1970.

Kanter, N. J., & Goldfried, M. R. Relative effectiveness of rational restructuring and self-control desensitization in the reduction of interpersonal anxiety. *Behavior Therapy,* 1979, *10,* 472–490.

Kantorowitz, D. A., Walters, J., & Pezdek, K. Positive versus negative self-monitoring in the self-control of smoking. *Journal of Consulting and Clinical Psychology,* 1978, *46,* 1148–1150.

Karol, R. L., & Richards, C. S. *Making treatment effects last: An investigation of maintenance strategies for smoking reduction*. Paper presented at the meeting of the Association for the Advancement of Behavior Therapy, Chicago, November 1978.

Kau, M. L., & Fischer, J. Self-modification of exercise behavior. *Journal of Behavior Therapy and Experimental Psychiatry*, 1974, *5*, 213–214.

Kazdin, A. E. Covert modeling and the reduction of avoidance behavior. *Journal of Abnormal Psychology*, 1973, *81*, 87–95. (a)

Kazdin, A. E. The effect of response cost and aversive stimulation in suppressing punished and non-punished speech disfluencies. *Behavior Therapy*, 1973, *4*, 73–82. (b)

Kazdin, A. E. Comparative effects of some variations of covert modeling. *Journal of Behavior Therapy and Experimental Psychiatry*, 1974, *5*, 225–231. (a)

Kazdin, A. E. Covert modeling, model similarity, and reduction of avoidance behavior. *Behavior Therapy*, 1974, *5*, 325–340. (b)

Kazdin, A. E. The effect of model identity and fear-relevant similarity on covert modeling. *Behavior Therapy*, 1974, *5*, 624–635. (c)

Kazdin, A. E. Effects of covert modeling and model reinforcement on assertive behavior. *Journal of Abnormal Psychology*, 1974, *83*, 240–252. (d)

Kazdin, A. E. Reactive self-monitoring: The effects of response desirability, goal setting and feedback. *Journal of Consulting and Clinical Psychology*, 1974, *42*, 704–716. (e)

Kazdin, A. E. Self-monitoring and behavior change. In M. J. Mahoney & C. E. Thoresen (Eds.), *Self-control: Power to the person*. Monterey, Calif.: Brooks/Cole, 1974. (f)

Kazdin, A. E. *Behavior modification in applied settings*. Homewood, Ill.: Dorsey, 1975. (a)

Kazdin, A. E. Covert modeling, imagery assessment, and assertive behavior. *Journal of Consulting and Clinical Psychology*, 1975, *43*, 716–724. (b)

Kazdin, A. E. Assessment of imagery during covert modeling of assertive behavior. *Journal of Behavior Therapy and Experimental Psychiatry*, 1976, *7*, 213–219. (a)

Kazdin, A. E. Effects of covert modeling, multiple models and model reinforcement on assertive behavior. *Behavior Therapy*, 1976, *7*, 211–222. (b)

Kirsch, I., Heatherington, L., & Colapietro, E. Negative effects of tangible self-reinforcement. *Cognitive Therapy and Research*, 1979, *3*, 49–53.

Kirschenbaum, D. S., & Karoly, P. When self-regulation fails: Tests of some preliminary hypotheses. *Journal of Consulting and Clinical Psychology*, 1977, *45*, 1116–1275.

Knapp, T., & Shodahl, S. Ben Franklin as a behavior modifier: A note. *Behavior Therapy*, 1974, *5*, 656–660.

Knox, D. *Marriage happiness: A behavioral approach to counseling*. Champaign, Ill.: Research Press, 1971.

Komaki, J., & Dore-Boyce, K. Self-recording: Its effects on individuals high and low in motivation. *Behavior Therapy*, 1978, *9*, 65–72.

Krop, H., Calhoon, B., & Verrier, R. Modification of the "self-concept" of emotionally disturbed children by covert reinforcement. *Behavior Therapy*, 1971, *2*, 201–204.

Krop, H., Perez, F., & Beaudoin, C. Modification of "self-concept" of psychiatric patients by covert reinforcement. In R. D. Rubin, J. P. Brady, & J. D. Henderson

(Eds.), *Advances in behavior therapy* (Vol. 4). New York: Academic Press, 1973.

Ladouceur, R. An experimental test of the learning paradigm of covert positive reinforcement in deconditioning anxiety. *Journal of Behavior Therapy and Experimental Psychiatry*, 1974, *5*, 3–6.

Lakein, A. *How to get control of your time and life.* New York: New American Library, 1973.

Lazarus, A. *Behavior therapy and beyond.* New York: McGraw-Hill, 1971.

Leitenberg, H., Agras, S. W., Thompson, L. E., & Wright, D. E. Feedback in behavior modification: An experimental analysis in two phobic cases. *Journal of Applied Behavior Analysis*, 1968, *1*, 131–137.

Leon, G. R. Cognitive-behavior therapy for eating disturbances. In P. C. Kendall & S. D. Hollon (Eds.), *Cognitive-behavioral interventions.* New York: Academic Press, 1979.

Lepper, M. R., Greene, D., & Nisbett, R. E. Undermining children's intrinsic interest with extrinsic reward: A test of the "overjustification" hypothesis. *Journal of Personality and Social Psychology*, 1973, *28*, 129–137.

Levendusky, P., & Pankratz, L. Self-control techniques as an alternative to pain medication. *Journal of Abnormal Psychology*, 1975, *84*, 165–168.

Levitt, E. E. Research on psychotherapy with children. In A. E. Bergin & S. L. Garfield, *Handbook of psychotherapy and behavior change: An empirical analysis.* New York: Wiley, 1971.

Lewinsohn, P., et al. *How to control your depression.* New York: Prentice-Hall, 1979.

Lewis, L. E., Biglan, A., & Steinbock, E. Self-administered relaxation: Training and money deposits in the treatment of recurrent anxiety. *Journal of Consulting and Clinical Psychology*, 1978, *46*, 1274–1283.

Lich, J. R., & Heffler, D. Relaxation training and attention placebo in the treatment of severe insomnia. *Journal of Consulting and Clinical Psychology*, 1977, *45*, 153–161.

Linehan, M. M. Structural cognitive-behavioral treatment of assertion problems. In P. C. Kendall & S. D. Hollon (Eds.), *Cognitive-behavioral interventions.* New York: Academic Press, 1979.

Lipinski, D. P., Black, J. L., Nelson, R. O., & Ciminero, A. R. Influence of motivational variables on the reactivity and reliability of self-recording. *Journal of Consulting and Clinical Psychology*, 1975, *43*, 637–646.

Lipinski, D. P., & Nelson, R. O. The reactivity and unreliability of self-recording. *Journal of Consulting and Clinical Psychology*, 1974, *42*, 118–123.

Lloyd, V. *Deep muscle relaxation as an aid to rock climbing.* Unpublished manuscript, 1976. (Available from the author, c/o Sierra Club, Los Angeles Chapter, Rock-Climbing Unit.)

Lovitt, T. C., & Curtiss, K. A. Academic response rate as a function of teacher- and self-imposed contingencies. *Journal of Applied Behavior Analysis*, 1969, *2*, 49–53.

Luria, A. *The role of speech in the regulation of normal and abnormal behaviors.* New York: Liveright, 1961.

Lutzker, S. Z., & Lutzker, J. R. A two-dimensional marital contract: Weight loss and household responsibility performance. Paper presented at the meeting of the Western Psychological Association, San Francisco, April 1974.

MacDonald, W. S. *Emotional life of college students.* Book in preparation, 1977.

Mahoney, M. J. The self-management of covert behaviors: A case study. *Behavior Therapy*, 1971, *2*, 575–578.

Mahoney, M. J. *Cognition and behavior modification.* Cambridge, Mass.: Ballinger, 1974.

Mahoney, M. J. On the continuing resistance to thoughtful therapy. *Behavior Therapy*, 1977, *8*, 673–677. (a)

Mahoney, M. J. Some applied issues in self-monitoring. In J. D. Cone & R. P. Hawkins (Eds.), *Behavioral assessment.* New York: Brunner/Mazel, 1977. (b)

Mahoney, M. J., & Bandura, A. Self-reinforcement in pigeons. *Learning and Motivation*, 1972, *3*, 293–303.

Mahoney, M. J., Bandura, A., Dirks, S. J., & Wright, C. L. Relative preference for external and self-controlled reinforcement in monkeys. *Behaviour Research and Therapy*, 1974, *12*, 157–163.

Mahoney, M. J., Moura, N. G. M., & Wade, T. C. Relative efficacy of self-reward, self-punishment, and self-monitoring techniques for weight loss. *Journal of Consulting and Clinical Psychology*, 1973, *40*, 404–407.

Mahoney, M. J., & Thoresen, C. E. *Self-control: Power to the person.* Monterey, Calif.: Brooks/Cole, 1974.

Mahoney, M. J., Thoresen, C. E., & Danaher, B. G. Covert behavior modification: An experimental analogue. *Journal of Behavior Therapy and Experimental Psychiatry*, 1972, *3*, 7–14.

Maletzky, B. M. Behavior recording as treatment: A brief note. *Behavior Therapy*, 1974, *5*, 107–111.

Mandler, G. Transfer of training as a function of degree of response overlearning. *Journal of Experimental Psychology*, 1954, *47*, 411–417.

Marholin, D., & Touchette, P. E. The role of stimulus control and response consequences. In A. P. Goldstein & F. H. Kanfer (Eds.), *Maximizing treatment gains.* New York: Academic Press, 1979.

Marlatt, G. A., & Marques, J. K. Meditation, self-control and alcohol use. In R. Stuart (Ed.), *Behavioral self-management.* New York: Brunner/Mazel, 1977.

Marshall, W. L., Boutilier, J., & Minnes, P. The modification of phobic behavior by covert reinforcement. *Behavior Therapy*, 1974, *5*, 469–480.

Matson, J. L. Social reinforcement by the spouse in weight control: A case study. *Journal of Behavior Therapy and Experimental Psychiatry*, 1977, *8*, 327–328.

Mayer, J. *Overweight.* Englewood Cliffs, N.J.: Prentice-Hall, 1968.

McFall, R. M. Effects of self-monitoring on normal smoking behavior. *Journal of Consulting and Clinical Psychology*, 1970, *35*, 135–142.

McKenzie, T. L., & Rushall, B. S. Effects of self-recording on attendance and performance in a competitive swimming training environment. *Journal of Applied Behavior Analysis*, 1974, *7*, 199–206.

Meichenbaum, D. H. Examination of model characteristics in reducing avoidance behavior. *Journal of Personality and Social Psychology*, 1971, *17*, 298–307.

Meichenbaum, D. H. Self-instructional methods. In F. H. Kanfer & A. P. Goldstein (Eds.), *Helping people change.* New York: Pergamon Press, 1975.

Meichenbaum, D. H. *Cognitive behavior modification: An integrative approach.* New York: Plenum Press, 1977.

Menges, R. J., & Dobroski, B. J. Behavioral self-modification in instructional settings: A review. *Teaching of Psychology*, 1977, *4*, 168–174.

Miller, N. E. Learning of visceral and glandular responses. *Science,* 1969, *163,* 434–445.

Miller, R. K., & Bornstein, P. H. Thirty-minute relaxation: A comparison of some methods. *Journal of Behavior Therapy and Experimental Psychiatry,* 1977, *8,* 291–294.

Miller, W. Behavioral self-control training in the treatment of problem drinkers. In R. Stuart (Ed.), *Behavioral self-management.* New York: Brunner/Mazel, 1977.

Mischel, W. *Personality and assessment.* New York: Wiley, 1968.

Mitchell, K. P., & White, R. G. Self-management of severe predormital insomnia. *Journal of Behavior Theory and Experimental Psychiatry,* 1977, *8,* 57–63.

Moss, M. K., & Arend, R. A. Self-directed contact desensitization. *Journal of Consulting and Clinical Psychology,* 1977, *45,* 730–738.

Nay, W. R. Parents as real-life reinforcers: The enhancement of parent-training effects across conditions other than training. In A. P. Goldstein & F. H. Kanfer (Eds.), *Maximizing treatment gains.* New York: Academic Press, 1979.

Nelson, R. O., Hay, L., & Hay, W. *Observational procedures in behavioral assessment.* Workshop at the annual convention of the Association for Advancement of Behavior Therapy, San Francisco, December 1975.

Nelson, R. O., Lipinski, D. P., & Black, J. L. The reactivity of adult retardates' self-monitoring: A comparison among behaviors of different valences and a comparison of token reinforcement. *Psychological Record,* 1976, *26,* 189–201.

Nelson, R. O., Sprong, R. T., Hayes, S. C., & Graham, C. A. *Self-reinforcement: Cues or consequences?* Paper delivered at the meetings of the Association for the Advancement of Behavior Therapy, San Francisco, December 1979.

Nicassio, P., & Bootzin, R. R. A comparison of progressive relaxation and autogenic training as treatments for insomnia. *Journal of Abnormal Psychology,* 1974, *83,* 253–260.

Nolan, J. D., Self-control procedures in the modification of smoking behavior. *Journal of Consulting and Clinical Psychology,* 1968, *32,* 92–93.

Novaco, R. W. Treatment of chronic anger through cognitive and relaxation controls. *Journal of Consulting and Clinical Psychology,* 1976, *44,* 681.

Nurnberger, J. I., & Zimmerman, J. Applied analysis of human behavior: An alternative to conventional motivational inferences and unconscious determination in therapeutic programming. *Behavior Therapy,* 1970, *1,* 59–69.

Passman, R. The reduction of procrastinative behaviors in a college student despite the "contingency fulfillment problem": The use of external control in self-management techniques. *Behavior Therapy,* 1977, *8,* 95–96.

Patterson, G. R., & Gullion, M. E. *Living with children: New methods for parents and teachers.* Champaign, Ill.: Research Press, 1968.

Paul, G. L. *Insight vs. desensitization in psychotherapy.* Stanford, Calif.: Stanford University Press, 1966.

Pawlicki, R., & Galotti, N. A tic-like behavior case study emanating from a self-directed behavior modification course. *Behavior Therapy,* 1978, *9,* 671–672.

Payne, P. A., & Woudenberg, R. A. Helping others and helping yourself: An evaluation of two training modules in a college course. *Teaching of Psychology,* 1978, *5,* 131–134.

Pechacek, T. F., & Danaher, B. G. How and why people quit smoking. In P. C. Kendall & S. D. Hollon (Eds.), *Cognitive-behavioral interventions.* New York: Academic Press, 1979.

Perkins, D., & Perkins, F. *Nail biting and cuticle biting.* Dallas: Self-Control Press, 1976.

Perri, M. G., & Richards, C. S. An investigation of naturally occurring episodes of self-controlled behaviors. *Journal of Counseling Psychology,* 1977, *24,* 178–183.

Perri, M. G., Richards, C. S., & Schultheis, K. Behavioral self-control and smoking reduction: A study of self-initiated attempts to reduce smoking. *Behavior Therapy,* 1977, *8,* 360–365.

Presbrey, T. *Social problem solving: Impact and effects of training on a normal adult population.* Unpublished doctoral dissertation, University of Hawaii, 1979.

Rachlin, H. Self control. *Behaviorism,* 1974, *2,* 94–107.

Rachlin, H. Reinforcing and punishing thoughts. *Behavior Therapy,* 1977, *8,* 659–665. (a)

Rachlin, H. Reinforcing and punishing thoughts: A rejoinder to Ellis and Mahoney. *Behavior Therapy,* 1977, *8,* 671–681. (b)

Rachman, S. *The effects of psychotherapy.* Oxford: Pergamon Press, 1971.

Rehm, L., & Marston, A. Reduction of social anxiety through modification of self-reinforcement: An instigation therapy technique. *Journal of Consulting Psychology,* 1968, *32,* 565–574.

Richards, C. S. Improving study behaviors through self-control techniques. In J. Krumboltz & C. Thoresen (Eds.), *Counseling methods.* New York: Holt, Rinehart & Winston, 1976.

Richards, C. S., & Perri, M. G. Do self-control treatments last? An evaluation of behavioral problem solving and faded counselor contact as treatment maintenance strategies. *Journal of Counseling Psychology,* 1978, *25,* 376–383.

Richardson, A. Mental practice: A review and discussion (Parts 1 and 2). *Research Quarterly,* 1967, *38,* 95–107, 263–272.

Roberts, R. N., & Tharp, R. G. A naturalistic study of school children's private speech in an academic problem-solving task. *Cognitive Therapy and Research,* in press.

Robinson, F. P. *Effective study* (4th ed.). New York: Harper & Row, 1970.

Romanczyk, R. G. Self-monitoring in the treatment of obesity: Parameters of reactivity. *Behavior Therapy,* 1974, *5,* 531–540.

Rosen, G. M. *The relaxation book.* Englewood Cliffs, N.J.: Prentice-Hall, 1977.

Rosen, G. M., & Orenstein, H. A historical note on thought-stopping. *Journal of Consulting and Clinical Psychology,* 1976, *44,* 1016–1017.

Rosenbaum, M. A schedule for assessing self-control behaviors: Preliminary findings. *Behavior Therapy,* 1980, *11,* 109–121.

Rozensky, R. H. The effect of timing of self-monitoring behavior on reducing cigarette consumption. *Journal of Behavior Therapy and Experimental Psychiatry,* 1974, *5,* 301–303.

Russell, R. K., Miller, D. E., & June, L. N. A comparison between group systematic desensitization and cue-controlled relaxation in the treatment of test anxiety. *Behavior Therapy,* 1975, *6,* 172–177.

Russell, R. K., & Sipich, J. F. Treatment of test anxiety by cue-controlled relaxation. *Behavior Therapy,* 1974, *5,* 673–676.

Rutner, I. T. The effects of feedback and instructions on phobic behavior. *Behavior Therapy,* 1973, *4,* 338–348.

Schachter, S. Some extraordinary facts about obese humans and rats. *American Psychologist,* 1971, *26,* 129–144.

Seidner, M. L. *Behavior change contract: Prior information about study habits treat-*

ment and statements of intention as related to initial effort in treatment. Unpublished doctoral dissertation, University of Cincinnati, 1973.

Shelton, J. Instigation therapy: Using therapeutic homework to promote treatment gains. In A. P. Goldstein & F. H. Kanfer (Eds.), *Maximizing treatment gains.* New York: Academic Press, 1979.

Sherman, A. R. Real-life exposure as a primary therapeutic factor in the desensitization treatment of fear. *Journal of Abnormal Psychology,* 1972, *79,* 19–28.

Sherman, A. R. Two-year follow-up of training in relaxation as a behavioral self-management skill. *Behavior Therapy,* 1975, *6,* 419–420.

Sherman, A. R., & Plummer, I. L. Training in relaxation as a behavioral self-management skill: An exploratory investigation. *Behavior Therapy,* 1973, *4,* 543–550.

Sherman, A. R., Turner, R., Levine, M., & Walk, J. *A behavioral self-management program for increasing or decreasing habit responses.* Paper presented at the Ninth Annual Convention of the Association for the Advancement of Behavior Therapy, San Francisco, December 1975.

Sieck, W. A., & McFall, R. M. Some determinants of self-monitoring effects. *Journal of Consulting and Clinical Psychology,* 1976, *44,* 958–965.

Skinner, B. F. *Science and human behavior.* New York: Macmillan, 1953.

Sloat, K. D. M., Tharp, R. G., & Gallimore, R. The incremental effectiveness of classroom-based teacher training techniques. *Behavior Therapy,* 1977, *8,* 810–818.

Snyder, A. L., & Deffenbacher, J. L. Comparison of relaxation as self-control and systematic desensitization in the treatment of test anxiety. *Journal of Consulting and Clinical Psychology,* 1977, *45,* 1202–1203.

Spates, C. R., & Kanfer, F. H. Self-monitoring, self-evaluation, and self-reinforcement in children's learning: A test of a multi-stage self-regulation model. *Behavior Therapy,* 1977, *8,* 9–16.

Speidel, G. *Self-reinforcement: A critical examination of the construct and the procedures.* Unpublished manuscript, 1977. (Available from The Kamehameha Educational Research Institute, Honolulu, Hawaii 96822.)

Spinelli, P. R., & Packard, T. *Behavioral self-control delivery systems.* Paper presented at the National Conference on Behavioral Self-Control, Salt Lake City, February 1975.

Staats, A. W. *Learning, language and cognition.* New York: Holt, Rinehart, & Winston, 1968.

Staats, A. W. *Social behaviorism.* Homewood, Ill.: Dorsey, 1975.

Stuart, R. B. Behavioral control of overeating. *Behaviour Research and Therapy,* 1967, *5,* 357–365.

Stuart, R. B. Self-help group approach to self-management. In R. B. Stuart (Ed.), *Behavioral self-management.* New York: Brunner/Mazel, 1977.

Stuart, R. B., & Davis, B. *Slim chance in a fat world: Behavioral control of obesity.* Champaign, Ill.: Research Press, 1972.

Stunkard, A. J. The management of obesity. *New York State Journal of Medicine,* 1958, *58,* 79–87.

Suinn, R. M. Body thinking: Psychology for Olympic champs. *Psychology Today,* July 1976, 38–40.

Sutherland, A. *Paddling my own canoe.* Honolulu: University Press of Hawaii, 1978.

Tharp, R. G., Watson, D. L., & Kaya, J. Self-modification of depression. *Journal of Consulting and Clinical Psychology,* 1974, *42,* 624. (Extended Report, University of Hawaii, 1974).

Tharp, R. G., & Wetzel, R. J. *Behavior modification in the natural environment*. New York: Academic Press, 1969.

Thase, M. E., & Moss, M. K. The relative efficacy of covert modeling procedures and guided participant modeling on the reduction of avoidance behavior. *Journal of Behavior Therapy and Experimental Psychiatry*, 1976, *7*, 7–12.

Thomas, E. J., Abrams, K. S., & Johnson, S. B. Self-monitoring and reciprocal inhibition in the modification of multiple tics of Gilles de la Tourette's syndrome. *Journal of Behavior Therapy and Experimental Psychiatry*, 1971, *2*, 159–171.

Thoresen, C. E. *Self-control*. Address delivered at the Southern California Conference on Behavior Modification, Los Angeles, 1975.

Thorpe, G. L., Amatu, H. I., Blakey, R. S., & Burns, L. E. Contributions of overt instructional rehearsal and "specific insight" to the effectiveness of self-instructional training: A preliminary study. *Behavior Therapy*, 1976, 7, 504–511.

Todd, F. J. Coverant control of self-evaluative responses in the treatment of depression: A new use for an old principle. *Behavior Therapy*, 1972, *3*, 91–94.

Turin, A., Nirenberg, J., & Mattingly, M. Effects of comprehensive relaxation training on mood: A preliminary report on relaxation training plus caffeine cessation. *The Behavior Therapist*, 1979, *2*, 20.

Ullmann, L. P., & Krasner, L. *A psychological approach to abnormal behavior* (2nd ed.). Englewood Cliffs, N.J.: Prentice-Hall, 1975.

Upper, D. Unsuccessful self-treatment of a case of "writer's block." *Journal of Applied Behavior Analysis*, 1974, *7*, 497.

Vygotsky, L. S. *Thought and language* (E. Hantmann & G. Vokar, Eds. and Trans.). Cambridge, Mass.: M.I.T. Press, 1965.

Vygotsky, L. S. *Mind in society: The development of higher psychological processes* (M. Cole et al., Eds.). Cambridge, Mass.: Harvard University Press, 1978.

Wallace, I., & Pear, J. J. Self-control techniques of famous novelists. *Journal of Applied Behavior Analysis*, 1977, *10*, 515–525.

Watson, D. L. *Psychology: What it is, how to use it*. San Francisco: Harper & Row (Canfield), 1978.

Watson, D. L., Tharp, R. G., & Krisberg, J. Case study of self-modification. Suppression of inflammatory scratching while awake and asleep. *Journal of Behavior Therapy and Experimental Psychiatry*, 1972, *3*, 213–215.

Watson, J. B., & Rayner, R. Conditioned emotional reactions. *Journal of Experimental Psychology*, 1920, *3*, 1–14.

Wedding, D. *A comparison of progressive relaxation and meditation as anxiety-reduction agents in college students*. M.A. thesis, University of Hawaii, 1976.

Weil, G., & Goldfried, M. R. Treatment of insomnia in an eleven-year-old child through self relaxation. *Behavior Therapy*, 1973, *4*, 282–294.

Weiner, H. R., & Dubanoski, R. A. Resistance to extinction as a function of self- or externally-determined schedules of reinforcement. *Journal of Personality and Social Psychology*, 1975, *31*, 905–910.

Williams, R. L., & Long, J. D. *Toward a self-managed life style*. Boston: Houghton Mifflin, 1975.

Wisocki, P. A. A covert reinforcement program for the treatment of test anxiety: Brief report. *Behavior Therapy*, 1973, *4*, 264–266.

Wolpe, J. *Psychotherapy by reciprocal inhibition*. Stanford, Calif.: Stanford University Press, 1958.

Worthington, E. L. Behavioral self-control and the contract problem. *Teaching of*

Psychology, 1979, *6*, 91–94.

Youdin, R., & Hemmes, N. S. The urge to overeat: The initial link. *Journal of Behavior Therapy and Experimental Psychiatry*, 1978, *9*, 339–342.

Zegiob, L. E., Arnold, S., & Forehand, R. An examination of observer effects in parent-child interactions. *Child Development*, 1975, *46*, 509–512.

Zemore, R. Systematic desensitization as a method of teaching a general anxiety-reducing skill. *Journal of Consulting and Clinical Psychology*, 1975, *43*, 157–161.

Zimbardo, P. *Shyness*. Reading, Mass.: Addison-Wesley, 1977.

Zimmerman, J. If it's what's inside that counts, why not count it? 1: Self-recording of feelings and treatment by "self-implosion." *Psychological Record*, 1975, *25*, 3–16.

Zitter, R. E., & Fremouw, W. J. Individual versus partner consequation for weight loss. *Behavior Therapy*, 1978, *9*, 808–813.

Name Index

Abrams, K. S., 68
Adams, S., 263
Agras, S. W., 67
Ainslee, G., 5, 6, 177, 204
Aitchison, R., 44, 267
Alberti, R., 45
Amatur, H. I., 110
Annon, J. S., 113
Arend, R. A., 156
Arkowitz, H., 161
Arnold, S., 78
Ascher, L. M., 175, 191, 192
Axelrod, S., 196
Azrin, N. H., 139, 140

Baer, J., 45
Bajtelsmit, J. W., 177
Baker, S. B., 175
Balance, W., 144
Bandura, A., 37, 161, 203, 204, 252
Barrera, M., 16, 203
Barrios, B. A., 147
Beaudoin, C., 183
Beck, A., 45
Beck, S. T., 131
Becker, W., 267
Bellack, A. S., 69, 166
Benson, H., 145
Bergin, A. E., 113
Berlin, F., 143
Bernard, H. S., 162
Biglan, A., 147
Billings, A., 67
Black, J. L., 67

Blakey, R. S., 110
Blanchard, E. B., 161, 175
Bootzin, R. R., 96, 153
Borden, B. L., 256
Boren, J. J., 247
Bornstein, P. H., 147
Boudreau, L., 145
Boutilier, J., 175
Bower, G., 45
Bower, S., 45
Bringman, W. G., 144
Brown, G., 144
Burns, L. E., 110

Calhoun, B., 175
Calkins, R. P., 85
Castaneda, C., 64
Castro, L., 204
Catania, A. C., 204
Cautela, J. R., 160, 175, 191, 192, 199, 200
Chambliss, A., 37
Ciminero, A. R., 67
Coates, T. J., 35, 36
Cohen, E., 162, 257
Colapietro, E., 203
Curtiss, K. A., 214

Danaher, B. G., 43, 162, 172, 206
Davis, B., 32, 44, 73, 129
deBaca, P. C., 172
Deffenbacher, J. L., 147
Devine, J. V., 172
DiCara, L., 100

Dirks, S. J., 204
Dobes, R. W., 25
Dobrowski, B., 17
Dodd, D., 162, 257
Dove-Boyce, K., 67
Draper, D. O., 175
Dubanoski, R. A., 214
Dubren, R., 188
D'Zurilla, T. J., 25, 30, 253

Efran, J. S., 162
Eimers, R. E., 44, 267
Ellis, A., 109, 183
Emmelkamp, P. M. G., 67
Emmons, M., 45
Epictetus, 39
Epstein, L. H., 59, 78, 175
Ernst, F. A., 153
Evans, I., 147

Fensterheim, H., 45
Ferguson, J. M., 57
Ferster, C. B., 113
Fischer, J., 16, 44, 186, 188
Fixen, D. L., 67
Flannery, R. F., 161
Flaxman, J., 162
Fo, W., 126
Forehand, R., 78
Fox, L., 118
Frankel, A. J., 29, 116, 117
Franklin, B., 58
Frederiksen, L. W., 67
Fremouw, W. J., 186
Freud, S., 8
Fuchs, C. Z., 57, 80, 130, 163, 184, 205

Gajdos, E., 161
Gallagher, J. W., 161
Galotti, R., 17, 18
Gelfand, D., ix, 162, 257
Gershman, L., 144, 161, 177
Girodo, M., 45
Glasgow, R. E., 16
Glogower, F., 251
Gochros, H., 44
Goethe, J. W. von, 144
Goldfried, A. P., 151, 159

Goldfried, M. R., 25, 30, 100, 109, 120, 130, 143, 147, 151, 154, 159, 175, 253
Goldiamond, I., 112, 173
Goldstein, A. P., 161, 254, 255, 262
Gonso, J., 44, 163
Gottman, J. M., 44, 67, 163
Gournay, K., 143
Graham, C. A., 204
Graziano, A. M., 38
Green, L., 81
Greenberg, R. L., 45
Greene, D., 203
Greenleaf, D., 254
Greiner, J. M., 215
Greist, J. H., 143, 159
Griffin, D. E., 41, 223
Gullion, E., 44, 267

Hall, R. G., 256
Hall, S. M., 256
Hall, V. R., 196
Hamilton, S., 17
Hanson, R. W., 256
Harris, G. S., 119
Hawkins, R. P., 25
Hay, L., 48, 62
Hay, W., 48, 62
Hayes, S. C., 204
Hays, V., 122
Heatherington, L., 203
Hefferman, T., 129, 206
Heller, K., 251
Hemmes, N. S., 129, 197
Hersen, M., 183
Higa, W. R., 85
Hoffman, A. M., 175
Hollon, S. D., 130
Homer, 5
Homme, L. E., 172
Horan, J. J., 174, 175
Hunt, W. A., 127

Israel, A. C., 186

Jagodzinski, M. G., 247
Janis, I. L., 36
Jeffery, R. W., 161
Jeffrey, S. B., 44

Jensen, J., 162, 257
Johnson, S. B., 68
Johnson, S. M., 67
Johnson, W. G., 174
June, L. N., 152

Kanfer, F. H., 42, 68, 86, 112, 144, 161, 203, 204, 215, 262
Kanter, N. J., 120
Kantorowitz, D. A., 81
Karol, R. L., 251
Karoly, P., 57, 86
Katz, R., 44
Kau, M. L., 16, 186
Kaya, J., 16, 57, 62, 116, 142
Kazdin, A. E., 6, 67, 69, 79, 114, 160, 161, 162, 190, 194, 199, 200
Kirchev, A., 144
Kirsch, I., 203
Kirschenbaum, D. S., 57
Knapp, T., 58
Knox, D., 212
Komaki, J., 67
Krasner, L., 7, 262
Krisberg, J., 16, 71
Krop, H., 175, 183

Ladouceur, R., 200
Lakein, A., 44, 129
Lazarus, A. A., 38
Leitenberg, H., 67
Leon, G. R., 129, 162
Lepper, M. R., 203
Levine, M., 16
Levitt, E. E., 8
Levitt, E. G., 113
Lewinsohn, P., 45
Lewis, D., 123
Lewis, L. E., 147
Lichtenstein, E., 43
Linehan, M. M., 129
Lipinski, D. P., 67, 78
Lloyd, V., 151
Long, J. D., 30
Loos, A., 267, 268
Lopez, N., 254
Lovitt, T. C., 214
Luria, A., 85
Lutzker, J. R., 195
Lutzker, S. Z., 195

MacDonald, W. S., 64, 65, 66
Mahoney, K., 44
Mahoney, M., 16, 32, 44, 54, 59, 68, 183, 194, 204
Maletsky, B. M., 68
Mandler, G., 255
Mann, L., 36
Marholin, D., 248, 252
Markman, H., 44, 163
Marks, I. M., 143
Marlatt, G. A., 145
Marques, J. K., 145
Marshall, W. L., 175, 200
Marston, A., 16
Matarazzo, J. D., 274
Matson, J. L., 186, 189
Mayer, J., 32
McFall, R. M., 67
McKenzie, T. L., 69
McReynolds, W. T., 119
Meichenbaum, D. H., 16, 85, 118, 160
Menges, R., 17
Miller, D. E., 152
Miller, N. E., 100
Miller, P. M., 59
Miller, R. K., 147
Miller, W., 43
Minnes, P., 175
Mischel, W., 6
Moss, M. K., 156, 161
Moura, N. G. M., 16, 194
Munoz, R., 43

Nader, R., 263
Nay, W. R., 251
Nelson, R. O., 62, 73, 78, 204
Nicassio, P., 153
Nisbett, R. E., 203
Nolan, J. D., 112
Noshirvani, H., 143
Notarius, C., 44, 163
Novaco, R. W., 16
Nunn, R. G., 139, 140
Nurnberger, J. E., 113, 195

Odysseus, 5–6, 7, 8, 38, 195
Orenstein, H. A., 123
Orgel, M., 263

Packard, T., 174
Passman, R., 39
Patterson, G. R., 44, 267
Paul, G. L., 149, 158, 159
Pawlicki, R., 17, 18
Payne, P. A., 16
Pear, J. J., 216
Pechacek, T. F., 162, 205
Perez, F., 183
Perkins, D., 16
Perkins, F., 16
Perri, M. G., 17, 80, 165, 206, 207, 254
Peterson, G. L., 175
Pezdek, K., 81
Phillips, E. L., 67
Phillips, J. S., 112, 262
Plummer, I. L., 151
Pomerleau, C., 43
Pomerleau, O., 43

Rachlin, H., 6, 183, 196, 204
Rachman, S., 8
Rehm, L., ix, 16, 57, 80, 130, 163, 184, 205
Richards, C. S., 16, 17, 80, 129, 165, 206, 207, 251, 254
Richardson, A., 157
Rickert, E. J., 172
Roberts, R. N., 85
Robinson, F. P., 44, 160
Rohrer, S., 196
Romanczyk, R. G., 67, 69, 81
Rosen, G. M., 16, 123, 203
Rozensky, R. H., 69
Rushall, B. S., 69
Russell, R. K., 152
Rutner, I. T., 67

Saccone, A. J., 186
Schacter, S., 81
Schultheis, K., 166, 254
Schwartz, J., 69
Seidner, M. L., 43, 223
Shelton, J., 162, 205, 254
Sherman, A. R., 16, 151, 161
Shigetomi, C. C., 147
Shodahl, S., 58
Shute, R. E., 175

Sieck, W. A., 67
Sipich, J. F., 152
Skinner, B. F., 9, 204
Sloop, E. W., 251
Snyder, A. L., 147
Spates, C. R., 215
Speidel, G., 204
Spinelli, P. R., 174
Spinoza, 37
Sprong, R. T., 204
Staats, A. W., 100, 204
Steadman, J. M., 144, 161
Steinbock, E., 147
Steinhorst, R., 172
Stuart, R. B., 32, 39, 44, 73, 114, 127, 129
Stunkard, A. J., 47
Suinn, R. M., 157
Sutherland, A., 120

Tharp, R. G., 16, 57, 62, 71, 85, 116, 142, 186
Thase, M. E., 161
Thomas, E. J., 68
Thompson, L. E., 67
Thoresen, C. E., 32, 35, 36, 48
Thorpe, G. L., 110
Todd, F. J., 174
Touchette, P. E., 248, 252
Tregerthan, G., 125
Trier, C. S., 147
Turner, C., 162, 257
Turner, R., 16
Twain, M., 137

Ullmann, L., 7, 262
Ultee, K. A., 67
Upper, D., 19

Verrier, R., 175
Volks, V., 44
Vygotsky, L. S., 85

Waddell, K. A., 122
Wade, T. C., 16, 194
Walk, J., 16
Wallace, I., 216
Walters, J., 81

Watson, D. W., 16, 41, 57, 62, 71, 116,
    142, 146, 223
Webster, J. S., 59
Wedding, D., 145
Weil, G., 151
Weiner, H. R., 214
Weiss, L., 196
Wetzel, R. E., 186
White, G., 67
Williams, R. L., 30
Wisocki, P. A., 158, 175, 177
Wolf, M. M., 67
Wolpe, J., 122

Worthington, E. L., 17, 78, 194
Woudenberg, R. A., 16
Wright, C. L., 204
Wright, D. E., 67

Youdin, R., 129, 197

Zeigob, L. E., 78
Zemore, R., 151
Zimbardo, P., 3
Zimmerman, J., 107, 195
Zitter, R. E., 186
Zorba the Greek, 267–268

Subject Index

A-B-C analysis, viii, 9, 11–12, 48–54,
  105–106, 143, 167, 191, 192,
  209–213 (*see also* Antecedents;
  Consequences; Recording of
  behavior)
Addiction, 256
Adjustment (*see also* Maladjustment;
    Medical model)
  and the behavioral model, 9–10
  definition of, 3
  and learning, 10–11
  and the medical model, 7–8
  and natural reinforcement, 246–247
  and values, 3–4
Alcoholism, *see* Topic Index:
    Overeating, smoking, drinking, and
    drug use
Alternative behaviors, *see* Incompatible
    behaviors
Antecedents (*see also* A-B-C analysis)
  arranging new, 96, 110, 118–125,
    125–131
  and avoidance behavior, 94–95, 143
  avoidance of, 13, 95, 106, 110–113,
    124–125, 198–199, 209–211,
    211–213, 217
  behavior of others as, 211–213
  beliefs as, *see* Beliefs
  classifications as, *see* Classifications
  control by, 96, 128, 130–131,
    209–211, 251–252
  identification of, 13–15, 47–54,
    106–110, 128
  narrowing, 96, 112, 125–126
  and operant behaviors, 93

Antecedents (*continued*)
  and respondent behaviors, 99–100
  rules as, 214
  thoughts as, 50–52, 53–59,
    118–125, 217
Approximations, *see* Shaping
Assertion, *see* Topic Index
Avoidance behavior:
  analysis of, 88–89, 167–168
  antecedent control of, 94–95
  definition of, 88
  learning, 88, 89

Baseline data:
  analysis of, 231–237
  definition of, 74
  of incompatible behaviors, 141
  length of, 32, 74–77
  on new categories, 236–237
  omitted, 78–79
  purpose of, 107, 225
  reactivity of, 67–70, 235
  reliability of, 77–78
  use in shaping, 133–137
Behavior modification, professional, vii,
    5, 260
Behavior therapy, vii–viii, 5, 265
Beliefs (*see also* Self-statements)
  changing, 109–110, 120–121,
    122–125, 130
  identification of, 109–110
  influence of, on success, 37–38,
    252–253
  irrational, 109–110
Brainstorming, 30, 31, 218–219

Chains of events:
  analysis of, 28–31, 107, 135, 138, 249
  changing, 29, 96, 106, 113–118, 130–131
  examples of, 28–30, 113–117, 135, 138
  recording and reactivity in, 69
Cheating, 201–202
Classifications, 109
Cognitive behaviorism, vii–viii
Cognitive restructuring, 109–110
Commitment, 35–43, 127–128, 197, 217, 247
Conditioned stimuli, 98–99
Conditioning, see Operant behavior; Respondent behavior
Consequences:
  arranging, 165–207, 218
  during baseline, 48
  of changing behavior, 35–36
  definition of, 87, 89
  effects of, 86–93
  observation of, 48, 166–168
  recording, 42–48
Consummatory behaviors, 111–113, 162, 167, 191, 206, 209–211, 256 (see also Topic Index: Overeating, smoking, drinking, and drug use; Sexual problems)
Contingency:
  definition of, 165
  evolving natural, 248–252
  in intervention, 165, 169, 172, 175, 176, 182
Contracts, 41–42, 186–188, 223, 264
Covert techniques, 18, 157–161, 175–176, 210, 218
Cues, see Antecedents; Discriminative stimuli

Daily log, 64–66
Depression, see Topic Index
Desensitization, clinical, 159 (see also Relaxation techniques)
Diary, structured, 47–54, (see also Recording of behavior)
Discriminative stimuli, 94, 125–131 (see also Antecedents)

Drinking, see Topic Index: Overeating, smoking, drinking, and drug use
Drug abuse, see Topic Index: Overeating, smoking, drinking, and drug use
Drugs, medical use of, 8

Emotions (see also Respondent behavior)
  conditioning of, 99–100, 101
  recording of, 62–63, 64–66, 72, 124–125
  and relaxation, 156
  and self-statements, 100, 121–125
Escape behavior, 88–89
Escape clauses, 39–41
Ethics, 5 (see also Values)
Exercise, see Topic Index
Extinction:
  arranging, 191
  and avoidance behavior, 94–95
  definition of, 91, 191
  imagined, 191–192
  and intermittent reinforcement, 91, 249–250
  versus punishment, 91
  resistance to, 91–93, 249–250

Fantasies, see Thoughts
Fears (see also Topic Index)
  and incompatible behaviors, 143–163, 177
  rating scales, 63
  reactivity of recording, 67, 115
  reinforcement in reducing, 177, 180
Feedback, 215–218, 225–226
Frequency counts, 54–59
Functional relationships, 86–87

Generalization, see Transfer of training
Goals:
  changing, 33–34, 219–222, 225, 234–237, 245–246
  nonbehavioral, 31–32
  reinforcing value of, 204
  reminding oneself of, 38–39, 121, 251
  selection of, 11, 20

Goals *(continued)*
  specifying, 25, 27, 28, 41, 42–43,
    214–223, 235–236
  subgoals, 33, 34, 163, 215–223
  unclear, 31, 245–246, 259–260
Graphs, 226–237
Group counseling, 262

Help from others *(see also* Models;
    Professional help)
  advice, 29–30
  and avoidance of punishment, 30, 39,
    71, 156, 188–190
  in being reminded of one's goals, 39,
    127–128, 251
  in dispensing punishment, 189,
    195–196
  in dispensing reinforcement, 126,
    185–190
  others as confederates, 219–222, 238
  in recording, 55, 71, 78
  in relaxation, 261
Helping others, 265–267
Hierarchies of feared situations,
    158–159
Higher-order conditioning, 98–99

Imagination, *see* Covert techniques
Imitative learning, *see* Models
Incompatible behaviors, 138–156
  as alternatives to punishment,
    138–139, 194
  definition of, 139
  recording as, 144, 145
  recording of, 140–141, 237
  and reinforcement, 141, 199, 218
  types of, 144–147, 151–154, 161,
    200–201
Intellectual curiosity, as incompatible
    behavior, 144

Karate, 145, 161
Kung fu, 144–145

Language:
  and conditioning, 100
  development, 84–86, 95–96
  directing behavior by, viii, 84–86
  and thinking, 83–86

Maintenance of behaviors, 248–252,
    254
Maladjustment, 3 *(see also* Adjustment)
Martial arts, 144–145, 161
Mediators, *see* Help from others
Medical model, 7–9
Meditation, 145, 146
Models for behavior, 101, 137,
    160–161

Narrowing stimulus control, *see*
    Antecedents
Negative practice, *see* Practice, negative
Negative reinforcers, *see* Reinforcement
    and reinforcers; Punishment
Neurotic behavior, 95
Nonbehavioral goals, 31–32

Observational learning, vii *(see also*
    Models for behavior)
Operant behavior:
  definition of, 86–87
  principles of, 87–97
  and respondent behavior, 100–101
Overeating, *see* Topic Index

Pauses, building in, 114–115
Phobias, *see* Topic Index: Fears
Plateaus, 136, 225
Point systems, *see* Reinforcement and
    reinforcers, token
Practice, *see* Rehearsal
  negative, 70–71
Precommitment, 127–128, 195–196,
    218, 241
Premack principle, 172–174, 179, 183,
    186, 218, 231
Problem solving, 25, 30, 238–239,
    252–254 *(see also* Brainstorming)
Professional help, 262–265
Psychiatrists, *see* Professional help
Psychotherapy, *see* Professional help
Punishment *(see also* Avoidance
    behavior; Escape behavior; Self-
    punishment)
  definition of, 90
  effects of, 90, 193–194
  of others, 184, 189, 212–213
  resistance to effects of, 193
  use of, 91, 189, 193–198

Rating scales, *see* Recording of behavior, rating scales
Reactivity, 67–70, 235
Recording of behavior (*see also* Baseline data)
  antecedents, 47–54
  apparatus for, 58, 59, 60
  daily log, 64–66, 230
  duration, 55–56
  frequencies, 54–59
  by intervals, 72
  during intervention, 178, 216, 225, 226–237
  and knowledge of results, 69–70, 215–217 (*see also* Feedback)
  prerecording, 69, 114
  publicly, 69–70
  rating scales, 62–67, 124–125, 215
  reinforcement for, 73
  reliability of, 77–78
  storage of, 60–61
  structured diary, 47–54
  after termination, 68, 255–257
  during thinning, 250
Reflexes, 97–98
Rehearsal, 156–163, 215, 254–255
  imagined (covert), 157–160, 192, 199–201, 210, 215, 241
Reinforcement and reinforcers:
  absence of, 177–178
  accessibility of, 166, 175, 176
  amount of, 184, 191
  cataloging, 168–170, 174
  covert, 175–176, 177–178, 180, 183, 199–201
  definition of, 87, 88
  discovering, 166–178
  imagined, *see* covert
  intermittent, 91–93, 167, 249–250 (*see also* Thinning)
  logical, 169, 176, 177, 188, 200
  "natural," 246, 247, 248–249, 251, 252
  negative, 88–89
  positive, 87–88, 93–94, 100, 166–178, 182–183, 198–203, 218
  potency of, 176–178, 184
  Premack-type, *see* Premack principle
  problems in, 184–185
  satiation, 184, 188

Reinforcement and reinforcers (*continued*)
  selecting, 166–178, 184–185
  self-reinforcement, 165–166, 174–176, 180, 182–184, 198–207, 218
  timing of, 178–181
  token, 180–182, 184–188, 195, 214–217, 219–222, 250
  verbal, 174–175, 177–178, 180, 189
  withdrawal of, *see* Extinction
Relaxation, 145–156, 158–160, 161–163, 177
  meditation method, 147–148
  practicing, 150–155, 158–159, 215
  reinforcing effects of, 177, 200–201
  tension-release method, 147–150, 215
Reliability, *see* Recording of behavior, reliability of
Reminders, 38–39, 121, 127–128, 251
Respondent behavior (*see also* Emotions)
  conditioning, 98–101, 173, 177
  definition of, 97
  and emotions, 98–100, 173
  and language, 100
  and operants, 100–101
Rules, 214–215

Satiation, 184, 188
Self-directed behavior:
  difficulties in, 252–257
  limits of, 259–262
  overview, 4, 11–12, 21
  in psychotherapy, 262–263
  research evidence, 16–17
  skills in, 260
  steps in, 11–12, 20, 42–43, 79–80, 102–103, 128, 161–162, 205, 222, 223, 242, 257
Self-instructions:
  as antecedents, 85–86, 252
  in behavior change, 96, 114, 118–121, 122–127, 130–131, 253
  in childhood, 84–85
  identifying, 108–109
  negative, 121–125, 253
Self-modification, *see* Self-directed behavior

Self-observation, *see* Baseline data;
    Recording of behavior
Self-punishment, 15, 193–197
Self-reinforcement, 165–166, 174–176,
    180, 182–184, 198–207, 218
Self-statements:
    beliefs as, *see* Beliefs
    classifications as, 108–109
    identification of, 106–110
    self-criticizing, 50–51, 53–54, 72,
        100, 107, 121
    self-instructing, *see* Self-instructions
    stopping, 122–125
    substitution of new, 120–122, 183,
        205
Sexual arousal, as incompatible
    behavior, 144
Sexual problems, *see* Topic Index
Shaping:
    antecedents, 210
    definition of, 133
    examples of, 33–34, 134, 135, 136,
        155–156, 201
    and reinforcement, 201
    and relaxation, 155–156
    rules for, 134, 137, 201
    and subgoals, 215
    and tokens, 201
    and willpower, 136–137
Shyness, *see* Topic Index
Signals, *see* Antecedents; Discriminative
    stimuli
Smoking, *see* Topic Index: Overeating,
    smoking, drinking, and drug use
Social anxiety, *see* Topic Index: Fears, of
    people; Shyness
Social workers, *see* Professional help
Sports, *see* Topic Index: Exercise and
    athletics
Stimulus control, 95–96, 125–128,
    198–199 (*see also* Antecedents)
Stimulus generalization, *see* Transfer of
    training
Structured diary, *see* Recording of
    behavior, structured diary
Studying, *see* Topic Index: Studying and
    time management
Subvocal speech, 83–85
Successive approximations, *see* Shaping

Symbolic reinforcers, *see* Reinforcement
    and reinforcers, token
Symptoms, 7–8

Termination:
    formal, 247–252
    informal, 246–248
    planning, 248–252
    and values, 246–247
Test anxiety, *see* Topic Index: Fears, of
    tests
Thinning, of reinforcements, 249–252,
    255
Thoughts (*see also* Antecedents,
    thoughts as; Self-statements)
    and fears, 154–155
    and language, 83–86
    recording of, 50–52, 53–54, 60, 68
    reinforcement of, 182–183
    as reinforcers, 170, 173, 175–176
    replacement of, 66, 141
Thought stopping, 122–125, 155
Tinkering, 237–242
Tokens, *see* Reinforcement and
    reinforcers, token
Traits theory, 6–7, 8
Transcendental meditation, *see*
    Meditation
Transfer of training, 126–127, 248–252,
    267
Troubleshooting, 237–242
Two-stage process, 112, 209–211

Values:
    and adjustment, 3–4
    and individual goals, 4–5, 246
    and reactivity, 67–68
    and termination, 245–247
Verbal self-control, viii (*see also*
    Language; Self-instructions)

Weight loss, *see* Topic Index:
    Overeating, smoking, drinking, and
    drug use
Willpower, vii, 5–6, 36, 136–137

Yoga, 147

Topic Index

Note that the topics listed in the following index include, but are not restricted to, those covered in the "Tips" sections of the book.

Assertion, 76, 119–120, 121–122, 123, 136, 160–161, 176, 200, 251
  "Tips" sections, 44–45, 80, 129–130, 162, 205
Depression, 28, 33–34, 50, 57, 62–63, 66, 68, 116, 130, 141–142, 171, 176, 183–184
  "Tips" sections, 45, 80, 130, 163, 205
Exercise and athletics, 38, 49, 59, 68, 121–122, 137, 151, 157, 168, 172, 179, 186–188, 239–241
Family, friends, lovers, and coworkers:
  "Tips" sections, 44, 81, 130, 163, 206
  couples, 31, 48, 54, 106–107, 109, 115, 127–128, 143, 165, 184–185, 192, 212–213, 250–251
  coworkers, 48–49, 53–54, 59–60, 73, 119–120, 139, 211–213
  friends, 24–25, 26, 52–53, 106–107, 109, 181, 213, 237–238, 248–249
  parents and children, 33, 50, 69, 106–107, 109, 114, 116–117, 120–121, 138–139
Fears:
  "Tips" sections, 80, 130, 162–163, 205
  of automobiles, 173
  of being alone, 145
  of birds, 155–156, 201

Fears (continued)
  of cemeteries, 144
  of closed places, 144–145
  of diseased organisms, 144
  of mental illness, 145
  of people, 261–262 (see also Shyness)
  of public speaking, 36–37, 63, 126, 155, 231–232
  of sex, 143
  of tests and exams, 143, 152–153, 154–155, 158–159, 176, 177
  of water, 261
Insomnia, 96, 151–152
The other sex, 10–11, 24, 26, 29, 63, 79, 106–107, 109, 119, 121–122, 123, 124–125, 135, 138–139, 199–200, 248
Overeating, smoking, drinking, and drug use:
  "Tips" sections, 43–44, 81, 128–129, 162, 206–207
  overeating, 25, 31, 32, 33–34, 36, 37, 38, 40, 47, 52, 57, 59, 67, 68, 69–70, 71, 96, 110, 111, 114, 115, 121–122, 126, 165–166, 175, 178–179, 186, 189, 193–194, 195, 197, 199, 230, 245, 247, 249, 254
  smoking, 25, 37, 38, 39, 52, 57, 59, 60, 61, 67, 69, 75, 77, 110,

Overeating, smoking, drinking, and
    drug use *(continued)*
    111–112, 115–116, 127–128,
    165–166, 176, 188, 195–196,
    197, 198, 199, 209–211,
    232–234, 254, 256–257
  drinking, 39, 73, 77, 107, 110, 113,
    127–128, 254
  drug use, 39, 111–112, 180, 198,
    254, 256
Reading improvement, 69, 173–174
Self-injurious habits:
  face picking, 218–219
  hair pulling, 16, 112
  knuckle cracking, 57, 60, 70, 139
  lip biting, 153
  nail biting, 14–15, 119, 139, 180
  scratching, 70–71, 139
  teeth grinding, 17–18

Sexual problems, 95, 111, 122, 123,
    143, 197, 198 (*see also* Fears, of
    sex)
Shyness, 3–4, 9, 24, 29, 30, 80,
    130–131, 137, 138–139, 216,
    219–222, 235–237
Studying and time management, 15,
    27–28, 38, 40, 42, 55, 56, 59, 75,
    79, 96, 126, 136–137, 165–166,
    169, 179, 185, 191, 195,
    226–230, 246, 248, 252–253,
    259–260
  "Tips" sections, 44, 81, 129, 163,
    206
Swearing, 12–15, 179
Urination, excessive, 115
Writing, creative and professional, 19,
    28, 51–52, 118, 125–126, 135,
    184, 216